219

TRADE UNIONS
AND THE GOVERNMENT

Trade Unions
and the Government

V. L. ALLEN

LONGMANS

LONGMANS, GREEN AND CO LTD
6 & 7 CLIFFORD STREET, LONDON WI

THIBAULT HOUSE, THIBAULT SQUARE, CAPE TOWN
605–611 LONSDALE STREET, MELBOURNE CI
443 LOCKHART ROAD, HONG KONG
ACCRA, AUCKLAND, IBADAN
KINGSTON (JAMAICA), KUALA LUMPUR
LAHORE, NAIROBI, SALISBURY (RHODESIA)

LONGMANS, GREEN AND CO INC
119 WEST 40TH STREET, NEW YORK 18

LONGMANS, GREEN AND CO
20 CRANFIELD ROAD, TORONTO 16

ORIENT LONGMANS PRIVATE LTD
CALCUTTA, BOMBAY, MADRAS
DELHI, HYDERABAD, DACCA

© V. L. Allen 1960
First published 1960

Printed in Great Britain by
Butler & Tanner Ltd,
Frome and London

CONTENTS

PART I

THE DEVELOPMENT OF A CONSTITUTIONAL RELATIONSHIP

PART II

THE GOVERNMENT AS AN EMPLOYER

PART III

THE GOVERNMENT AND STRIKES

PART IV

TRADE UNIONS
AND LABOUR GOVERNMENTS

ACKNOWLEDGEMENTS

THE advertisements on pp. 178–184 are reproduced from *The Times*: those on pp. 180, 181, 182 *(left)* and 183 by permission of *The National Union of Railwaymen*; pp. 178, 179, 182 *(right)* and 184 are Crown Copyright and are reproduced by permission of the Controller of H.M. Stationery Office.

PREFACE

THE purpose of this study is to provide an analysis of the relationship between trade unions and the Government so that the effect of unions on Government decision-making can be revealed and evaluated. Only central Government and national trade union activities are examined, therefore no assessment can be made from this study of the influence which unions exercise either at local Government level or in industry.

Two points need to be made about the analysis. First, all decisions are made in an environment of competing interests which are hard to disentangle and more difficult to evaluate. This is particularly so of the individual decisions of Ministers and the collective decisions of the Cabinet. The second point is a technical one. Cabinet decisions are subject to the Official Secrets Act which restricts the use of a major source of material. Nonetheless there is a substantial body of evidence which can be used in the examination of Government decision-making and which allows useful conclusions to be drawn from it.

In addition to using documentary evidence, much of which came from primary sources, I had discussions with trade union leaders and politicians. A number of former Conservative and Labour Cabinet Ministers talked freely and at length with me about the Government's relationship with trade unions and they provided me with details about some of the most important of the relationship problems which have occurred. Some of the conversations were held on the express understanding that they should be confidential and should serve only to build up a background of knowledge. I have respected this confidence.

The Government and the State are treated here as synonymous terms. The State, for the purposes of practical administration, is the Government and when the Government acts it does so always in the name of the State. Governments, however, change between elections and because of elections. They contain different personnel and pursue varying policies. Where these differences are reflected in a change of attitude towards trade unions one Government is distinguished from another in the text, otherwise the word Government is used to represent a continuous function.

The study is part of a larger one concerning the impact of trade unions in Britain since 1918 which the Nuffield Foundation enabled me to begin by providing me with a research fellowship for the three years 1955–1958. The fellowship was held at the London School of Economics. The history of trade unionism in Britain since 1918 is in the process of being written as another part of the project and later an examination will be made of the part which trade unions play in industry.

I wish to thank the Nuffield Foundation for making it possible for me to write this book. I am grateful to the Trades Union Congress for allowing me to consult its records; to Miss Crowther, the T.U.C. librarian; and to Miss Blackwell and Mr. Murphy of the T.U.C. Filing Department for their help in sorting out material. My thanks, too, go to Mrs. Sheila Williams who assisted me in collecting material for Chapters III and XI, undertook the arduous task of checking the references, and made a number of constructive suggestions for the text. I am grateful to the many people who have discussed many of the issues raised in the book with me and who have provided me with information. Among these are Lord Attlee, Lord Monckton and the late Lord Waverley who are acknowledged in the text, and the other equally prominent people who must remain anonymous.

I wish to thank my wife, Peggy Allen, who did all the typing, helped me to redraft the first copy of the typescript, and compiled the index, that most unenviable of tasks. I also want to record here my gratitude to Mr. C. C. Blagden for the constant help and encouragement he has given me over the last seven years. For the opinions expressed in the book, which are numerous and definite, I alone am responsible.

The University,   V. L. ALLEN
  Leeds.

1

THE DEVELOPMENT OF A
CONSTITUTIONAL RELATIONSHIP

Chapter One

TRADE UNIONS AS PRESSURE GROUPS

TRADE unions, throughout the greater part of their existence, have tried to influence Government behaviour in relation to their own special interests. In a general way they have acted like other voluntary societies with strong political interests. They have treated the need to influence the Government as a specific function which has required organization and finance; they have used the prevailing methods to exert pressure and have been motivated by self-interest.

Pressure groups are usually interest groups which are independent of political parties and which prefer to exert an influence upon all parties in order to guide them in the direction of their own special interests. There are some pressure groups in Britain which neatly fit this description, but those with predominant economic motives normally find that they get a more sympathetic hearing from one party than another. Trade unions have even established their own political party, but they have not thereby ceased to be pressure groups. They have found that a Government formed by the Labour Party simplifies the means of trade union access to it but that it does not remove the need of unions to put their viewpoint.[1]

Early Pressure Group Activity

When workers first combined in the eighteenth century their relations with masters were covered by various statutes dating from the fourteenth century. The movement of labour, wage assessment, apprenticeship regulations and working conditions were all subject to regulation by the state. The mainspring of this legislation was the Statute of Artificers, 1563, which gave the state control over industrial matters which had hitherto been mainly under municipal and craft jurisdiction.

It had always been difficult to apply this legislation because of the lack of an effective central and local government administration; and the extent to which it was applied is a matter of some controversy. At the beginning of the eighteenth century much of it had fallen into disuse. But the attitude that it was a proper function of the state to intervene in industry continued to prevail, so that when workers

[1] The relationship between trade unions and Labour Governments is discussed in Part IV.

3

obtained the conditions for combining it was to Parliament that they looked for the redress of their grievances. Acting collusively in their crafts, they petitioned Parliament to apply those statutes which concerned them.

There are many examples of petitions. A few, such as the petition by silk and woollen weavers against the use of printed linens and calicoes in 1720, were undoubtedly undertaken in connivance with employers and stood a good chance of success. In this case the Government passed an Act to do as the weavers requested. Occasionally petitions which were initiated by the workers themselves against employers succeeded. For instance, in 1756 the Gloucester weavers obtained legislative approval for the fixing of wages by magistrates.[1] But the chances of success were considerably reduced when the petitions were opposed by the employers, for, as Adam Smith wrote in 1776, 'Whenever the legislature attempts to regulate the differences between masters and their workmen, its counsellors are always the masters.'[2]

The expense of financing petitions encouraged workers to combine. Usually counsel had to be employed and the expenses of witnesses to London had to be met. It was the stated object of the Cloth Workers' Society in Yorkshire in 1805 'to effect and conduct the application to Parliament for preventing the Repeal of Laws . . .'[3] The cloth workers were organized in each of the principal woollen manufacturing towns of the country during the few years each side of 1800 and collaborated in petitioning Parliament. The Committee 'On the State of the Woollen Manufacture of England' in 1806 reported about the Societies: 'A stated weekly contribution, greater or less according to existing circumstances, is required from every Member; and of course the sum raised in this way may be, and in fact has been, very considerable. From this Fund was defrayed a very considerable part of the expenses of several different applications to Parliament, as well as of that which is now pending. . . .'[4] One witness before the Committee stated that between 1803 and 1806 the Cloth Workers in Yorkshire must have spent from £10,000 to £12,000 on making applications to Parliament. The hatters who submitted a counter-petition in 1777 against their employers' plea to Parliament for protection, though organized in separate local societies, also acted on a national basis for the purpose of petitioning Parliament. Petitions came in from London, Manchester and other centres including

[1] *The Cotton Trade and Industrial Lancashire, 1600–1780*, by A. P. Wadsworth and Julia de L. Mann, p. 361.
[2] *The Wealth of Nations*, vol. I, 2nd edn. (edited by J. E. Thorold Rogers), p. 149.
[3] Report and Minutes of Evidence on the State of the Woollen Manufacture of England, 4 July 1806.
[4] ibid.

Newcastle-under-Lyme, Burton-upon-Trent, Derby, Bristol, Liverpool and Chester.[1]

The Combination Acts, 1799 and 1800, made all workers' combinations illegal but did not unduly hinder them in financing petitions to Parliament. The position was altered by the repeal of the Tudor legislation under which workers sought protection. All the Tudor Labour statutes were repealed by 1813.[2]

Trade societies had always been much more concerned with reviving moribund legislation than with demanding new measures. When there was no legislation to revive, their relations with the Government almost ceased. They did not even act as an organized force to obtain the repeal of the Combination Acts;[3] and they left to philanthropists the task of demanding factory legislation.[4] The petition, in this situation, fell into disuse as an organized pressure-group method.[5]

A NEW PHASE AND NEW METHODS

No significant relationship between the Government and trade unions existed from 1825 until the 1860s. During that period unions changed their outward form and to some extent their purpose. They developed from loose alliances of local societies into national organizations; they dropped all pretensions about changing the nature of society; they emphasized their friendly society functions, imposed high contributions, and became exclusive organizations for relatively well-paid, thrifty craftsmen. To fulfil their new function, unions needed to accumulate central funds but they were prevented from doing this by the state of the law, which gave them no protection against defaulters. Trade unions re-emerged as pressure groups in the 1860s to press for legal protection.

The task of William Allan, Robert Applegarth and other leaders

[1] Wadsworth and Mann, op. cit., p. 382.

[2] Occasionally workers looked to Parliament for help afterwards, as did the journeymen paper-makers who petitioned in 1816, alleging distress and asking for relief and for the suppression of newly introduced machinery. ('Combinations of Capital and Labour in the English Paper Industry, 1789–1825', by D. C. Coleman, *Economica*, February 1954.)

[3] The repeal was obtained by Francis Place, a tailor, in a most unconventional manner. He succeeded in getting a number of his own nominees on to the Select Committee of the House of Commons which examined the Acts; he briefed the trade society witnesses with questions and answers and rigged the proceedings of the Committee in a painstaking ingenious and unscrupulous manner. See *Francis Place*, by Graham Wallas.

[4] The miners were an exception. See below.

[5] The petition remained to be used by what S. E. Finer calls 'Promotional Groups' —that is, by societies whose sole *raison d'être* is lobbying 'for improving this and pulling down that' (*The Twentieth Century*, October 1957, p. 372).

T.U.G.—B

of these 'New Model' unions was a complicated one, for they had to convince their own members of the value of political agitation, gain public support for their demands, and then persuade the Government to make concessions. The trade union movement was small, concentrated in a few urban areas, divided in opinion and operating in an antagonistic environment.

Trade unions became disillusioned with political action after the failure of the Chartist Movement in 1848, and an early task of the 'New Model' union leaders was to dispel the disillusionment. They did so by agitating over political issues which were related to the struggle for liberty. They publicly supported the Northern States in the American Civil War and encouraged the Polish insurrection against Tsarist Russia in 1863. When Garibaldi came to England in 1864 they arranged a popular welcome for him. And they displayed their enthusiasm for international solidarity by helping, with Karl Marx, to form the International Working Men's Association in 1864.

The task of gaining public sympathy was much more difficult. Unions at that time were eschewed by many people because they were considered to be disreputable, coercive organizations. This view was given credence by the violence which occurred in Sheffield and Manchester in the 1860s in the name of trade unionism. The 'New Model' leaders tried to make trade unionism look respectable. They deprecated strike action and took steps to curtail it; and they denounced the Sheffield outrages. Applegarth asked the Government to send a Commission to Sheffield to investigate the outrages and thus clear the name of trade unionism. A Royal Commission was in fact set up in February 1867 but its terms of reference extended beyond the outrages to the whole question of trade unionism. It seemed for a time that the intentions of the 'New Model' leaders would go awry, for many people looked on the inquiry as a means of initiating repressive labour legislation on the lines of the Combination Acts.

The unions stood little chance of persuading the Government to make concessions so long as they were divided amongst themselves, and they were divided throughout the 1860s. The formation of trades councils in some of the large cities, notably London, Manchester, Glasgow and Sheffield, was a first step towards united action. The 'New Model' leaders worked through the London Trades Council which had been formed in 1860 'to watch over the general interests of labour, political and social, both in and out of Parliament'. But the effectiveness of pressure in London was impaired by rivalry amongst union leaders, which reached such lengths that rival deputations went to the Home Secretary in 1867, each advocating the same changes in labour law.[1]

A number of attempts were made in the 1860s to achieve national unity among unions, but not until 1868 was any real success achieved. The unity, though not at first complete, was welded under the threat of repressive legislation and in conditions of an economic depression. In June 1868 the Trades Union Congress met for the first time to express the opinion of all British trade unions on matters of general interest to them. It met again in 1869 but postponed its 1870 meeting until the Government had fulfilled a promise to introduce a Trade Union Bill giving unions legal recognition. The third Congress, convened in March 1871, was dissatisfied with the Bill and appointed a committee of five members to organize political agitation against it.[2] The Congress met annually after that and the committee became its permanent Parliamentary Committee.

The Royal Commission, instead of recommending repressive legislation, suggested giving unions legal recognition with certain powers and rights. The Government broadly embodied the Commission's proposals in the Trade Union Act of 1871, but through the Criminal Law Amendment Act of the same year it restricted union activities by penalizing peaceful picketing. The Trades Union Congress in 1872 instructed the Parliamentary Committee to work for the complete repeal of the Criminal Law Amendment Act. The Parliamentary Committee formed a number of deputations to the Government to protest against the Act, while at the same time its secretary, George Howell, bargained secretly and discreditably with the Liberal Government to get the Act amended, not repealed.[3] Independently of the Parliamentary Committee a general trade union agitation against the Act developed in 1873. The Liberal Party was defeated in the general election in 1874 and the following year the Conservative Government completely repealed the Criminal Law Amendment Act. Unions then relaxed for twenty-six years under the impression that they were immune from the law.[4] The Parliamentary Committee spent most of its time intriguing and pressing for industrial reforms, mainly involving amendments to the Factory Acts.

[1] *The Congress of 1868*, by A. E. Musson, p. 21. On the one side were the 'New Model' leaders and on the other George Potter, controller of the *Beehive*. The first deputation ever to wait on a Chancellor of the Exchequer, in March 1864, went because of this rivalry. Mr. Gladstone had referred to Potter as 'the far-famed Secretary of the Trade Unions' and the 'New Model' leaders went to disabuse him of Potter's importance and official status (*London Trades Council, 1860–1950, A History*, p. 14).
[2] Musson, op. cit., p. 47.
[3] 'Practical, Capable Men', by Royden Harrison (*New Reasoner*, Autumn 1958, pp. 111–115).
[4] See Chapter VII, p. 120.

Deputations

The Parliamentary Committee developed a formal routine for making representations to the Government. After each Congress the Committee met to sort out the resolutions which Congress had passed. It embodied some in the form of Parliamentary Bills and relegated the remainder to what was known as the 'omnibus' deputation. It arranged to meet the Ministers of the Government Departments concerned, all at the same time, and to present its views to them on all the issues. These representations were hurried, cramped, inadequate affairs. There was not even time for formal answers to many questions. The annual deputations were mass ones, too, consisting of from 200 to 400 delegates from different trades. The Parliamentary Committee dispensed with the 'omnibus' deputation in 1895 because of its inadequacy, and made arrangements with the respective Ministers separately, at different places and on different dates. The deputations remained large annual affairs and were concerned with wide-ranging topics. For instance, the first deputation of this kind on 13 November 1895, consisting of 250 trade union representatives, met Sir Matthew White Ridley, M.P., the Home Secretary, and put questions to him concerning the Employers' Liability Bill, Factory Legislation, Dangerous Trades, the right of workmen to be represented at Coroners' Inquests, the Truck Act Amendment, Youths joining Trade Unions, Bakers and Unhealthy Trades' Schedule, Law of Conspiracy, Compulsory Weighing, Payment of Councillors, Representation on Governing Bodies, Poor Law Amendment, and the right of postal workers to combine.[1] The deputation could hardly say more than that these were questions which worried trade unionists.

The relative ineffectiveness of its deputations continued to perturb the Parliamentary Committee. It reported in 1897 that

> from casual observations made during these interviews it would appear that there is a divergence of opinion as to the utility or otherwise of these annual deputations to Ministers. Your Committee have given great consideration to this matter, and although they are bound to acknowledge that up to the present the existing methods are not only expensive, cumbrous, and generally unsatisfactory, yet they have not been able to devise any better process of bringing their labour grievances before the Government than that which is now open to them, and they would therefore recommend the Congress to still use these opportunities of urging on Government departments the great necessity of changing the laws for the benefit of labour.[2]

[1] T.U.C. Report, 1896, pp. 20–21.   [2] ibid., 1897, p. 18.

By 1901 the Parliamentary Committee made up the deputations out of its own number and only occasionally co-opted other trade unionists to speak in support. But criticisms continued to be made about deputations for many years. They dealt with too many subjects and speakers had too little time to develop a case.[1]

The annual deputations did not become a recognized channel of communication between trade unions and all Government Departments. Trade unions were always suppliants and on occasions Ministers emphasized this by refusing to receive deputations. The Rt. Hon. G. J. Goschen, M.P., Minister for War, refused to meet a Parliamentary Committee deputation in 1899 to discuss the operation of the House of Commons Fair Wages Resolution. The Parliamentary Committee was indignant. Goschen's action, it stated, 'is unworthy of a British Minister, is discourteous to the working classes of the country, and contrary to the treatment which the Parliamentary Committee invariably receives at the hands of high Government officials, especially when dealing with important labour questions'.[2] Lord Stanley, when he was the Postmaster-General in Balfour's Conservative Government in 1905, consistently refused to meet a trade union deputation about the recognition of postal workers' unions. But the hostile attitude of a few Ministers was more than counter-balanced by the sympathetic and favourable approach of others. From Gladstone's first Ministry the attitudes and personalities of Government Ministers in general, and Prime Ministers in particular, deeply influenced the accessibility of trade unions to the Government. The Prime Minister often set the tone of the relationship.

Mr. Gladstone's interest in industrial relations was a marginal one but it was so far in advance of that of any previous Prime Minister as to create substantial political precedents, and to make it much easier for trade unions to approach the Government. When he was Chancellor of the Exchequer, Gladstone received at least two trade union deputations and on 4 July 1868 he presided at a meeting of the Social Science Association on relations between capital and labour. After he became Prime Minister in December 1868 he left labour matters mainly to others. Two prominent union leaders, Henry Broadhurst and Thomas Burt, became junior members of his Governments but they had little political influence.[3] A. J. Mundella, whom Gladstone made President of the Board of Trade in his last

---

[1] *The Railway Clerk*, 15 April 1918.   [2] T.U.C. Report, 1899, p. 32.
[3] Henry Broadhurst, general secretary of the T.U.C. 1875–1885 and 1886–1890, became Under-Secretary of State for the Home Department in 1885; Thomas Burt, a Northumberland Miners' leader 1864–1914, became Parliamentary Secretary to the Board of Trade in 1892.

two Governments, was the most competent and influential trade union sympathizer of his time.[1]

The other Prime Ministers between 1871 and 1905, Mr. Disraeli, Lord Rosebury, Lord Salisbury and Mr. A. J. Balfour, had only a tactical political interest in trade unions. The last of these, Mr. Balfour, was under intensive pressure to make union funds immune from the law and to tackle the problem of unemployment, but he did not respond satisfactorily. The Parliamentary Committee asked him in November 1904 to receive a deputation to discuss unemployment. Unions had rarely before taken their complaints to the Prime Minister. Balfour was slow to reply, but eventually he agreed to meet a combined deputation from the Parliamentary Committee, the Labour Members of Parliament and the General Federation of Trade Unions on 7 February 1905. Nothing came of the meeting.

In December 1905 a Liberal Government was formed which contained a number of Ministers who were interested in social policy and who had some concern about the role of trade unions. The new Prime Minister, Mr. H. Campbell-Bannerman, appointed John Burns, the mellowed socialist trade union leader, as President of the Local Government Board and member of the Cabinet. Then on 15 February 1906 he and Mr. Asquith, Chancellor of the Exchequer, met a deputation of union leaders to discuss the rights of combination among Government workers—the matter over which Lord Stanley had refused to meet a union deputation earlier on—old age pensions, and the deposit of trade union funds in the Saving Banks. It was novel enough for union leaders to be met by such high-powered Government representatives; it was almost revolutionary for them to be received so cordially.[2]

Receiving deputations was more than an act of courtesy on the part of Campbell-Bannerman and Asquith. Mr. Asquith had already, in 1895, fulfilled a promise he had given to a large union deputation to amend the Factory and Workshop Acts of 1878–1891.[3] Mr. Campbell-Bannerman responded to the arguments of trade unionists in 1906 by reversing a decision of his Cabinet about a clause in the Trade Disputes Bill.[4]

---

[1] Mundella formed the Labour Bureau of the Board of Trade in 1886, the forerunner of the Ministry of Labour. See Chapter III.

[2] Mr. Asquith spoke of 'the pleasure which it gives us to meet you today, and have this frank interchange of opinion upon matters which are especially interesting to all those whom you represent . . .' (T.U.C. Report, 1906, p. 88).

[3] The deputation saw Mr. Asquith, who was the Home Secretary, on 16 January 1895 and he introduced a Bill to amend the Acts on 1 March 1895 (T.U.C. Report, 1895).

[4] See below, p. 18.

In 1906 neither of these politicians was compelled to placate trade unions. The Liberal Party had emerged from the December 1905 election with an overall majority in the House of Commons of 132. There were only fifty-three Labour members in this Parliament and of these twenty-four were allied to the Liberal Party. Trade unions were actively agitating against the severe restrictions of the Taff Vale decision of the House of Lords, but they were weak and could have been kept so. A significant political factor, however, was the need of the Liberal Party to obtain and retain the allegiance of the working-class voters. A conciliatory attitude towards unions and electoral collaboration with the Labour Representation Committee contributed towards fulfilling that need. But it was quite apparent that both Mr. Campbell-Bannerman and Mr. Asquith brought into the Government a new, not wholly uninhibited, but liberal conception of trade unions which was sufficiently pervading to alter and improve its communications with unions.

The part which personal attitudes played in moulding these communications was emphasized during the tenure of the war-time and post-war Coalition Governments when Mr. D. Lloyd George was Prime Minister. Mr. Lloyd George, first as President of the Board of Trade in December 1905, then as Chancellor of the Exchequer, and later as Minister of Munitions, displayed an unprecedented propensity to intervene in industrial disputes and an exceptional willingness to talk with union leaders. When he went to 10 Downing Street as Prime Minister in 1917 he took these qualities with him. Hitherto, British Prime Ministers had either ignored industrial disputes or had intervened only in times of acute stress, as did Mr. Asquith in 1911 and 1912. They had received union deputations only on matters of national importance. Mr. Lloyd George altered this pattern. He received deputations on a wide range of issues—some were of national significance and some were clearly within the provinces of his Ministers. He even sent for union leaders to hear their views or to use his persuasiveness on them. He enjoyed acting as the arbitrator, albeit often a partial one, for the Government itself was usually the employer. And he delighted in making dramatic announcements about trade union visits to 10 Downing Street, with a content and in a manner which clearly intended them for posterity rather than as contributions to the solution of current disputes.

The attitude of subsequent Governments to trade union representations was altered permanently by Mr. Lloyd George's behaviour. It continued, of course, to be basically determined by the national character of issues, by their intensity, by the power of trade unions. But a pattern of expectations and reactions had been established which remained and became aspects of normal behaviour. On certain issues union leaders expected to talk with the Prime Minister and he, in turn, reacted as if the expectation were justified. Access to Ministers of Departments became correspondingly easier. Union leaders continued to meet Ministers after each Trades Union Congress to present them with Congress resolutions, and saw them on other occasions, too, whenever matters arose which demanded Government action.

The range of issues which the Government considered proper to discuss with trade unions extended slowly. Education, old age pensions, unemployment, the nationalization of industry, and aspects of foreign policy were gradually added to the confined field of labour law, factory acts and workmen's compensation which was the trade unions' in the nineteenth century. But not until the Second World War and after did unions extend their scope to cover the whole field of social activity.

No established right of access to the Government was conceded to unions, however, until the Second World War when circumstances and personalities combined to improve their status. The main personality in this case was Ernest Bevin who became Minister of Labour in May 1940. He made it the practice for unions to have open access to all Government Departments because he believed firmly in their right to it. The practice was not established irrevocably but it became sufficiently ingrained to be retained in some form despite circumstances. The long duration of the war and the much longer duration of post-war economic problems encouraged its establishment. Indeed, communications often moved in the opposite direction. Frequently it was the Prime Minister or one of his Ministers who wanted to meet the trade union leaders. The significance of deputations, however, had decreased by this time because the channels of communication had become diverse and more effective. But they remained as a means of bringing the official opinion of the trade union movement to the notice of the Government.

Nowadays deputations to Ministers are part of a process. It is no longer the practice for a union deputation to put its case to a Minister, retire and hope for the best. A deputation is preceded by meetings of a General Council policy-making sub-committee, by preparation of memoranda on the contentious matter, by correspondence with the Minister. Frequently the General Council issues a policy statement so that in any event the Government will know its views. Only matters not settled by correspondence are argued out by a deputation. If the deputation gets no satisfaction, correspondence may continue and further deputations put the union case.

The submission of trade union memoranda is now a significant supplement to the protests and arguments of deputations. The memoranda which are submitted by the General Council to the Government are detailed and documented statements prepared by specialist members of the Trades Union Congress staff. Today, deputations can go to the Government as well briefed by the Trades Union Congress as Government representatives are by the civil service. The existence of this trade union research service has rendered it unnecessary for deputations to argue lengthy, detailed cases. The arguments of each side can be studied beforehand through the exchange of memoranda.

The need for equipping deputations with adequate information seems obvious now, but for many years it was not so. Occasionally during early agitations to get the law changed the help of intellectuals was sought, but not until 1900 did the Parliamentary Committee appoint a legal adviser.[1] The development of Trades Union Congress research facilities occurred much later. For fifty years the spokesmen for deputations relied upon their own semi-skilled efforts to compile their cases. They had neither the time nor facility for the collection and collation of facts.

The Trades Union Congress appointed its first full-time clerk in 1902. He, with the secretary, performed all the administrative work of Congress until February 1918 when Fred Bramley became an assistant in the office.[2] Bramley was put in charge of a research department in 1919 but he was its only member. Radical administrative changes occurred in 1921 which resulted in the establishment, on 1 January 1922, of research, press and publicity, and international departments, jointly with the Labour Party. The Trades Union Congress did not find this arrangement satisfactory and in March 1926 it set up its own departments. These have expanded and increased in number so that now the Trades Union Congress can supply to its affiliated unions a research and information service on a wide range of subjects. The division of the Congress administration into specialist departments, and of the General Council into corresponding specialist sub-committees comprising people with a close day-to-day interest in the subjects they cover, has improved the quality of deputations. It is quite possible that they will meet Government Ministers who are less familiar with their subjects and more dependent upon specialist advice.

---

[1] T.U.C. Report, 1900, p. 32. He was Edmund Browne, L.C.C., Barrister-at-Law.

[2] Bramley was an organizer for the National Amalgamated Furnishing Trades Associatiou and a member of the Parliamentary Committee of the Trades Union Congress, 1916–1917. He subsequently became General Secretary of the T.U.C. 1923–1925.

The efficiency of a deputation, however, may have little or no connection with the Government response. As unions are concerned
with results, they have had to exercise more persuasive means of
pressure than reason or sentiment. How they have done this is
described below.

Constitutional Pressure on Parliament

The re-emergence of unions as pressure groups coincided with the
passing of the Reform Act in 1867, which extended the franchise to
householders in cities and boroughs. Between 1866 and 1869 the
electorate in the United Kingdom increased from 1,364,000 to
2,448,000.[1] Urban workers voted for the first time in such numbers
that they were able to swing some election results in the direction
they desired. Trade unions then assumed a new significance, for they
represented the most politically alert section of this new electorate. If
unions could influence the political behaviour of their members then
clearly they were candidates for the favours of the political parties
who were competing for votes. It was not known what influence
unions carried in this direction—indeed this has never been accurately
assessed—but this did not detract from their political significance.

It was not an entirely new phenomenon for trade unions to be considered for political favours. Where, under old forms of franchise,
craftsmen had been freemen with a right to vote, their organizations
had been deferred to by politicians. The shipwrights of Liverpool
were well organized from the very beginning of the nineteenth century.
One of the factors which gave their society power 'was the fact that
the shipwrights were all freemen, and their influence was necessary
to the success of a candidate. In the evidence before the committee
of the House of Commons, 1824, it is mentioned that it was customary
for both sides (political parties) to send down large donations to the
Union when there appeared to be a probability of an election. . . .'[2]
On one occasion in 1790 when the two political parties agreed not to
contest an election in Liverpool but to re-elect the sitting members,
the shipwrights nominated their own candidate for one of the seats
and had him elected. The framework knitters of Nottingham had
acted similarly. The framework knitter 'though he was poor he was
still a burgess and had the vote, hence the election of 1778 when the
stockingers . . . fight an election on the question of wages, get their
man in, and through him introduce a bill to regulate the wages in

---

[1] *Life of W. E. Gladstone*, by John Morley, vol. II (New Edition, 1906), p. 365. The
total population was more than twenty-six million.

[2] *Trades' Societies and Strikes* by the National Association for the Promotion of
Social Science, 1860, p. 480.

the stocking industry'.[1] But it was new for unions to receive wide political favours in return for their support.

The New Model union leaders took part in the agitation for electoral reform which preceded the passing of the 1867 Reform Act. Before the Act could be of use to unions the new working-class voters had to be induced to use their votes in the interests of their own class. This was a slow process. A few working men stood for Parliament in the 1868 election but, despite exhortations to voters from George Potter's London Working Men's Association, they were heavily defeated.

The Labour Representation League was formed in September 1869 as a serious attempt to obtain labour representation. On its executive council sat all the prominent union leaders of the day. It stated in its manifesto:

> There are in the United Kingdom above twenty millions of people belonging to the working classes, whose welfare as citizens depends on a correct understanding and wise treatment by the British Parliament of questions in which they are specially interested; and yet not one actual workingman has found a seat in the present Parliament—a Parliament reformed professedly for the purpose of securing an equitable representation of every section and every interest in the community. . . .[2]

The League aimed 'to organize fully the strength of the operative classes as an electoral power, so that when necessary it may be brought to bear with effect on any important political, social or industrial question in the issue of which their interests are involved'.

The significance of the new labour vote to the established political parties was brought home by the result of the 1868 election when the Liberal Party was returned with a majority of 112, replacing a Conservative Government, and ending its long era of political torpor.[3] The Conservative Party fought the 1874 election obviously determined to win labour votes, while the Trades Union Congress, engaging in its first general election, endeavoured to ensure that those votes were not won without cost. As the election was approaching the Trades Union Congress issued a list of seven questions which it asked working men voters, regardless of their party politics, to put to Parliamentary candidates. It testifies to the immaturity of the new voters and the electioneering fervour of the Conservatives that only

---

[1] *Nottinghamshire in the Eighteenth Century* by J. D. Chambers, p. 34. The Bill was defeated, largely due to the efforts of a powerful master hosier, whereupon the stockingers rioted for about ten days.

[2] The manifesto is reproduced in *'Labour's Formative Years' 1849–1879*, vol. II, edited by James B. Jefferys, pp. 147–150.

[3] Morley, op. cit., vol. I, p. 885.

two working men were elected to Parliament and the Conservatives displaced the Liberal Government.

The electoral device of putting questions to candidates irrespective of party became common trade union practice. The threat of causing voters to switch their allegiance in sufficient numbers to remove a Parliamentary majority was the only pressure unions could impose on the Government during the last quarter of the nineteenth century. The Government fear of losing a majority was real, for the election results in Great Britain in the general elections after 1868 showed marked swings.

In other ways trade union pressure on the Government was negligible. The attempt to compete with the established political parties by building an independent labour party was carried on without the wholehearted support of the Trades Union Congress until 1899, and even then the two dominant trades in the Congress, the miners and cotton textile workers, chose to act unilaterally as they had done before. Trade unions were not strong enough to bring industrial pressure on the Government; the economy was not sufficiently integrated to make this possible in any but a few trades, even if unions had been better organized.

So unions, in isolated cases on their own account but mostly through the Trades Union Congress, pressed Members and prospective Members of Parliament to support their demands on the Government. The Parliamentary Committee frequently went to the House of Commons to persuade friendly M.P.s to ballot for Private Members' Bills. It was often a thankless task. In 1898 the Parliamentary Committee reported:

> We may state that this year, although a goodly number of members of the House who are friendly to labour were kind enough to ballot, yet their names came out in every case in a hopeless position and even in regard to 'The Miners' Eight Hour Bill', for which over thirty members put down their names to ballot, and the Miners' Federation sent up over sixty delegates to lobby members on behalf of their Bill, they only got the seventh place. . . . It is sincerely to be hoped that all trades who are primarily interested in the legislative proposals relegated to the Parliamentary Committee will do their best to assist the Committee in performing the lobbying work and writing members of Parliament to secure their balloting for Bills. . . .[1]

Much lobbying and agitating was done in the first few years of the twentieth century on behalf of postal workers who claimed Government recognition of their right to combine and wanted an inquiry

[1] T.U.C. Report, 1898, p. 40.

into Post Office wages. The Postmaster-General in the Conservative Government refused outright to meet deputations from the Parliamentary Committee to consider recognition. He also refused to appoint a Select Committee of the House of Commons to examine the question of wages. He said in April 1905:

> I hold as strongly as I have ever done that a House of Commons Committee is not a body for such an inquiry. . . . Hon. Members know and it is no use blinking our eyes to the amount of pressure which is brought to bear or is attempted to be brought to bear upon Members on both sides of the House by public servants and by Post Office servants especially . . . and even if the machinery by which Select Committees are appointed were such as to enable us to secure a Select Committee composed of thoroughly impartial men who had committed themselves by no expression of opinion to one side or the other, I still think it would not be fair to pick out fifteen Members of this House and make them marked men for the pressure which is now exercised more or less over the whole Assembly.[1]

A committee of business men was formed to examine Post Office wages for the Government. In a debate on the report of this committee, the Postmaster-General made further complaints about the lobbying activities of civil servants who wanted wage increases.[2] He quoted from a circular which asked civil servants to write to their M.P.s for support. This, he said, 'was nothing more nor less than blackmail. It was nothing more nor less than asking Members to purchase votes for themselves at the general election at the expense of the public Exchequer. Both sides would have to make up their minds that some means should be devised by which there should not be this continual blood-sucking on the part of the public servants. . . .'

The last major issue on which unions sought the help of members of all parties was during the agitation for the reversal by legislation of the 1901 House of Lords decision on the Taff Vale dispute.[3] The agitation was conducted by the Parliamentary Committee of the T.U.C. At the outset a Trade Disputes Bill was drawn up by the Parliamentary Committee and a Member of Parliament who had been successful in the ballot for Private Members' motions was induced to move it. The Bill was defeated in 1902 so the Parliamentary Committee set about canvassing support for it. The campaign lasted until late in 1906.

The Parliamentary Committee circulated each affiliated union to persuade its members to press their local M.P.s to vote for the Bill.

---

[1] Parliamentary Debates, Fourth Series, 1905, vol. 148, cols. 1354–1355.
[2] ibid., col. 1365.
[3] See Chapter VII, p. 120, for the House of Lords decision.

It arranged meetings throughout industrial centres to discuss the Bill and at each meeting a motion was moved which stated that trade unionists would not 'support any Parliamentary candidate who fails to declare his intention to vote for the Bill'.[1] Then, late in December 1904, all Members of Parliament were circulated with a request to ballot for the Bill, and for a Workmen's Compensation Act Amendment Bill which the Parliamentary Committee had drafted. Just over 100 M.P.s replied to the circular and seventeen agreed to ballot for one of the Bills.

The campaign to put pressure on M.P.s continued, but with little success. The Government set up a Royal Commission on Trade Disputes but did not appoint a Labour representative to serve on it. The 1903 Trades Union Congress protested 'against the Government's insult to Labour' and the Parliamentary Committee refused to accept the Commission's report. The establishment of the Royal Commission was a well-worn delaying tactic which proved useful to the Conservative Government until Mr. Balfour's resignation in December 1905.

During the ensuing election campaign, the Parliamentary Committee drew up a list of reforms it desired, such as a Trade Disputes Bill, Workmen's Compensation, Truck Act, Unemployment Act, a State pension fund, adult suffrage and an eight-hour working day. And it urged all trade unionists and wage-earners to vote only for those candidates who were pledged to support the Trades Union Congress version of these measures. In effect these candidates were endorsed Labour candidates.

The Parliamentary Committee set about influencing the new Liberal Government more optimistically than it had tried to influence the Conservative Government beforehand. The early optimism, however, was dispelled by rumours that the Cabinet was divided over the Trade Disputes Bill. So, early in February 1906, the Parliamentary Committee again circulated all Members of Parliament to ballot for its Bill in the forthcoming session. On 22 February 1906 its Bill was introduced again but the Government countered by presenting a Bill of its own on 28 March. The two Bills differed in important respects, so the Members of Parliament who sat on the Parliamentary Committee interviewed the Prime Minister, Mr. Campbell-Bannerman, and, unexpectedly, obtained his support for the union sponsored Bill.

The Government Bill was not withdrawn, but when it came up for a second reading on 25 April 1906 the Government announced that it would make a concession. The Solicitor-General said that the

[1] Parliamentary Committee Minutes, 28 September 1904.

Government had asked for the opinion of trade union leaders, and having done so, the Government was bound to take it into account. The Government Bill was modified, though not entirely in accord with trade union wishes, and became law late in 1906. The Parliamentary Committee was sufficiently joyful to hold a dinner in honour of David Shackleton, its most active member in pressing the Bill through Parliament.

Sectional Activities

In the last quarter of the nineteenth century various trades wanted legislation to regulate some aspects of their work, such as sanitation, overcrowding, safety from accidents, the number of working hours, payment of wages in kind, overtime and holidays. The National Union of Boot and Shoe Operatives wanted the exclusion of alien immigrants, and the compulsory provision of workshop accommodation by employers; the Amalgamated Society of Tailors demanded the legal abolition of home work; while the Seamen's Union had a long list of legal requirements.[1] Shop assistants pressed year after year, often with influential Parliamentary support, for the regulation of shop hours.

The unions in most trades did not construct any special machinery to obtain their demands for legislation. Most of them did not constitute formidable interest groups in their constituencies. As the Webbs stated:

> to bring any proposal effectively before the legislature, that is to say, to persuade members of Parliament to take the matter up, Trade Union leaders must convert, not the employers and workmen in their own industry wherever carried on, but the electors of particular constituencies, to whatever trade they belong. An organization according to localities has, therefore, to be superimposed upon an organization according to trades.[2]

Only trade unionists in two trades, mining and cotton textile, had the conditions to do this, and the political acumen to realize that it ought to be done.

The miners were the most fortunate in this respect for once they had the right to vote[3] they were congregated in such numbers in constituencies as to be able to send their own representatives to Parliament. They possessed a political consciousness which was more highly developed than that in any other trade. No Parliamentary candidate in a mining constituency could hope to be elected unless

---

[1] *Industrial Democracy*, by Sidney and Beatrice Webb, pp. 252–253.
[2] ibid., p. 258.   [3] After 1885.

he supported the miners' demands which usually included legislation
to regulate safety in the mines, hours of work and minimum wages.
The miners formed their own lobby, independent of the Parliamentary Committee of the Trades Union Congress, and made up their
own deputations to the Government.

The miners, however, impaired their political effectiveness by
differences among themselves. The Miners' Federation of Great
Britain, for some years after its formation in 1889, had to fight on
two fronts, for whatever it proposed to the Government would be
opposed by the Northumberland and Durham miners' unions. A
deputation from the Miners' Federation to the Prime Minister in
1893 about an Eight Hour Bill was followed by counter-deputations
from the other miners' group.[1]

The miners' agitation for the Eight Hour Bill consumed their
political energy until circumstances brought them into closer alliance
with the Parliamentary Committee. Their Bill was introduced into
the House of Commons on every possible occasion but each time it
was defeated until 1906. In December of that year the executive committee of the Miners' Federation met the new Liberal Prime Minister
and found him in a conciliatory mood, just as the deputation over the
Trade Disputes Act had done. He agreed to tackle the question of
hours in the mines. Nevertheless the miners introduced their own
Bill into Parliament and, for the first time, accepted help from the
Parliamentary Committee in making parliamentary arrangements.[2]
Finally, in December 1908, a Government Mines Eight Hours' Bill
became law.

The miners had not only acted independently in the lobbies but
had also kept apart from any attempts to form an independent
labour organization and had refused to affiliate to the Labour
Representation Committee. The Socialists, however, were winning
ground. They were aided by the relative success of the Labour
Representation Committee in winning twenty-nine seats during the
general election in January 1906 and by the advocacy of some
miners, notably Robert Smillie. The following year a miners'
conference agreed to affiliate to the Labour Party, as the Labour
Representation Committee was called, and in 1908 a ballot of the
membership gave the same result. The miners did not wholly alter
their inclination to take independent action, but after 1908 they
became much more a part of the political machine of the Labour
Movement.

Like the miners the cotton operatives were sufficiently concentrated
within a small number of constituencies to enable their organizations

[1] *The Miners*, vol. I, by R. Page Arnot, p. 197.   [2] ibid., p. 334.

to exercise electoral pressure. Three-quarters of the 132,000 members of the unions of the cotton operatives in 1890 lived in ten constituencies within twenty miles of Bolton.[1] The cotton workers had devised a political machine, totally independent of their industrial organization, to press their views in Parliament. The societies of spinners, weavers, card-room operatives, beamers and overlookers, became federated in 1886 in the United Textile Factory Workers' Association which had as its sole object 'the removal of any grievance . . . for which Parliamentary or Governmental interference is required'.[2] This Association conducted the political campaigns for cotton workers within the constituencies, lobbied Members of Parliament, and endeavoured to obtain Parliamentary seats for some of its members. It tended to be Conservative but was allied to no particular party. Its leadership reflected its political composition for the general secretary of the weavers' union was a Liberal, whereas the general secretary of the cotton-spinners stood for Parliament as a Conservative in 1900 and in 1906. It thus lobbied freely.

The methods the United Textile Factory Workers' Association employed were clearly illustrated by a report of its Legislative Council in February 1895. First the Council had been instructed by a representative meeting to make arrangements to secure Parliamentary seats for members of the Association. It recommended that two candidates, David Holmes and James Mawdsley, Liberal and Conservative respectively, should stand for Parliament and that an effort should be made to secure them two seats by arrangement with the two principal political parties, so as to avoid a contest if possible. The Report added:

> The Legislative Council consider that an effort should be made to make our influence felt much more than it hitherto has been in Parliamentary Elections. At present we find that some M.P.s for constituencies containing thousands of textile workers simply ignore, and even oppose, many of our proposals. The Council consequently think that it would be an advantage if the Local Committees of all our Branches were to write to their present members, and any other candidates that might be in the field, a letter something like the draft below. Any answers that may be received should be sent to the General Office, and they will then be collated, and our members advised to support our friends, and try to defeat our opponents. It is useless trying to make headway with such proposals as the Abolition of Steaming, and the Extension of the Particulars Clause, so long as those interested vote for men opposed to our views. It is consequently hoped that our members will be honest enough to put politics on one side, and vote for those who will return the compliment.

[1] *Industrial Democracy*, p. 258. [2] ibid.

T.U.G.—C

Cotton operatives had less political sagacity than the miners: they voted neither uniformly nor progressively; they resented the intrusion of party politics into the affairs of their trade societies and believed, in a sense, that they could separate political opinions from political action. Consequently, they were slow to become an integral part of the Labour Movement. But they, like the miners and the Parliamentary Committee of the Trades Union Congress, were compelled by circumstances to alter their pressure-group methods after the return of the 1906 Liberal Government and to work closely with the Labour Party.

THE END OF PRIVATE POLITICAL BARGAINS

All trade union political pressure groups in the last quarter of the nineteenth century had a mixed bag of political patrons; they canvassed support from all parties and unhesitatingly used it regardless of the particular allegiances of their leaders. In order for this situation to exist it had to be possible for individual politicians to make private bargains with interest groups in their constituencies. That is, party alignments in the House of Commons had to be flexible, permitting party members to hold independent views with freedom to vote accordingly. The political system before 1906 permitted this rather free and easy behaviour. The Conservative and Gladstonian Liberal Parties opposed each other, sometimes acrimoniously, but the opposition was often on a personal level or was generated by policies over which there were no deep-seated class feelings. The two main political parties in the nineteenth century often stole each other's clothes without arousing a lot of public interest.

The situation changed in 1906. The Liberal Governments under Mr. Campbell-Bannerman and Mr. Asquith possessed strong radical elements which focussed attention on domestic social policy. Through their attitude towards trade unions, social insurance, property and the House of Lords, they aroused bitter class antagonisms which closed the ranks of the political parties. The parties became identified with class interests and the unity of each party had a positive correlation with the success of a class cause. Members of Parliament rapidly lost their freedom for independent action. This process was accentuated by the emergence of the Parliamentary Labour Party, which, though it had no clearly defined legislative programme until 1918 to mark it off from the Liberal Party, had its *raison d'être* in the class conflict.

The enforcement of Parliamentary party discipline affected all pressure groups and drove those with prime economic interests to ally themselves with one or other of the political parties. The trade union movement naturally looked to its own political party, the Labour Party, to press its point of view, but it also continued to give general support to the Liberal Party which, after all, possessed the political power of the Government.

This last point was a cardinal one for unions. They were concerned with promoting the interests of their members and the legislative changes they desired were directed to that end. They had formed the Labour Party as a means of expediting these changes, but even the greatest of optimists thought it would be many years before the Labour Party could get sufficient electoral support to form a Government. So what in the meantime should the unions' attitude to a Government be? If they refused to collaborate with Conservative or Liberal Governments they delayed their prospects of getting legislative concessions. If they did collaborate they were guilty of adopting an equivocal attitude, of bolstering up a system which through the Labour Party they were aiming to alter.

Quite soon after the formation of the Parliamentary Labour Party the Trades Union Congress stated its position. In 1907 the question of rationalizing the work of the Labour Party and the Trades Union Congress was considered by their executives at a joint meeting. J. Ramsay MacDonald wanted the work of the two bodies to be strictly defined. The T.U.C. Parliamentary Committee would not hear of it. 'The Labour Party', David Shackleton said, 'is naturally antagonistic to every Government: the Parliamentary Committee are in a somewhat different position, and are of the opinion that it would weaken the power of labour generally to give up their right to approach Ministers year by year with the different resolutions passed at Congress.' [1]

This attitude became firmer as trade unions developed a more complex relationship with Governments, and it was reiterated and re-emphasized by individual trade union leaders and by the General Council of the Trades Union Congress. For instance, after the Conservative Party had been returned to office in October 1951 the General Council stated: 'It is our long standing practice to seek to work amicably with whatever Government is in power and through consultation jointly with Ministers and with the other side of industry to find practical solutions to the social and economic problems facing this country. There need be no doubt, therefore, of the attitude of the T.U.C. towards the new Government.' [2] Arthur Deakin, stating his view in 1953, said: 'If our policy as a Movement

[1] Minutes of Joint Meeting, 19 December 1907.
[2] T.U.C. Report, 1952, p. 300.

is to be that we shall have no part in anything that does not completely conform to our own political theories then, in my view, we are going to have a pretty thin time.' [1]

The trade union movement came to use the Labour Party as a prime, but nevertheless limited, means of exercising Parliamentary pressure despite its preference to deal with the Government direct. But first it went through a spell of disillusionment over the Labour Party and constitutional political action generally. The high expectations raised by the results of the 1906 election were not maintained and before the First World War unions were already concentrating on militant industrial action. The war re-orientated some union views towards party politics, but the election set-back which the Labour Party suffered in 1918 convinced many union leaders that union destinies were safer in their own hands than in those of politicians. How this conviction operated can be seen clearly in Chapter X.

The emphasis on militant industrial action was short-lived. Trade unions were weakened first by the depression in 1921 and then by the General Strike. From 1926 until the Second World War they lacked the resources to engage in extensive strike action and, in any case, were disillusioned about its effectiveness. They had to turn to constitutional means of exerting pressure on the Government. Trade unions, however, were so powerless that the Government was able to ignore their direct representations and they had no alternative to using the Parliamentary Labour Party as a means of contact with the Government. The war altered this situation by making the interests of unions and the Government touch at many points. It was not necessary to convince the Government that this was so or that trade union interests ought to receive attention, for labour had become a vital factor in the solution of wartime and post-war problems. The Government even began to approach unions to try to influence their behaviour and responses. Fresh means of contact between unions and the Government developed to meet this new situation.

Parliamentary pressure then went into relative disuse though unions continued to sponsor Parliamentary candidates. Some unions attached more importance to having their own Parliamentary representation than others. In the inter-war period railway unions had developed the technique of opposing private bills promoted by the railway companies so that they could secure some industrial concessions from them. [2] Shopworkers had been interested in using legislation to achieve their aims and possessed an appreciable group

[1] *Trade Union Leadership*, by V. L. Allen, p. 149.
[2] *British Pressure Groups*, by J. D. Stewart, p. 178.

of union members in Parliament. Other unions had virtually no
interest in Parliament, though they had sponsored candidates because
it was a trade union practice to do so. So, although the need for
specific representation in the House of Commons had declined, there
were in the 1951 general election as many trade union sponsored
candidates as in 1929.[1]

[1] ibid., p. 177.

Chapter Two

TRADE UNIONISTS ON GOVERNMENT BODIES

It is inevitable that in any national community only a fraction of the population can be in a position to participate in the national and local decision-making which constitutes the government of the community. Ordinary people are circumscribed by economic, political and industrial forces over which they have no control. The ruling minority is strongly influenced but not controlled by the same forces. It reacts to the pressures which they create and makes decisions as a result of them.

The composition of the ruling minority is principally determined by one factor—the possession of economic power. In the past economic power entailed the possession of land and stock, so the minority consisted of the land-owning groups: the aristocracy, the monarchy and the established church. Power between these groups was distributed unevenly and it altered with time. In the eighteenth century when trade unions were emerging, the landed aristocracy was in the ascendant. As manufacturing industry expanded the essential qualification for holding economic power changed; land ownership declined in importance and was replaced by the ability to control economic organizations. A new group, members of the manufacturing class, joined the ruling minority. The political history of Britain in the nineteenth century is in reality the history of the manufacturers' successful struggle for political power. The other minorities, however, were not wholly displaced from their positions of authority. They came to terms with the new class of manufacturers.

During the eighteenth and most of the nineteenth century minority control was not disturbed by such things as human rights and universal suffrage. Governments represented the dominant economic class, acted according to its dictates, protected and nurtured it. When Governments sought advice they did so from those with a vested interest in preserving the status quo. There was no question of a Government consulting members of the working class or its representatives about its courses of action. It did not depend upon working-class votes for its existence for most members of the working class did not have votes. This situation changed after the franchise was extended to workers but the change was slow, uneven and grudgingly conceded.

The Development of Committee Work

It was a rarity for a workman to be appointed or elected to any public body before 1870. It was contrary to tradition. Robert Applegarth's suggestion in 1866 that two experienced trade unionists should be appointed to the Royal Commission on Trade Unions was considered to be preposterous.[1] It was a concession even to permit workers to give evidence for themselves before Select Committees or Commissions. And although there were elections for Improvement Boards, Burial Boards, Vestries, and Municipal Corporations, the financial qualifications candidates had to possess were such as to preclude working men from standing, unless special provisions were made for them. The Government even opposed suggestions that miners should become members of Coroners' Juries which inquired into fatal accidents in the mines.

The first significant Government recognition of a trade union leader was Robert Applegarth's appointment as a member of the Royal Commission on the Contagious Diseases Acts in September 1870.[2] Thereafter at fairly long intervals union leaders became members of Royal Commissions. Thomas Burt, who was a Member of Parliament as well as a miners' leader, sat on one to inquire into accidents in coal mines in 1879; the Royal Commission on Housing the Poor in 1884 included Henry Broadhurst, general secretary of the Trades Union Congress, and the Prince of Wales—a unique combination for those days. The Royal Commission on Education in 1887 had George Shipton, secretary of the London Trades Council, amongst its members. Whereas the Royal Commission on Trade Unions in 1867 had no labour men on it, out of the twenty-seven members of the 1891 Royal Commission on Labour seven were trade unionists. This indicated a change in attitude but it did not represent a wholly consistent trend.[3] A Government could still ignore labour representatives if it so minded, just as the Conservative Government under Mr. A. J. Balfour did in 1903 when it appointed a Royal Commission on Trade Disputes and Trade Combinations.

Trade unionists, during the same period, entered various decision-making spheres. Their entry into Parliament enabled them to sit on Select Committees. From 1885 it was possible for them to be appointed as justices of the peace, and, as a result of the Local Government

---

[1] *Robert Applegarth*, by A. W. Humphrey, p. 144. [2] Allen, op. cit., p. 19.

[3] Beatrice Webb thought the composition of the 1891 Commission was a 'gigantic fraud. Made up of a little knot of dialecticians *plus* a carefully picked parcel of variegated Labour men, and the rest landlords or capitalists, pure and simple. The dialecticians . . . have had it their own way . . .' (*Our Partnership*, p. 40).

Acts of 1888 and 1894, they qualified to sit as local government representatives. Between 1882 and 1892 the total number of representatives on local bodies rose from 12 to 200. By 1895 on borough councils alone there were 600 working-class representatives.[1]

There developed a ladder of public service up which working men could climb. Few ever reached the top rungs. The highest point was membership of the Cabinet and only one working man, John Burns, got there before 1914. The Trades Union Congress in that year had a membership of more than $2\frac{1}{4}$ million, comprising about 25 per cent of the total working population. Some of its affiliated unions were national organizations whose actions had widespread repercussions. In general, unions in 1914 were in a relatively strong industrial bargaining position. They also possessed some political power. There was national male suffrage, and through the Labour Party unions were endeavouring with some slight success to organize and obtain the votes of the working class.

These were reasons, it seemed, for their leaders to be drawn into the fringe, at least, of the power élite. But they were not so drawn. What power trade unions had was new and the country had not grown accustomed to it. It was still regarded as an act of rash and excessive equalitarianism to treat self-educated trade union leaders as men of power and to accord them commensurate status. The tradition of plutocracy died hard even among trade unionists themselves. In 1914 the power of trade unions was most probably greater than it had ever been but industrialists remained firmly in control. A form of political democracy had come to Britain but it had not yet found a practical expression in the decision-making processes of the Government.

The First World War had three characteristics which altered the whole relationship between trade unions and the Government and gave unions a new status. The first was the realization of the value of labour power as a war commodity. The second was the need of the Government to intervene in economic and industrial affairs to ensure that scarce commodities, including labour, were used fully and effectively for the sole purpose of prosecuting the war. The last characteristic was the extensive use of the committee system to supplement existing Government organizations, creating a complex administrative machine through which many decisions were made which in peacetime had been made by private industry. The combination of the three factors resulted in trade unionists being drawn into decision-making processes from which they had traditionally been excluded.

[1] *History of Labour Representation*, by A. W. Humphrey, p. 97.

Before this could happen the trade union movement had to assure the Government of its support. Such an assurance was necessary because many union leaders had publicly expressed their opposition to war on political or pacifist grounds and because the war had interrupted a period of militant union activity in which the Government as well as employers had figured as villains. The assurance was given promptly by the ordinary trade unionists who volunteered in large numbers to fight against Germany and by the Parliamentary Committee of the Trades Union Congress in September 1914 when it issued a public statement in support of the war policy of the Liberal Government. When the Trades Union Congress met in September 1915—its first meeting after the declaration of war—it endorsed by an overwhelming majority a patriotic motion submitted by the Parliamentary Committee.[1]

The Prime Minister, satisfied with the assurances, invited Labour to be represented in the Government in 1915. It accepted the invitation. Arthur Henderson (Friendly Society of Ironfounders) became a Cabinet Minister and William Brace (Miners' Federation) and G. H. Roberts (Typographical Association) were appointed junior Ministers. In the course of the war five other trade union leaders joined the Government. John Hodge (British Steel Smelters) became the Minister of Labour and G. N. Barnes (formerly Amalgamated Society of Engineers) became the first Minister of Pensions—they later changed places; and J. R. Clynes (N.U. of General Workers) ended the war as Food Controller. The other two had junior posts. Henderson resigned in 1917 as a member of the War Cabinet, in which he had acted as a labour adviser, and was replaced by Barnes. A new stage in the evolution of British trade unionism had begun. The first three trade unionists to be members of a Government, namely Broadhurst, Burt and Burns, had not been drawn in as representatives of organized labour; they had been working-men Liberals. The wartime Labour members of the Government represented the Labour Movement though they were, of course, obliged to accept decisions reached by a Government which was dominated by other political parties.

The entry of labour representatives into the Government overshadowed the Government committee work undertaken by other trade unionists; it was publicized ostentatiously by those who saw in it an advance and denigrated by those who did not. But in substance it was the less important of the two developments. Wherever the Government intruded into the affairs of private industry it set up a committee or a series of committees with mixed memberships

[1] Only seven delegates out of three hundred voted against the motion.

representative of the main interests concerned. It was a radical departure from the practice of private industry to permit groups involved in industrial activities to participate in decision-making; it was revolutionary to have union officials sitting with industrialists and civil servants, helping to reach decisions which had been the jealously guarded prerogative of industry.

The Government committees on which trade unions were represented are too numerous to mention in detail.[1] They were to be found in all the main departments of Government but, as one would expect, they were concentrated in the industries most directly connected with war; in agriculture, mining, transport, engineering. In agriculture there were committees at national and county level to advise on the production and distribution of agricultural produce, on the wages of farm workers and on the employment of female labour. In mining the committees dealt with labour disputes, retail coal prices, working hours, output, transport costs, recruitment. The committees in engineering came mainly under the jurisdiction of the Ministry of Munitions which, although it was not established until June 1915, had more than sixty departments divided into ten groups at the close of the war. Labour was represented on many of the committees advising the departments at national and local level.

As the wartime network of controls was discarded so the advisory committees which formed a part of it were dissolved. The systematic consultation between trade unions and the Government ended and was not replaced. Unions had not established a right, as a result of war practices, to be consulted and their advice was sought only when the Government thought fit to seek it.

The attitude of Mr. Lloyd George towards consultations with trade unions over matters other than actual industrial disputes was equivocal. He preferred to give advice rather than receive it, but he liked the ceremony of consultation, particularly when it was marked by a sense of urgency. For instance, on 4 October 1921 the Parliamentary Committee of the Trades Union Congress received a telephone message from the Prime Minister asking it to appoint eight members to have a 'confidential chat' with him on the subject of unemployment.[2] He wanted a quick reply, yet the country had been troubled with acute unemployment since late in 1920 and there had been many union deputations to him about it.

The Lloyd George Government was undoubtedly influenced in its view of trade unions by the acute industrial unrest of the immediate

---

[1] *A Dictionary of Official War-Time Organizations*, by N. B. Dearle, gives a list of Government wartime committees of all kinds, with their origin, purpose, representation, and other details.   [2] Parliamentary Committee Minutes, 5 October 1921.

post-war years. Its attitude for a time was tempered by the continuation of full employment which perpetuated the wartime value placed on labour and increased the power of unions through raising their memberships to the unprecedented aggregate, in 1920, of 8,334,000. After the middle of 1920, however, unemployment increased and by 1921 had reached mass proportions. Trade unions lost members and financial resources. Between 1920 and the end of 1921 their membership had been reduced by 20·5 per cent. It fell further throughout the 1920s. The Government, under those conditions, had no need to consult with unions. Moreover, Government changes in personnel brought in men who had played little or no part in the wartime practice of consultation and who assessed unions as they saw them. So, with the exception of the two spells of Labour Government, union leaders were rarely to be seen on Government committees until the 1930s.[1]

This situation was not altogether of the Government's making. The dominant union leaders after the war deliberately eschewed anything which savoured of collaboration with the Government. Until 1921 they advocated direct action to influence Government policy and then, until 1925 when the miners, mine-owners and the Government became involved in dispute, they preoccupied themselves with domestic union and industrial affairs. Other union leaders, not so aggressively anti-Government, gradually adopted the same attitude after the experience of the National Industrial Conference in 1919.

At Labour Conferences on unemployment in December 1920 and January 1921 decisions were taken against collaborating with the Government, although unions were demanding state action to solve the problem. There were few union misgivings about the absence of their leaders from Government advisory bodies. This attitude continued for a while after the General Strike. In 1928, Ernest Bevin said he would rather sit down with capitalists to discuss the problem of unemployment than with Government representatives.[2] A similar opinion was expressed over the task of achieving industrial peace after the General Strike. The president of the Trades Union Congress in 1927, George Hicks, spoke of the value of direct negotiations between national representatives of employers and workers, and said it would be of far greater significance than a spectacular national conference under the Government.[3] Then gradually the trade union view about relations with the Government altered, and economic conditions changed to make the new viewpoint a practical possibility.

[1] The annual Trades Union Congress directory of committees on which members of the General Council sat recorded nothing resembling a Government Committee for the years 1925–1929, apart from statutory wages boards.
[2] T.U.C. Report, 1928, p. 450.   [3] ibid., 1927, Presidential address.

In September 1926 W. M. Citrine became the general secretary of the Trades Union Congress. It was a Congress of disillusioned, nearly bankrupt, trade unions with declining memberships and beset with recrimination after the General Strike. The new authority which the Congress sought in the trade union movement after its re-organization in 1920 had not materialized. In the face of this situation Citrine set about making the Trades Union Congress into the central co-ordinating agency for the whole Movement.

The Congress, by providing research and publicity services to its affiliated members, slowly gained their confidence. As it did so, the Government became more willing to take notice of the many representations which it made under Citrine's influence. It displayed an interest in a wide range of Government activities which impinged on the welfare of trade unionists. It showed concern about the Government's plans for reducing unemployment, establishing industrial development councils, introducing tariffs, rationalizing industry, and so on. It prepared memoranda on these issues. It took every opportunity of submitting evidence to Royal Commissions and Government advisory committees and pressed for trade unionists to be represented on them.

The development of the Trades Union Congress was inevitably slow for it depended upon an improvement in the membership of trade unions, which in turn was influenced by the level of employment. The employment position worsened during the first few years of Citrine's tenure in office: 9·7 per cent of the insured population in the United Kingdom was unemployed in 1927, whereas in 1931, 1932, and 1933 the percentages were 21·3, 22·1, and 19·9 respectively. The membership of trade unions in Great Britain was already down to 4,919,000 in 1927 but it fell further to 4,392,000 by 1933. Then conditions improved. The level of unemployment fell after 1933, though it was never less than 10·8 per cent until 1940; and the total membership of trade unions increased. Thus it was that after 1933 Citrine's efforts were reflected in positive results.

The Trades Union Congress directory of committees listed only one Government committee on which the General Council was represented during 1931–1932,[1] but named six committees for 1934–1935.[2] Each year some committees lapsed and others were formed, but each year the number on which trade unionists were represented

[1] The National Advisory Council for Juvenile Employment. There was also trade union representation on the Macmillan Committee on Finance and Industry.

[2] They were the National Advisory Council for Juvenile Employment, the Committee on Overseas Exhibitions and Fairs, the Unemployment Insurance Statutory Committee, the Committee of Inquiry into the British Industries Fair, the Transport Advisory Council, and the Coal Mines National Industrial Board.

increased until, in 1938–1939, there were twelve. Most of them dealt with matters which closely affected the interests of labour.

When war was declared in 1939 trade unions had not regained the members they had lost since 1920, but they had become so consolidated in their relations with employers and the Government that, within limits, their absolute membership was irrelevant. The authority of the Trades Union Congress was firmly established. The Movement was no longer militant, or intent on pursuing political ends through industrial action. It acted through constitutional channels in most matters. It was powerful but in a way which was different from that in 1920. Its power in 1920 was based mainly on the threat of force, whereas in 1939 it had power derived from being an established, orthodox institution, with a recognized function to perform. So without asking for assurances about trade union intentions the Government drew union leaders into consultation as soon as the Second World War began.

Government Committees after 1939

As in the First World War, trade union collaboration after 1939 was sought at two levels. First, union leaders, through the Labour Party, were drawn into the Government and given responsibility for Government decisions. As a piece of political strategy this was aimed to gain the allegiance of workers to a Government for which they had not necessarily voted. But it also enabled trade union opinion to be brought to bear on uppermost Government decisions and added competent men to the Government's ranks. At the other level, trade union leaders became members of the large number of wartime committees which took over functions previously fulfilled by private industry and tackled new ones arising out of war needs.

It was never expected that union relations with the Government would return after the war to their precise pre-war state. But even the most optimistic of union leaders did not envisage such a favourable situation as did occur. The Trades Union Congress claim to have a say in all Government matters affecting workers, recognized under the exigencies of war, was granted in peacetime too. It became normal Government practice to accept trade union representation on the majority of its advisory committees.

A number of factors were responsible for the continuation of the wartime practice. First a Labour Government, influenced deeply by Bevin and generally sympathetic towards trade union aspirations, succeeded the wartime Coalition Government and through its policy of planning perpetuated many of the wartime bodies. Secondly, the war emergency was replaced by an economic emergency. Thirdly, the trade union movement increased its wartime membership gains and enhanced its power position. It had 7,875,000 members in 1945 and 9,320,000 members in 1948.

The number of Government committees on which trade unions were represented rose from twelve in 1939 to sixty in 1948–1949. Eight of these committees were important Joint Reconstruction Committees containing Government representatives and industrialists. The others were mainly concerned with labour and related matters. Some intruded into general economic policy. One such committee was the Economic Planning Board established in 1947 to advise the Government on the best use of national economic resources. This body had as members the Government's Chief Planning Officer, who was its chairman, the Permanent Secretaries of the Ministries involved, specialist members of the Cabinet's staff, and trade union and employer representatives. A number of these committees owed their origin to the post-war economic crisis: there were, for example, committees on 'Commercial Load Spreading' and 'Export Guarantees'. Others were formed for specific purposes and the remainder were continuous, though not necessarily permanent.

It would not have been surprising if the number of Government committees had decreased after the Conservative Government was formed in 1951. The new Government was opposed to planning and controls, and gradually dispensed with committees in that sphere. It had no emotional bond with the trade union movement and did not feel impelled to give unions as wide and pervasive a say in Government affairs as a Labour Government was expected to give. But there was no apparent change in the relationship. Sir Winston Churchill and his Minister of Labour, Sir Walter Monckton, accorded to unions the form of representation to which they had grown accustomed since 1939. Indeed, the stage was reached under this Government when hardly any Government committee was formed without someone in authority asking for the trade union view to be represented on it. Trade union leaders sat on eighty-one Government committees in the year 1953–1954, covering a wide range of subjects. This state of affairs was undoubtedly influenced by personalities in the Government. But even after Sir Winston Churchill and Sir Walter Monckton had left the Government and antagonism had developed between it and some union leaders, the formal relationship remained virtually unaltered. In 1957–58 union leaders sat on sixty-five Government committees.[1]

---

[1] See Appendix I for a list of these committees.

The most prominent of these committees have been the two general advisory committees, the National Joint Advisory Council to the Minister of Labour and the National Production Advisory Council on Industry. These bodies have fairly wide functions and their members are free to raise matters for discussion. It is worthwhile looking briefly at their activities.

The National Joint Advisory Council has nineteen of the senior and most dominant members of the General Council on it. It was formed in October 1939 by the Minister of Labour, Mr. Ernest Brown, to provide a means of consultation between the Government and national representatives of industry on a wide range of labour problems. When Ernest Bevin became Minister of Labour in 1940 he used a sub-committee of the Council, the Joint Consultative Committee, to advise him from day to day. The sub-committee displaced the full Council from 1941 until 1946 and became an influential body. Its members discussed the many proposals for legislation affecting working conditions which Bevin submitted and bargained with him over the price of collaboration with the Government.

The National Joint Advisory Council was revived in 1946 but, although the need for close and constant consultation between unions and the Government continued, the Council deteriorated into a platform for the Minister of Labour to air his views or to test the feelings of trade unionists and employers on contentious matters. It was the body to which the Minister of Labour went in 1951 and 1958 when the Government intended to make changes in the Order relating to compulsory arbitration. The Council discussed restrictive practices in industry when the Minister was under pressure to legislate for them in 1957. And when, also in 1957, a Private Members' Bill was introduced into the House of Commons which proposed that manual workers should be paid by cheque, the Minister of Labour tested the feeling about it on the Council. The notice taken of trade union views on the council has varied. The advice of the trade union representatives about the payment by cheque was accepted and the offending section in the Bill was withdrawn. On the other hand the Government abolished compulsory arbitration in October 1958 despite opposition from the union members of the Council. Sometimes the Council is consulted, not over a proposed decision, but over the implementation of a decision.

The Council is undoubtedly useful to the Government though sometimes it merely gives a formal endorsement to earlier informal discussions which have taken place between the parties. But it is not operating wholly satisfactorily for trade unions because the Trades

Union Congress rarely uses it to press its suggestions on the Government. If it were not for the Ministry of Labour the Council might cease through default. Even with a Ministry interested in perpetuating the Council it is often difficult to find enough items to constitute an agenda.

The National Production Advisory Council for Industry has nine leading members of the General Council on it and is also attended by employers' representatives, a galaxy of Ministers or their representatives and civil service advisers. Altogether it has about sixty members and is too heavily weighted with officials. Like the National Joint Advisory Council it is principally a platform for Government views. At each meeting the Chancellor of the Exchequer presents a survey of economic and industrial affairs and he has frequently used the occasion to make pleas for wage restraint. This was particularly so during 1956 and 1957. Various production matters are raised but normally they are too wide ranging to be discussed adequately. It is possible for representative groups to raise matters, as the unions did in May 1957 when they asked for a committee of inquiry into British roads, but the size of the Council and its mixed composition limit the extent to which any one group can participate.[1]

The Effectiveness of Trade Unionists on Government Bodies

Once a political party has received a mandate to govern from the electorate it can implement its election policy and introduce new measures regardless of group protests. In so far as the principles of its policy are concerned it has a duty to the electorate to ignore group protests. But in the detailed formulation and implementation of its policy a Government should take cognizance of the different viewpoints of those people affected by the policy. To do otherwise is contrary to the standard of representative Government. So until the Government was prepared to accept the representatives of workers as its advisers British political democracy was incomplete.

The mere entry of trade union leaders, however, into the circle of Government did not automatically make the Government more democratic in practice; though it did give it a more democratic façade. What happened in practice depended upon the contribution which union leaders were able to make in the determination of detailed policy.

[1] In May 1959 the T.U.C. General Council expressed its dissatisfaction with the way in which the N.P.A.C.I. functioned and sent a memorandum to the Chancellor of the Exchequer containing suggestions for improved working. It wanted the Government to use the N.P.A.C.I. more effectively in an endeavour to increase the pace of industrial development. (T.U.C. *Industrial News*, 29 May 1959.)

Trade union leaders, in the vast majority of cases, are men who have worked in manual jobs after a formal elementary-school education. Most have been too busy with union work to be able to spare part of their adult lives for any continuous, disciplined education. They start with a rudimentary education and develop their intellectual capacity through their experiences in industry, unions, and local politics. Educational ability is not, and never has been, a prime qualification for their work. It assists them in the administrative side of union activity and may influence their movement through the hierarchy, but other qualities relating to the exercise of power over men and negotiating prowess predominate. If intellectual ability is revealed in this prowess it usually lacks the qualities of thoroughness and disciplined thinking which an academic training aims to provide. It appears more as intuition and less as a process of reasoning; it is reflected in an understanding of the essential points of a case without involving, necessarily, the logic which may have gone into its construction.

Normally, trade union leaders do not easily marshal facts, argue logically from them, or follow closely-reasoned arguments of others. This is due not only to the lack of intellectual training but also to the presence of fixed loyalties and traditions which comprise the trade union ethical code. This factor influences all union leaders in their decision-making. It tends to make them stubborn. Like others with an ethical basis for their behaviour, union leaders can adopt positions upon which fact and reason may have no effect.

Such men as these sit on Government committees with people who either have had extended courses of formal education, often including university training, or who work in occupations where educational ability figures prominently. Invariably trade unionists are outnumbered for, though they are representative of many people, they only represent one interest. In addition, the composition of a committee frequently reflects the result which the Government would like it to produce. So it may be that trade unionists will have to counter a bias as well as intellectual dialectics. The bias, of course, could be in their favour.

It is unwise to generalize about the impact trade unionists have made as Government advisers. There is always a striking divergence in the quality of union leaders, in the composition of committees, and in the subjects under discussion. There is, moreover, little written evidence to go on, and some of the verbal evidence is contradictory. But enough is known to give an indication of the effectiveness of the trade union advisory role.

The first intimate description of Government committee work is

T.U.G.—D

provided by Beatrice Webb. She was a biased observer, for she was intolerant of many trade union qualities, but her observations are revealing. When she sat on a Statutory Pensions Committee in 1916 she wrote: 'My Labour colleagues are Gosling and Barnes,[1] neither of them strong men. It is pathetic to watch the "Labour man" struggling with an environment that he cannot master. However, he is a portent, foreshadowing the coming of social equality. . . .'[2] After members of the Labour Party had joined Mr. Lloyd George's Coalition Government at the end of 1916 she wrote: 'Neither as individuals nor as a class do Labour men realize that they are mere office-mongers when they serve with men of trained intelligence or even with middle-class administrators.'[3] Mrs. Webb described in some detail most of the members of the influential Reconstruction Committee which was formed in 1917. But of the Labour members she simply, cryptically, reported that they seldom attended.[4]

None of the trade unionists who sat alongside Beatrice Webb would have professed a claim to intellectual ability—the quality for which she was looking. Nor would their keenest supporters. They were noted for their stubbornness.[5] This can be a useful quality in negotiations with employers over a straightforward wage issue, but on a committee whose task is to collect data and formulate opinion on the basis of it, stubbornness is a negative quality unless it is accompanied by the ability to reach independent, rational decisions. In the case of the trade union leaders of the First World War it is likely that Beatrice Webb's assessment was correct. Most of the men concerned belonged to a generation which was nearing the end of its functional role in the trade union movement. They were mainly orators who were more capable of shouting a single-point argument to a mass of men than becoming effectively immersed in committee work.

The experience of committee work in the First World War had little positive influence on trade union leaders who were already set in their ways; but for some of their immediate subordinates it provided a means for intellectual development. Ernest Bevin, Arthur Pugh of the Iron and Steel Trades Confederation, and Frank

---

[1] Harry Gosling was the general secretary of the Watermen, Lightermen and Bargemen's Union and President of the National Transport Worker's Federation. George Barnes had been general secretary of the Amalgamated Society of Engineers, 1898–1908.
[2] *Diaries, 1912–1924*, pp. 54–55.   [3] ibid., p. 73.
[4] ibid., p. 85.
[5] This was made clear at the Labour Party Conference in 1917 when the entry of trade union leaders into the Government was debated. Arthur Henderson, John Hodge and the others concerned could not 'be shaped and moulded in any way', J. R. Clynes maintained, for they were 'of the most stubborn kind and once they took their stand on any question they were immovable' (Labour Party Conference Report, 1917, p. 96).

Hodges of the Miners' Federation emerged from the war as able committee men. But these belonged to the giants in the trade union movement. The war had merely hastened their development.

Before these men sat on a committee they acquainted themselves with the subject of its deliberations, took the elementary step of reading its agenda and briefed themselves in readiness. It was sometimes found that their rough form of intellectual capacity supplemented the efforts of fellow committee members with trained minds. This was illustrated during the deliberations of the Royal Commission on the Coal Industry in 1919. Then Robert Smillie and Frank Hodges worked closely with the intellectuals, Sidney Webb and R. H. Tawney. Another case was the Macmillan Committee on Finance and Industry, appointed in 1931, when Ernest Bevin served effectively in an illustrious intellectual company, including John Maynard Keynes.[1]

When the Government wants a trade unionist to serve on a committee the Government department in which the committee falls takes the initiative to obtain him. In some cases legislation requires that trade unions should be consulted about the appointment, in which case the Trades Union Congress is asked for names. The Minister of the department concerned is not bound to accept the suggestions, but in practice he does accept them. Where consultation is not stipulated the Government department either approaches a union leader who is thought suitable for the appointment—usually a General Council member—or asks the Trades Union Congress for nominations, sometimes in excess of the number required so that the Government can make its own choice. With the present procedures the onus of Government committee work falls almost entirely on to the shoulders of General Council members, for the General Council normally confines the nominations to its own ranks.[2]

There are thirty-five members on the General Council. All but one[3] are full-time union officials whose General Council work is additional to that of their own unions. As General Council members they sit on about 150 committees between them. There are General Council sub-committees and standing committees, Labour Party joint committees, joint committees with various outside bodies, and Government committees. Many union leaders sit on committees in which they have little or no interest. Only to a small extent can they choose

[1] *Ernest Bevin*, by Francis Williams, p. 166.
[2] Occasionally past members of the General Council are left on unimportant committees, or trade union officials who are not on the General Council sit with General Council members in a sense as technical advisers.
[3] One member from the Transport and General Workers' Union is a rank and file trade unionist.

which to sit on, for the General Council operates mainly on lines of seniority. The leaders of large unions claim some privileges, so they and the senior members sit on the most important ones; others are given committees partly to coincide with their special fields and partly to ensure an equitable distribution of the work. Most of them do so much committee work that they have barely any time to study agendas, to read the relevant documents or to prepare briefs. They may only have time to consider committee business on the way to a meeting. No wonder that when they get there they act in a limited and somewhat negative fashion—preventing decisions being taken which are inimical to the interests of trade unions more by being present than by argument.

The General Council could improve its effectiveness as a Government adviser by reducing the burden of committee work on its members, thus enabling them to be placed where they could exercise most influence. It could do this either by using union leaders who were not members of the General Council or by restricting its interests.

Neither of these courses is likely to be taken. First, the General Council will not go outside its ranks for committee members, except in a very limited way, because only its members can act as representatives of the trade union movement. A spread of committee work might weaken the already tenuously held authority of the General Council. The individual members of the General Council might like to see a reduction in the number of their commitments but not necessarily in the Government committees on which they sit. They derive some satisfaction from the experience and in a few cases they are paid. Secondly, the Trades Union Congress has become more intent on preserving the prestige derived from having representatives on a large number of Government committees than on ensuring that its interventions in Government are genuinely effective. This has become a misplaced emphasis. Now that the right to express its opinions on all Government matters has been secured, the Trades Union Congress is in a position to discriminate in its interventions. It should concentrate on those committees which deal with individual industries or with specific matters which are of direct interest to unions, along with the two general advisory committees which bring trade union representatives into direct contact with Ministers.

There are, then, two main aspects in an assessment of the effectiveness of trade unionists on Government committees. One relates to the interest which the Trades Union Congress takes in the preparation of the agendas for meetings. In cases where items can be submitted for discussion the Trades Union Congress should make sure that it utilizes the facility. The other concerns the interventions of individual trade unionists in the discussions. In two respects these interventions are dependent upon the efficiency of the Trades Union Congress: they depend upon the quality of the briefs with which the organization can supply the members and upon the volume and nature of committee work the members are called upon to undertake. Basically, the impact of the interventions depends upon the intellectual quality of union leaders in relation to other members of the committees. Here trade union leaders are normally at a disadvantage. They are not intellectuals nor are they required to be so for the main purpose of their work.

Appendix I

THE GOVERNMENT BODIES ON WHICH THE TRADES UNION CONGRESS WAS REPRESENTED
1957–1958

Joint Committees with Representatives of Government Departments and National Employers' Organizations.
1. Joint Consultative Committee to Minister of Labour.
2. National Joint Advisory Council to Minister of Labour.
3. National Production Advisory Council on Industry.
4. British Productivity Council.

Government Committees to which Representatives of the General Council are appointed or nominated by the General Council or are appointed after Consultation:
5. Agricultural Machinery Advisory Committee.
6. Agricultural Marketing Act, Consumers' Committee.
7. Agriculture and Fisheries Advisory Committee on Standard Grades and Packs for Home-Produced Fruit and Vegetables.
8. Anthrax, Committee of Inquiry.
9. British Travel and Holidays Association.
10. Building Material Prices, Standing Committee.
11. Catering Wages Commission.
12. Census of Distribution, Advisory Committee.
13. Census of Production, Advisory Committee.
14. Central After-Care Association (E. &. W.) Council.
15. Cinematograph Films Council.
16. Cinematograph Films Act, 1948, Selection Committee.
17. Civil Defence Services, Advisory Committee on Publicity and Recruitment.

18. Clean Air Council.
19. Coal Consumers' Councils.
20. Coal Distribution Costs, Inquiry Committee.
21. Colonial Labour Advisory Committee
22. Companies Act, Board of Trade Standing Committee on Administration.
23. Consultative Committee for Industry, Board of Trade (International Trade Questions).
24. Cost of Living Index, Ministry of Labour Advisory.
25. Council for the Provision of Rest-Break Houses for Nurses and Midwives.
26. Decontrol of Fatstock, Joint Advisory Panel.
27. Council for Scientific and Industrial Research.
28. Disabled Persons (Employment) Act.
29. Duty Free Entry of Machinery Consultative Committee.
30. Economic Planning Board.
31. Education, Ministry of, Central Advisory Council.
32. European Community for Agriculture, Trade Union Advisory.
33. European Productivity Agency.
34. Exports Credits Guarantee Department.
35. Fairs and Exhibition Overseas Advisory Committee, Board of Trade.
36. Food Hygiene Advisory Council.
37. Industrial Health Advisory Committee.
38. Industrial Injuries Advisory Council.
39. Industrial Sub-Committee of I.I.A.C.
40. Industrial Safety Sub-Committee of N.J.A.C.
41. Insurance Advisory Committee, National.
42. Legal Aid and Advice Act, Advisory Committee.
43. Merchandise Marks Act (Statutory) Committee.
44. Migration Board—Commonwealth Relations Office.
45. Monetary System—Committee on the Working of the.
46. Monopolies Commission.
47. National Savings Committee.
48. National Youth Employment Council.
49. Nurses and Midwives, Ministry of Labour, National Advisory Council.
50. Oil Consumers' Council.
51. Pig Reorganization Commission.
52. Pneumoconiosis and Byssinosis Benefit Board, Ministry of National Insurance.
53. Radio-Active Substance Advisory Committee.
54. Recruitment and Training of Young Workers N.J.A.C. Sub-Committee.
55. Regular Forces Resettlement Service Advisory Board.
56. Revolving Loan Fund, Board of Trade Committee.
57. Road Safety Committee.
58. Royal Society for the Prevention of Accidents (Committee on Industrial Safety).

59. Rubber Consultative Committee, Board of Trade.
60. Territorial Army, Advisory Committee.
61. Tidal Thames, Inter-Departmental Committee on the Condition of the.
62. Transport Consultative Committee, Central.
63. Transport Tribunal, General Panel.
64. United Nations Food and Agriculture Committee.
65. Workmen's Compensation Supplementation Board.

Chapter Three

THE GOVERNMENT AS CONCILIATOR
AND ARBITRATOR

So far we have been concerned with the attempts of trade unions to establish a relationship with the Government. Now we turn to the other side of this process.

The dominant political view of Government in the nineteenth century was that it should assume the minimum of functions in the economy and concern itself primarily with the maintenance of law and order. This is what was attempted in practice. The Government endeavoured to stand aloof from industry and to ignore its domestic troubles. Throughout the century, however, social reformers demonstrated that in the light of actual conditions this view was untenable and they succeeded in getting the Government to pass industrial legislation for the protection of workers.

The orthodox view of Government changed gradually under the impact of more penetrating social investigations and as the structure of the economy altered to consist of large interdependent units. The Government came to be regarded as the custodian of the community's wide interests. Whatever issue touched the welfare of the community was considered to be the concern of Government. In the evolution of this role the field of industrial relations came within the Government's purview.

Industrial Legislation

The Government has reduced the area of possible conflict between trade unions and employers by a series of legislative acts. Early in the nineteenth century the Government legislated to regulate the working conditions of apprentices. Later, in 1819 and 1820, it passed Acts to protect child workers as distinguished from apprentices, but only those employed in cotton mills. In 1833 the first Factory Act was passed to cover the working hours and conditions of children and young persons in almost all textile mills.[1] A distinguishing feature of this Act was that it introduced the principle of Government inspection of factories. Thereafter the scope of inspection widened. The employment of women and girls was regulated. Industries other than textiles were covered by Factory Acts and, in the case of the mines,

[1] *The Worker and the State*, by Sir Frank Tillyard, p. 108 et seq.

by separate legislation. The Government gave itself the authority to impose standards of safety, of health and of welfare in most industries and trades. It enforced its authority through the Factory Inspectorate which became subject to the control of the President of the Board of Trade. Another aspect of this form of intervention arose from the Government's concern about industrial injuries. Through the Workmen's Compensation Act, 1897, successive Amending Acts, and then the National Insurance (Industrial Injuries) Act, 1946, an insurance against injuries was established which placed responsibilities on employers and workmen.

Industrial legislation intervenes in the conduct of industry mainly by imposing statutory obligations on employers. Only to a slight degree do workers carry any statutory responsibility. Its results are similar, then, to the consequences of successful trade union pressure on employers, except that industrial legislation is more pervasive and obligatory. The similarity is made greater by the close identity between the industrial issues which the Government and trade unions have pursued.

The Government, by forcing employers to implement standards which trade unions endorse as their own, has assumed a function of trade unionism. Much of the early legislation, however, occurred in the absence of union activity; in the absence, sometimes, of unions themselves. Industrial legislation, moreover, has often covered matters which unions have been unable to tackle, such as workmen's compensation. It has sometimes resulted from or has been the subject of trade union pressure.

Only rarely have unions been apprehensive about the Government's legislative incursions into industry. In 1941 and 1942 some unions, amongst them the Transport and General Workers' Union, were concerned about a proposal to introduce family allowances by legislation lest it should interfere in any way with employer and trade union wage-bargaining.[1] But then unions have always been prepared to resist proposals for Government incursions into wage determination. It may be argued that all extensions of the state welfare provisions have a bearing on wage determination but so far they have created no special relationship problem. The effect up till now has simply been to reduce the number of issues over which unions and employers could argue.

Legislation for Settling Industrial Disputes

The Government could not legislate to settle labour disputes which involved trade unions until it had recognized collective action by workers and employers. This recognition was not given until

[1] See T.U.C. Report, 1941, pp. 372–376.

1824 when the Combination Acts were repealed. Arbitration provisions had appeared in Acts containing various other labour regulations before 1747, and between then and 1824 they had been provided for by special enactments; but in all cases the provisions referred solely to individual disputes. The Cotton Arbitration Acts of 1800, 1803, 1804, and 1813 were enactments of this type.[1]

Shortly after the Combination Acts were repealed the Arbitration Act, 1824, was passed. This aimed to consolidate and amend all the laws relative to the arbitration of disputes between workers and employers. The Act excluded the determination of wage rates unless the mutual consent of both parties was obtained. It was amended in 1837 and 1845 but it was never applied. It was outdated almost from its beginning for the disputes it aimed to cover had ceased to be important by 1824, and the determination of wages which it excluded had become a primary cause of disputes.

The next legislative intervention by the Government was in 1867, after the subject of conciliation and arbitration had been examined by a number of Government committees. The Councils of Arbitration Act, 1867, aimed to encourage the growth of conciliation, which had already begun to be practised in a few industries.[2] There was no provision for Conciliation Councils to establish wage rates. The Act was forgotten almost as soon as it was passed.[3] The Arbitration (Masters and Workmen) Act of 1872, though its scope was wider and included wage determination, met a similar fate.

There are various reasons to account for the failure of the Acts. On each occasion the Government illustrated how futile legislation could be unless it was attended by certain developments in the environment where it was to be applied. The Government could not force workers and employers to be conciliatory in their dealings; they had to evolve their own procedures and possess confidence in the results. Conciliation machinery could only be built by representative organizations for workers and employers which could command the loyalty of their members to the decisions they jointly reached. There were few representative employers' organizations until the last quarter of the nineteenth century. Trade unions were much more numerous, but until the 1860s and 1870s they were immature, unstable organizations, largely incapable of adhering to a procedural settlement of disputes.

Most employers, however, had no desire to be conciliatory, and refused to negotiate with trade union representatives. Conciliation

---

[1] *Industrial Conciliation and Arbitration*, by I. G. Sharp, p. 273 et seq.
[2] See Final Report of the Royal Commission on Labour, 1894, Appendix III.
[3] Sharp, op. cit., p. 286.

entailed compromises and concessions which employers in their strong bargaining positions felt it unnecessary to concede. The state of mind to make conciliation work usually came to employers only after much experience of organized industrial action. Trade unionists were always much more willing to come to terms with employers.

The idea of achieving industrial conciliation through legislation in the absence of strong trade unions was misplaced. But even if it had not been, the Acts as constituted would still not have worked. It was a prime motive of trade unions to free themselves of legal restrictions during the nineteenth century and the penal provisions of the Arbitration Acts were inconsistent with this intention. The Acts were not intended to supplement voluntary machinery but aimed to provide alternative means for settling disputes. A witness to the Royal Commission on Labour, 1891, claimed that this factor was responsible for the failure of the legislation.[1] Another defect was that, until 1872 the Acts did not cover wage determination and thus excluded an important cause of disputes. Lastly, the Government did not possess its own labour administration to encourage the acceptance of the provisions of the Acts and to supervise their operation.

Most of the conditions which had frustrated the intentions of legislators began to show a marked change in the last two decades of the nineteenth century. Trade unionism spread to the hitherto unorganized groups of unskilled and semi-skilled workers, it became consolidated in the crafts, and employers learned to act collectively. The two sides focused the attention of the Government and the public on their relationship by engaging in bitter disputes. The Government found itself intervening directly in industrial disputes, not to maintain law and order, but to conciliate.

THE FORMATION OF A LABOUR ADMINISTRATION

The Labour Bureau

No member of the Government or the civil service had the appointed task of dealing with labour matters until 1886. In March 1886 Mr. Charles Bradlaugh, M.P., set about rectifying this deficiency in a small way. With the approval of Mr. A. J. Mundella, the President of the Board of Trade, he moved in the House of Commons 'that . . . immediate steps should be taken to ensure in this Country the full and accurate collection and publishing of Labour Statistics'.[2] The suggestion that labour statistics should be collected was not new. It had been made by a Departmental Committee of Parliament in 1883

---

[1] Royal Commission Report, op. cit., p. 376.
[2] Hansard, 1886, vol. CCCII, col. 1768.

and in parts of Canada and the United States of America it was
already implemented. Mr. Bradlaugh's case was that a good collection of labour statistics would make arbitration and conciliation
more effective. The motion was accepted.

Later in the same month a Bureau of Labour Statistics was formed
to inquire into the organization, remuneration and expenditure of
the working classes. It was organized under the supervision of
Mr. R. Giffen, the chief of the Statistical Department of the Board
of Trade, and had one Labour Correspondent, John Burnett, to do
its work.[1] The first apparent result of Burnett's appointment was the
publication in November 1887 of two articles by him in the Board of
Trade Journal which was founded by Mundella in July 1886. One of
the articles was on the 'State of the Skilled Labour Market', a subject
on which Burnett wrote frequently afterwards. By 1890 he was
publishing a monthly article in the Journal.

The functions of the Bureau were discussed by the Royal Commission on Labour in 1891. At that time these consisted of the compilation
and publication of wage statistics, strike and lock-out returns,
statistics relating to alien immigration, and of special reports on
relevant topics, such as sweated labour, profit sharing and the cost
of living.[2] Various witnesses before the Commission submitted ideas
for the extension of the Bureau's activities. Some wanted a more
extensive collection of labour statistics published in a Labour
Journal, others proposed that certain separate functions of the
Government which concerned labour should be amalgamated into a
distinct department or ministry. Mr. Sidney Webb, for instance,
wanted the Labour Bureau and the Factory and Mining Sections
of the Home Office amalgamated; while Mr. Ben Tillett[3] thought
there should be a Labour Department, under the control of a Labour
Minister, which should be obliged to confer with the Parliamentary
Committee of the Trades Union Congress over amendments to the
Factory Acts.[4]

Ben Tillett, Sidney Webb, and Tom Mann each proposed that a
Labour Department should be formed to arbitrate in trade disputes.
Tillett wanted the Labour Department to issue awards which would
be legally binding on the parties; Webb preferred it simply to conduct
inquests into the causes of disputes and to publish the results. Tom
Mann advocated a middle course which entailed the formation of a

---

[1] John Burnett resigned from the general secretaryship of the Amalgamated Society
of Engineers to do this job.
[2] Royal Commission Report, op. cit., p. 363.
[3] General Secretary of the newly formed Dock, Wharf, Riverside and General
Workers' Union.
[4] Royal Commission Report, op. cit., p. 363.

central board of mediation for the whole country, under the jurisdiction of a Labour Department, to which voluntary boards of
conciliation could submit the issues over which they failed to agree.
Advice from the Labour Department of the United States, initially
formed in 1885, was that the functions of a labour department should
be confined to the compilation of statistics.[1]

The Labour Bureau was reorganized while these suggestions were
being offered and before the Commission had reached its own conclusions. Industrial relations had suffered an upheaval through the
rapid and unprecedented growth of trade unions for general workers.
These unions rejected the moderate policies and friendly society
functions of the older established craft unions. They owed their
origin to strike action and they showed their gratitude by pursuing
an aggressive policy which was only slackened when their funds were
exhausted and their organizations shaken. It was estimated that in
1888 there were 509 stoppages of work. In 1889 the strikes at the
London docks and the South Metropolitan Gas Company occurred
and the total number of strikes increased to 1,145.[2] In the following
year the number was 1,028. It was this high pitch of industrial unrest
which prompted the Government to set up the Royal Commission
and then form a Labour Department.

The Labour Department

The ideas of Tillett, Webb, and Mann found expression in Parliament. In 1892 and 1893, a Bill to establish a Labour Department
under the control of a Labour Minister, was presented in the House
of Commons but it was unsuccessful.[3] The Government introduced its
own, less ambitious Bill early in 1893 and then set up a Labour
Department without a Labour Minister and with limited functions.

The work of collecting, digesting, and publishing statistical and other
information bearing on questions relating to the conditions of labour
[a Government Memorandum stated] will in future be entrusted to a
separate branch of the Board of Trade. This branch will take over the
work of the present Commercial Department at the Board of Trade,
and will consist of three departments—commercial, labour, and statistical—the whole thing being under the superintendence of Mr. Giffen
as Comptroller-General.[4]

The Labour Department remained within the Board of Trade but

---

[1] ibid., p. 364.   [2] Sharp, op. cit., p. 290.
[3] The Bill received opposition from an odd quarter. Sir Charles Dilke, a friend of
labour, said it was 'one of those sham remedies, to which many of us object very much
in the interests of labour' (Hansard, vol. VIII, 15 February 1893).
[4] Memorandum on the Progress of the Work of the Labour Department, Board of
Trade, April 1893.

was given its own buildings and separate staff. It had a Commissioner for Labour, H. Llewellyn Smith; a Chief Labour Correspondent, John Burnett; three Labour Correspondents, Miss C. E. Collett, J. J. Dent, and C. J. Drummond; an Assistant Superintendent of Statistics, F. H. McLeod; and about thirty clerks of all grades. Part-time Local Correspondents were appointed in a number of large provincial towns, coincident with the centres selected for factory inspection. Their job was to keep the Department in touch with local events. Arrangements were made with secretaries of trade unions, trades councils, employers' associations, chambers of commerce, and district associations of the Co-operative Union, to supply the Department with information. A monthly *Labour Gazette* became the official publication of the Department.[1]

There were criticisms of the new Department. It was said that a few of its Local Correspondents held extreme political views, and that seventeen out of twenty-five were Gladstonian propagandists. A more important criticism was that Mundella had simply taken the Commercial and Statistical Department of the Board of Trade, added four inspectors and renamed it.[2] All its functions, except the publication of the *Labour Gazette*, were concerned with inquiry. The question was raised whether a Department of State was needed to inquire into special problems. The Government's initial attempts to extend the powers of the Department to enable it to work with existing Boards of Conciliation in settling disputes came to nothing. A Bill dealing with conciliation was presented by the Government in April 1893 but it was not proceeded with owing to the lack of Parliamentary time. A similar Bill suffered the same fate in 1894. The Labour Department did, at first, seem to be an extravagant means of collecting statistics.

It was soon revealed that the Labour Department would perform diverse tasks. Early in its life questions were asked in Parliament about conciliation and arbitration boards, destitute aliens, home and foreign labour, trade union reports, unemployment, unhealthy industries, women's wages, strikes, and employers' liability. The Labour Department had to provide the answers. In its task of collecting information about strikes the Labour Department sometimes deputed its officials to make on-the-spot inquiries instead of relying on its Local Correspondents. This had a far-reaching consequence. Once the officials were on hand both strikers and employers sought their advice. The information which was collected in some

---

[1] It was priced at 1*d.* and sold 20,000 copies on the first day of publication (Hansard, vol. XII, 18 May 1893).

[2] Hansard, vol. XVII, 8 September 1893.

cases, 'appeared to point to the possibility of lessening the conflict by conciliation, [and] the Board of Trade was enabled to assist informally and unofficially in smoothing over difficulties and generally bringing the forces of conciliation to bear'.[1] Strikes in the cotton industry, in shipping at Hull, and in the coal industry in the Midlands were named as ones in which the Labour Department conciliated informally.

No details of these interventions were given because of their new and unofficial character. The Labour Department became more forthright about its activities later on. It learned of disputes from newspapers, its Local Correspondents, or other sources. Then it sent 'a detailed series of questions to each of the parties involved in the dispute, in order that both sides [might] have an opportunity of fully stating their own case'.[2] This was in addition to the efforts of individual members of the Labour Department. Thus before the Department had been entrusted by Parliament with the job of conciliating it was doing it.

The Conciliation Act of 1896. From 1893 until 1896, A. J. Mundella tried, but unsuccessfully, to get a Conciliation Bill passed by the Government of which he was a member. On 7 August 1896 the Conservatives, only recently returned to office, made a Conciliation Bill law. The terms of the Bill followed the recommendations of the Royal Commission. The Commission stated that the Government could undertake conciliation work without legislation but that a statutory provision 'would probably be of use as giving the Department a better *locus standi* for friendly and experienced intervention'.[3] The Department could help, too, by nominating persons to act as arbitrators but the decisions of those nominated should not be legally binding.

The Conciliation Act, 1896, removed all elements of legal compulsion from the procedures for settling trade disputes and it conferred on the Board of Trade the statutory authority to intervene in an industrial dispute.[4] The Board of Trade had the following powers:

(*a*) to inquire into the causes and circumstances of the difference;
(*b*) to take such steps as the Board may consider expedient for the purpose of enabling the parties to the difference to meet together . . . under the presidency of a chairman mutually agreed upon or nominated by the Board of Trade, or by some

---

[1] First Report of the Labour Department, 1894.
[2] Seventh Annual Report on Labour Disputes, 1895.
[3] Committee on Industry and Trade, Survey of Industrial Relations, 1926, p. 255.
[4] The Board of Trade was the Ministry responsible to Parliament for labour matters. The Labour Department was merely an administrative section of the Board of Trade.

other person or body, with a view to the amicable settlement
of the difference;

  (c) on the application of the employers or workmen interested,
and after taking into consideration the existence and adequacy
of means available for conciliation in the district or trade and
the circumstances of the case, to appoint a person or persons
to act as conciliator or as a board of conciliation;

  (d) on the application of both parties to the difference to appoint
an arbitrator.

The Act did not alter the course of the activities of the Labour
Department. As is mentioned above, it was already conciliating.
What the Act did was to enable the Department to publicize its
activities and to point out to conciliation boards the desirability of
keeping in close touch with it. The Labour Department, however,
had to act cautiously in its new public role. There were still employers
who regarded the Act as a means to enable the Government to make
unwarranted intrusions into their private affairs. This was illustrated
when the Board of Trade intervened in the Penrhyn Quarries dispute
soon after the Act was passed.

The dispute, initially about the terms and conditions of employment, turned on to union recognition when Lord Penrhyn suspended
all the workers' representatives in the quarries. The quarrymen came
out on strike late in September 1896, and on 30 September appealed
to the Board of Trade for help under the Conciliation Act. One of
the quarrymen's requests was for a Board of Trade representative
to be present at the negotiations. Lord Penrhyn rejected this condition flatly. He wrote 'my acceptance of it would establish a precedent for outside interference with the management of my private
affairs'.[1] The Permanent Secretary of the Board of Trade, Sir
Courtenay Boyle, replied:

> I am to state that there is no desire to press the matter against your
> wishes, but I am to point out that in view of the provisions of the Concilia-
> tion Act, the Board cannot admit that the settlement of a prolonged
> dispute affecting some thousands of men and their families, can be
> rightly regarded as a matter of private interest only.[2]

This reply evoked protests from some Members of Parliament and
raised questions concerning the interpretation of the Conciliation
Act, the right of the Government to intervene in industrial disputes
and the wisdom of any interventions which could be construed as

---

[1] Hansard, vol. XLV, 1897, col. 694.   [2] ibid.

political. The questions were not answered and they continued to crop up periodically.[1]

The conciliation service of the Labour Department was used increasingly despite opposition from employers like Lord Penrhyn. In 1896 it assisted in the settlement of eleven disputes. In the following year this figure rose to thirty-seven and until 1908 it fluctuated between eleven and thirty-nine.[2] In many other cases the Department assisted informally. The activities of the Department depended not only on the demands made on it by workers and employers but upon its ability to initiate inquiries and upon the willingness of successive Presidents of the Board of Trade to intervene in industrial affairs. The Department was small, with no one member being able to devote his whole time to conciliation. Much of the work of conciliation, therefore, was necessarily delegated to independent persons. Some politicians have a disposition to intervene in disputes, whether they be between countries, classes, or individuals. Whenever such a person was the President of the Board of Trade the activities of the Labour Department expanded. They expanded under the direction of Mr. Lloyd George and Mr. Winston Churchill.

It was Mr. Lloyd George who appointed the first full-time conciliator for the Board of Trade. Sir George Askwith had been used frequently as an independent person to arbitrate during the early years of the Conciliation Act. He was invited by Lloyd George to enter the Board of Trade in August 1907 as an Assistant Secretary in control of the Railway Department in anticipation of industrial unrest on the railways.[3] In January 1909 Askwith became the Comptroller-General of the Commercial, Labour, and Statistical Departments of the Board of Trade. He gave expression to his own interest in the Government's conciliation service by encouraging and assisting its expansion.

The Government had no consistent labour policy. What was done depended on and varied with the whims of the successive Presidents of the Board of Trade. Askwith did not like Ministers who intervened in the affairs of his Department. 'However disinterested a Minister may be in fact,' he wrote, 'suspicion is aroused, and suspicion is fatal to the success of advice.'[4] But it was Askwith's fate to be associated with Ministers who interfered frequently. Indeed, his

---

[1] The dispute was not settled by conciliation; it dragged painfully on for about eleven months but it is doubtful whether this was caused, or had any connection with, the Government's attempt to intercede. Lord Penrhyn was faced by a large degree of hostile criticism from the press, the church and from Parliament, yet he refused to make concessions.

[2] Report of the Ministry of Labour, Cmd. 2481, p. 33.

[3] *Industrial Problems and Disputes*, by Lord Askwith, p. 110.

[4] ibid., p. 129.

rise was to a large extent dependent on that association. His predecessor as Comptroller-General in the Board of Trade, Mr. Arthur Wilson Fox, died prematurely, Askwith maintained, because of worry over the activities of Ministers in the engineering and shipbuilding disputes in 1908.[1]

The Industrial Council, 1911. On 15 August 1911 the Prime Minister, the President of the Board of Trade, Askwith and some other Government officials, met a number of employers and trade union leaders 'for the purpose of an informal exchange of views as to the present state of unrest in the labour world, and the possibility of improving the means available for preventing or shortening industrial wars'.[2] They discussed a plan for a special business court, consisting of employers and trade union leaders, to deal with industrial disputes.[3] The discussions were cut short by a deterioration in an already bad industrial situation. On the day the meeting was held, the railway unions threatened to call a national strike and the Government reverted to its traditional role of protector of private property.[4] The discussions were resumed in September and resulted in the formation of an Industrial Council with a membership of twenty-six divided equally between employers and trade unionists acting in their individual capacities. The Industrial Council's function was to settle industrial disputes. It was not equipped with compulsory powers.[5]

Mr. Sidney Buxton, the President of the Board of Trade, elaborated the reasons for setting up the Council at its first meeting on 26 October 1911. He said:

> One disadvantage of the existing system is undoubtedly that it brings into action and prominence the Parliamentary Head of the Board of Trade, who is necessarily a politician . . . and a member of the Government, in disputes and conciliations which ought to be purely industrial. It has been my policy, and, I hope, my action, during my two years at the Board of Trade to efface as far as possible my personality as a political President, and I believe my department has won the confidence of the public and of the two industrial sides to a remarkable degree. At the same time, I realize that, if the action of the department in these matters could be still further removed from the sphere of politics or the suspicion of politics, it would give even greater confidence, and there would be greater willingness by the parties to a dispute to seek the assistance of the Board of Trade. The President, cannot, of course,

[1] *Industrial Problems and Disputes*, by Lord Askwith, pp. 127–128.
[2] ibid., p. 161.
[3] Proposed by Sir Charles W. Macara (ibid.).
[4] See Chapter VII for the Government's use of troops at this time.
[5] Ninth Report by the Board of Trade of the Proceedings under the Conciliation (Trade Disputes) Act, 1896, 1911.

dissociate himself from all responsibility, and in certain circumstances the Government may have to intervene as a last resort. But such cases would be few and far between.[1]

The membership of the Industrial Council was impressive and if appearance had been the main ingredient for success it would have succeeded.[2] But the Council failed. It acted unsuccessfully in a few disputes and issued a report on the fulfilment and enforcement of industrial agreements which the Government did not accept as authoritative but referred instead to the Trades Union Congress for its opinion. The members were appointed for one year. After the first renewal of tenure the Council lapsed and was soon forgotten.

The Industrial Council was the first Government attempt on a grand scale to prevent strikes. Sir George Askwith submitted his reasons for its failure.[3] The idea, he wrote, of having a tribunal to which employers and trade unions could go voluntarily before engaging in strike action was prematurely applied. It was not the result of a growth of an idea by those immersed in industrial relations but an act imposed by the Government. Those who were opposed to Government interference looked askance at it. Others considered it to be a political move, and therefore to be discountenanced. The Government itself failed to treat the Industrial Council seriously once the phase of intense industrial unrest had passed. It was quietly but deliberately dropped.

The members of the Industrial Council were unable, or unwilling, to utilize its services in disputes involving their own organizations. There were strikes on the docks and in the mines in 1912 and the unions in both of these industries had leading figures on the Council. A more obvious case involved Sir Charles Macara, who conceived of the idea of the Council. Employers in his industry would have nothing to do with it; moreover, he was the chairman of the cotton employers who declared a lock-out in 1912 and ignored it completely.

The inauguration of the Industrial Council, however, had one positive consequence. In December 1909, because of the expansion in its conciliation work and its accretion of new duties, Mr. Churchill, the President of the Board of Trade, had divided the Labour Department into three sections. One section dealt with wages, arbitration, conciliation and trade boards; another section confined itself to

---

[1] Askwith, op. cit., p. 183.
[2] On the trade union side it contained Thomas Ashton, general secretary of the Miners' Federation; C. W. Bowerman, general secretary of the Trades Union Congress; Harry Gosling, president of the National Transport Workers' Federation; J. E. Williams, general secretary of the Amalgamated Society of Railway Servants; John Hodge, general secretary of the British Steel Smelters; and others of similar repute.
[3] *Industrial Problems and Disputes*, pp. 183-184.

statistics, special inquiries, and the *Labour Gazette*; and the third section supervised Labour Exchanges and unemployment insurance. This sub-division was carried further in 1911. Sir George Askwith and some of his immediate officers had been spending so much time on conciliation work that they were unable to carry on the proper control of other branches of the Board of Trade for which they were responsible. This was overcome by the appointment of Askwith as a specialist in charge of conciliation work. He became the chairman of the Industrial Council and was called the Chief Industrial Commissioner. He was given the rank of a Permanent Secretary and had charge of a special department for labour problems called the Chief Industrial Commissioner's Department.

The development of the new Department in the Board of Trade was accelerated by the war in 1914. The Government introduced measures to prevent strikes. It imposed compulsory arbitration and set up additional machinery to deal with it. These are described in Chapter VIII dealing with the Government attitude to strikes in wartime. The number of industrial disputes settled with the assistance of Askwith's department increased to 397 in 1915 and 1,412 in 1916. But the increase in the volume of conciliation and arbitration work was not sufficient by itself to compel the Government to devote more of its attention and resources to labour matters. The Government had to exercise control over labour in the war by every possible method. Coercion and persuasion and bribery were used, and in the process a Ministry of Labour was formed.

The Ministry of Labour

The first Government sop to obtain trade union concessions in the First World War was the appointment of Arthur Henderson[1] in May 1915 as a labour adviser with a seat in the Cabinet. Henderson did not have a department. He participated in the conciliation and arbitration work of the Labour Department but his interventions were considered to be unhelpful.[2] As the war progressed various Government Ministries dabbled in labour affairs. The Ministry of Munitions particularly had close though not usually amicable dealings with labour. There was an obvious need for the co-ordination of the Government's labour activities.

The Government was re-formed under the Premiership of Mr. Lloyd George in December 1916 and representatives of the Labour Move-

---

[1] The Secretary of the Labour Party. Henderson's nominal title was President of the Board of Education. After a time he shed this title and became known as Labour Adviser.

[2] Askwith, op. cit., pp. 412 and 413.

ment were invited to join it. A strong minority in the Labour Movement wanted to refuse this invitation. If it had succeeded the national character of the Government would have been spoiled. To prevent this happening Lloyd George offered to enhance the status of Labour in the Government. He said that Labour could have a seat in the War Cabinet and that he would form two new Ministries, one for Labour and the other for Pensions, with a Labour man at the head of each. Labour accepted. Thus suddenly, without protracted preliminary inquiries or planning, a Ministry of Labour was formed. No details had been arranged. The decision to establish the Ministry was taken after a few minutes' consideration.[1]

The Ministry of Labour started to exercise its duties on 11 January 1917. It was formed by the transfer from the Board of Trade of the Chief Industrial Commissioner's Department, the Office of Trade Boards, the Labour Exchanges and Unemployment Insurance Department. It was given the Department of Labour Statistics in July 1917. The Minister of Labour acquired the functions of Labour Adviser to the Government. Later in 1917 a Joint Industrial Councils Branch was formed. A new Appointments Department to provide employment for ex-Servicemen was created in 1918.[2] Much of the work which the new Ministry took over from other Departments arose out of the war and was temporary.

Not all the activities of the other Ministries which fell within the scope of a Ministry of Labour were transferred to it, however. There remained much untidiness within the field of conciliation and arbitration during the remaining years of the war. Sir George Askwith described the situation in a memorandum to the Prime Minister. He wrote:

> The Engineering Employers' Federation have formally complained to the Prime Minister of the lack of co-ordination and the necessity for one authority on labour matters. . . . Trade unions and employers everywhere are in uncertainty and confusion, and are unable to look to any one central or responsible authority in the number of over-lapping Government Departments. . . . The Ministry of Munitions has established a Disputes Department. The Admiralty has at least two. There is nothing to prevent officers of the Board of Agriculture, the Shipping Controller, the Controller of Mines following the same course. The Ministry of Labour is itself divided. Under the plea of being the employers, some of these Departments are seriously impairing the relations and responsibility of actual employers and workpeople to settle their own differences; are causing unrest in the ranks of labour; are weakening

---

[1] Askwith, op. cit., p. 414.
[2] Special Investigation Committee on Staffs, Cmd. 1069, p. 2.

the authority of trade union leaders; are spreading bureaucracy throughout the country; are pitting one Department against another. . . .[1]

The situation remained confused until after the war, despite Askwith's
protests.

The National Industrial Conference. The First World War had
started with a trade union movement which was insular, class-bound,
distrustful, and distrusted. When it ended the trade union movement
was changed in some of these respects. Some of the insularity and
prejudices were lost through the wartime intimacy of trade union
officials with employers, civil servants, and Conservative and Liberal
politicians. But much class tension remained. This was obvious before
the war ended. As soon as the Armistice was signed trade unions
released their demands and a period of intense industrial unrest
began.

In February 1919 the Government invited leading trade unionists
and employers to confer with it on the action to be taken to achieve
industrial peace. As in 1911, the Government appeared at the outset
to be genuinely concerned about seeking advice from trade unions
and employers; and it went outside its conciliation machinery to
deal with industrial disputes.

A National Industrial Conference met on 27 February 1919. There
were 800 delegates present representing the most prominent trade
unions and employers. G. H. Stuart-Bunning, chairman of the
Parliamentary Committee, represented the Trades Union Congress;
J. H. Thomas attended as spokesman for the Triple Industrial Alliance; and Arthur Henderson acted for the Friendly Society of Ironfounders. The Minister of Labour, Sir Robert Horne, was chairman
of the conference. Its feeling was amicable and the tenor of its
debates was moderate. Critics of moderation were dismissed as
irresponsible elements. A Joint Committee was appointed, consisting
of equal numbers of employers and workers, and a chairman
appointed by the Government, to consider:

(1) Questions relating to hours, wages and general conditions of
    employment.
(2) Unemployment and its prevention.
(3) The best methods of promoting co-operation between Capital
    and Labour.

The representative nature of the Conference was seriously impaired
by the refusal of the miners, railwaymen, transport workers, and
engineers to be associated with it after its first meeting, but the

---

[1] Askwith, op. cit., pp. 423–424.

Government nevertheless pressed on with the arrangements for the Joint Committee.

The Minister of Labour had stated at the first Conference that the Government would consider introducing legislation to fix hours and a national minimum wage. The Joint Committee took him at his word and submitted a report in April 1919 containing a number of proposals for legislation. It also proposed that a permanent National Industrial Council, consisting of 400 members equally representative of employers' organizations and trade unions, should be established; and that it should be recognized as the official consultative authority to the Government upon industrial relations.[1]

The report was received sympathetically by Mr. Lloyd George, while the Minister of Labour called it 'the most momentous document which had been presented to the country in a long number of years . . .' But with the easing of its troubles on the railways and in the mines, the Government began to lose interest. It refused to apply the Joint Committee proposals for hours and minimum wages. It acted dilatorily in summoning meetings. Even Sir Allan Smith, representing the Engineering and Shipbuilding Employers' Federation, said that the Government was asking for trouble and would get it.[2] The Government was willing to establish ostentatiously the permanent National Industrial Conference but the employers and unions wanted evidence of the Government's good faith before they embarked on anything of a permanent nature. The Government by 1920 was not even making a pretence at consultation with the Conference. It was formally dissolved on 19 July 1921. The Government was completely unconcerned.

The Trade Boards Act. The use of the Ministry of Labour conciliation machinery depended upon their being in existence a high degree of organization among workers and employers. The Government had assisted in the development of this organization by passing the Trade Boards Act in 1909.

It had been interested in the wages and working conditions in 'sweated' trades since the establishment of the Labour Department. One of John Burnett's early reports was about these industries and the Royal Commission on Labour devoted much of its time to them. Outside the Government the Anti-Sweating League engaged in persistent propaganda to get legislation.

The Act enabled the Government to set up Trade Boards which

---

[1] Report of Provisional Joint Committee. Presented to Meeting of Industrial Conference, 4 April 1919, Cmd. 139.

[2] Minutes of Proceedings of the National Industrial Conference Provisional Joint Committee, 13 June 1919.

could fix legal minimum wage rates; it was only to be applied in those trades where 'sweating' was an exceptional problem, namely in ready-made and wholesale bespoke tailoring, paper-box making, machine-made lace and net finishing, and chain-making. The Board of Trade, however, was empowered to establish boards in any trade, subject to parliamentary confirmation, where the rate of wages was exceptionally low in comparison with wages in other employments. Four Trade Boards were formed under this provision in 1914.

Mr. Winston Churchill, when introducing the 1909 Bill into Parliament, said: 'The principles on which we are proceeding are to endeavour to foster organization in trades in which, by reason of the prevalence of exceptionally evil conditions, no organization has yet taken root, and, in which, in consequence, no parity of bargaining power can be said to exist. . . .' [1] This reasoning was taken further by the Trade Boards Act in 1918 which aimed to extend the trade board system to those industries where there was little or no organization among workers and employers 'pending the development of such degree of organization as would render possible the establishment of a national council or district councils'. The Ministry of Labour was entrusted with the task of operating the Trade Boards Acts.

The Industrial Courts Act, 1919. Another legislative act designed to assist trade union organization was the Industrial Courts Act, 1919. In October 1916 the Cabinet had appointed a committee 'to make and consider suggestions for securing a permanent improvement in the relations between employers and workmen' and 'to recommend means for securing that industrial conditions affecting the relations between employers and workmen shall be systematically reviewed by those concerned, with a view to improving conditions in the future'. The committee was called the 'Committee on Relations between Employers and Employed', but it became widely known as the Whitley Committee after its chairman, J. H. Whitley, M.P.

The Cabinet intended the Committee to examine permanent measures and not to inquire into wartime unrest, though undoubtedly wartime strikes were largely responsible for its formation. The Committee issued five reports. The first report recommended the voluntary formation of standing national and district industrial councils composed entirely of employers and workers' representatives. It wanted a uniform development of voluntary negotiating machinery. The Government accepted this recommendation and the officials of the Ministry of Labour were given the task of assisting its implementation. A Joint Industrial Councils Division of the Ministry of Labour was created in 1918 which arranged conferences between the two

[1] Hansard, vol. II, cols. 1791–1792, 24 March 1909.

sides of industry, helped to draw up constitutions, smoothed out difficulties whenever possible, and convened the first meeting of each new Joint Industrial Council. By the end of 1918 twenty Joint Industrial Councils had been formed.[1]

The fourth report made suggestions about what should be done when voluntary negotiations failed. It stated:

> We desire to emphasize the advisability of a continuance, as far as possible, of the present system whereby industries make their own agreements and settle their differences themselves. . . .
>
> We are opposed to any system of Compulsory Arbitration; there is no reason to believe that such a system is generally desired by employers and employed, and in the absence of such general acceptance, it is obvious that its imposition would lead to unrest. . . . For the same reason we do not recommend any scheme relating to conciliation which compulsorily prevents strikes or lock-outs pending inquiry. . . .
>
> We further recommend that there should be established a Standing Arbitration Council for cases where the parties wish to refer any dispute to arbitration, though it is desirable that suitable single arbitrators should be available, where the parties so desire. . . .
>
> We suggest that the Ministry of Labour should be authorized to hold a full inquiry when satisfied that it was desirable, without prejudice to the power of the disputing parties to declare a strike or lock-out before or during the progress of the inquiry. . . . Presumably the existing Act [the Conciliation Act, 1896] empowers the Ministry of Labour to publish reports made as a result of inquiries of this character, but, if not, the necessary power should be obtained, so that there may be immediate publication, for the information of those affected by the dispute and of the public generally, of an independent and authoritative account of the matters in difference.[2]

This recommendation did not break new ground. Single arbitrators were a successful feature of the Conciliation Act, 1896, and the Standing Arbitration Council resembled the wartime Committee on Production without its compulsory powers.[3] But it did contain a positive proposal to facilitate the settlement of industrial disputes in peacetime which the Government embodied in legislation.

The Industrial Courts Act established a permanent tribunal consisting of independent persons and members representing employers and workers. Cases could be heard by one or more members of the Court. Any dispute could be referred to the Minister of Labour for his attention, but he could only submit it to the Industrial Court if it satisfied three conditions. First, it had to be a trade dispute as

[1] Sharp, op. cit., p. 329.
[2] *Industrial Relations Handbook*, H.M.S.O., 1953, p. 123.
[3] cf. Sharp, op. cit., p. 348.

defined in the Act; secondly, the reference had to be consented to by both parties to the dispute; and lastly the negotiating machinery in the industry must have been used fully beforehand. Given that these conditions were satisfied the Minister could, if he wished, refer a dispute to a single arbitrator appointed by himself or to a Board of Arbitration set up for that purpose. The Minister, it should be emphasized, had no freedom of action until a dispute had been referred to him.

Under Part II of the Act the Minister had the power to appoint a Court of Inquiry into a dispute, whether or not it had been reported to him, and without the consent of the parties to it. Thus he was able to inform Parliament and the public of the facts of a dispute whenever he thought it expedient to do so. A Court of Inquiry could make recommendations for a settlement but it had no means of enforcing one. It was anticipated, however, that the publication of a detailed investigation of a dispute would contribute towards a settlement.

The initial reaction of the trade union movement to the Industrial Courts Bill was hostile. The Parliamentary Committee of the Trades Union Congress complained that it had not been consulted about the Bill and warned the Minister of Labour that legislation designed to secure industrial peace could not be successful without the co-operation of unions.[1] The Parliamentary Committee thought the Bill was premature and wanted most of its clauses withdrawn. It succeeded in one case only. There had been a clause in the Bill to make decisions of the Industrial Court legally binding for about four months, but it was deleted after strong union opposition. The Bill became law on 20 November 1920, and, with the Conciliation Act, 1896, which still remained on the statute book, was the authority for most of the Minister of Labour's interventions in industrial disputes until 1940.

A Period of Inactivity. The Ministry of Labour, then, after the First World War, formally intervened in industrial relations in order to initiate conciliation, arbitration, or inquiries. It assisted in the formation and maintenance of joint voluntary negotiating machinery in industry and it operated the trade board system. It performed a variety of other functions too. Its expansion in some directions was so rapid that it was not accompanied by adequate administrative preparations. All in all, the immediate post-war growth of the Ministry of Labour was unco-ordinated and untidy. Then it stopped and contracted.

The number of conciliation settlements declined after the war but

---

[1] Minutes of Joint Meeting of the Parliamentary Committee of the T.U.C. and the Labour Party Executive, 12 November 1919.

remained high by pre-war standards. In 1919 and 1920 there were 1,323 and 920 settlements. This was a period of full employment. After the middle of 1920 unemployment started to increase and the number of conciliation settlements decreased to 272 in 1921, then to 167 in 1923.

As the trade recession intensified so the enthusiasm for expansion within the Ministry of Labour declined. After the publication of the Geddes Committee reports on National Expenditure in 1922 the Ministry of Labour abandoned its drive for the formation of joint industrial councils. The Joint Industrial Councils Division was merged into the Industrial Relations Department of the Ministry. The idealism which the Whitley Report had inspired receded and disappeared. From 1921 until the start of the Second World War only one new council was formed in private industry.[1] The Ministry's staff, which in May 1919 was approximately 26,000, had fallen to 15,000 by May 1924.[2]

The absence of zeal in the inter-war years was a more serious deficiency in the Ministry of Labour than the contraction of its machinery. The Ministry was not developed on the basis of a consistent policy, for there was no such thing. Ministers were rarely in office long enough to impress any positive quality on it. In any case it was a second-rate Ministry which did not offer attractions to aspiring politicians. The bright and ambitious studiously avoided it. Only one of the inter-war Ministers of Labour reached high office.[3] The office was occupied by stodgy, uninspiring people. The development work which had preceded the formation of the Ministry had been done largely by civil servants recruited for their exceptional qualities, with the help of enthusiastic Presidents of the Board of Trade. In the 1920s career civil servants began to take over. These by temperament and training worked harmoniously with Ministers regardless of their ineptness.

THE CHANGING RELATIONSHIP BETWEEN TRADE UNIONS AND THE MINISTRY OF LABOUR

When trade unions were losing members through the effects of a high rate of unemployment and their funds were spent through strikes and excessive claims for benefits, demands on the conciliation service decreased. Solutions to disputes were forced on to trade

---

[1] Sharp, op. cit., p. 331.
[2] Ministry of Labour Report, 1923 and 1924, Cmd. 2481.
[3] Sir Robert Horne, Minister of Labour in 1919, became Chancellor of the Exchequer in 1921.

unions by employers. Normally the Government, in this situation, adhered to a policy of leaving the participants in industrial disputes to settle their differences unaided. It did not initiate additional measures to conciliate over-powerful employers.

In the inter-war years, too, with a brief exception in the mid-1920s, Governments felt no need to attempt to force or induce trade unions to adopt any particular industrial policy. Trade unions were in the grip of economic pressures which removed the impact of their actions on national economic welfare. In national terms it was largely irrelevant what industrial policy they pursued.

This situation was altered by the Second World War. The in-difference with which the Government had viewed the labour scene when employers were powerful was replaced by a deep consideration for industrial relations. The Government desired not only to concili-ate but also to influence trade union policy. As in the First World War, legislation was introduced to prohibit strikes and enforce arbitration.[1] The Government's consideration for Labour continued after the war. It wanted unions to be moderate in their demands and conciliatory in their approach to industrial differences in order to assist in the solution of national economic problems created by inflation and an adverse balance of foreign trade.

The Ministry of Labour became a key Government department in the new situation. This was obvious when Ernest Bevin was the Minister of Labour from 1940 till 1945. It was not so obvious from 1945 to 1951 when the Labour Government had so many high level contacts with unions that the importance of the Minister of Labour was reduced. The willingness of the trade union movement to co-operate with the Government also helped to keep him in the background. But the importance of the Ministry as the department responsible for labour affairs was unimpaired.

When the Conservative Party took office in 1951 the same economic problems remained to be solved and the co-operation of trade unions was required for their solution, but there no longer existed a wide range of connections between the trade union movement and the Government. Any member of the Government could appeal to workers to work harder, but none was in a position to make a speech which could not be regarded as party propaganda. The Conservatives required a person with high status in the Government to handle their labour affairs and, in order to retain the confidence of the employers and trade unions in the Government's conciliation machinery, that person had to be able to isolate himself from the practical operation of the Government's economic policy. Clearly a Minister of Labour

[1] See Chapter VIII for wartime strike legislation.

in a Conservative Government in 1951 was faced with a perplexing assignment.

The Conservative Prime Minister, Mr. Winston Churchill, attempted to get over the difficulty by appointing as Minister of Labour a person of high standing without obvious party political affiliations. Sir Walter Monckton was his choice. Monckton accepted the job on the understanding that he would largely have a free hand and that if the Prime Minister objected to the policies he was pursuing then he would resign.[1] The arrangement between Monckton and Churchill worked satisfactorily. Two or three times each week Monckton gave a brief report to the Cabinet to keep Ministers informed about labour matters, but in the main Churchill supported Monckton's desire to have little or no discussion of industrial relations either in the Cabinet or in Parliament. Churchill intervened directly in a dispute on only one occasion and then it was with Monckton's support.[2]

The Minister of Labour, however, is a member of the Government and he cannot act in disregard of that Government's policies. He is a member of the Cabinet and is bound by the collective responsibility for Cabinet decisions. He may not actively propagate Government policy but he has a duty to pursue it in practice. The more the Government's policies involve wages, productivity, and industrial behaviour and the more the Government has to win the support of trade unions, the closer does the Minister of Labour have to associate himself with the implementation of policy. Sir Walter Monckton, with a professed disinterest in party politics, discovered this in late 1951 and 1952.

Under the Wages Councils Act, 1945, which amended earlier Trade Board Acts, the Minister of Labour had the statutory right to refer back decisions of Wages Councils for further consideration. A decision referred back could not be applied. Normally Wages Council proposals were only referred back for technical reasons and this was accepted by trade unions. But if a proposal was not accepted by the Minister on political grounds his action was construed by unions as undue interference in the wage-determining structure.

Sir Walter Monckton referred back two Wages Council proposals in December 1951—shortly after his entry into the Government. They each contained a provision for a cost of living sliding scale and Monckton thought it was 'undesirable under present economic conditions to fix statutory minimum wages at an undetermined level

---

[1] Lord Monckton emphasized this point during meetings I had with him in 1957.
[2] When a railway strike was threatened in December 1953. See below, pp. 97–98.

varying with the cost of living'.[1] The General Council of the Trades Union Congress protested to the Minister that his action was likely to harm the Wages Council machinery, but Monckton replied that as he had a statutory responsibility for enforcing Wages Council decisions the public interest required him to take account of wider economic considerations.[2] Public interest and Government policy were regarded as synonymous terms. The protests petered out because the two Wages Councils submitted new proposals which omitted any mention of sliding-scale arrangements.

The Minister of Labour rejected further Wages Council proposals in the early summer of 1952. On 15 May 1952 the Chancellor of the Exchequer, Mr. R. A. Butler, spoke to the National Joint Advisory Council to the Minister of Labour about the possible effects which a general increase in wages would have on the export drive and, consequently, on the level of employment, and appealed for wage restraint. The Economic Committee of the Trades Union Congress considered the Chancellor's statement and decided it could do nothing to support it in the circumstances. It added, however, that trade unions would continue to act with a sense of responsibility.

The Minister of Labour felt that the statement should be given serious consideration by unions, so in May and early June, without consulting other members of the Government, he referred back twelve Wages Council proposals to give the Wages Councils more time for reflection. The General Council of the Trades Union Congress protested to the Prime Minister, who adopted the same attitude as Monckton. The incident was concluded when the Minister of Labour gave an assurance that he had no desire to interfere with the functions of Wages Councils and said that he was prepared to issue a statement explaining that he just wanted to be sure that the Councils had considered the Chancellor's words. The General Council accepted this assurance. The proposals were resubmitted unchanged and were endorsed by the Minister.

No real damage was done to the Government's relations with the trade union movement at this time. The Conservative Government was new in office and had a surprising amount of official trade union goodwill. Moreover, Monckton's word was believed by the most influential union leaders with whom he had already established good relations. Finally, all types of wage-determining machinery were subsequently left alone by the Churchill Government, except when the Government wished to make a concession to unions. The two incidents served, however, to indicate the difficult position the

[1] T.U.C. Report, 1952, p. 291.
[2] ibid., p. 292.

Minister of Labour could get into by trying to reconcile the incompatible functions of head of a conciliation department and advocate of the Government's policy.

After the retirement of Sir Winston Churchill, industrial interests in the Cabinet were strengthened and the Government pursued a new and independent industrial policy in which they were prepared to be tougher with trade unions. This coincided with the adoption of a militant industrial policy by the Trades Union Congress in September 1956. From that time on the relations between the trade union movement and the Government deteriorated.[1]

The Government was involved in the relationship in three ways: as a conciliator and arbitrator, as the nation's largest single employer, and as the overseer of the community's interests. Priority was given to the last role. Unable to obtain the collaboration of trade unions the Government attempted to enforce a policy of wage restraint on its own employees. The Minister of Labour occupied a pivotal position in this action. In consequence his judgements were suspected of political bias and so were those of some of the arbitrators whom he appointed to act for his department. Whether this bias existed or not was irrelevant, for once the suspicion arose, the confidence of trade unionists in arbitration decisions fell and the institution of arbitration was endangered.

In October 1958 the Government announced that the compulsory arbitration system which had originated in 1940 was to be terminated, and that it was reverting back to voluntary arbitration under the Industrial Courts Act of 1919. This system of arbitration presupposed that the Government's only interest in industrial relations was in the amicable settlement of disputes. This was no longer so. The question was raised as to whether the Government could continue to operate an arbitration service based on the 1919 Act. It seemed that the time had come for the Government's relationship with trade unions in this respect to be changed.

[1] See Chapters V and VI below for a description of the situation after 1955.

2

THE GOVERNMENT AS AN EMPLOYER

THE three chapters in this Part show how the Government in its role as an employer has worked with the trade unions which organize its employees. The first chapter describes some of the problems which have arisen in the civil service; the next chapter extends the description to cover the public sector in industry created by the Nationalization Acts after 1945. The third chapter is about the predicament of the Government as the nation's largest single employer endeavouring to run a conciliation and arbitration service and to supervise the community's interests at the same time.

In these chapters the Government is regarded as the employer of a labour force if it is ultimately responsible for financing it. The Government is most obviously an employer of civil servants. These have been described by successive Royal Commissions on the civil service as 'servants of the Crown, other than holders of political or judicial offices, who are employed in a civil capacity and whose remuneration is paid wholly and directly out of monies voted by Parliament'. The Government is also an employer if it has assumed the functions of shareholders, as in the nationalized industries; and if it has taken over the financial responsibility of an industry in order to acquire control for a specific time and purpose, as it did during the two World Wars.

But what is the function of a Government which grants a subsidy to an industry to enable it to meet workers' demands? It is not an employer in the accepted sense nor is it acting simply as a bank which makes advances to industry. The Government is much more deeply and widely implicated than a bank would be. This is obviously a marginal case. In this book the Government in such an instance is treated as an employer.

Chapter Four

LABOUR PROBLEMS IN THE
CIVIL SERVICE

THE Government's peacetime labour force until 1945, with the exception of a brief period after the First World War, was concentrated in the civil service. It consisted of industrial workers employed on munitions, in dockyards, in the Office of Works and the Stationery Office; and non-industrial workers in the Post Office and Government administrative departments. All these workers were employed as civilians and were wholly paid by money granted by Parliament.

The civil service first brought the Government in its capacity as an employer into contact with trade unionism. Through its industrial workers the Government met various trade unions which also organized non-Government workers. Through its non-industrial workers it met unions which knew no other employer than the Government and which tested its qualities as an employer through struggling to organize, to gain recognition as bargaining agents, and then to bargain.

This chapter is concerned only with non-industrial workers.[1] Its purpose is to show the kind of relationship the Government endeavoured to establish with trade unions when its interests were those of an employer, and to indicate its responses to some of the problems which organized civil servants raised. It is neither a detailed analysis of the relationship nor a complete account of its development. Most of the chapter is concerned with a period following the First World War when the relationship was embryonic and when, in consequence, the labour issues which arose were of acute significance to organized civil servants. Once recognition was secured and collective bargaining machinery established the most persistent problem was that of wage determination. This is described to the present. But it should not be assumed that the relationship in other respects has been, and is, a consistently comfortable one. Like the relationship between trade unions and private employers it has been subject to variations.

Early Organizations of Civil Servants

The Government was not confronted by trade unionism in the civil service until late in the nineteenth century. Until 1855 entry

---

[1] In 1914 there were 282,402 non-industrial civil servants (Cmd. 276). The number rose to 387,400 in 1939 (Cmd. 3388), increased rapidly during the war and remained

into the civil service was based exclusively on patronage and not until 1870 was open competition for admission established. Inevitably it was some years after 1870 before the effects of patronage were eliminated and there existed an environment in which unions could be organized.

Civil service trade unionism first appeared in the Post Office which was by far the largest Government department. In March 1902 the Post Office employed 77,035 persons out of a total of 105,888 established in the civil service and working for the central Government. A high proportion of the Post Office workers were in the manipulative grades: letter carriers, sorters and telegraph clerks, and were not influenced in the same way by patronage or its legacy as were other sections of the civil service.

Although Parliament had accorded legal recognition to unions in 1871, the Government opposed the attempts of the postmen to form unions for some years afterwards. Nevertheless, postal unions began to appear from 1881 onwards. The Postal and Telegraph Clerks' Association was established in 1881; then came the United Kingdom Postal Clerks' Association in 1887, the Fawcett Association in 1890 and the Postmen's Federation in 1891. There were nine postal unions in 1902.[1]

Postal workers in the 1880s and 1890s were not openly victimized for forming unions but they were not granted the right to negotiate through their unions. The Postmaster-General said in 1899 that he would receive representations provided they were made by postal workers through the normal Post Office administrative machinery.[2] This restriction was modified by later Postmaster-Generals but not until 1906 did the Postmaster-General, Mr. Sidney Buxton, agree to recognize any duly constituted Association or Federation of postal servants and consent to negotiate with their full-time officials.[3]

The growth of trade unionism in the other grades of the civil service was much slower. Various organizations for clerks were formed dating from the 1890s, but their activities were restricted and largely ineffective. Most of them, such as the Association of Tax Clerks and the Customs Officers' Federation which appeared in 1892 and 1894 respectively, were based on departments. Departmental associations appeared because, in the main, concessions were easier to obtain if departmental autonomy was respected.

This development was interrupted in 1903 when the Assistant Clerks' Association was formed by clerks from all the principal

---

at a high level in the post-war period. In 1957 the number was 635,700 (*Annual Abstract of Statistics*, 1957).

[1] *Whitley Councils in the British Civil Service*, by L. P. White, p. 245.
[2] *Clerical Unions in the Civil Service*, by B. V. Humphreys, p. 40. [3] ibid., p. 41.

Government offices in London. Individual branches of this union acted within departments to obtain specific concessions, but the main concern of the union was to recruit as many clerical workers in the civil service as possible, and to justify its right to deal directly with the Treasury.[1] The Assistant Clerks' Association cast aside 'humble memorials' for pay increases and submitted wage demands; it disregarded tradition and recognized procedures in the civil service. Its nonconformity was welcomed by the clerks. The membership of the association rose from 554 in twenty-two departments in 1904 to 2,223 in fifty-two departments in 1912. Its total potential membership in 1912 was 2,400.[2]

When the war broke out in 1914 trade unionism in the civil service was widespread if not very effective. There were seventy-three active associations with memberships varying from 75 to 100 per cent of their potential total memberships. But they possessed no full-time officers, no offices, and no staff. Their spokesmen did not have access to Heads of Departments, or to the Treasury. Their activities were largely confined to organizing 'round-robin' petitions, and occasionally getting a question asked in Parliament about civil service matters.[3]

The war altered the whole character of the civil service. Normal practices were abandoned, women replaced male labour, new departments were established and others were reorganized, temporary workers came in who knew nothing of and cared as little for civil service traditions. And then at the end of the war ex-service men returned to their civil service posts in a state of high expectancy. When they found that their expectations were not realized they became disgruntled and expressed their dissatisfaction through trade unions. The war helped to break down the departmental mentality of the civil service administrative heads, who began to think in terms of the civil service as a whole and to recognize that functions and classes of workers were not limited to departments. Full recognition of the civil service unions' right to bargain collectively for their members was an inevitable outcome of this situation. The publication of the Whitley Committee Report in 1917 assisted this end.

Whitleyism in the Civil Service

The recommendations for creating joint industrial councils at local and national levels which were contained in the Whitley Committee Report were not intended for the civil service.[4] The civil service unions, however, quickly pressed to have the recommendations applied to them, as a solution to their negotiating problems, and

---

[1] Humphreys, op. cit., p. 51. [2] ibid.
[3] *So Far*, by W. J. Brown, p. 79. [4] White, op. cit., p. 4.

they grew impatient when the Government did not immediately respond. They considered that the Government should put into practice what it was recommending private employers to adopt. The Committee itself subsequently supported this view. An initial concession was made in October 1918 when the Cabinet accepted modified Whitley proposals for Government industrial workers.[1] By 1920 there were national joint councils, departmental joint committees, and works joint committees in the shipbuilding, engineering, building, and miscellaneous trades in Government establishments. The unions involved were those which catered for trades generally outside of the Government service. At that time the Government's industrial staff formed a substantial proportion of its total staff but it was inflated by war needs.[2]

In February and March 1919 there was acute industrial unrest throughout Britain. Dissatisfaction with the Government's immediate post-war policies was rife and it was contagious. Clerical civil servants were influenced by this atmosphere. They became militant. They even talked of strike action.[3]

In the midst of this agitation a Government Inter-Departmental Committee reported on the application of the Whitley recommendations to the administrative departments. It approved of the formation of a national council but excluded from its functions the determination of salaries and working conditions because, it stated, the 'fact that the State is the ultimate employer of Government servants through the Heads of Departments who consequently have not the freedom of decision in regard to wages and conditions enjoyed by the private employer' means that the ultimate decision about wages and conditions must remain, unimpaired, in the hands of Ministers responsible to Parliament.[4]

The unions were dissatisfied. This was not the kind of Whitley system they had envisaged. They pressed to have the proposals altered and met the Chancellor of the Exchequer, Mr. Austen Chamberlain, in a conference to put their view on 8 April 1919. Mr. Chamberlain, it turned out, did not have fixed ideas. He pressed the conference to accept the report in his opening speech but allowed the conference to accept a proposal, without comment, which referred the disputed sections of the report for the consideration of

---

[1] Humphreys, op. cit., p. 107.

[2] *The Growth of Public Employment in Great Britain*, by Moses Abramovitz and Vera Eliasberg, p. 43. 455,500 workers out of a total central Government civilian labour force of 852,000 belonged to the Government's industrial defence staff in November 1918. The number in April 1928 was only 77,400.

[3] Humphreys, op. cit., p. 109.

[4] 'Report on the Application of the Whitley Report to the Administrative Departments . . .', Cmd. 9 (1919).

a National Provisional Joint Committee. A revised constitution was subsequently drawn up which gave the Council the function of negotiating general conditions of service including wages and working conditions. The Council's decisions were to become operative after they had been reported to the Cabinet. The Cabinet accepted the new constitution without demur on 13 June 1919. The unions were elated at their success.

The first properly constituted National Whitley Council for the Civil Service met on 23 July 1919. It was followed by the creation of an elaborate system of conciliation at all levels of the civil service. The system was far more complex and firmly fixed than anything attempted in private industry. It had a hierarchy of consultative committees neatly organized and synchronized to work as a unit.

At the second meeting of the National Whitley Council on 14 October 1919 the staff side pressed for a reorganization of the grades because it realized that civil-service wide bargaining units could not work effectively so long as the service was organized tightly into departments. A reorganization committee was set up and with great speed a new civil service structure consisting of four functional grades was proposed and implemented.[1] New pay scales were agreed upon and the task of altering departmental practices was tackled. The reorganization was completed in the main by 1924.[2] The structure has remained largely unchanged to the present day.

The institution of the Whitley system forced the civil servants to look at their own organizations. There were far too many associations to have each one represented on the Whitley Councils and there was too great a division of opinion between them to make for effective negotiations with the official side. Moves were made to amalgamate many of the 200 unions which existed. The formation of the Union of Post Office Workers in January 1920 brought together most of the significant unions which organized postal workers; a series of amalgamations among those catering for clerical workers resulted in the creation of the Civil Service Clerical Association in 1922. Amalgamations concerning the clerical unions went on throughout the inter-war years. Some departmental unions retained their identity and flourish still; the Inland Revenue Staff Federation and Ministry of Labour Staff Association are the most prominent examples. By 1930 the Society of Civil Servants had secured complete representation for members of the executive class. As a result of this tidying-up process the number of associations represented

[1] The four grades were: (*a*) Writing Assistant Class; (*b*) Clerical Class; (*c*) Executive Class; (*d*) Administrative Class.
[2] Humphreys, op. cit., p. 123.

directly or indirectly on the staff side of the Whitley Councils fell from 200 in 1919 to twenty-five in 1956.[1]

The acceptance of Whitley Councils by the Government resulted in its having relatively harmonious relations with the civil service unions. The Government encouraged its employees to be members of unions because 'the existence of fully representative associations not only promotes good staff relations but is essential to effective negotiations on conditions of service'.[2] Minor grievances did not accumulate but were dealt with systematically; while large issues were decided by the National Council. The Whitley system developed its faults; it became perhaps too rigid and formal; its hierarchical form encouraged the official side at the lower levels to pass up difficult problems instead of tackling them themselves. These faults were irritants but they did not result in bad employer/employee relations in the civil service. Some problems, however, could not be solved by the Whitley system. The main ones are described below.

Some Significant Problems

(i) *Accountability to Parliament*. All the issues described here relate to the difference between the Government and private employers. It will be remembered that the Government's special position as an employer was used as a reason for refusing to establish a system of free negotiations in the civil service. The Government was accountable to Parliament; private employers were accountable only to themselves. Nevertheless, the Cabinet accepted a formula which permitted final decisions to be reached by a National Whitley Council. This, however, was not the end of the matter. The official side, at an early meeting, wanted to clarify the finality of the decision-making process to make sure that the final authority still rested with Parliament. The National Whitley Council itself declared in October 1921 that

> The establishment of Whitley Councils cannot relieve the Government of any part of its responsibility to Parliament, and Ministers and Heads of Departments acting under the general or specific authority of Ministers must take such action as may be required in any case in the public interest. This condition is inherent in the constitutional doctrines of Parliamentary Government and Ministerial responsibility, and Ministers can neither waive nor escape it. It follows from this constitutional

---

[1] The principal unions in 1956 were the Union of Post Office Workers; the Post Office Engineering Union; the Association of First Division Civil Servants; the Civil Service Union; the Society of Civil Servants; the Society of Technical Civil Servants; the Institution of Professional Civil Servants; the Civil Service Clerical Association; the Inland Revenue Staff Federation; the Ministry of Labour Staff Association.

[2] *Staff Relations in the Civil Service*, 1949, p. 3.

principle that while acceptance of the Whitley System as regards the Civil Service implies an intention to make the fullest possible use of Whitley procedure, the Government has not surrendered, and cannot surrender, its liberty of action in the exercise of its authority and the discharge of its responsibilities in the public interest.[1]

That this was an agreed declaration indicated that the trade union representatives were clearly aware of the limitation which Government employment imposed on them.

It followed that as Parliament had the final power to impose a decision, then civil service unions had to take steps to influence it. They endeavoured to get their own representatives into Parliament and they lobbied members of all parties in the manner of any other pressure group, in order to exercise influence over Parliament. In the incident described below they lobbied so successfully that they secured the defeat of the Government.

(ii) *The Starting-Pay Issue.* During the First World War the normal methods of entry into the civil service were suspended. Many temporary clerks were admitted into the service without first taking an examination and the vacancies in the established grades created by wastage were not filled. After the war the problem arose of how to fill the vacancies and meet the claims of the temporary clerks to be absorbed into the service. A sub-committee of the National Whitley Council proposed in February 1920 that 75 per cent of the vacancies in the established grades should be filled by recruitment from the temporary clerks, and that the selection should be based on the results of a simple examination which they would be required to take.[2] There was some opposition to requiring adults to sit an examination and the matter was re-examined by a Government committee. The unions had been divided in their opposition to the examination. A fresh proposal was made which united them. The committee suggested that the starting pay of newly established temporary clerks should be £80 per year, plus bonus. This was the salary which would be paid to an eighteen-year-old recruit to the clerical class. The clerical unions opposed the introduction of this measure. They took the issue to the National Whitley Council but the official side refused to adjudicate. It then went to the Civil Service Arbitration Board and was rejected. W. J. Brown, general secretary of the Assistant Clerks' Association, led a deputation to the Financial Secretary to the Treasury, staged a demonstration of

---

[1] White, op. cit., p. 18.
[2] Treasury Memorandum submitted to the Royal Commission on the Civil Service (1929), p. 151.

civil servants in Trafalgar Square, and used every reasonable means of pressure at his disposal. But he was unsuccessful.

The 'Starting-Pay' case was pressed on. Candidates in the 1922 general election were asked for their support and after the new Government had been formed the issue was raised in the House of Commons. W. J. Brown recalled:

> First, we approached the Labour Party and secured a promise of support from the Party as a whole. Next, for a period of some weeks, we flooded the House with 'Lobbyers'. Each 'Lobbyer' was equipped with a clear statement of the case, and his job was to extract a pledge that, when the motion for the appointment of a Committee of Enquiry came before the House, the Member he was canvassing would support it. The list of pledges grew longer every day. . . . Simultaneously with this canvassing of individual Members, I got into touch with every organized group in the House which I thought could be influenced in our favour. . . .[1]

A Liberal Member, Mr. Duncan Millar, agreed to use his place in the ballot for Private Member's Motions to get a motion submitted by the civil service unions before the House of Commons. The motion asking for the appointment of a Select Committee to examine the 'Starting-Pay' issue was debated on 10 April 1923, and although the Government opposed it, the motion was carried. The Government, after its defeat, appointed a Special Committee of Inquiry so as not to acknowledge the defeat fully, but composed it mainly of Members of Parliament. The Special Committee reported in June 1923 and recommended increases in the pay of the men concerned.

(iii) *Political Rights*. In the 'Starting-Pay' case the civil service unions and the Labour Party worked closely together. This collaboration arose not only because Labour Members of Parliament agreed with the unions' view of the case, but also because some of the unions were affiliated to the Labour Party and regarded it as an additional means of exerting pressure on the Government.

The unions, up to 1927, were free to decide whether they should have political affiliations, but restrictions were imposed on individual civil servants. Before 1884 some civil servants were prevented by statute from becoming Members of Parliament. A Treasury minute in 1884 extended this disqualification to apply to the whole civil service. No written rule prevented civil servants as a class from taking part in political activities generally, but there was an unwritten rule mentioned by the Government occasionally. An Order in Council in 1910 stated that 'employees of the civil service should take no overt part in public political affairs'.[2] Some departments trans-

---

[1] *So Far*, by W. J. Brown, pp. 100–101.
[2] Humphreys, op. cit., p. 174.

lated this into a specific instruction, others left it unwritten. It remained a matter of departmental discipline.[1]

The political rights of the unions were altered after the General Strike. The civil service unions did not engage in the strike, but the Union of Post Office Workers and the Civil Service Clerical Association pledged themselves to support it by giving financial aid, and the Staff Side of the Whitley Council expressed sympathy with its aims. Some of the unions for higher grades openly opposed the strike and withdrew from the National Whitley Council in protest against the attitude of the Staff Side.

In 1927 the Government re-defined the political rights of individual civil servants through the Servants of the Crown (Parliamentary Candidature) Order. It excluded industrial staffs in industrial establishments from the 1884 ruling but extended the ruling to cover all other civil servants, whether permanent or temporary, established or unestablished. It added in the Order that 'The public interest demands the maintenance of political impartiality in the Civil Service and of confidence in that impartiality as an essential part of the structure of Government in this country.'[2]

The Government, also in 1927, took steps to ensure the political impartiality of the civil service unions through Clause V of the Trade Disputes and Trade Unions Act, 1927. The clause prohibited civil servants from belonging to any organization which had political objects or which was associated, directly or indirectly, with any political party.

No civil service union could affiliate to the Labour Party or to the Trades Union Congress. Nor could it officially give financial support to a Parliamentary candidate. In May 1927 the Attorney-General amplified the Government's reasons for introducing the clause, when he said:

> The situation which was developed in May last was that organizations of civil servants, whose undivided allegiance the State has a right to claim, were, in fact, through their officials, actively engaged in fomenting a rebellion against the State. That, in the judgment of the Government, is an intolerable situation in which to find the established civil servant.[3]

Some of the affected unions and the Trades Union Congress protested unsuccessfully about the Act.[4] During the Second World War the Union of Post Office Workers even decided to defy it. Its

---

[1] Treasury Memorandum, op. cit., p. 37.
[2] Quoted in Humphreys, op. cit., p. 175.
[3] Hansard, vol. CCV, col. 1332.
[4] See Chapter XIV below for a description of the attempts to repeal the Act during the Second Labour Government.

annual conference in 1943 proposed that its branches should affiliate
to trades councils and authorized its executive to discuss reaffiliation
to the Trades Union Congress with the General Council. The
General Council agreed to accept an application for reaffiliation if it
should be made, and pressed the Government, through the Prime
Minister and the Labour members of the Cabinet, to make defiance
unnecessary by altering the Act. The Government made no concessions for the Conservative Party, on which it depended for
parliamentary support, wanted to retain the Act as it was. The
Government announced, moreover, that if the Union of Post Office
Workers affiliated to the Trades Union Congress its members
would be automatically disestablished. The Act was not defied and
the situation continued unaltered until the Labour Government
unconditionally repealed the Act in 1946.[1] Only the Union of Post
Office Workers, however, reaffiliated to the Labour Party after 1946.

Individual civil servants are still subject to regulations covering
their political activities. There are three rough categories. The first,
consisting of the industrial staff and the non-industrial staff in the
minor and manipulative grades, is politically free. The second, comprising typists, clerical assistants, clerical officers and comparable
grades, is free to engage in most political activities provided departmental permission is first obtained. The last category includes all
the remaining civil servants. They are prevented from engaging in
national politics but are free to take part in local political activities
with departmental permission.[2] The officials of many of the civil
service unions are directly involved in party politics but then they
are not civil servants.

(iv) *The Supercut Case.* Whenever the Government has considered
it necessary to curtail its expenditure or to reduce the national wage
bill, it has had a tempting and easily accessible target in the civil
service. In practice, however, the Government had been restrained
from using the civil service thus. This may have been because the
conception of the state as a model employer has had a real and
perpetual meaning irrespective of the composition of the Government of the day or of its political complexion. Or it may have been
due to more practical matters. From the end of the First World War
civil service unions maintained a vigilance in case the Government
contravened the standards of a good employer, and gave immediate
publicity to the acts which did. The Government, like a private
employer, had to consider the recruitment of its labour force.

---

[1] The relations between the T.U.C. and the Labour Party during this incident are
described below in Chapter XV.

[2] Humphreys, op. cit., p. 175n.

Behaviour which victimized its employees would have had an adverse effect on the quality and volume of this force.

These factors, however, did not entirely prevent the Government from using the civil service as an easy way of cutting its expenditure. In May 1920 a cost-of-living sliding scale bonus system was instituted for permanent civil servants whose salaries did not exceed £500 a year. It was accepted by the National Whitley Council that people with annual salaries higher than £500 lay outside the scope of the Whitley machinery, but the Treasury agreed to apply the bonus system to those receiving salaries up to £1,000 a year.[1] In fact, officials receiving up to £2,000 a year received some proportion of the bonus but the inclusion of the higher paid ones was not a part of the constitutionally negotiated agreement. When the bonus system was introduced Britain was still experiencing the prosperity which came with the post-war expansion in trade. But by the spring of 1921, Britain was in the grip of a severe economic depression and from various quarters there were demands that the Government should take action to counteract it. The Government, in a manner consistent with the advice it received from misguided economic theorists, cut its expenditure.

On 25 July 1921 representatives of the civil service unions were informed that the Government had decided to reduce the bonus payments in varying degrees to all civil servants receiving salaries higher than £500 a year. Protests were made at the National Whitley Council and continued until the end of 1925, but no agreement was reached. The 'supercut' case, as it was called, was then referred to the Industrial Court. The unions maintained that the cut was in violation of an agreement; while the Government insisted that there had been no such agreement. The Industrial Court gave a written explanation of its decision. The agreement, it stated, was for salaries not exceeding £500 a year, but an honourable undertaking had been given to the National Whitley Council concerning salaries over £500. It added:

> Such undertaking could be withdrawn by the overriding authority of Parliament, but it was only natural in the circumstances of the present case that feelings of resentment would be aroused when the 'Supercut' was put into force without consultation on the Whitley Council.
>
> The Court are of opinion that as there is in existence a Whitley Council for Civil Service matters, every effort should be made to bring forward all questions within its jurisdiction for discussion before executive action is taken.[2]

[1] White, op. cit., p. 126.
[2] Quoted in White, op. cit., p. 127.

The Court, however, did not remove the 'supercut'. It contended that the country's financial state had to be considered and there had not been a sufficient change in that state since 1921 to warrant its removal. This was an early instance of independent arbitrators considering matters other than those involved in the merits of the case.

When Mr. Winston Churchill, the Chancellor of the Exchequer, was questioned about the Industrial Court decision in March 1927, he emphasized the Government's responsibility. He said:

> The decision reached by the Government in July 1921 regarding the civil service bonus was announced to and received the approval of the House of Commons, and while the Government have every intention of continuing to make the fullest possible use of the machinery of Whitley Councils in Civil Service matters when it is appropriate, they cannot in the exercise of their responsibility to this House surrender their liberty to take such action as may appear to them in any case to be required in the public interest. This discretion is a recognized condition of the establishment of Whitley Councils in the civil service and the Government do not intend to waive it.[1]

The case was not finally settled until 1934.

(v) *Compulsory Arbitration.* Another instance of a unilaterally imposed act of economy occurred shortly after the 'supercut' case had started. At the end of 1916 the War Cabinet decided to apply the principle of independent compulsory arbitration to civil service matters. This created a new situation, for the Government, by giving the Arbitration Board the right to reach a final decision, protected civil servants against Treasury dictation. When the National Whitley Council was formed, the Civil Service Arbitration Board was continued in being though not as an integral part of the Whitley machinery.

The Geddes Committee, appointed in 1921 to investigate ways of curtailing the national expenditure of the Supply Services, recommended that the Civil Service Arbitration Tribunal should be abolished to save £1,886 a year.[2] It stated that compulsory arbitration was inconsistent with the development of voluntary negotiating machinery and that the Chancellor of the Exchequer lacked control over the decisions of the Board, which could authorize expenditure. The Government implemented the recommendation in February 1922. The National Whitley Council was not consulted before the Board was abolished. Civil service unions, W. J. Brown stated, 'were thus left without any appeal from the decisions of the Treasury and

[1] Hansard, vol. CCIII, col. 2186, 17 March 1927.
[2] Treasury Memorandum, op. cit., pp. 93–94.

of Departments, other than appeals to the House of Commons—
where the Government reckoned that it could safely rely on its
Parliamentary majority'.[1]

The unions protested strongly to the Government and formed an
ad hoc Civil Service Joint Defence Committee to organize a political
campaign to get the Board restored. The Defence Committee
submitted two questions to 615 Parliamentary candidates in the 1922
general election. They were: '(1) Are you in favour of the principle
of arbitration in regard to Civil Service pay and conditions of
employment?' and '(2) Do you agree that the machinery of arbitration
should be a body composed of an equal number of representatives
of both sides with an independent chairman?' 427 replies agreed to
both questions: 89 agreed to the first question; 36 refused to accept
either question and 63 sent no reply.[2] The Government was unmoved
by this campaign. But after its defeat over the 'Starting-Pay' case
it changed its mind and in May 1923 Mr. Stanley Baldwin, the
Chancellor of the Exchequer, agreed to accept the principle of arbitration for the civil service and appointed a committee to prepare a
scheme. In 1925, after much delay, the committee proposed that
civil servants should be covered by the Industrial Courts Act, 1919.
The jurisdiction of the Industrial Court was redefined for civil service
cases so that arbitration became compulsory upon a demand from
either party.[3] This situation continued until 1936, when a separate
Civil Service Arbitration Tribunal was again established. Arbitration for the greater part of the civil service has remained compulsory
in the sense that the Government cannot refuse to allow claims to
be submitted to arbitration unless these raise issues of major policy;
and it has agreed to be bound by Tribunal awards 'subject to the
overriding authority of Parliament'.[4]

A Civil Service Wage Policy

After the First World War there was always some concern about
criteria for determining the level of civil service wages. Government
departments were not profit-making concerns, so therefore the
standard of private industry could not be used. The search for a
standard, and its application when one was obtained, were to some
extent responsible for preventing interferences by the Government
with civil service wages. Between 1947 and 1950 civil service wage
claims were rejected, but even this was done according to a standard.

[1] Brown, op. cit., p. 104.
[2] White, op. cit., p. 103n.
[3] Industrial employees were excluded from this provision.
[4] Report of the Royal Commission on the Civil Service, 1953–1955, Cmd. 9613,
pp. 8–9.

When the 1909 Fair Wages Clause was first operated the Government undertook to apply its terms to its own labour force.[1] The Government thus stated by implication that civil service wages should keep pace with the wages paid for comparable work in private industry by 'good' employers. This did not constitute a wage policy in practice, for until 1920, when the civil service was reorganized, wages were determined by individual departments and they varied, depending upon the interaction of many factors such as departmental budgets and established differentials.

The establishment of wage grades in 1920 which cut across departments caused Government administrators to turn seriously to the principle of fair relativity. It seemed reasonable and was simple to operate. The unions raised no objections, for at the time incomes in non-Government occupations were rising. The Treasury departed from the principle to some extent when it accepted the cost-of-living bonus system in 1920, but as prices were rising no objections were raised against that either. Fair relativity, nonetheless, remained the main principle of civil service wage determination for some years.[2]

In years of prosperity it was fair to compare wages paid for similar jobs in public and private employment. When there was full employment all workers had a comparable degree of security and other non-monetary advantages. Workers in private industry who lost their jobs could get new ones. Because the employment market operated in their favour their bargaining position was enhanced and their ability to gain non-monetary benefits increased. Security and non-monetary benefits were characteristic of state employment.

This situation was radically altered as unemployment increased. Workers in private industry lost their security and suffered a general deterioration in their working conditions, whereas Government employees experienced little change in these respects. Was it fair, then, to compare only money wages? When civil service wages were being assessed, ought not the non-monetary advantages of Government employment to be considered? If they were, then it meant that civil service wages could fall below the wages paid for comparable work in outside industry and yet still be fair wages.

The increased complexity of civil service wage determination was described by the Industrial Court in a 1927 Post Office case. It stated:

In their consideration of the claims and counterclaims the Court have taken the view that the broad principle which should be followed in

[1] See Appendix II at the end of this chapter.
[2] In May 1924 the Prime Minister confirmed that the Fair Wages Clause applied to Government employees (Royal Comission Report, 1929-1931, p. 82).

determining the rates of wages of Post Office servants, is that of the maintenance of a fair relativity as between their wages and those in outside industries as a whole, and as between the various classes within the Postal Service, with due regard to the adequacy of the payment for the work done and the responsibilities undertaken.

Any direct comparison with outside industries presents some difficulty owing to the fact that in the postal service the duties and conditions of employment are in general dissimilar from those obtaining in outside industries.

In any such comparison, it has to be remembered that the appointment of Post Office employees as established officers to one or other of the different classes, whose claims are under review, brings with it all the advantages of a Civil Service career. Such an employee has security of employment, annual leave with pay, free medical attendance and sick pay, is relieved of Health and Unemployment Insurance contributions, has some prospect of promotion and is qualified for a pension on retirement.

These factors are not, in general, characteristic of outside employment. . . .

On the other hand, it is to be borne in mind that in the Postal Service the hours of attendance are in general irregular. The incidence of the work entails a good deal of night duty, and split attendances. . . .

The relativity, therefore, which in the view of the Court should obtain between the wages of Post Office employees and those in outside industries involves the consideration of many factors. The importance to be attached to the different factors may vary from time to time. . . . Accordingly, no hard and fast rule can be laid down which would be capable of automatic application. Changes in either an upward or downward direction may be necessary in order to maintain a due consonance with general national or industrial conditions. . . .[1]

The civil service unions regarded this explanation as being incomplete. The Civil Service Clerical Association considered that the Government recruited not only good employees, but the best of their kind; that it ought to think in terms of long-run wage stability in the civil service and, above all, 'it ought to be tempered by the reflection that the State cannot take its morals from below, but should set standards of itself from above which should be an example for the private employer to follow'.[2]

The Government, by this time, had become essentially pragmatic in its handling of civil service matters. In any case, so long as it was mistakenly believed that economic recovery from a depression would come through economy, the Government could hardly use the taxpayers' money to set wage standards in advance of those in outside industry.

[1] Award 1325, July 1927. Quoted in White, op. cit., pp. 121–122.   [2] ibid., p. 122.

T.U.G.—G

A number of views about the basis of renumeration in the civil service were heard when the Royal Commission on the Civil Service met under the chairmanship of Lord Tomlin from 1929 to 1931.[1] The staff side of the National Whitley Council wanted the Government to be a model employer—a function which was incompatible with the principle of fair relativity. The higher grades, represented by a Joint Consultative Committee, desired rates of pay which were sufficient to recruit men of the right calibre and to act as an incentive throughout their service-life; they wanted, too, a long-run stability. The Treasury view was, briefly, that many non-monetary factors needed to be considered alongside wages which were adequate to recruit and retain a fully qualified staff. This meant that wages should bear a reasonable relationship with wages paid in competing occupations. But they should not be unduly high because that would have the effect of making the civil service into a privileged class and 'of doing an injustice to the community which *ex hypothesi* would be worse off, and has always to foot the bill'.[2]

The Commission rejected the proposal that the Government should be a model employer because it considered the phrase was meaningless. It concluded that if there was fair relativity between civil service and comparable outside rates of pay a satisfactory staff would be recruited and retained. It did not agree with the staff side of the National Whitley Council which thought that meaningful comparisons could not be made. 'In effecting such comparisons the State should take a long view. Civil Service remuneration should reflect what may be described as the long-term trend, both in wage levels and in the economic condition of the country.' The principle of paying what the trade could bear was rejected. These conclusions became known as the Tomlin Formula and were used by official negotiators to justify their attitude to wage claims until 1953.

In practice, the official negotiators were not successful in applying the formula. The unions consistently claimed that the wages of their members lagged behind those in outside industry and in the main their claims were justified. Dr. Humphreys, who made some statistical comparisons for the years 1932–1953, concluded that after the adoption of the Tomlin Formula fair relativity was definitely not maintained so far as general rates were concerned, in either money or real terms, and 'on the basis of the limited information available on outside clerical rates it seems questionable that fair relativity has been accomplished on this test either'.[3]

[1] Royal Commission on the Civil Service Report, Cmd. 3909.
[2] ibid., p. 84.
[3] op. cit., p. 208.

A number of reasons accounted for this situation. First, though in their approach to negotiations the official side may have been guided by the Tomlin Formula, in actual negotiations they acted like custodians of the public purse. 'If there is a danger,' it was said, 'it is that members of the official side, owing to their sense of responsibility to their political chiefs, to a natural taste for the exercise of authority over subordinates, and to their traditional sense of honour, shall be even more Governmental in their attitude than the Cabinet itself.' [1] After the Second World War, when the Government was exhorting workers to exercise wage restraint, this attitude was particularly important. Secondly, the Tomlin Formula aimed at long-term stability, as well as fair relativity. In times of rapidly rising prices these aims were inconsistent and fair relativity was the one which suffered. Thirdly, civil servants were among the inevitable economic victims of an inflationary situation.

The principles of civil service wage determination were again examined by a Royal Commission in 1953–1955. This Commission viewed a civil service and an economic and political environment which had changed appreciably since 1931. The labour force of the civil service had grown from 340,000 to 720,000; there had been sharp changes in price levels; through full employment many of the non-monetary advantages of civil service employment were enjoyed by comparable workers in non-Governmental jobs; and the Government was regulating the economy more than ever before in peacetime.

The 1953 Commission substantially rejected the Tomlin Formula.[2] 'We think', its Report stated, 'that in the conduct of wage and salary negotiations concepts of fairness and of the existence of a wage and salary framework not governed solely by "the law of the market" play a large and increasing part.' [3] The intention should be, it added, to obtain a civil service, 'recognized as efficient and staffed by members whose remuneration and conditions of service are thought fair both by themselves and by the community they serve'.

The Commission's conclusions were dominated by the concept of 'fairness', which had no precise meaning. Its definition varied with every interest group in civil service affairs, so a Civil Service Pay Research Unit was established to assist negotiators to reach an agreed definition. But civil service negotiators were operating within a situation dominated by external factors which neither concepts of fairness nor a juggling with statistics could overcome.

---

[1] White, op. cit., p. 14.
[2] See Royal Commission on the Civil Service Report, 1953–1955, Cmd. 9613.
[3] ibid., para. 94.

In so far as there was such a thing as a civil service wages policy in the post-war period it was one which was consistent with the Government's treatment of the whole public sector, which in turn was an integral part of the Government's economic policy. If it had been otherwise the purpose of the Government's economic policy would have been defeated, for the public sector was large and the effects of its treatment pervaded the whole economy. It is to the rest of this sector that we must turn to get a more pronounced view of the Government as an employer.

Appendix II

THE FAIR WAGES CLAUSE OF THE HOUSE OF COMMONS

Before the Government conceded collective bargaining rights to its own employees it concerned itself with the wages of workers on Government sub-contracts, and sought to give them fair treatment. On 13 February 1891, Mr. Sidney Buxton, M.P., raised a motion in the House of Commons about labour practices on Government contracts. He asked that the State as a capitalist and employer should set a good example. He said he wanted to apply the maxim that property has its duties as well as rights to labour relations. In the past the Government had declared that it had no need to look beyond the solvency of the sub-contractor.

The Government was sympathetic and it introduced an amendment, closely resembling Buxton's motion, which stated:

> That in the opinion of this House, it is the duty of the Government in all Government contracts to make provision against the evils recently disclosed before the Sweating Committee, to insert such conditions as may prevent the abuse arising from sub-letting, and to make every effort to secure the payment of such wages as are generally accepted as current in each trade for competent workmen.[1]

The clause was amended slightly in 1893, but in neither the original nor the revised form was the clause effective, and in August 1907 the Treasury appointed a Committee consisting of representatives of the various contracting departments to consider the matter.

The Committee's recommendations were incorporated in a new clause which was adopted by the House of Commons on 10 March 1909. The new clause read as follows:

> That, in the opinion of this House, the Fair Wages Clauses in Government contracts should be so amended as to provide as follows:— The Contractor shall, under a penalty of a fine or otherwise, pay rates of

[1] Hansard, vol. CCL, 1891, col. 614 et seq.

wages and observe hours of labour not less favourable than those commonly recognized by employers and trade societies (or in the absence of such recognized wages and hours, those which in practice prevail amongst good employers) in the trade in the district where the work is carried out. . . .[1]

An Advisory Committee on the Fair Wages Clauses of Government Contracts was established to advise Government departments in their dealings with contractors, and the Government gave an undertaking to apply the terms of the clause to labour directly employed by it.[2]

The Advisory Committee recommended a common form of Fair Wages Clause to be used by all Government departments, which omitted the words 'under a penalty of a fine or otherwise' owing to the difficulty of applying them. Thereafter the Government, assisted by the vigilance of trade unions who were quick to report unfavourable deviations from the clause, endeavoured to apply the principle of fair wages. The clause remained unaltered until October 1946. It had been realized in 1937 that it needed to be amended to suit a situation in which there was a developed form of trade unionism and an established system of collective bargaining, and a committee was set up to perform this task. The war started before the committee reported. Nothing was done until the war ended, because Government contractors were largely covered by the Conditions of Employment and National Arbitration Order, 1940.

A long and detailed Fair Wages resolution was adopted by the House of Commons in 1946. It stated that what the 'good employers' paid was no longer a criterion of what was a fair wage. Only wages negotiated by trade unions were fair. Amongst other things the 1946 resolution stated that 'The contractor shall recognize the freedom of his workpeople to be members of Trade Unions'.

The position now is as follows. The departments of the Government attempt to apply the resolution in their dealings with contractors. Where an allegation is made, normally by a trade union, that the resolution is not being observed, the offending contractor is reminded of his obligations and informed of the complaint. The matter is dealt with by the Ministry of Labour which attempts to arrange an amicable settlement. If it fails to do so the question is referred to an independent tribunal, usually the Industrial Court, for a decision. The procedure which follows is governed by the Industrial Courts Act.

---

[1] *Industrial Relations Handbook*, H.M.S.O., 1953, p. 139.
[2] The undertaking was given in a debate on the Army estimates, 8 March 1910 (Royal Commission Report, 1929–1931, Cmd. 3909, p. 82).

Chapter Five

THE NATION'S LARGEST EMPLOYER

THIS chapter is about the normal behaviour of the Government as a peacetime employer of labour other than civil servants. It briefly describes the position in the nationalized industries and the national health service and shows how the Government has responded when labour difficulties have arisen. It does not describe actual strikes.[1] No detailed account is provided for the years after 1955, for then a new set of factors began to operate and complicate the situation. This account is given in the following chapter.

The Government first became a large employer of labour in peacetime after 1918. It continued the wartime control of the railways until August 1921 and of the coal industry until 31 March 1921. It continued to have a financial interest in the coal industry until after the General Strike. The years of control, however, were turbulent ones in which the Government had neither the respite nor the desire to act as a normal employer. It had rejected the proposals to nationalize the railways and the mines, and was simply biding time until these industries could be handed back to private control.

The situation after 1945 was wholly different and this chapter is concerned only with that period. Legislation between 1945 and 1951 placed civil aviation, the coal industry, transport industry, the gas, electricity, and the iron and steel industries and health services in the public sector of the economy. These industries and services employed more than 2½ million people, all of whom, to varying extents, came under the control of the Government but did not acquire civil service status. The industries and services were national in scope and were largely basic ones in the British economy.

When the Nationalization Acts became operative there already existed strongly organized trade unions in most of the affected industries. They possessed the right to strike and some of them had had much practice in using it. There were well-established negotiating procedures in existence too. These were altered when the nature of the employer changed but the practice of free collective bargaining continued. Most of the unions were affiliated to the Trades Union Congress and to the Labour Party and were able thereby to take political action.

[1] See Chapter XI for 'Strikes Against the Government as an Employer'.

The industries, except the national health service, were continued as profit-making concerns, so it was not expected that the problem of establishing a new criterion against which to measure wage claims would arise. But just as civil servants expected the Government to be a model employer so workers in nationalized industries looked for treatment which was exemplary and did not depend on profit-and-loss accounts. They had been informed through decades of propaganda that under nationalization workers as well as the community at large would be better served.

The Nationalized Industries

The iron and steel industry came into public ownership in 1951, but it was denationalized soon afterwards by the Conservative Government and by 1955 was largely back in private hands. It was a prosperous industry and its workers were relatively highly paid. Nationalization had no effect on the management of the industry; it simply entailed a transference of ownership. The Government at no stage appeared as an employer to iron and steel workers.

The gas and electricity industries had been subjected to Government regulations before nationalization. They were among the 'sheltered' industries of the inter-war years; the workers in them had no cause to regard nationalization as a panacea for they had no large problems to solve. They suffered a relative decline in real earnings during the war but were able to move back towards their pre-war position by 1950 without attracting public attention.[1] The electrical supply workers were aided in this recovery by the small proportion which their wages constituted in total costs.

Railway transport was a declining industry. This was reflected not in a contraction of its services but in a decline in working conditions and railway wages. The services were maintained because they constituted a public service and were of military value. Railway men rightly resented having to bear a cost which should have been a national responsibility. They entered the phase of nationalization with an accumulation of bitterness which many thought would be dissipated by the benefits from a national transport organization. But they were destined to be disappointed. The Railway Executive had a recurring annual deficit and was unable either to meet the wage demands of the railwaymen or to improve working conditions. To pay wage increases it had either to increase productivity, increase prices, or receive a subsidy from the Government. As productivity could not easily be increased in the short run and price increases

---

[1] 'Nationalised Industry', by H. A. Clegg, in *The British Economy 1945-1950*, edited by Worswick and Ady, p. 443.

and subsidies were determined at Cabinet level, the railway unions and the Government were brought into contact with each other whenever the railwaymen demanded a wage increase.

The road haulage industry consisted of a large number of diverse undertakings. Its nationalization involved the imposition of uniform practices and conditions of work. For many workers uniformity improved working conditions but reduced earnings; occasionally it evoked outbursts of resentment. The Government, however, was not the target. Road haulage was denationalized, along with the steel industry, before any large issues supported by the unions arose.

The whole of the road passenger transport services in London and some services in the provinces were nationalized. The majority of the provincial bus workers remained in municipal and private undertakings. For London passenger transport workers nationalization was no more, at first, than a change in a letter-head from London Passenger Transport Board to London Transport Executive. The same controlling personnel remained in charge; the same negotiating procedures were used. There were changes, however, which were not created by the post-war Nationalization Act but which contributed towards bringing London busmen into conflict with the Government, their ultimate employer. In the war years London busmen moved away from the relatively highly paid position with good working conditions which they had held in the inter-war years. This movement was accentuated after the war. Their industry did not expand and prosper as did manufacturing industry, so it was not able to give wage advances to keep pace with price movements. So long, however, as official wage demands from the busmen were consistent with what was being currently granted in the annual round of wage increases, and provided the Transport and General Workers' Union which organized the London busmen was disposed to co-operate with the Government, then no issues arose involving the Government which could not be settled unobtrusively. When these conditions altered the relationship between London busmen and the Government become overt and potentially disruptive.

The coal-mining industry was different from any other nationalized industry. There was a long continuous history of protests by miners against private ownership of the mines, so that nationalization was regarded not simply as a means of making the industry more efficient for all concerned but also as a victory for the miners. But victory and acclamation could not remove the bitterness which years of struggle against employers, deplorable working conditions, and large-scale unemployment, had engendered. Nor could they alter traditions which influenced the miners' collective behaviour. Miners remained independent in their group reactions, disregarded central authority, acted spontaneously and aggressively. They continued to strike at local level after nationalization in much the same way as they had struck before. The miners' relative earnings rose during and after the war so much that they were among the highest paid manual workers in the country. The miners had none of the grievances of the railwaymen or London busmen. The nation needed coal so much that the Government was prepared to give the industry and its workers priority of treatment. The National Union of Mineworkers made only moderate demands and collaborated, as far as it was able, in encouraging means for increasing productivity, expanding the labour force, and reducing absenteeism; and it desisted from threatening or taking national strike action. So the miners, oddly and unexpectedly, had no obvious relations with the Government in its capacity as an employer.[1]

Methods of Control. Each industry was put under the control of a public corporation which had a wide area of freedom from Government intervention. Unlike the civil service departments they were not under close and continuous supervision by Parliament. A Minister could not be questioned about them except on matters of general public interest. The industries did not have to present estimates to Parliament, but they did have to publish detailed annual reports which were submitted to Parliament. They were charged, averaging good and bad years, with balancing revenue and expenditure.

The Boards were the bargaining counterparts to the trade unions and were responsible for applying labour policies. In order to assist them a statutory provision was made for joint consultation. The machinery of joint consultation varied between industries but in all cases it covered questions relating to safety, health, and welfare. It was the most elaborate and at the same time most effective in the electricity industry. Consultation was used with purpose in civil aviation, though not always in the manner intended by the legislators. In all cases negotiations about conditions of employment and consultation were separate processes. The unions concentrated their attention on the negotiating procedures and it was through these that the policies of the Government in respect of nationalized industries were discussed.

The Government, within the limits set by statute, could influence the behaviour of the boards of nationalized industries in their dealings

---

[1] Since this was written a number of uneconomic pits have been closed in various parts of the country and miners have protested to the Government about it. But the protests have concerned the Government's general economic policy, not its policy as an employer.

with unions, through using persuasion or by actual interference. It could interfere through its ultimate control of the price policy of the boards; thus, by refusing to agree to a price increase, it could make it very difficult for a board to grant a wage increase, regardless of the merits of the claim. Or it could regulate the borrowing policy of the boards and thus prevent them from incurring a deficit or an increased deficit to meet trade union claims which involved finance. All the nationalized industries, with minor exceptions, required Treasury approval as well as the consent of the appropriate Minister before they could borrow money.[1] When the Select Committee of the House of Commons on Nationalized Industries examined this form of Government control in 1957, it was told that the boards had to tell the Treasury at the beginning of the year what their financial needs would be and that their estimates could not be varied without Treasury permission.[2]

There was no overt connection between the Government's control of the boards' finances and trade union action, with one exception, until 1956. The trade union movement broadly co-operated with the Government until that year and there was in consequence little friction between the Government and unions in nationalized industries. There were strikes but they were unofficial and were not directed against the Government. In the mines they were local and endemic; elsewhere they mostly assumed the characteristics of intra-union disputes.

The railways provided the exception. From 1950 the railway unions found that a complete acceptance of the Government's policy for the railways involved too high a cost for their members. They rejected the policy of collaboration and the Government found itself directly implicated as an employer. The consequences are described below.

Railway Troubles. The first railway dispute in which the Government was involved obviously as an employer after railway nationalization, occurred when Labour was in office late in 1950. The three railway unions had submitted separate wage claims. The National Union of Railwaymen asked for a 10 per cent increase; the Associated Society of Locomotive Engineers and Firemen wanted 15 per cent; while the Railway Clerks' Association asked for a $7\frac{1}{2}$ per cent increase. The Railway Executive made a conditional offer in November. The unions refused to discuss an offer hedged by conditions, so the Minister of Labour, Mr. George Isaacs, appointed a Court of Inquiry into the dispute. This was just before Christmas.

---

[1] Appendix I, Report from the Select Committee on Nationalized Industries (Reports and Accounts) 29 October 1957.

[2] ibid., pp. 4–5.

While the Court of Inquiry was sitting there were threats of unofficial strike action. The Midland district council of the footplate men's union, for instance, recommended a forty-eight-hour token strike if the report did not meet their claim. The report was published on 13 February 1951 and as it did not meet the railwaymen's claim the demands for strike action were intensified. In Scotland arrangements were made by footplate men to strike on 3 March.[1] In Liverpool almost 1,000 goods workers began working to rule. Railwaymen of various manual grades in other parts of the country called for strike action too. There were reports of weekend strikes and working to rule. And to make the Government's position more uncomfortable, when the new Minister of Labour, Mr. Aneurin Bevan, asked the National Union of Railwaymen to advise its members not to take precipitate strike action, the union refused to do so.[2]

The Railway Executive's offer for the lowest grades on the railways amounted to a 5 per cent increase if added to increases already received in August 1950. The Court of Inquiry recommended that this offer should be accepted, subject to minor modifications which gave slightly larger increases for the higher grades. It stated that the offer should be made subject to the unions accepting proposals for economizing in manpower and increasing efficiency.[3] The Railway Executive had accumulated a deficit of more than £50 million over three years and this undoubtedly had influenced the attitude of the Court.

The three railway unions rejected the Court of Inquiry's recommendations. It had been a long time, the Railway Clerks' Association stated, since a Court of Inquiry 'issued findings so nearly identical with the employers' point of view'.[4] The reception given to the recommendations was so hostile that the Minister of Labour arranged an early interview with the three unions. From then the unions, traditionally antagonistic towards each other, worked together.

Mr. Bevan arranged meetings between the Railway Executive and the unions but the difference between what one offered and the others demanded, amounting to only £500,000 in a claim involving £9¼ million, remained. There was also the matter of railway efficiency to settle. The negotiations broke down on 21 February and, although the unions had not threatened to call an official strike, the possibility of a strike taking place by default was serious.

The following day Mr. Bevan met the representatives of the unions and told them that in the national interest it was imperative that

[1] *The Times*, 15 February 1951.   [2] ibid., 17 February 1951.
[3] Cmd. 8154.   [4] *Railway Service Journal*, March 1951.

everything possible should be done to reach an amicable settlement.[1]
Then a series of meetings was hurriedly held. The Minister and the
chief officials of the British Transport Commission and the Railway
Executive were all involved. On 23 February the Railway Executive
met the executives of the three railway unions and made an offer
which bridged the difference.

The Court of Inquiry's recommended wage increase was raised to
$7\frac{1}{2}$ per cent, although the Railway Executive had previously insisted
that it could not pay more than 5 per cent without placing an
intolerable financial burden on the railways. And no conditions were
attached to the offer. The question of efficiency on the railways was
referred for examination by a special joint committee. The revised
offer was accepted by the unions. They agreed to co-operate in
eliminating the waste of manpower and in improving productivity.
The general secretary of the National Union of Railwaymen dispatched 1,600 telegrams to branches urging the members to resume
normal work.[2] The settlement had come only just in time.

The dispute raised a number of points. It showed that so long as
the railways were incurring a deficit, free collective bargaining
between the Railway Executive and the railway unions in their mood
of dissatisfaction could not exist. It revealed the possibility of the
Government getting its various roles mixed up. If the railwaymen
had extended their strike action the railway unions catering for the
operative grades would have been forced to take charge and give the
strike official recognition. The Labour Government had not had a
large official strike to contend with before. For prestige as well as
practical reasons it wanted to avoid one. In particular, it did not
want a railway dispute, because of the possible adverse effects on
trade and the inconvenience it would cause to the public. Thus it was
difficult for the Government to act as a hard-headed employer.
Indeed, it did not want to appear as the employer at all but as a
conciliator. Even at the most critical stage of the dispute Bevan told
the railwaymen's representatives that he could not take part in the
wage negotiations.[3] The façade, however, was transparent. The
Government was stating the employer's terms.

Lastly, it was shown that in its desire to avoid a dispute the Government was willing to disregard its own conciliation machinery. There
was no legal obligation for either party to accept the recommendations of the Court of Inquiry, but there was a strong practical and
moral reason why the Government should do so. The Government's
act in disregarding the recommendations set a precedent which was

---

[1] *Railway Review*, 2 March 1951.   [2] *The Times*, 24 February 1951.
[3] ibid., 23 February 1951.

damaging to the structure of conciliation. 'We have succeeded', the National Union of Railwaymen proclaimed, 'in overturning for the first time in history the recommendations of a Court of Inquiry.' [1]

The 1951 railway dispute was repeated in some essentials at the end of 1953. There was a Conservative Government in office by that time, but it was pursuing a deliberate policy of conciliation towards unions. The railwaymen remained badly paid and justifiably were still dissatisfied. In July 1953 the National Union of Railwaymen submitted a claim for a 15 per cent increase in wages. This was rejected by the Railway Executive and in November it came up before the Railway Staff National Arbitration Tribunal.

The Arbitration award, issued on 3 December, was for a 4s. a week increase. The union leaders were angry. The General Secretary of the National Union of Railwaymen called it a 'meagre award' and said 'It seems clear to me that many outside factors have had a bearing on the conclusions.' [2] The awards of a number of Arbitration Courts that year had been for similar amounts.

The award was repudiated and a national strike was called for 20 December if no satisfactory settlement had been reached by then. The railway unions sent representatives to meet the British Transport Commission, but it was clear that without Government permission a revised offer could not be made. The chairman of the British Transport Commission, like the chairman of the Railway Executive in 1951, declared that the Tribunal's award represented the limit of the Commission's financial capacity. At this point the Government had to assess various factors. There was a general feeling of sympathy for the railwaymen and a recognition of the inadequacy of the Arbitration Award. A strike at Christmas, however, would have been unpopular with the public and it might have caused such public inconvenience that the Government might have felt it necessary to take steps to avoid it. Whatever the time of year, a national railway strike was economically undesirable. On the other hand the railway union had rejected an Arbitration Award. If this were practised frequently, confidence in Awards would be destroyed and the arbitration machinery would cease to function. The union, moreover, was attempting to get a wage increase by coercion.

Sir Walter Monckton decided to conciliate and brought the parties together soon after the award was rejected. The resumed negotiations reached an impasse, so on 16 December the dispute was reported to the Prime Minister, Sir Winston Churchill. The Prime Minister, in his only direct intervention in industrial disputes during his post-war spell in office, decided that the railwaymen should be given extra

[1] *Railway Review*, 2 March 1951.   [2] ibid., 11 December 1953.

pay to avert a strike. The Tribunal's offer of 4*s*. was increased to
7*s*. and although it only amounted to about one-third of the
demand the railwaymen accepted it. A settlement was reached again
by the Government over-riding the normal procedures for determining wages.

The railway unions continued to have disputes involving the
Government. They were unavoidable so long as the unions' claims
exceeded the capacity of the Railway Executive to pay. This situation could not be resolved until either the railways were sufficiently
reorganized to make a profit, or the Railway Executive was released
from its statutory obligation to pay compensation to former railway
shareholders.

The Government had been criticized since 1951 by private employers and by some trade union leaders for going above the established negotiating machinery. It had also faced criticisms for the
irresponsible way in which railwaymen were treated. There was not,
as there was in the civil service, a wage formula which was intended
to provide fair treatment. The Government did not seem to consider
itself to be responsible for the welfare of the railwaymen.

It was reminded that it had responsibilities during a dispute in
January 1955. An agreement over wage rates was reached on 8
October 1954 between the British Transport Commission and the
three railway unions. The agreement was ratified by the executive of
the National Union of Railwaymen on 12 October and was put into
operation. There was an immediate and spontaneous protest from
the ordinary railwaymen. So strong was the protest that the executive
of the National Union of Railwaymen informed the Transport
Commission on 11 November 1954 that the agreement was unacceptable to its membership and asked it to re-open negotiations to
obtain the balance of the 15 per cent increase in wages it had origin-
ally asked for in July 1953. The Transport Commission refused to
do this and the Minister of Transport declined to intervene on the
grounds that the normal processes of negotiations had not been
exhausted. The Transport Commission was willing to consider a
fresh application for a wage increase but the union would not agree
to this delay as it considered its existing claim was still to be met.
In consequence, on 22 December the union executive gave notice of
a national strike to be called on 9 January 1955.

On the day the strike notice was posted the Cabinet discussed the
railway dispute. The next day Sir Walter Monckton appointed a
Court of Inquiry into the dispute and appealed for the strike to be
called off. The union refused to do this because it considered that
the Court of Inquiry was a time-buying device, but it nonetheless

agreed to co-operate with the Court and give evidence. An Interim Report was issued on 3 January and on 6 January the strike was cancelled because the Transport Commission gave an assurance that there would be future wage talks. The Report made two important points:

> It is clear that the delay in reaching agreement, and the nature of the contentions urged by the B.T.C. in the course of these negotiations, had caused a sense of exasperation and frustration in the minds of the negotiating members of the N.U.R. Executive. There was reason for such exasperation. Throughout the negotiations, and indeed in the discussions before us, the B.T.C. were maintaining two apparently contradictory positions. First, that the offers made by them have represented fair and reasonable wage rates, and second, that they were not able to offer such wages as they would have desired to offer because of the financial limits placed upon their freedom of action by the terms of the Transport Act, 1947. It is little surprising that, faced with arguments so mutually contradictory, negotiators on the other side of the table should have little faith in either.
>
> At this point we come very close to the core of the matter, and we feel that we must state in the plainest of terms what we apprehend to be the proper approach. The Nation has provided by statute that there shall be a nationalised system of railway transport, which must therefore be regarded as a public utility of the first importance. Having willed the end, the Nation must will the means. This implies that employees of such a national service should receive a fair and adequate wage, and that, in broad terms, the railwayman should be in no worse case than his colleagues in a comparable industry.[1]

The Minister of Labour announced that the Government accepted all the implications of the statement and added that any wage increases negotiated between the British Transport Commission and the railway unions would be paid even if they involved the Commission in a financial deficit. But no significant change in Government policy occurred. The hand-to-mouth policy for the railways continued. So did the repudiation of arbitration awards.

The Railway Staff National Tribunal rejected a claim from the National Union of Railwaymen for a 10 per cent increase in wages in March 1957 and recommended a 3 per cent increase. The recommendation was immediately rejected by the railwaymen. A shipbuilding strike had started and an engineering strike was about to begin.[2] Road transport facilities were restricted because of petrol rationing. A railway strike would have been an intolerable additional national economic burden. A hurried unofficial meeting was held

[1] Cmd. 9352.   [2] See below, p. 105.

between the railwaymen's leaders and the chairman of the Transport Commission, followed by official meetings. On 22 March the Transport Commission offered the railwaymen a 5 per cent increase which was accepted. In effect the level of the yearly round of wage increases was set with the approval of the Government.[1] A similar situation occurred in June 1958 when the Government made an offer to the railwaymen during the bus strike after the Tribunal had rejected their claim.[2]

The Government, through disregarding railway arbitration awards, has provided the means but not in the manner envisaged by the Court of Inquiry. It has not formulated a satisfactory wages policy for the railways. Nor has it made the railways any the less an industrial trouble spot. But the situation is not simply in the hands of the Government. The whole body of railwaymen are relatively poorly paid; the poorest paid railwaymen are underpaid in absolute terms. Any attempt to improve the position of the lowest paid group, however, without corresponding improvements for the other groups, interferes with jealously guarded established differentials. A strike of footplate men did in fact take place over differentials at the end of May 1955.[3] It is possible that when the railways were first nationalized prompt action, which remunerated railwaymen because they were public servants, would have contributed towards industrial peace. Initially it would have been costly, but the long-run gains would have been substantial.[4] As it is, not only has delay made railway wages more difficult to regulate satisfactorily, but it has brought even the negotiating machinery into disrepute.

National Health Service Employees

National health service employees compare more closely with civil servants than with workers in the nationalized industries. They do not work in a profit-making organization; they consist of a relatively high proportion of female workers who are notoriously difficult to organize; apart from the male mental-hospital nurses, they possess no militant traditions; and in the main they eschew the strike weapon. Most of them do not possess the status of civil servants nor do they receive comparable remuneration. The health service consists of many grades, differentiated in some cases by class barriers; there are doctors, hospital administrators, hospital tech-

[1] See *The Employers' Challenge*, by H. A. Clegg and Rex Adams, pp. 89–90.
[2] This situation is described in Chapter VI, pp. 112–113, and in greater detail in Chapter XI, pp. 204–207.
[3] See Chapter XI for a brief description of this strike.
[4] It would have entailed statutory provision which removed from the British Transport Commission the need to act like a private industrial undertaking.

nicians, male and female nurses, manual maintenance staffs, and others. Unity between these is inevitably difficult to achieve. They are dispersed geographically and experience contrasting local conditions.

The National Health Service Act of 1946 gave the Minister of Health the task of establishing a comprehensive health service in England and Wales which was to be financed almost entirely by public funds and for which he was to be responsible to Parliament. About four-fifths of the health service employees were hospital workers and these, excluding workers in teaching hospitals, worked under the instructions of local Hospital Management Committees and had their wages paid by the Treasury. But by law they were employed by the fourteen Regional Hospital Boards established under the Act.

There was no uniform collective bargaining system in the health service before 1946. Some bargaining procedures had existed before the war, but they had left many workers without protection. The position was improved during the war by Government intervention, but it was still necessary to create a system with complete coverage which corresponded in some way with the organization of the health service. Collective bargaining machinery based on the Whitley system was established. A General Council was formed to act as a central joint body to cover certain issues involving the whole service, while eight Functional Councils dealt with matters appertaining to the main occupational groupings.[1] The Functional Councils had the right to 'determine remuneration'. On each Council were representatives of the staff and management.

The constitution of the management sides presented a problem. There were four managing groups: the Regional Boards, Boards of Governors of teaching hospitals, Local Authorities, and Executive Councils which controlled general practitioner services, dentistry, supplementary ophthalmic services, and pharmaceutical services. But these groups could not engage in free collective bargaining because all except the Local Authorities were dependent upon the Government for finance. The Ministry of Health was accordingly represented on all the Functional Councils except the Dental Council which organized dentists in the local health and education services. These representatives could be outvoted on all the management sides but their number was irrelevant for no management side could pay a

---

[1] The following Councils were established: The Ancillary Staffs Council; the Nurses and Midwives Council; the Administrative and Clerical Staffs Council; the Professional and Technical Councils; the Pharmaceutical Council; the Medical Council; the Optical Council; and the Dental Council.

wage increase without the sanction of the Minister of Health. He in turn had to consult the Treasury about any increase in the expenditure of his department.

The wage policy which was pursued in the health service until the mid-1950s compared with that practised in the civil service. It was 'something like a qualified Tomlin formula'.[1] The Government, perhaps, was in a greater dilemma than over civil service wages. It could not give preferential treatment to its own workers when it was appealing for restraint from others; on the other hand, the pressure for fair relativity was greater than in the case of civil servants, because health service employees in the main were relatively poorly paid and were so obviously performing a public service. The dilemma was resolved, it has been maintained,[2] by the device of failing to agree over wage claims which were reasonable according to the Tomlin Formula and submitting the cases to arbitration, where the Government knew that the formula would most probably be applied. When the Government was not so rigorous in its pursuit of wage restraint it had no need to use this device. Nor was it used when the Government was prepared to risk the political consequences of interfering directly to effect wage stability, as happened in the autumn of 1957.[3]

The Consequence of Neglect

Once the Labour Government had made statutory provisions for the industries and services it wished to nationalize, its attitude towards them was determined primarily by economic factors. In assessing the remuneration of workers and their conditions of work, it took no account of their contribution to the welfare of the community nor of the high expectations of workers which formed a part of the case for nationalization. It did not even behave as a good employer. The inadequacy of the Government's attitude was shown clearly by the dissatisfaction of the railwaymen. It had, however, a more general consequence. The Government was able to discriminate as it pleased in its treatment of its employees after 1956, because no co-ordinated and principled way of determining the wages of Government workers had been devised and operated. The following chapter describes the situation which occurred.

---

[1] *Wage Policy and the Health Service*, by H. A. Clegg and T. E. Chester, p. 81.
[2] ibid., Chapter VI.
[3] See Chapter VI below for a description of the national health service overtime ban.

Chapter Six

THE GOVERNMENT EXPLOITS ITS POSITION
1955–1958

SIR WINSTON CHURCHILL ceased to be Premier in April 1955 and was succeeded by Sir Anthony Eden. No major changes were made in the Cabinet until December of that year, when Mr. Harold Macmillan became the Chancellor of the Exchequer and Mr. Iain Macleod replaced Sir Walter Monckton as Minister of Labour. After the changes had been made the emphasis in the Government's policy changed too. The new Conservative leaders desired to forge their own independent industrial policy and were prepared to be tougher in their attitude towards trade unions.

The economic position of the country deteriorated during the autumn of 1955, and the pressures to restrict credit and stabilize wages which had been relaxed earlier in the year were reintroduced. The Chancellor of the Exchequer exhorted unions to be moderate while the Prime Minister appealed for price stability.

The nationalized industries came in for much criticism. The Chairman of the London Electricity Board, in a controversial letter to *The Times* on 14 February 1956, blamed them for starting the annual round of wage increases. He criticized particularly the former union leaders on nationalized boards for failing to 'deal with wage claims in a judicial way'. The British Employers' Confederation repeated his contention about the nationalized industries but with a different slant.[1] It stated that the Government was not prepared to accept responsibility for the actions of the nationalized industries yet serious repercussions followed in private industry from actions in the public sector. Increased wage costs were passed on to the consumer through higher prices for coal, transport, electricity, and gas.

The Government took notice of the criticisms. On 19 March 1956 it refused to sanction an increase in passenger transport fares and it limited an increase in freight charges to 5 per cent instead of the 10 per cent, which, along with the fares increase, had been approved by the Transport Tribunal.[2] But this was not considered to be enough. At a meeting in June, employers' representatives insisted to the Prime

[1] 14 March 1956; cf. *The Employers' Challenge*, by H. A. Clegg and Rex Adams, p. 52. [2] ibid., p. 54.

Minister that more effective action should be taken over the nationalized industries.[1] It was taken. One by one the chairmen of the
nationalized boards made declarations about maintaining price
stability in their industries, at the cost, it seemed, of wage increases.

There had been an important change in the personnel of trade
union leaders. Arthur Deakin, the general secretary of the Transport
and General Workers' Union, had died on 1 May 1955. He had been
moderate and conciliatory with Conservatives as well as Labour; he
had been a close friend of Sir Walter Monckton; and he had exercised
more influence in the trade union movement than any other individual. For a year after his death there was no settled leadership in his
union and his place in the Movement was not filled. His successor in
his union, Arthur Tiffin, died without holding effective office. In the
spring of 1956 Frank Cousins became general secretary of the
transport union and immediately set about impressing his own mark
on his union and on the Movement. He introduced a phase of militancy into trade union affairs which had been absent since before the
war. The Government's policy provided him with admirable material
and cause.

The impact of Mr. Cousins was not felt until the Trades Union
Congress met in September 1956, and he introduced a motion which
censured the Government for its inflationary policy. It stated that the
Congress 'asserts the right of Labour to bargain on equal terms with
Capital, and to use its bargaining strength to protect the workers
from the dislocations of an unplanned economy. It rejects proposals
to recover control by wage restraint, and by using the nationalized
industries as a drag-anchor for the drifting national economy. . . .'[2]
In a terse speech, Mr. Cousins attacked the Government, to the
delight of the delegates. This was a motion the General Council
dared not oppose, even though a number of its members profoundly
disagreed with it. Had it done so the Council clearly would have been
defeated. Its collective opinion remained unheard at the Congress and
the motion was acclaimed. The tone of trade union relations with
the Government, which had been changing gradually during the year,
was set at this Congress.

The Congress coincided with the British attack on Egypt which
placed an additional burden on the British economy. There were
subsequent changes in the Government. Mr. Harold Macmillan
became Prime Minister in January 1957 and Mr. Peter Thorneycroft
took his place as Chancellor of the Exchequer. Industrial interests
in the Cabinet were strengthened. The return to doctrinaire Con-
servatism became more marked. The Government did not take con-

[1] *The Employers' Challenge*, p. 59.   [2] T.U.C. Report, 1956, p. 398.

troversial action over wages as an employer until some months after the changes, but in the interim much happened which was of direct relevance.

It must have been clear to the Government that its policy of encouraging the boards of nationalized industries and private employers to resist wage demands could not be pursued without taking a strong risk of its ending in strike action. It must, therefore, have had its priorities arranged: measures to counter inflation first; industrial peace second. Until the Suez crisis this order was realistic from the Government's point of view. The economy appeared to be strong enough to bear one or two strikes but it could not stand continued inflation. The Suez crisis upset this order, but the Government did not realize, until after the national shipbuilding and engineering strikes had started on 16 and 23 March 1957, that the country could no longer afford national strikes.[1] As soon as this fact dawned upon the Government, it set about trying to persuade the employers to make concessions to the unions.[2] The Minister of Labour set up two Courts of Inquiry: one for shipbuilding after the shipbuilding strike had lasted for nine days; and one for engineering when its strike was seven days old. The strikes were called off on 2 April pending the reports of the Courts of Inquiry. These came out on 2 May and recommended pay increases comparable with the amount the union leaders had been willing to accept during the strikes. The Government had, in effect, taken away its support from employers in their resistance to wage demands.

The Courts of Inquiry, in their recommendations, reiterated a proposal which had been made by similar Courts in 1954.[3] It was that an authoritative and impartial body should be established to consider the wider problems of a wage policy in an inflationary setting.[4] The proposal arose out of the inability of the Courts to adjudicate on the recognized and accepted merits of a claim as they would arise in joint negotiations and, at the same time, take cognizance of the wider issue of inflation. The Government welcomed the suggestion. During May and June the Ministry of Labour was mainly preoccupied with the impartial body: with its size, composition, and terms of reference. Employers, chairmen of nationalized industries, and the General Council of the Trades Union Congress were consulted but the Government had already made up its mind to establish a body before it met these organizations. Consultation

[1] For a detailed explanation of the Government's part in these strikes see Clegg and Adams, op. cit.
[2] ibid., p. 148.
[3] Report of a Court of Inquiry into a Dispute in the Engineering Industry, Cmd. 9084.
[4] Cmd. 159 and Cmd. 160.

was only about form. A number of unions opposed the proposal and the General Council of the Trades Union Congress entered upon discussions with the Government only with reluctance and after some delay. The Government ignored the union attitude and on 12 August 1957 it announced the composition of the new body. It had three members,[1] whose task was 'Having regard to the desirability of full employment and increasing standards of life based on expanding production and reasonable stability of prices to keep under review changes in prices, productivity and the level of incomes (including wages, salaries, and profits) and to report thereon from time to time.'[2] The body was not a wage court and was not to be concerned with specific disputes.

The Government, having failed to restrain wages in the engineering and shipbuilding industries, seemed to be reconciled to price increases. Its efforts to get voluntary price stability had failed. In June and early July 1957 price increases had been announced or forecast for coal, rail freight and fares, docks and canal charges, cement, gas, electricity, and postal rates.[3] The upward trend seemed likely to continue. The problem of inflation was widely debated in the newspapers and in Parliament. The Parliamentary Labour Party raised the issue but, more important for the Government, there were 'rumblings of angry disapproval from some Conservative back benchers'[4] and the Chancellor of the Exchequer had to meet the Conservative 1922 Committee on 11 July to explain the Government's policy.

The danger of inflation increased during the summer months and the external confidence in the pound declined. There were large losses in Britain's gold and dollar reserves in August which left them lower than they had been in earlier economic crises. The Trades Union Congress in September 1957 re-affirmed its opposition to the Government's monetary policy and to wage restraint. The Government, compelled by the adverse economic situation to take action, with no hope of trade union co-operation, and precluded by its philosophy from introducing physical controls, turned to a more stringent application of monetary control. It declared a standstill in the capital expenditure of nationalized industries and public authorities. On 19 September the bank rate was raised dramatically from 5 per cent to 7 per cent to discourage internal spending.

[1] Lord Cohen, Lord Appeal in Ordinary (age 69 years); Sir Harold Howitt, chartered accountant (age 70 years); and Sir Dennis Robertson, formerly Professor of Political Economy in the University of Cambridge (age 67 years).
[2] *The Times*, 13 August 1957.
[3] *The Financial Times*, 10 July 1957.
[4] *The Times*, 12 July 1957.

Trade unions regarded the measures as a direct attempt to weaken them through encouraging employers to be more aggressive and through increasing unemployment. The Chancellor of the Exchequer tended to confirm this opinion in a speech he made in Washington. He said that the Government must be prepared to deny the extra cash to match the upward spirals 'whatever other painful consequences may follow'.[1] Mr. Thorneycroft was prepared to subordinate full employment to a sound currency. The hard lines of the Government's policy were revealed further by the Minister of Labour on 5 October when he said, 'although no one welcomes strikes, we must not be afraid of them'.[2]

The policy was taken a stage further when in a motion for the adjournment in the House of Commons on 29 October, Mr. Thorneycroft said:

> Economies have been achieved and must be rigorously sought. . . . Instructions have been given wherever possible that increased costs, whether of materials or wages, should be offset by reduced services or administrative economies. . . . Wages increases unrelated to and going far and beyond the general growth of real wealth of this country are by far the greatest danger we have to face. . . . Those who ask for wage increases, those who grant wage increases, and those who adjudicate on wage increases should have this well in the forefront of their minds. . . . If costs, including wage costs, go up, activity will have to be reduced, and this will be so also where the Government is looked to as the source of cash.[3]

This statement was direct advice to arbitrators and a plain indication where the Government was going to act. It aroused controversy in the House of Commons and opposition from trade union leaders. Railwaymen construed it as an intention to interfere in their negotiations. The general secretary of the National Union of Railwaymen said:

> It appears that, instead of being able to enter into simple straightforward negotiations, the Transport Commission must now have the kind permission of the Chancellor of the Exchequer and the National Union of Manufacturers. . . . There is already growing doubt about the impartiality of wage tribunals. . . . A period of arbitration based on Government instructions is being ushered in. The trade union movement will not stand for this.[4]

On the day after the Chancellor's statement was made Mr. Macleod was asked for clarification. About the railway negotiations

---

[1] ibid., 25 September 1957.   [2] *Manchester Guardian*, 5 October 1957.
[3] ibid., 30 October 1957.   [4] ibid., 31 October 1957.

he said: 'We do not intend to usurp the functions in negotiations of the Transport Commission; but we do intend to make clear to them and to everyone else our continuing determination that we will not finance inflationary awards, however they are secured, either through negotiation or arbitration.' He added: '. . . we are not attempting to instruct arbitration tribunals. Indeed, it would be inconsistent with their function if we attempted to do so. The Government are the largest employer. . . . In wage claims where we are the direct employer we will apply—and be seen to apply—the most stringent tests. . . .'[1] This is in fact what the Government did.

Discrimination Against Government Workers

On 1 November 1957 the Minister of Health and the Secretary of State for Scotland refused to confirm a pay increase for National Health Service employees. It had been agreed by the National Whitley Council for the Health Service that employees earning less than £1,200 a year should receive a 3 per cent increase and that employees earning over that amount should have a 5 per cent increase. The refusal applied only to the lower-paid employees.

Although the Minister had a statutory right to act as he did it was a right which had not been exercised before. Indeed, in February 1956 the Government had said it would be inconsistent with the proper operation of collective bargaining for the Minister to intervene in health service negotiations.[2] Mr. Walker-Smith was reminded of this assurance by trade union leaders. His retort was that his decision had been made in the light of conditions in October 1957 not February 1956. Moreover, since the Ministry of Health representatives on the National Whitley Council were in a minority and as it was the Ministry of Health which footed the bill, Mr. Walker-Smith considered that the normal principles of collective bargaining did not apply.[3]

Civil service trade unions were the next to be affected by the Government's policy. The Treasury intimated to a few civil service unions which had reached wage settlements that it intended to insert a new paragraph in the establishment circulars which gave authority for the payment of wage increases. The paragraph read: 'In making provision for the cost of the pay increase authorised below, departments should be governed by the Government's general policy that pay increases are to be offset by corresponding economies.'[4] Negotia-

---

[1] *The Times*, 31 October 1957.
[2] cf. ibid., 2 November 1957.
[3] ibid. See Chapter V above for a description of the composition of the National Whitley Council.
[4] *Manchester Guardian*, 19 November 1957.

tions in the civil service were thus inhibited by the threat of redundancy.

A claim for a $7\frac{1}{2}$ per cent wage increase for 12,000 employees of the British Broadcasting Corporation was rejected on 12 December 1957. The Governors of the B.B.C. explained that the Government had informed the Corporation 'that it would not be possible for the Government to finance wage increases either by increasing the B.B.C.'s percentage of licence revenue during the term of the present agreement or by augmenting the grant-in-aid for external services. ... In the light of these factors, the governors are unable ... to accede to the claim for an increase in salaries and wages.' [1] A pay settlement for probation officers, agreed by a body similar to the National Whitley Council for the Health Service, was rejected by the Government on 29 January 1958 and a small increase was substituted. And in February 1958 a pay increase for 450 firewomen was refused by the Home Secretary, though he agreed in principle that firewomen should be paid more. [2]

Trade unions reacted in various ways to the application of the Government's policy. Many of them had wage claims in the process of negotiation. Some refused to submit their claims to arbitration because they believed that the arbitrators were influenced by the Government. The Civil Service Alliance, representing 120,000 clerical officers, reacted in this manner early in November. So did the five unions which organized Co-operative Society workers. Mr. Alan Birch,[3] the spokesman for these unions, informed the National Wages Board for the Co-operative Union that their members would not allow their claim to be decided by arbitration. This attitude, he claimed, was justifiable in view of the Government's actions and present policy.[4] The Transport and General Workers' Union, which had requested an increase of 25s. a week for London busmen, was more aggressive in its attitude towards the Government. 'It would be a sorry day', its general secretary, Mr. Cousins, stated, 'when the trade union movement took its direction from any government, whatever its political faith.' [5] In his union journal he explained that 'we have a number of current wage claims. We are satisfied that they are completely justified and it will therefore be our intention to pursue them to a conclusion.' 'Like other sensible

---

[1] *The Times*, 13 December 1957.   [2] ibid., 15 February 1958.

[3] General Secretary of the Union of Shop, Distributive and Allied Workers and member of the General Council of the T.U.C.

[4] *Manchester Guardian*, 22 November 1957. The National Wages Board responded by awarding a general wage increase of 12s. a week for men and 6s. 6d. a week for women.

[5] *The Times*, 13 December 1957.

people,' he added, 'we hope this can be done without conflict.' [1] The general secretary of the United Society of Boilermakers, Mr. E. J. Hill, was more explicit. 'The Tory Government', he wrote, 'has decided to declare war on the trade unions of this country in a more vicious way than any former Government. It has decided to use its political power in purely industrial issues and, therefore, the trade unions are free to use their industrial power in political issues.' [2]

The unions in the health service were in a difficult position. They naturally wanted to make an effective protest but they had no quarrel with the hospital management boards and they did not want to do anything which might injure patients. In any case they had traditionally rejected strike action. The Government, however, was so determined in its attitude that verbal protests in public, in deputations, or through Parliament, were unlikely to have much effect. The unions could not report a dispute to the Minister of Labour for arbitration because they had no dispute with the official side of the National Whitley Council.

The union with most members involved in the health service was the National and Local Government Officers' Association. Very quickly protests came in from its branches. Members in the north-east, north-west, and north Wales within two days called on the union to apply an overtime ban and in the last resort to withdraw labour. Other groups sent in similar protests a little later on. There was no doubt that the ordinary members did not want the issue to be lost in a welter of words. Hospital workers lobbied Members of Parliament on 7 November and a deputation of union and management representatives saw the Minister of Health on 11 November. The Government made no concession. Also on 11 November the executive of the National and Local Government Officers' Association decided that its 30,000 health service members should operate an overtime ban from 18 November. Other unions with fewer members in the health service agreed to join in implementing the ban.

The purpose of the ban was to hurt the Government and not the patients. This was plainly difficult to execute and some members felt that the Government had taken this into account when reaching its decision to refuse their pay increase. The relative ineffectiveness of banning overtime was recognized by the unions. They knew it would be some time before the Government felt the effects of the ban, and that it would only be felt through administrative deficiencies such as failing to get reports and statistical returns. But the ban was carried out nevertheless.

[1] *The Record*, February 1958.
[2] November Circular to members of the United Society of Boilermakers.

It was supported by other measures. A protest about the principle of the Government's pay veto from doctors, dentists, and other health service workers not directly affected by the veto was made to the Prime Minister; a motion signed by sixty Labour Members of Parliament was tabled in the House of Commons, condemning 'the actions of Her Majesty's Government in abusing its political power by destructive interference with the established processes of collective bargaining in nationalized industries';[1] and the National and Local Government Officers' Association advertised its grievance in *The Times*. The Government was unmoved. '[I] have no evidence', the Minister of Health said, 'of any detriments to patients or interruptions of services. . . . It is not for me to do anything about the ban. I have said from the start that I deprecate this ban. It would be entirely inconsistent with the duty of Ministers if they allowed themselves to be coerced in the exercise of their statutory duty by such means as this.'[2] If the unions had persisted in the ban for a long period the Minister may have changed his mind. But they were bound by their assurance to patients that they would do nothing to endanger their welfare and the ban had to be called off late in December 1957.

Divide and Rule

The Prime Minister had said on 22 November 1957 that the Government meant to see its anti-inflationary measures through 'no matter how much we are abused or our actions are misrepresented'.[3] The protests at that time, apart from the national health service ban, were confined to words. But there was no guarantee that they would remain so. The Government had amongst its employees some of the most militant sections of the trade union movement. The London busmen, the railwaymen, and the miners had pay claims in the course of negotiation. A complete and final rejection of each of these claims could result in industrial strife comparable to that of the early 1920s. If the unions involved united in their opposition the whole authority of the Government would be challenged. This situation was speculative at the end of 1957 but it had to be reckoned on by the Government.

When the Chancellor of the Exchequer, Mr. Thorneycroft, and his two Parliamentary assistants at the Treasury, resigned from the Government early in January 1958 because they felt that the Government was not adopting a sufficiently strong anti-inflationary policy,

---

[1] *Manchester Guardian*, 27 November 1957.
[2] *The Times*, 17 December 1957.
[3] *Manchester Guardian*, 23 November 1957.

it seemed that the Government had decided not to risk a widespread industrial conflict.[1] These men had been the most persistent advocates of a firm approach to wages, and without them the Government was expected to be more flexible.

An understanding of the Government's attitude was confused, however, by the publication on 21 February 1958 of the Cohen Council's first report on prices, productivity, and incomes. The report advised the Government to remain firm in handling wage claims and endorsed all the facets of the Government's economic policy. This may have counter-balanced the departure of Mr. Thorneycroft. Certainly some union leaders thought it did. They were afraid that the Government would use the report to interfere more persistently in the wage negotiations of nationalized industries, which were at critical stages. The mine workers had had a pay claim for a 10s. a week increase for 350,000 day-wage workers rejected by the National Coal Board on 19 February. The London busmen's claim for a 25s. a week increase was being heard by the Industrial Court on 24 February. And the following month the Railway Staff National Tribunal was considering the wage claims of the railwaymen.

The subsequent course of industrial relations depended upon three things: the timing of the stages of conciliation and arbitration in the three industries concerned; the attitudes of the trade unionists and their leaders; and the applied policy of the Government. The Government was in the favourable position of being able to adapt its policy to changes in the first two.

The time factor was beyond the control of the Government, for the claims were being dealt with by different procedures. Fortunately for the Government the claims conveniently separated themselves. The miners' claim was long in coming to a conclusion. It was 29 May 1958 before the pay claim was rejected by the National Reference Tribunal. By then the claims in the other industries had been disposed of and the unions' policies declared. The miners, moreover, had three claims and only one was rejected outright. It was hard for them to get heated in this situation, particularly as the coal-face workers who gave the union its rank and file leadership were not affected by the rejection of the pay claim. The Government, then, had only to contend with the railwaymen and London busmen.

The railwaymen and busmen were capable of taking independent militant action if the results of negotiations and arbitration were un-

---

[1] Mr. Nigel Birch, Economic Secretary to the Treasury, who resigned with Mr. Thorneycroft, said, 'The Treasury Ministers were out to win the battle of inflation and the others were not . . .' (*The Times*, 9 January 1958).

favourable to them, but they were influenced strongly by the advice of their leaders. The union leaders were a mixed bag. Mr. Cousins, leading the busmen, was an aggressive critic of the Government. Mr. Webber, general secretary of the Transport Salaried Staffs' Association, and Mr. A. Hallworth, the general secretary of the Locomotive Engineers and Firemen, were both moderate in their approach to the Government. The leadership position in the National Union of Railwaymen was unpredictable. Mr. J. Campbell, the general secretary of the union, who had initiated the railwaymen's wage claim and who had persistently opposed the Government's policy, had been killed in a road accident in Russia on 6 November 1957. The railwaymen's case was taken over by a hitherto unknown assistant general secretary, Mr. S. F. Greene, and it was not known what advice he would give to his executive or whether the advice would be accepted.

The Government decided to separate the railway unions from the London busmen by discriminating treatment. After prolonged and diverse negotiations the London busmen declared a strike on 5 May 1958. This was the first industrial dispute of any significance which had resulted from the Government's wage policy. The railwaymen who reached the point of striking whilst the bus strike was on, were given a wage increase by the Government in contravention of an arbitration tribunal award which had rejected the men's claim. The increase was accepted and the London busmen were isolated. Mr. Cousins made an attempt to widen the area of the strike but he was discouraged by the General Council of the Trades Union Congress, which refused to support him. The busmen continued the strike with a remarkable display of solidarity and only ended it after the Government had made concessions which at the outset it had opposed.[1]

The Government's anomalous position as a large-scale employer, conciliator, and regulator-in-chief of the economy was clearly shown after 1955. The Government gave priority to its role as regulator of the economy. Where this, in the Government's opinion, required a policy of wage restraint, the Government applied the policy directly to its own employees. It did so not only because it was the easiest course to take but also because it acted as an example to private industry. The Government was better able to advocate a policy which it operated itself. It could not, however, risk having almost 18 per cent of the country's labour force in revolt against it, especially as more than half of these workers were employed in basic industries. So it applied its policy to the sections of its labour force which had the least ability to harm the economy through strike action.

[1] The strike and the treatment of the railwaymen are examined in detail in Chapter XI.

The economic situation changed during the summer of 1958. Even before the bus strike was over the Bank Rate was reduced to 5½ per cent. Then, on 3 July, credit restrictions were eased and the Government relaxed its wages policy. Later in the summer pockets of unemployment began to appear which grew and multiplied. The problem for the Government and unions at the end of 1958 was how to cope with a recession, not inflation. This change in economic conditions removed the Government's role in industrial relations from the field of immediate controversy, but it did not remove the problem which is inherent in the Government's economic activities. If the trend of this century continues, the Government will become increasingly implicated in applying national economic policy and it will become a larger employer of labour. The Government will again be tempted to discriminate against its employees, thus increasing the possibility of strike action against itself and reducing its effectiveness as a conciliator.

3

THE GOVERNMENT AND STRIKES

THE intention of Part III is to show the general development of the attitude of the Government towards strikes, to describe how it has reacted in different moods and under various circumstances and to distinguish between strike motives in so far as they have concerned the Government.

Chapter Seven

THE SIGNIFICANCE OF STRIKES TO THE GOVERNMENT[1]

A STRIKE is a collective protest expressed by withdrawing labour from work. It is the most aggressive form of industrial protest—apart from sabotage, which has rarely occurred in Britain since the days of machine-breaking and rattening in the nineteenth century. Violence against persons or property may occur during strikes if the strikers are provoked through a deliberate use of blackleg labour, or if they are unable to get united support.

There is a potential subversive element in all strike action. At any time strikes are capable of being directed against the state and therefore of having some impact on the authority of a Government. The inherent threat to the Government comes from the organized character of strikes and from the emotional stimulus which they generate. To the extent that the activities of the strikers can be controlled by strike leaders they can be directed at the Government. For this reason the personalities and ambitions of strike leaders are important.

The threat to the Government's authority from strike action may appear to be theoretical in a modern democratic community. But under unstable economic and political conditions the threat is real. Successive totalitarian Governments have realized that large strikes can lead to political disturbances and they have promptly either suppressed trade unions or controlled their strike activities.

This chapter deals with the development of the Government's attitude to strikes in general and describes the emergence of new implications as unions and the economy have grown in complexity. The chapter does not show a trend, for the Government's attitude to strikes has been singularly changeable, even reversible.

There were strikes and riots over industrial discontent during the eighteenth century in Britain, but they were largely of local significance only and engendered no fear in the minds of statesmen that they would have revolutionary consequences. The French Revolution in 1789, however, left few British statesmen in doubt about the collective strength of the middle and working classes or about their ability to overthrow an established Government by force. Afraid of a revolution in Britain on the French pattern, the Government

[1] This chapter deals only with peacetime strikes.

adopted a policy of repression which, so far as trade unions were concerned, found expression in the Combination Acts of 1799 and 1800, which made unions into illegal organizations and strike action a criminal act.

The treatment of strikes in Britain as if they were insurrectionist movements continued until 1824, when the Combination Acts were repealed. Then followed an intensive spell of striking and rioting which resulted in the re-imposition of restrictions on strike action in 1825 through the Combination Laws Repeal Act Amendment Act. This Act penalized violence, threats, intimidation, molestation, and obstruction in the calling of a strike and during its course. Peaceful picketing was illegal and remained so for many years. The Government was alarmed by the unprecedented growth of the Grand National Consolidated Trades Union in 1834, by violence in the late 1830s, and then by the Chartist agitation, though trade unions had played an insignificant role in the Chartist Movement.

Some slight changes in the law were made by the Molestation of Workmen Act of 1859, but such terms as 'threats' and 'intimidation' remained undefined and the sphere of lawful strikes was a restricted one. Strikes which did not have the determination of wages or hours of work as their objects were covered by the common-law doctrines of conspiracy and restraint of trade. In the category of conspiracy came all strikes with political aims.

The Government did not have the administrative machine to enforce legal suppression and widespread suppression by force would have been dangerously provocative. Troops were used for various activities during strikes in the nineteenth century until the police forces, which were formed in the second half of the century, assumed the general function of protecting property and maintaining order. Troops were then left either to act as blacklegs or for occasional use to provide a display of force by protecting blacklegs.

There was a limited number of trades where troops could be used as blacklegs. In 1861, during a strike of London building workers, the War Department permitted sappers of the Royal Engineers to work for the builder of the new Chelsea barracks. The sappers were withdrawn, however, after protests to the Government by the newly formed London Trades Council.[1] Troops were also used to help farmers get in the harvest during a lock-out of farm workers in Oxfordshire in 1872. Again the London Trades Council protested successfully and even succeeded in getting a new article inserted in the Queen's Regulations forbidding the use of troops in harvest work 'where strikes or disputes between farmers and their labourers exist'.[2]

[1] *London Trades Council 1860–1950. A History*, pp. 17–18.   [2] ibid., p. 43.

The responsiveness of the Government to union protests in the two cases quoted above reflected signs of a change in the Government's attitude to strikes, which were confirmed by alterations in the law. Through the Criminal Law Amendment Act of 1871 vague terms, such as intimidation, were defined and restricted in application, and it ceased to be a statutory offence merely to threaten to strike. The Act, however, imposed severe restrictions on the conduct of strikes. It was repealed in 1875 by the passing of the Conspiracy and Protection of Property Act. After 1875 there were no legal difficulties in the way of calling trade disputes until the Courts intervened in 1901.

Political strikes remained illegal under the Conspiracy and Protection of Property Act of 1875. The Act also made it illegal for a worker employed in the supply of gas or water, to break his contract of service with his employer. It had previously been a criminal offence for any worker to break his contract. This was an early indication that the Government was regarding the provision of essential services as one of its functions.

The eagerness with which the 'New Model' union leaders condemned strikes in public and discouraged them in practice may have influenced the Government to adopt a more liberal attitude towards strikes. These leaders, however, were replaced by men who viewed strike action in a wholly different light and who, starting with the London dock strike in 1889, conducted widespread strikes intensely and bitterly. In these circumstances the Government directed its attention to maintaining law and order and in 1891 set up a Royal Commission on Labour. While the Commission was sitting troops were used on two occasions.

The first occasion was at Hull in April 1893 during a strike of dockers and seamen. The Shipping Federation, taking advantage of the high level of unemployment in the country, had moved 1,000 blacklegs from London to Hull. The appearance of blacklegs led to disturbances, and three companies of Dragoons were drafted to the strike area; two gunboats were dispatched to the Humber in case the strikers interfered with the shipping; and extra police were moved in. The disturbances petered out and Mr. Asquith, the Home Secretary, who had been responsible for giving armed protection to the blacklegs, was congratulated for his 'prompt action'.[1]

Troops were used again when some miners overturned several loaded wagons during a lock-out at Featherstone, Yorkshire, in September 1893. Twenty-eight infantrymen and a captain, who had been summoned from York by an order of Justices of the Peace,

---

[1] *The Times* stated: 'A small troop of Dragoons has been invaluable: the men have only had to show themselves for order to be restored' (11 April 1893).

fired on the miners, and others who had collected, after they had failed to disperse when the Riot Act was read to them. Two men were killed and sixteen were wounded. This was said to have been the first occasion since Chartist times that troops had fired on civilians.[1] Troops and police were drafted to other areas during the lock-out. The Miners' Federation of Great Britain stated in protest: 'While we strongly denounce all who take part in rioting as the worst enemies of the miners' cause, yet we cannot help believing that the pressure of imported police and military in such large numbers acts as a forcible incentive to rioting and disorder, and hereby urges on the Government to withdraw at once all newly imported soldiers and police from the various counties affected.'[2]

The phase of strike action after 1889 did not induce the Government to re-impose legal restrictions on the right to strike. On the contrary it accepted the advice of the Royal Commission to use conciliatory measures and in 1896 passed the Conciliation Act. This was a sign not only of public tolerance but also of recognition that unions were established institutions. These two factors, however, did not protect unions from the Courts. In 1901 two House of Lords' decisions were made which curtailed strike action. The first decision made it illegal for a combination to strike for any purpose a Court considered to be 'unjustifiable' or not in pursuit of the legitimate interests of the members of the combination.[3] Then, in deciding the issue in the Taff Vale case, the House of Lords held that any trade union could be sued in its registered name for torts committed by its officials. In other words if a trade union called a strike it could be sued for damages.

The two decisions were reversed by Government legislation in 1906. Under the Trade Disputes Act of 1906 peaceful picketing became clearly lawful, and so did persuasion to strike. The Act defined 'trade dispute' so as to include sympathetic strike action as well as the focal dispute.

A number of factors influenced the nature of strike action after 1906. The advent of the militant politically conscious union leaders after 1889 coincided with the beginning of a phase of theorizing about the strike weapon as a determinant of the relationship between unions and the state. The theorizing, started by Marx, emerged at the beginning of the twentieth century as Syndicalism. This gave unions a much more vital role to play in the struggle against capitalism than Marx had done. Its greatest practical significance in Britain was in the years leading up to the First World War.[4]

---

[1] cf. *The Miners*, by R. Page Arnot, pp. 236–241.   [2] ibid.
[3] *Trade Union Law*, by N. A. Citrine, pp. 15–16.
[4] See Chapter X for details about the effect of Syndicalism on strike behaviour.

As unions became more conscious of the class struggle their economic position in society was changing. The economy was developing into one consisting of large interdependent units, so that the well-being of substantial sections of the community depended increasingly upon the private decisions of small groups of people. Many unions became national organizations or national federations with jurisdiction over whole industries. For the first time, they waged national strikes and they did so on the docks, the railways, and in the mines, where the welfare of the community was affected most.

The Government could not remain detached from strikes in such circumstances; nor did it. More than in any other period it used troops during strikes, in order, it stated, to protect the interests of the public. Its interventions, however, were provocative because more than anything else they protected blacklegs and the property of employers.

Its first intervention in this phase was during a miners' strike in South Wales in November 1910. The Cambrian Combine declared a lock-out at one of its coal mines, so in retaliation the South Wales Miners' Federation called all of the 12,000 miners employed by the Combine out on strike.[1] During the strike, the miners at a pit near Tonypandy, thinking that blacklegs were being introduced, took precautions which brought them into conflict with the police. At this point the Chief Constable of Glamorgan applied to the local army command for troops to aid the police. He wanted 200 cavalry and two companies of infantry.[2] The Army Council issued instructions for the 18th Hussars to be sent to the strike scene if necessary.[3] The Home Secretary, Mr. Churchill, consulted with the War Minister, Lord Haldane, and decided that Metropolitan policemen should be sent instead of troops. About 800 policemen went from London in three contingents and, despite Churchill's decision, 3,000 infantry moved in too.[4] Major-General Nevil Macready, Director of Personal Services at the War Office, was sent to South Wales to take command of the civil and military forces.[5] There was no bloodshed; just a use of bayonets as 'gentle persuasion' to drive stone-throwers into the arms of the police.[6]

The Government now seemed intent on preserving its authority because it feared insurrection. Troops were deployed widely during

---

[1] cf. *The Miners—Years of Struggle*, by R. Page Arnot, pp. 57–67.
[2] *The Times*, 9 November 1910.
[3] ibid., 8 November 1910.
[4] There have been many contradictory reports about the number of police sent to South Wales. This number is taken from a Home Office statement issued at the time.
[5] cf. *Annals of an Active Life*, by Sir Nevil Macready, vol. I, pp. 136–158.
[6] ibid.

the national dock strike in 1911. In Liverpool the railwaymen struck in sympathy with the dockers, and when the dockers' claim was settled they refused to go back to work until their own outstanding claims were settled too. The strike in Liverpool spread until it included all transport workers. The police clashed with the strikers and troops were drafted to the city. The Riot Act was read but the disturbances continued, during which, on 15 August, two men were shot and killed.

By this time railwaymen throughout the country were striking. The railway employers refused to meet the representatives of the railwaymen to discuss their grievances, so on 18 August 1911 a national railway strike was called. The Government assured the employers that they would be given ample protection to enable them to carry on their services. It threatened to use troops to run the trains, but, as there were only three companies of the Royal Engineers in the country which it could use, the threat was an empty one.[1] Instead, non-union labour was used with Government-provided protection.

There was one other outbreak of violence. On the day a settlement of the strike was agreed upon a group of workers in Llanelly, South Wales, tried to stop a train being run. Soldiers of the Worcester Regiment were ordered to intervene and in the process two men were killed and others injured. Feelings ran high after the shooting and a large body of strikers and other workers moved on to attack a train and to raid some trucks in a siding. One of the trucks, containing gunpowder, carbide, and gelatine, was fired on and in the explosion five people were killed and many injured.

Approximately 58,000 troops were put at the disposal of strike area commanders. All other troops stood by. The military authorities had always had the power to move troops about the country but the employment of troops in cases of disorder was restricted. During the railway strike this restriction was lifted and military commanders were allowed to use their own initiative in protecting railway property, preserving order, and maintaining traffic.[2]

The day before the railway strike took place Mr. Churchill, the Home Secretary, had made a statement about the use of troops in strikes. He said:

There can be no question of the military forces of the Crown intervening in a labour dispute in the proper sense of the words. That so far as it can be done by the Government, is a function of the Board of Trade. It is only when a trade dispute is accompanied by riot, intimidation, or

[1] *The Times*, 18 August 1911.
[2] Mr. Churchill in the House of Commons (*The Times*, 23 August 1911).

other violations of the law or when a serious interruption is caused or likely to be caused to the supply of necessary commodities, that the military can be called on to support the police; and then their duty is to maintain the law, not to interfere in the matter in dispute.[1]

In fact, of course, the Government did intervene in the railway dispute by using troops. The presence of troops at the strike-centres itself implicated the Government; their use to protect blacklegs undoubtedly intimidated the strikers and created a bitterness in the minds of trade unionists which has remained to this day.

The Government did not use troops so provocatively in the national coal strike in 1912. The strike was fought over a simple trade union issue, a minimum wage, and the Government played a prominent part in the negotiations but without open military support. During the strike Tom Mann was arrested under the Incitement to Mutiny Act of 1895 for distributing a leaflet imploring troops not to shoot at strikers.

Protective Devices

The strike trend was continued after the First World War. There were national strikes and much more frequent strike threats for political and economic reasons. Troops were used occasionally to provide a show of force, but never on the scale of the pre-war period.[2] The Government, instead, equipped itself with special protective powers through legislation and administrative measures. This process was tackled in four main stages.

(*i*) *The Police Act 1919.* After the war there was widespread disaffection in the police.[3] There had been a successful strike of London policemen on 30 August 1918. A national union was formed and the union leaders became involved in the political and industrial activities of the trade union movement. The Government was not prepared to tolerate this or another strike. So when a strike threat was made by the National Union of Police and Prison Officers in May 1919, the Commissioner of the Metropolitan Police stated that policemen were not workmen under the Trade Disputes Act of 1906 and were not entitled to picket. If they picketed or interfered with policemen on duty they would be guilty of an offence under the Crimes Act, 1885. Then on 8 July the Government introduced a Police Bill in the House of Commons which prohibited policemen from joining a trade union and made it unlawful for policemen to strike. The Bill stated

---

[1] ibid., 18 August 1911.

[2] See Chapters X and XI below for details of the post-war strikes.

[3] For a description of this see 'The National Union of Police and Prison Officers', by V. L. Allen, in *The Economic History Review*, vol. XI, no. 1, 1958.

that any person found guilty of causing disaffection among the police, or of inducing 'any member of a police force to withhold his services . . . shall be liable . . . to imprisonment with or without hard labour, for a term not exceeding two years . . .'[1] Before the Bill became law on 15 August 1919 there was a police strike of small dimension and all the strikers were dismissed from the service.

Oddly, the first intervention by troops in a post-war strike was to stop disturbances during this strike. Its main impact was in Liverpool, Birkenhead, and Bootle where more than half of the police forces went on strike. Strikers intimidated non-strikers and assaulted constables on duty. The strike created an opportunity for an orgy of looting and rioting. A thousand troops were drafted to Liverpool and fought with the rioters, using their rifles as clubs or with fixed bayonets.[2] There were casualties and one man was killed. Five hundred troops were sent to Birkenhead to deal with the rioting there. Other groups of workers in Liverpool were on strike at the same time. The situation was comparable to that in Liverpool in 1911. Under instructions from Mr. Bonar Law, some warships were moved into the River Mersey as a precautionary measure.[3]

An attempt was made by the National Union of Manufacturers to get the Government to extend the provisions of the Police Act. It resolved at a special meeting on 16 September 1919: 'In order to make good government and administration of this country more secure, the Government be requested to extend the provisions of the Police Act to all nationalized public services, including the telegraph, telephone, postal, and excise services, together with the mines and railways if and when nationalized. . . .'[4] The Government did not respond to this call, except to extend the restrictions concerning strike action by workers in the gas and water industries to electricity supply workers. This was done in the Electricity (Supply) Act of December 1919.

(*ii*) *The Emergency Powers Act.* The next step was taken the following year when the Government passed the Emergency Powers Act. The Bill was introduced into the House of Commons during the 'Datum Line' coal strike and passed through all its stages in a week. It became law on 29 October 1920. The Act permitted the Government to declare a state of emergency, but it did not make strikes unlawful even when this had been done. The Act stated:

If at any time it appears to His Majesty that any action has been taken or is immediately threatened by any persons or body of persons of such

---

[1] Police Act 1919, 9 and 10 Geo. 5, Ch. 46.
[2] *Salvidge of Liverpool*, by Stanley Salvidge, p. 177.   [3] ibid.
[4] *British Trades Union Review*, September 1919.

a nature and on so extensive a scale as to be calculated, by interfering with the supply and distribution of food, water, fuel, or light, or with the means of locomotion, to deprive the community, or any substantial portion of the community, of the essentials of life, His Majesty may, by proclamation . . . declare that a state of emergency exists. . . .[1]

The Government was empowered to deal with the situation and to take over and run essential services by emergency regulations, but it had no power to impose any form of compulsory military service or industrial conscription. The Emergency Powers Act was essentially an anti-strike measure. It was first used during the 1921 coal dispute, when army leave was cancelled, reservists were called up, and troops moved into the coal fields.

(iii) *Administrative Measures.* During the war an emergency organization was formed for the maintenance of supplies in case of a dislocation of services through enemy activities. The organization was equipped with military transport. At its head was Sir Eric Geddes. For a time after the war this 'Supply and Transport Service' was maintained and was used by the Government during the 1919 railway strike. Geddes remained in charge of it and at the same time was the chairman of the Cabinet sub-committee which was responsible for preparing against strike contingencies.[2] The Cabinet also had a Protection Committee, formed early in 1919, to provide protection for blacklegs, docks, road convoys, and the like.

The Government's Supply and Transport Service disintegrated as war organizations were disbanded, and no effective civilian counterpart was immediately established in its place. Instead, in 1920 and 1921, the Government took *ad hoc* strike precautions involving the withdrawal of troops from overseas commitments, the displacement of the police and the recruitment of a volunteer defence force. In those years it was faced with a number of strike possibilities: a single national coal or railway strike, a strike with varying degrees of sympathetic action, a Triple Alliance strike or a general strike. When Mr. Baldwin became Prime Minister in 1923 he set up an interdepartmental committee to examine the Government's emergency strike precautions.[3] The Labour Government, the following year, constructed a skeleton scheme under the control of Josiah Wedgwood, but no serious permanent provisions were made until after the Conservatives had been returned to power in the autumn of 1924.

---

[1] Citrine, op. cit., pp. 549–550.
[2] The sub-committee appeared to be called by different names at different times, but each name indicated its function. It was the Cabinet Committee of Public Safety, or the Industrial Unrest Committee, or the Cabinet Strike Committee.
[3] *Stanley Baldwin*, by G. M. Young, p. 59.

Then a scheme for maintaining supplies and transport was devised which rested on the Emergency Powers Act. Each Government department was made responsible for defined spheres of action; the country was divided into eleven areas, each under the control of a Civil Commissioner. The whole was administered by a Civil Commissioner who was responsible to a Cabinet committee. In practice the task of creating this emergency organization was tackled by the Home Secretary, Sir W. Joynson Hicks. It was done with such secrecy that even Ministers were unaware of what was being done.[1]

The wisdom of keeping the preparations secret was questioned in the Government during August 1925.[2] Hitherto it had been the Government policy to maintain the strictest secrecy about its strike precautions, to avoid being provocative. But an effective scheme depended upon local helpers and if secrecy were maintained these were kept in ignorance of their detailed duties and of each other. To be in a greater state of preparedness the Government had to be more open about its plans. Nonetheless the Government did not make public any of its plans. It simply dropped occasional hints. During the General Strike the Government organization operated under the façade of the Organization for the Maintenance of Supplies, a voluntary strike-breaking body formed in 1925. The Government's administrative measures in 1926 were effective and did not depend on military support. Troops were dispatched to the main industrial areas, but they were kept in the background in all places except London, where an army convoy system moved food from the London docks to a depot in Hyde Park.[3]

(*iv*) *The Trade Disputes and Trade Unions Act of 1927.* Before the General Strike there had been Conservative pressure on Mr. Baldwin to change the law relating to trade unions, but he had resisted it. Once the Strike had started he could no longer do so. A Bill to deal with sympathetic strikes was prepared by the Government before the Strike had ended, but it was delayed because of the danger of taking precipitate action and was introduced in 1927. In general it followed the suggestions made to the Government by employers' representatives.

The Trade Disputes and Trade Unions Act, 1927, altered the provisions of the 1906 Trade Disputes Act. It excluded from the protection of the 1906 Act sympathetic strikes and strikes designed

---

[1] Lord Waverley, in conversation with the writer in November 1956. Lord Waverley, formerly Sir John Anderson, was Permanent Under-Secretary at the Home Office at the time.

[2] Young, op. cit., p. 119.

[3] See Chapter XI for a description of the General Strike.

or calculated to coerce the Government either directly, or indirectly, by imposing hardships on the community. Thus it made a general strike illegal and because neither hardship nor community were defined, national strikes could be declared illegal too. The law relating to picketing was changed and confused. The Act also extended the provisions of the Conspiracy and Protection of Property Act, 1875, by stating:

> If any person employed by a local or other public authority wilfully breaks a contract of service with that authority knowing or having reasonable cause to believe that the probable consequence of his so doing, either alone or in combination with others, will be to cause injury or danger or grave inconvenience to the community, he shall be liable, on summary conviction, to a fine not exceeding ten pounds or to imprisonment for a term not exceeding three months.[1]

Thus, civil servants and local Government workers were classified with gas, water, and electricity supply workers.

The Significance after 1945

Strikes ceased to have any insurrectional significance to the Government after the General Strike. The law had been made more stringent; trade unions were financially weakened and largely incapable of large-scale strike action; and trade unionists at all levels were disillusioned. Not until after 1945 did the Government again have cause to be concerned about strikes. The Labour Government repealed the 1927 Act in its entirety by the Trade Disputes and Trade Unions Act of 1945 and restored the pre-1927 position with regard to trade union law. The situation in other respects was wholly different from the 1920s.

Britain's economic difficulties after 1945 were so serious that any strike which dislocated trade or production had national repercussions. The Government was drawn to intervene frequently, and in 1948, 1949, 1951, and 1955 it invoked the Emergency Powers Act; on some occasions it employed troops to move food supplies. The Government's primary concern was to maintain essential services. Its interventions, however, were not markedly dissimilar from interventions before 1926. Troops who moved food supplies were employed in the interests of the community, but in fact they were blacklegs who reduced the effectiveness of the strikes. Strikers did not openly resist as in earlier years; instead they resisted indirectly by extending the duration of the strikes, and making it difficult for a compromise settlement to be reached. Whatever the motives of the

---

[1] Citrine, op. cit., pp. 559–560.

Government, troops invariably appeared as strike-breakers and as protectors of the interests of employers.

The Labour Governments after 1945, with the official support of the trade union movement, had no need to fear highly organized strikes or strikes with political aims. Nevertheless, they always treated strikes seriously and anxiously and intervened promptly, equipped with emergency measures. The Conservative Governments since 1951, on the other hand, have been almost nonchalant in their treatment of strikes, despite some belligerent talk between them and union leaders. They have been less disposed to use emergency powers or troops.

Strikes in general only bother the Government if they interfere with the provision of essential services or if they endanger the nation's economic welfare. There are few unions, however, which can make such a marked impact on the economy as to compel the Government to intervene, unless they act in concert. The economy is viable and people in general are adaptable, so that the worst effects of strikes can be avoided. This is the situation now. The significance of strikes, however, can quickly change. They can easily become subversive or be regarded so. A change in union leadership as in 1889, the rise of authoritarian politicians, a further centralization of economic power, or just a change of mood, could each alter the significance of strikes to the Government.

Chapter Eight

WARTIME STRIKE LEGISLATION

The First World War

The declaration of war against Germany on 4 August 1914 interrupted the phase of acute industrial unrest which had been going on since 1910. Whereas in the period from April to June in 1914, 238,865 men were involved in strikes with a loss of 5,219,200 working days, in the period October to December 1914 only 21,128 men went on strike with a loss of 161,437 working days.

Trade union leaders readily substituted national patriotism for class patriotism. An industrial truce was declared between many unions and employers. The Joint Board, representing the Trades Union Congress, the Labour Party, and the General Federation of Trade Unions, at its meeting on 24 August 1914 decided 'That an immediate effort be made to terminate all existing trade disputes, whether strikes or lock-outs, and whenever new points of difficulty arise during the war period a serious attempt should be made by all concerned to reach an amicable settlement before resorting to a strike or lock-out.' [1]

The prime concern of the Government in the early months of the war was with the size of its army, and it indiscriminately recruited all manner of skilled workers. Early in 1915, however, it became clear to the Government that an army was being trained which could not be equipped and that priority treatment would have to be accorded to the munitions industry. It regulated the recruitment of skilled workers from the munitions industry and persuaded a number of unions to suspend some of their most valued industrial practices for the duration of the war. The success of the Government's labour policy, however, depended on the maintenance of the industrial peace which so many unions had promised earlier on.

The Government started with industrial attitudes in its favour. Most trade unionists were emotionally on its side at the outset of war and were willing to make concessions to win the war. But this situation was unstable for three reasons: (*a*) the industrial conditions against which workers had revolted before the war tended to worsen; (*b*) workers had been subjected to years of anti-Government propaganda and some of the politicians with whom they were asked to

[1] *Labour Supply and Regulation*, by Humbert Wolfe, p. 115.

129

collaborate were men who had been involved in using troops against strikers; and (c) the concessions the Government desired were in workshop practices which workers themselves had devised for their own material protection.

It was far easier for patriotic trade union leaders to sign away restrictive practices than it was for trade unionists at their work benches to see the logic of such concessions. This tended to create a dichotomy between union officials and the rank-and-file members which impaired the authority of the officials. It gave rise to a powerful shop-stewards' movement under the influence of unofficial leaders who were staunchly and consistently antagonistic towards the Government. The movement first showed its strength on the Clydeside where, on 16 February 1915, about 8,000 engineers came out on strike over a wage grievance. The strike was repudiated by the executive council of the Amalgamated Society of Engineers and its leadership was assumed by the local shop-stewards who formed a 'Labour Withholding' Committee, later called the Clyde Workers' Committee.[1] The strike ended on 4 March after the Government had issued an ultimatum to the strikers. The grievance was submitted to arbitration under which the strikers were given half of what they asked for.

On 4 February 1915 the Government had appointed a Committee on Production consisting of the Chief Industrial Commissioner, a representative from the War Office and one from the Admiralty. Its task was 'To inquire and report forthwith, after consultation with the representatives of employers and workmen, as to the best steps to be taken to ensure that the productive power of the employees in engineering and shipbuilding establishments working for Government purposes shall be made fully available so as to meet the needs of the nation in the present emergency.' Four days after the Clyde strike started the Committee issued its first report on 'Avoidance of Stoppages of Work', which stated:

> Whatever may be the rights of the parties at normal times, and whatever may be the methods considered necessary for the maintenance and enforcement of those rights, we think there can be no justification whatever for a resort to strikes or lock-outs under present conditions, when the resulting cessation of work would prevent the production of ships, guns, equipment, stores, or other commodities required by the Government for the purposes of the War.
>
> We therefore submit for the consideration of His Majesty's Government the desirability of the immediate publication of the following

[1] *Revolt on the Clyde*, by William Gallacher, p. 43 et seq. Gallacher said that the name 'Strike Committee' was avoided to escape prosecution under the Defence of the Realm Act.

recommendation to Government contractors and sub-contractors and to Trade Unions, and to request their adhesion to this recommendation, viz.:

Avoidance of Stoppages of Work for Government Purposes

With a view to preventing loss of production caused by disputes between employers and workpeople, no stoppage of work by strike or lock-out should take place on work for Government purposes. In the event of differences arising which fail to be settled by the parties directly concerned, or by their representatives, or under any existing agreements, the matter shall be referred to an impartial tribunal nominated by His Majesty's Government for immediate investigation and report to the Government with a view to a settlement.[1]

The task of arbitrating in the Clyde strike was given to the Committee on Production before its function had been defined or even discussed with union leaders. So when representatives of some important unions met the Chancellor of the Exchequer, Mr. Lloyd George, on 11 March 1915 to discuss the Committee's recommendation they had an example of the operation of successful arbitration before them. The recommendation was accepted and written into the Treasury Agreement on 19 March along with an assurance that the unions would suspend restrictive practices.[2]

The Agreement did not eliminate unofficial strikes. Indeed, they became more numerous after the Agreement had been signed. The Government obviously needed to re-appraise its approach. It had no statutory power to exercise compulsion over labour in industry, and it was this which the Government regarded as the next step in its endeavour to prevent strikes.

The task of equipping the armed forces with munitions was allocated to a new Ministry on 9 June 1915 and put under the control of Mr. Lloyd George. On the day following his appointment Lloyd George summoned a conference of representatives from the trade unions which had signed the Treasury Agreement and a few other unions such as the Miners' Federation, to state the case for giving the Government statutory powers in matters covered by the Agreement. Arising out of this and subsequent meetings a Munitions of War Bill was drafted which made arbitration compulsory and strikes, therefore, illegal. There were protests against the use of compulsion and some unions asked to be left outside the Bill's scope.

---

[1] *Trade Unionism and Munitions*, by G. D. H. Cole, pp. 62–63.

[2] The Amalgamated Society of Engineers was not party to the original Agreement. It entered into separate negotiations with the Government and, in return for a series of guarantees, signed a Supplementary Treasury Agreement a week later. See Cole, op. cit., pp. 73–74.

The Miners' Federation, in particular, was most strongly opposed to being subjected to compulsory arbitration. It sent two of its members as observers to the first conference summoned by the Minister of Munitions. They returned convinced that Lloyd George's proposals 'would seriously interfere with the individual rights of trade unionists, and with the fundamental principles of trade unionism itself'.[1] The miners, therefore, took no further part in the subsequent meetings. At one of these meetings when Lloyd George was explaining the industrial scope of the Bill the question arose as to whether it ought to include the miners. A number of delegates pressed to include them and as there were no miners' representatives present to object, this was done.

Immediately Robert Smillie, the president of the Miners' Federation, heard about this he rushed off to see Lloyd George. He told him:

> There is one clause in the Bill which makes it a criminal offence to incite workers to strike. . . . You may take it from me that if that clause goes through, and the miners are included in this Act, there will not be sufficient prisons in the country for the accommodation of the miners' leaders who will incite to strike. . . . The miners are willing to continue giving full service to the country during the present crisis, but they are not prepared to come under the coercion which you propose in this Bill. . . .[2]

Smillie said that Lloyd George agreed there and then to leave the miners out of the Bill but it did not turn out to be the case. The Bill's provisions relating to industrial disputes covered work outside munitions work if 'in the opinion of His Majesty the existence or continuance of the difference [dispute] is directly or indirectly prejudicial to the manufacture, transport, or supply of Munitions of War'.[3] The Bill was to be applied to such disputes by Royal Proclamation.

The 1915 Munitions of War Act[4] applied directly to all those on munitions work, which was defined as 'the manufacture or repair of arms, ammunition, ships, vehicles, aircraft, or any other articles required for use in the war, or of the metals, machines, or tools required for that manufacture or repair'. This definition was extended and amplified in 1916. The Act provided for the reference of industrial disputes in munitions work to the Minister of Labour

---

[1] *My Life for Labour*, by Robert Smillie (1924), pp. 156–162.
[2] ibid., p. 159.
[3] The Bill is reproduced in Wolfe, op. cit., Appendix 3.
[4] The 1915 Act was added to and amended by Amendment Acts in 1916 and 1917 but it remained unchanged in its strike and arbitration provisions.

(until 1917 the Board of Trade), who would refer the dispute to arbitration if the parties were unable to effect a settlement through their voluntary negotiating procedures. Any awards made under such a settlement were binding on the parties concerned. Three types of arbitration tribunals were established: there was the Committee on Production; a single arbitrator agreed upon by the parties or, if they were unable to agree, one appointed by the Minister of Labour; or a court of arbitration consisting of an equal number of persons representing workers and employers, with a chairman appointed by the Minister. A strike in work covered by the Act was illegal unless the dispute was reported to the Minister and he failed to refer the matter to arbitration within twenty-one days. Workers who contravened this regulation could each be fined up to £5 for each day of the strike. It was possible for workers to be imprisoned for the non-payment of fines.

The Act did not apply to strikes against such things as dilution on private work or the operation of the Military Service Acts.[1] The penalties could be enforced only against workers on strike; not against workers inciting others to strike. There were other regulations to deal with such persons. Under the Defence of the Realm Act the competent Military Authority had the right to remove suspected people from any area. In March 1916 this Act was applied to deport six members of the Clyde Workers' Committee to Edinburgh and other parts of the country. But in the main the Government relied on the Munitions Act to keep industrial peace. It remained in force until 21 November 1918. With its repeal went all the elements of control over labour, good and bad. There was no transition to peacetime conditions.

The Second World War

Manpower problems were of special significance to the Government in the Second World War for precisely the same industrial and military reasons as in the 1914–1918 War. The prevention of strikes was as necessary in the Second as in the First World War, but the need to take legislative action was not so great. The Government in 1939 had no immediate cause for concern over trade union behaviour. Since the General Strike, unions had pursued conciliatory industrial measures and official strikes had been exceptional. There was neither a militant spirit in the rank-and-file nor a disposition to evoke one in the minds of the leaders of trade unions. Unions were in a state of institutional development which was inconsistent with revolutionary

[1] Wolfe, op. cit., p. 122.

T.U.G.—K

tactics; they were deeply entrenched in the economic system, seeking to spread their influence through formal constitutional channels, prepared to deal with any properly elected Government.

The Government made no legislative attempt to prevent strikes until Mr. Churchill formed his Coalition Government in May 1940 and Mr. Ernest Bevin became Minister of Labour. Then the maintenance of industrial peace became a part of the Government's comprehensive manpower policy. Two schemes for the control of manpower were drawn up for the War Cabinet. The one for which Bevin was responsible 'excluded the use of compulsory powers and . . . limited control of engagement to the munitions and building industries'.[1] The other one, devised by the Lord President of the Council, Neville Chamberlain, and his advisers, was based on the full use of compulsion by the Government over persons and property. The War Cabinet accepted the second, more drastic, scheme on 20 May 1940 and two days later the Emergency Powers (Defence) Bill embodying the scheme became law. Under the Act the Government was statutorily given arbitrary powers of direction. The first Defence Regulation under the new Act placed the Minister of Labour in full control of the country's manpower and authorized the promulgation of Orders by which that control could be executed.

Six days after Parliament had given the Government emergency powers, Ernest Bevin met the Joint Consultative Committee of the National Joint Advisory Council to ask for 'advice as to the best means of removing wage problems from the field of prompt controversy during the next few months'.[2] He put three suggestions to the Committee: (a) that it might be possible to have a uniform basis of adjustment of wages to be applied to all industries by a special tribunal; (b) that an independent element might be introduced into the normal negotiating machinery; and (c) that arbitration might be made compulsory after the negotiating machinery had failed to produce a settlement.

The trade union members of the Joint Consultative Committee rejected the first two suggestions mainly because they wanted to retain as much as possible of the voluntary machinery. They and other members of the Committee approved the third suggestion, which in all essentials was like the Munitions of War Act provision of twenty-five years before. In a unanimous report of 4 June the Committee recommended that where voluntary negotiating machinery

[1] *Manpower* (History of the Second World War), by H. M. D. Parker, p. 93. See Chapter V for a description of the acquisition of new power by the Government to control Labour in 1940.

[2] T.U.C. Report, 1940, p. 171.

failed to produce a settlement, the matter in dispute should be submitted to arbitration for a decision which would be binding on all
parties. Where no provision for arbitration existed the parties could
either set up one for themselves or refer the dispute to a National
Arbitration Tribunal appointed by the Minister of Labour. 'In
return for accepting compulsory arbitration, the Joint Consultative
Committee asked that the Minister should take powers to secure that
wages and conditions of employment settled by negotiation or
arbitration would be binding on all employers and workers in the
trade or industry concerned.' [1] In general the recommendations made
by the Committee were accepted and appeared in the Conditions of
Employment and National Arbitration Order, 1940, commonly
known as Order 1305.

Part I of the Order dealt with Arbitration. Under it the Minister set
up a National Arbitration Tribunal for the purpose of settling trade
disputes which could not otherwise be determined. Any existing or
apprehended dispute could be reported by either party to the
Minister, who could refer it either for settlement according to existing provisions or to the National Arbitration Tribunal. The agreements, decisions, or awards made under the Order were binding on
the employers and workers to whom they applied. Part II on 'Lock-
outs and Strikes' stated:

> An employer shall not declare or take part in a lock-out and a worker
> shall not take part in a strike in connection with any trade dispute,
> unless the dispute has been reported to the Minister in accordance with
> the provisions of Article 2 of this Order and twenty-one days have
> elapsed since the date of the report and the dispute has not during that
> time been referred by the Minister for settlement in accordance with the
> provisions of that article.

Order 1305 was not limited to munitions work. Its overall scope
was a recognition of the interdependence of the parts of an economy
in total war. But it only covered trade disputes; there were some
disputes, such as those about demarcation problems, which were not
covered by this definition. Nor did the Order cover those who
incited and instigated strike action. To cover this type of person,
who could be motivated by political as well as industrial reasons, a
new Defence Regulation was made by Order in Council in April
1944. Under this Regulation it became an indictable offence to
'instigate or incite any other person to take part in, or otherwise act
in furtherance of, any strike among persons engaged in the per-
formance of essential services. . . . Any person convicted of an

---

[1] Parker, op. cit., p. 426.

offence against this Regulation shall, if convicted on indictment, be liable to penal servitude for any term not exceeding five years, or to a fine not exceeding five hundred pounds, or to both such penal servitude and such fine.'[1] In addition the Defence Regulation IA which prohibited acts calculated to prevent or interfere with persons carrying on essential services was amended to make peaceful picketing illegal.[2] This was the limit of the statutory regulation of strikes in the Second World War.

[1] *Industrial Relations Handbook* (H.M.S.O.), 1944, Appendix V, p. 245.
[2] Parker, op. cit., p. 470.

Chapter Nine

WARTIME STRIKES

THE strikes which are examined in this chapter took place during the two World Wars. They were not all of the same type: some were against employers, others were against the Government as an employer or against it for political reasons. The strikes in both wars had common characteristics: after a brief spell at the beginning of each war they were illegal; with few exceptions they occurred without the support of trade union executives; they were condemned from all quarters as being anti-patriotic; and they were called under extreme conditions of war which evoked the best and the worst passions in men. Given these factors it would be misleading to classify wartime strikes along with apparently similar peacetime strikes involving the Government.

But these things apart it is necessary to examine wartime strikes together to see how effectively the Government, with all the conditions in its favour, could prevent strikes, and conversely, how trade unionists behaved when strikes were illegal.

Wartime strike legislation was first effectively tested by the South Wales miners in 1915. The miners, it will be remembered, were covered indirectly by the Munitions of War Act through a clause which permitted the Government to apply the Act to industries other than munitions if conditions warranted it.

The South Wales Miners' Federation, on 3 March 1915, submitted proposals to the South Wales coal-owners for a revision of their Conciliation Board agreement which had run for five years from 1910.[1] The proposals covered wage-rates. The owners replied that it was undesirable to begin a new agreement while the war was on but that they would offer the miners a 10 per cent war bonus. The South Wales Miners refused the offer so the employers ended the negotiations. The Government ignored the situation until June. When it did intervene, even with the help of the three Labour members of the Government, it was unable to effect a settlement.[2] The Conciliation Agreement had been terminated for over three months when a delegate conference of the South Wales miners' declared: 'We do

---

[1] See *The Miners—Years of Struggle*, by R. Page Arnot, pp. 164–170, for a description of the dispute which followed; also see Wolfe, op. cit., pp. 126–127, and Smillie, op. cit., pp. 162–163. [2] Arnot, op. cit., gives details of the negotiations.

not accept anything less than our original proposals, and . . . we stop the collieries on Thursday next until these terms are conceded.' [1] 200,000 miners struck work at the appointed time. The Government hastily issued a proclamation to force the miners back to work. It was then in a dilemma. If it did not enforce the Munitions Act it might reduce, perhaps destroy, the effectiveness of the Act. If it did enforce the Act how could 200,000 miners be penalized? If the Government chose to use force it might prolong and spread the dispute. Lloyd George asked Robert Smillie for help. Smillie told him that it 'might have been possible to have secured a settlement by joint conference had you not taken the step of having the strike proclaimed by the King; but I am convinced that it is now impossible to make peace except by conceding the terms demanded by the men'. [2] He added that the Miners' Federation executive believed in the justice of the men's claim and that unless the Government were careful the strike would spread to other districts.

The Government had acted unwisely, unless it had really believed that the threat of penalties would deter the miners from striking. But the Government knew about the uncompromising temper of the South Wales miners from past experience and it knew that the miners were in a powerful bargaining position as suppliers of steam coal for the Royal Navy. There was no practical alternative to negotiations. On 20 July after the strike had lasted for seven days the Minister of Munitions went to South Wales and reached a settlement on the miners' terms.

This was the first indication of the fact that if a large enough number of workers in a vital industry ignored anti-strike legislation there was nothing the Government could do about it except behave as if no such legislation existed. Experience in the Second World War supported this view.

The National Reference Tribunal for the coal industry under the chairmanship of Lord Porter issued a report of its assessment of a miners' claim for higher wage rates and piece rates on 22 January 1944. [3] It raised the national minimum wage for underground and surface workers, though not to the level demanded by the miners, but rejected the claim for higher piece rates. [4] Lower-paid workers gained from the Award but it was of little benefit to higher-paid coal-face workers or workers from the coal-fields with the highest wage rates. [5] The Award created confusion and dissatisfaction all

---

[1] Arnot, op. cit., p. 168.   [2] Smillie, op. cit., pp. 162–163.
[3] National Conciliation Board for the Coal Mining Industry, National Reference Tribunal, Fourth Award, 22 January 1944.
[4] See *Coal*, by W. H. B. Court, p. 253 et seq.   [5] Parker, op. cit., p. 458.

round; in the better-paid districts such as Yorkshire, and in the poorly-paid coal-fields such as South Wales. Because it did not touch piece rates, it upset conventional differentials.

The dissatisfaction was expressed through a series of unofficial strikes. On 24 January 1944, 19,000 miners in Lancashire went on strike for twelve days; smaller strikes started on the same day in Glamorgan and Ayrshire; four days later 17,000 miners struck in Staffordshire. Each of these strikes ended on or before 5 February. A phase of larger strikes began in March. In South Wales and Monmouth 100,000 miners were on strike from 6 to 18 March; 15,000 struck in Scotland from 8 to 20 March; and for varying periods between 14 March and 1 April 120,000 miners were on strike in Yorkshire.[1] Each of these strikes was contrary to Order 1305.

The stoppages occurred at a crucial stage in the preparations for the invasion of the Continent and were of such dimensions that the Government could not permit them to continue; nor could it afford to attempt to suppress them.[2] While they were actually in progress a new wages structure with substantial increases for the higher-paid miners was hastily drawn up.[3]

In both wars, workers in small-scale strikes were prosecuted. An example from each war shows the difficulties the Government encountered even in this process.

On 26 August 1915, there was a nine-day strike of 431 shipwrights at Fairfields shipyard on the Clyde over the dismissal of two shipwrights. Under Section VII of the Munitions of War Act a worker on munitions work had to receive a leaving certificate from his last employer before he could obtain further employment. The two dismissed shipwrights claimed that the words 'not attending to work' were going to be inserted on their leaving certificates and as the management would not give a satisfactory assurance that this was not the case the strike began. Seventeen of the strike leaders—not the body of the strikers—were prosecuted under the Act on 3 September and were fined £10 each, with twenty-one days to pay. Failure to pay was to be punished by thirty days' imprisonment. Work was resumed and on 23 September fourteen of the accused paid their fines. The remaining three refused to pay, were arrested and sent to prison. There was much agitation on the Clydeside for the release of the men and a widespread Clydeside strike was threatened. The Government appointed a Commission to investigate the cause of the agitation but

---

[1] *Ministry of Labour Gazette*, February and April 1944.
[2] $2\frac{1}{2}$ million tons of coal were lost through industrial disputes in the four months ending 30 April 1944 (Court, op. cit., pp. 370–371).
[3] Parker, op. cit., p. 458.

the men were dissatisfied with its report. They then sent a telegram to the Minister of Munitions, in the name of 97,500 workmen, threatening a general stoppage unless the three men were released from prison within three days. In the face of this Mr. Lloyd George and the Secretary of State for Scotland met a deputation of Clyde-side workers on 26 October but without resolving the issue. When the meeting resumed next day the fines had been paid, reputedly by union officials, and the men were released.[1]

The example from World War II took place at Betteshanger, a colliery in Kent, late in 1941 and early 1942.[2] The trouble there started when sixty coal-face workers failed to get satisfactory rates for two difficult coal-faces. In retaliation they started a go-slow movement with the consequence that early in December 1941 the management ordered them out of the pit. Other miners in the pit came out in sympathy. The matter was then referred to arbitration but the men remained dissatisfied, and on 9 January 1942 the whole pit stopped work and remained out until 28 January.

When conciliatory efforts to get the miners back to work failed, summonses were taken out against each of the 1,050 coal-face workers in the pit,[3] and on 23 January the cases were heard and sentences were meted out. The Lodge chairman received a sentence of two months' imprisonment; the secretary and a committee member were each sentenced to one month's imprisonment. The miners on one coal-face were each fined £3, with an alternative of one month's imprisonment, while the rest were each fined £1 with two months to pay or fourteen days in gaol in default of payment. The miners did not return to work for another five days—until the management made a satisfactory offer to the coal-face workers over whom the dispute had started.

Many protests were made to the Home Secretary, who, after consulting with the Justices, released the three miners from prison. The fines, however, remained to be paid, except in nine cases, and in May the police had warrants for the arrest of the defaulters. At this stage Order 1305 could not easily be enforced. It was administratively difficult to make so many arrests and if they were made they were likely to have repercussions in the form of another strike covering a wider area. The Government advised the Justices not to cancel the fines but to hold the arrest warrants in abeyance. The fines were not paid.

---

[1] *Story of the Engineers*, by J. B. Jefferys, p. 178.

[2] See Parker, op. cit., pp. 460–462, for a full description of the incident.

[3] According to the *Ministry of Labour Gazette*, February 1942, 1,600 miners went on strike. The number of prosecutions is given by Parker, op. cit., p. 461.

The Enforcement of Legislation in Practice

The Munitions of War Act and Order 1305 were only enforced when either a relatively small number of men were involved or the accused strikers were not prepared to resist, as the Betteshanger men did. According to the Munitions Tribunals Returns to the Ministry of Munitions there were fifty-six prosecutions between July 1915 and July 1916;[1] 1,612 workers were involved, 1,006 were convicted, and £1,365 was collected in fines.[2] But these prosecutions represented only a very small number of the prosecutions which could have been made under the Act. A similar story can be told about the Second World War. The strikes then were mainly short and small but they were numerous. There had been about 1½ million strikers by January 1944, yet proceedings had been taken against only about 5,000 of them and less than 2,000 convictions were secured.[3] It was obvious that in both wars the Government was loath to apply the legislation it had devised to prevent strikes.

The evidence from strikes during both wars shows that workers were not unduly influenced in their use of the strike weapon either by the statutory regulations governing strike action or by the fact that because of that legislation and the conditions of war they were, in effect, striking against the Government. Indeed, they became accustomed to looking upon the Government as their adversary in industrial disputes.

Political Strikes

The engineering industry, because it felt the brunt of the Government's legislation, provided the greatest scope for political strikes during the First World War. This scope was fully utilized by the engineering shop-stewards' committees. The most notorious of these, the Clyde Workers' Committee, was rightly suspected of political motives whenever it acted. It disseminated highly-charged political propaganda through leaflets[4] and its newspaper, *The Worker*; it organized a 'down tools' protest in November 1915 against increased rents and, in consequence, hastened the introduction and passage of

[1] Imprisonment for illegal wartime striking was abolished by the Munitions of War (Amendment) Act 1916 which amended a clause in the original Act to read 'A person employed or workman shall not be imprisoned in respect of the non payment of a fine imposed by a munitions tribunal for an offence within the jurisdiction of a tribunal . . .'

[2] *Strikes*, by K. C. J. C. Knowles, p. 118.

[3] ibid., p. 119.

[4] A passage in its first leaflet stated: 'The support given to the Government by the Trade Union leaders is an act of grossest treachery to the working class' (*Revolt on the Clyde*, by William Gallacher, p. 52).

a Rent Restriction Bill through Parliament; and when the Government seized *The Worker* at the end of January 1916 2,000 engineers struck in protest. Three people connected with the paper were arrested under Article 42 of the Defence of the Realm Regulations, two of whom, William Gallacher and John Muir, militant shop-stewards, were each sentenced to one year's imprisonment.

In March 1916 David Kirkwood, a member of the Clyde Workers' Committee, was refused privileges as a convener of shop-stewards which he had long enjoyed at his factory, and there was another strike. It spread at the instigation of members of the Clyde Workers' Committee until 2,000 men working on vital munitions work were affected. The Government accused the Clyde Workers' Committee of embarking on a 'policy of holding up the production of the most important munitions of war in the Clyde district, with the object . . . of compelling the Government to repeal the Military Service Act and the Munitions of War Act, and to withdraw all limitations upon increases of wages and strikes, and all forms of Government control'.[1] After the strike had lasted for twelve days the Government arrested six members of the Committee under Regulation 14 of the Defence of the Realm Regulations and deported them from the Clydeside. The Clydeside engineers were left leaderless and though they engaged in further strikes they lacked political direction until after the war. The Government's attention was then diverted to engineering strikes south of the Scottish border.

Conscription for the armed forces was applied to single men when the first Military Service Act came into operation on 2 March 1916 and, to ensure that men in essential jobs remained in industry, lists of reserved occupations were issued at varying intervals of time. Hitherto dilution had been applied to increase production; after 2 March 1916 it was also used to release more industrial workers for the army. By the middle of 1916 craft unions were disturbed at the recruitment of skilled men and on 22 July their representatives protested to the Government, but with no success.

What the unions failed to get by negotiation, 12,000 engineers from Sheffield obtained by strike action in November 1916. The engineers struck because a skilled fitter was recruited for the army while dilutees remained behind. The man was released from the army and the Government met the Amalgamated Society of Engineers to devise a 'Trade Card Scheme' whereby the union was entitled to issue a card of exemption to each of its skilled members.[2]

The Scheme was abruptly withdrawn by the Government in April

[1] 81 H.C. Deb. 5s., 28 March 1916.
[2] See *Trade Unionism and Munitions*, by G. D. H. Cole, p. 129 et seq.

1917 on the ground that it was preventing the army from getting sufficient skilled men. At the same time the Government introduced a Bill to extend dilution to private work. These two factors gave rise to the biggest engineering strike of the war on 29 April 1917. 60,000 engineers stopped work in Lancashire; then the strike spread to all the main engineering centres except the Clydeside and Tyneside. This was an unmistakable political strike which could not be dealt with under the Munitions Act. The Government invoked the Defence of the Realm Regulations and arrested eight of the strike leaders after the strike had lasted for almost three weeks. The men returned to work with some concessions. The Trade Card Scheme remained withdrawn but the Munitions of War Bill was suspended and dilution on private work was not permitted by statute.

The political situation in the 1939–1945 War was much more settled and it was difficult to impute strikes to political motives. The Labour Party was a full coalition partner; a trade union leader, Ernest Bevin, held a Cabinet post which in terms of power was second only to that of the Prime Minister; and, after Russia entered the war in 1941, Communists in industry who would have been the natural leaders of unofficial movements lent all their energies to supporting the war. The Gallachers and the Kirkwoods of the Second World War were preventing strikes and were pressing Joint Production Committees for still greater production. It is significant that the only political strike worth recording in World War II was attributed to Trotskyists, a Communist splinter group.

Mr. Bevin, however, believed that many of the strikes in the engineering and coal-mining industries which were called in the autumn of 1943 and early in 1944, were politically inspired, and it was in this belief that he obtained the agreement of the Cabinet to make it an indictable offence to incite or instigate strikes. There was little evidence to support Mr. Bevin's belief. It appeared that he had developed what amounted to an obsession that the true explanation of strikes was political.[1]

The strike which was purportedly instigated by Trotskyists took place on 28 March 1944 against the application of a coal-mining ballot scheme to engineering apprentices. Under the scheme, men in all but a few trades who were liable to be called up could be drafted to the mines on the result of a ballot. The strike started when three Tyneside apprentices were directed to coal-mining.[2] A Tyneside Apprentices' Guild wrote to the Minister of Labour threatening to take strike action unless legislation exempting apprentices from the scheme was introduced within three weeks. No legislation was

---

[1] Parker, op. cit., pp. 470–471.   [2] ibid., pp. 465–466.

introduced and the Minister of Labour arranged for every apprentice who went on strike to be called up for the army if medically fit. The strike was called and within two days it involved nearly 11,000 apprentices from the Tyneside, the Clyde and Huddersfield. It spread further, then gradually broke up and ended unsuccessfully by 12 April. Four members of the Trotskyist Movement were prosecuted for 'conspiring to act in furtherance of an illegal strike. . . .' They were found guilty and sentenced to terms of imprisonment, but on appeal they were discharged for a technical reason.[1]

[1] Knowles quotes MacRae ('Organized Labour in War-Time', *Fabian Quarterly*, January 1945) as stating that only the strike 'on the Tyne could possibly have been Trotskyist influenced . . .' Bevin claimed he had evidence that Trotskyists were exploiting unrest amongst the apprentices (Parker, op. cit., p. 465).

Chapter Ten

INDUSTRIAL ACTION FOR POLITICAL ENDS

THIS chapter starts with a brief description of revolutionary strikes in British trade union history. Then, in detail, it describes the activities of a group of trade union leaders during the three years immediately after the First World War. Following no particular theory, this group captured the initiative for industrial action from the wartime unofficial shop-stewards' movement and directed it against the Government. The chapter ends by showing how the approach to industrial action for political ends has changed.

Revolutionary Strikes

These are the most extreme form of political strikes and they have usually been conceived of as means to remove a Government or to change a social and economic system. They have been given prominence in revolutionary literature but have been inconsequential in practice.

The general strike, or national holiday as it was called, was the first form of revolutionary strike to be advocated in Britain. In 1831 William Benbow wrote a pamphlet called 'the Grand National Holiday and Congress of the Productive Classes' in which the idea of a passive general strike was expounded.[1] He believed that if all the wage-earning class simply stayed at home the ruling classes, including the Government, would either surrender altogether or meet the demands of the workers. Benbow's idea attracted the Glasgow weavers, for in 1833 they resolved, but without effect:

> That it be recommended to the united weavers in England, Ireland and Scotland, also the various united operatives of these realms, that they take into early consideration the propriety of fixing a day when the whole shall simultaneously suspend work for a month, or till the rights of labour and property are properly ascertained and adjusted, a certain provision of the real necessaries of life established for the truly industrious to the extent of our national resources, and till every sane and active member of the community be invested with the elective franchise.[2]

[1] *History of Trade Unionism*, by S. and B. Webb (Trade Union edition, 1920), pp. 163–164.
[2] *Attempts at General Union, 1818–1834*, by G. D. H. Cole, p. 98.

145

Early in 1834 the executive of the Grand National Consolidated Trades Union, with which William Benbow was associated, proposed a general strike to achieve the kind of reorganization in society it desired. It soon retreated from this proposal and, in May 1834, advised workers to keep in constant employment on the best terms they could obtain until the Consolidated Union was able by other means to 'liberate all the producing classes from the slavery and degradation in which they have hitherto been and now are'. One of the keenest advocates of the general strike in 1834, certainly the most vocal, was James Morrison, a leading member of the Consolidated Union and editor of *The Pioneer*. The use of the general strike was suggested again in July 1839, but this time by Chartists because they could think of nothing else.[1] The suggestion did not have trade union support. Trade unions were to be asked for their co-operation for they were not an integral part of the chartist movement.[2] By the end of July the decision to hold the strike had been rescinded.

The general strike was displaced from revolutionary theory by Karl Marx. Trade unions, in Marx's opinion, were class organizations and every struggle they engaged in against employers was a class struggle. Every class struggle, he said, was a political one and all that was required was a body to centralize the many local struggles of the same character into one large-scale national struggle—a class revolt.[3] The centralizing body, however, was not a trade union but a political organization, and trade unions and strikes were subsidiary to it and the methods it advocated.

Syndicalism, a development of Marx's theory, gave trade unions greater importance in the class struggle than Marx did. It treated strikes as the only means of overthrowing capitalism and re-established the general strike as the prime means. Revolutionary Syndicalists, Georges Sorel wrote, 'restrict the whole of Socialism to the general strike; they look upon every combination as one that should culminate in this catastrophe; they see in each strike a reduced fascimile, an essay, a preparation for the great final upheaval'.[4] And so they did. In their propaganda they continually referred to small strikes as dress rehearsals for the big one which was to be the actual Social and Industrial Revolution—the climax of revolutionary struggle.[5]

Attempts were made to apply Syndicalism at the beginning of the twentieth century. The Industrial Workers of the World tried to

---

[1] cf. *The Chartist Movement*, by Mark Howell, pp. 164–170. William Benbow, by now an aged radical, was active in the Chartist agitation.   [2] ibid., p. 165.
[3] *The Manifesto of the Communists* (International Publishing Company, 1886), p. 9.
[4] *Reflections on Violence*, p. 127.
[5] Tom Mann in *The Industrial Syndicalist*, March 1911.

practise Syndicalism, but it was confined mainly to the U.S.A. and was small and of little significance. The theory was applied on much the largest scale by the General Confederation of Labour in France from 1902. In Britain before 1910 the Industrialist League agitated for 'The General Lock-Out of the Master-Class' and published pamphlets on the subject.[1] Pamphlets on Syndicalism by Daniel De Leon and Eugene V. Debs had a circulation in Britain, but it was not until Tom Mann returned from the Dominions in 1910 that a concentrated propaganda movement got under way. He published *The Industrial Syndicalist*, which first appeared in July 1910.

Although Syndicalism had virtually no support from official trade union leaders it influenced union activities for a number of years after 1910. It emphasized the right of workers to control industry and encouraged them to take prompt industrial action to redress their grievances. Many strikes after 1910 in the mines, on the railways, on the docks, and in the building and engineering industries, were initiated without official union support and were led by men who believed in some form of Syndicalism. The significance of the theory lay in the encouragement it gave to rank and file action and not in directing that action to overthrow capitalism. Few strikers had the revolutionary motives which their unofficial leaders may have possessed.

The influence of Syndicalism declined as variations of the theory were developed and its supporters branched off in pursuit of one or other of them. The idea of using the general strike as a legitimate union weapon persisted, however, and received much more serious attention from official union leaders after 1918 than at any other time in the history of trade unionism. But it was discussed as a means of coercing the Government to adopt given policies, not as a means of overthrowing the Government.

TRADE UNION ATTEMPTS TO CHANGE
GOVERNMENT POLICY, 1918–1921

These years formed a unique phase in trade union and Government relations. They were characterized by a contempt for parliamentary democracy which stopped short only at deposing the Government. The year of the General Strike, by comparison, was politically innocuous. There were several broad reasons for the trade union emphasis on industrial action after 1918 which need to be described briefly before tackling a description of that action in practice.

[1] *Revolutionary Unionism!*, by E. J. B. Allen, 1909, p. 23.

Emphasis on Industrial Action

(1) Trade unions in 1918 possessed a new-found numerical strength. Their membership had reached the unprecedently high figure of 6,533,000, which was 19 per cent higher than the previous year's total, and almost 2,400,000 more than in 1914. The increase in membership affected all industrial groups, but it was greatest in those consisting of transport workers, dockers, and general labourers. The membership of the Workers' Union increased from 160,000 to 379,000 in the war years; during the same period the National Union of General Workers expanded its membership from 134,500 to 302,400, while the membership of the Dock, Wharf, Riverside, and General Workers' Union rose from 43,700 to 80,000. Other less important unions in the same groups had comparable proportionate increases. The miners and railwaymen were already highly organized in 1914 but they too had gained members. The Miners' Federation membership rose from 500,000 to 650,000 and that of the National Union of Railwaymen from 267,600 to 402,000.

(2) There was a new alignment of trade union forces. The craft and cotton textile unions which had dominated the trade union stage for decades were displaced by highly disciplined and strike-conscious unions in the mines, on the railways, and on the docks. On the initiative of the Miners' Federation the new alignment assumed a constitutional form during the war. In 1912 the Miners' Federation delegate conference had authorized its executive to enter into relations with other unions with a view to taking joint action for mutual assistance, and its executive had approached the National Union of Railwaymen[1] and the National Transport Workers' Federation.[2] The three bodies held a conference in April 1914 at which they appointed a committee to draw up a working agreement, and on 9 December 1915 they formed the Triple Industrial Alliance with a membership of about 1,350,000. More important than its absolute size was the fact that in one strike the Triple Alliance could close the mines and docks and stop all forms of public transport.

The constitution of the Triple Alliance was devised to secure concerted industrial action, but it in no way interfered with the autonomy of the individual unions. It stated that:

> (1) Matters of a national character or vitally affecting a principle may be submitted to the joint body, co-operation not to be called upon or expected until the matter in dispute has received the endorsement of the National Executive of the organization concerned.

[1] Formed from an amalgamation of railway unions in 1913.
[2] Formed in 1911, it embraced all the important transport and dockers' unions.

(2) Joint action to be taken when two of the three Executives have decided in favour of such a course at a meeting specially called.

(3) Complete autonomy to be reserved for any one of the three bodies to take action on their [its] own behalf.

(4) . . . joint action can only be taken when the question at issue has been before the members of the three organizations and decided by such methods as the constitution of each organization provides. A conference shall then consider and decide the question of taking action.

No steps were taken to create a separate organization, or to give the Alliance its own administration or even separate offices. Its headquarters were those of the Miners' Federation. The constitutional arrangements clearly possessed important defects. The Alliance could only lumber into action after its constituent unions had gone through all the checks and balances which each had devised to prevent hasty decisions. The National Transport Workers' Federation was itself hampered by its lack of control over its own affiliated unions. The elements of surprise and spontaneity, and the facility to take action at the moment when the workers were emotionally prepared—matters vital in industrial conflict—were impossible under the constitution. But these defects were not recognized when the Triple Alliance was formed. To the trade union movement the Triple Alliance was an endeavour to close the ranks of labour in the class conflict. To the Government and employers it appeared as a blatant show of force. It played no part in industrial activities during the war except to meet occasionally and pass resolutions of a controversial nature, over such matters as demobilization, industrial conscription, and equality of sacrifice in the war.

(3) This factor concerns the personalities who directed the affairs of the Triple Alliance. In the first year after the war the Triple Alliance had a Consultative Committee of six, consisting of C. T. Cramp and J. H. Thomas, president and general secretary of the National Union of Railwaymen; Robert Smillie and Frank Hodges, president and general secretary of the Miners' Federation; and Harry Gosling and Robert Williams who held similar positions in the National Transport Workers' Federation. Thomas was the only Parliamentarian among them. Four of them, Cramp, Smillie, Hodges, and Williams, believed firmly in industrial action and were supported by executives which were equally contemptuous of parliamentary action in practice if not in theory.

(4) Many trade unionists were impressed by the Bolshevik Revolution in November 1917. It was bloody and cruel and not at all like the imagined acquisition of power by labour through a general

strike. But it gave the Russian workers power to reorganize their society after a relatively brief struggle.

By comparison, the progress of British Socialists was negligible. Those who had worked for the election of MacDonald and Burt to Parliament in 1874 and were living in 1918 still could not realistically foresee the creation of a Labour Government for very many years. The Labour Party had made few electoral gains since 1906. At the beginning of the war it held forty-two seats in the House of Commons, and was almost devoid of vitality outside. During the war some optimism was generated about the future of Democratic Socialism, but it was dashed by the results of the General Election in 1918. The Labour Party was returned to Parliament with fifty-nine members to oppose a Coalition Government with 484 supporters. The Labour Party was back, roughly, to its pre-war position and unions reverted to their pre-war attitudes.

Direct industrial action appeared to suffer from none of the defects of political democracy or violent revolution. It possessed the qualities of battle without bloodshed and its end was decisive.

(5) During the war the members of the Triple Alliance were busy formulating national programmes to be submitted to the Government and employers as soon as the war ended. So, simultaneously, a number of demands covering a variety of industrial matters were made which provided much material for agitation.

Signs of Alarm

Within a setting which had the above factors operating and interacting the Government faced a series of challenges to its authority. The year 1919 started with a number of large-scale strikes. About 250,000 miners in a number of coal-fields struck work in January and February. Then 40,000 engineers on the north-east coast, 50,000 in Belfast, and 50,000 in the West of Scotland, went on strike for a shorter working week. The engineering strikes were unofficial and were led by shop-stewards. The one in the West of Scotland lasted for fourteen days and was the last fling of the Clyde Workers' Committee. All of these strikes helped to create a general atmosphere of unrest. The Government was faced with a national strike threat by the miners in February. In March, the railwaymen also threatened to strike. The miners were temporarily placated by the establishment of a Royal Commission to investigate hours, wages, royalties, profits, and other questions raised by the miners' programme, including state ownership of the mines. The railwaymen, with backing from the Triple Alliance, obtained a partial settlement of their grievances and called off their strike.

The Government showed signs of alarm at the growing unrest, and an inclination to see sinister motives behind it all. When industrial unrest was discussed in the House of Commons in February 1919, the Prime Minister, Mr. Lloyd George, said that anarchy

> was the object of some of those men who were seeking to destroy not merely Trade Unionism but the State. Every demand which was put forward by any body of workmen would be examined fairly and carefully by the Government with a view to removing any legitimate grievance, but the Government were determined to fight Prussianism in the industrial world as they had fought it on the Continent of Europe, with the whole might of the nation. . . .[1]

He said he would welcome an investigation into the causes of industrial unrest.

Other members of the Government expressed their opinions about industrial action. Lord Birkenhead lamented that 'men neither insignificant in numbers, nor contemptible in influence had become converts to that inscrutable disease, the bitter enemy of democracy, Bolshevism'.[2] Birkenhead was always liable to exaggerate a trade union dispute, but not so Mr. Bonar Law, Lord Privy Seal and Leader of the House of Commons. Yet even he spoke strong words about the Triple Alliance in March 1919. In a memorandum to Lloyd George, who was unable to attend a Cabinet meeting, he wrote that he would make a statement to the House of Commons outlining the negotiations and disputes involving the transport workers, the miners, and the railwaymen. 'I shall then add', he wrote, 'that both miners and railwaymen are servants not of employers but of the State: that a strike would be against the State and that the State must win and must use all its power for that purpose, otherwise it would be the end of Government in this country. . . .'[3] Law declared that he was prepared, if a strike occurred, 'to pass legislation empowering the Government to seize strike funds and arrest the leaders . . .'[4]

The indiscriminate use of the strike weapon came in for criticism from trade union leaders too. In January, Mr. J. R. Clynes urged organized labour to accept the verdict of the polls and deprecated the use of the 'industrial weapon'. He said that there was no change in the social order that labour could not obtain on the floor of the House of Commons, if it sent its representatives there in sufficient

---

[1] *Annual Register*, 1919, p. 13.
[2] *Lord Birkenhead*, a biography by his son, the Earl of Birkenhead, vol. II, p. 118.
[3] *The Unknown Prime Minister*, by Robert Blake, p. 413.
[4] ibid.

strength.[1] And on 12 February the Parliamentary Committee of the Trade Union Congress circulated a statement about industrial unrest, complaining in particular about the engineering strikes over hours in violation of a recently signed agreement.

Trade Union Opposition to Foreign Policy and Conscription

Shortly after the general election in 1918 the Parliamentary Committee of the Trades Union Congress and the Executive of the Labour Party sent a joint letter to the Prime Minister asking for information about British policy with regard to Russia, and requesting an assurance that the British armed forces would be withdrawn from Russia at the earliest possible moment.[2] Apart from an official acknowledgement no reply to the letter was received, so on 3 January 1919 another letter was sent and the Minister of War was asked to receive a deputation on the subject of allied intervention in Russia. Neither the Prime Minister nor the Minister of War replied.

The Miners' Federation then took up the issue. When it met in conference on 26 March 1919 to discuss the Sankey Commission Report on the coal industry, its executive submitted a motion calling on the Government to withdraw all British troops from Russia and to abandon the Military Service Bill by which compulsory military service was to be continued, otherwise the Miners' Federation would take such steps in conjunction with the organized labour movement as would compel the Government to give way.[3] The motion was carried unanimously.

When a Special Conference was held jointly by the Trades Union Congress and the Labour Party on 3 April to consider the Covenant of the League of Nations, Smillie raised a similar motion. 'Was there ever', he said, 'such a betrayal of people as has taken place during the last few months . . . The Government did not care a rap for resolutions. The only thing to which the Government paid heed was votes at election times and the industrial power of the workers.'[4] The section of the motion calling expressly for action to enforce its opinion on the Government was deleted at the request of the chairman, G. H. Stuart-Bunning. It asked, instead, for a joint national conference to be convened to consider the possibility of taking industrial action to force the Government to give way. The motion as amended was carried.

The Parliamentary Committee of the T.U.C. decided not to call a conference as requested. Most of its members felt that there had been too many national conferences. Moreover 'as such a Conference

[1] *Annual Register*, 1919, p. 5.   [2] Labour Party Report, 1919, p. 25 et seq.
[3] *The Times*, 16 April 1919.   [4] ibid., 3 April 1919.

had not the power to order a General Strike, to declare such a threat without the certainty of its being carried out would reduce the prestige of the Labour Movement'.[1] The Parliamentary Committee decided instead to recommend that a joint deputation should meet Mr. Bonar Law, and then review the position.[2] This was arranged.

There was a succession of meetings between different Labour bodies. The discussion of the issues involved, particularly conscription, spread through the Movement and was accentuated by a press campaign initiated by the War Office in April in favour of conscription, and by the appeal for a relief force to rescue British troops at Archangel. A conference of the Miners' Federation met again on 16 April to receive the result of the ballot vote over the Sankey Commission Report, but the really important business of the conference was the reconsideration of the anti-conscription motion. The motion was endorsed again, but opinion this time was almost evenly divided.[3] This division was not disclosed to the press, for *The Times* reported a unanimous decision.[4] Also on 16 April, but later in the day, the Triple Alliance met and fully supported the Miners' Federation in its resolve to get the Parliamentary Committee to convene a national conference.

The Government was disturbed by the portending challenge to its authority. The threatened strikes on industrial matters on the railways and in the mines had been cancelled for one reason or another, but the new threat had a dimension which could not be reduced by talk of industrial peace or by a Royal Commission. The Government concentrated on internal defence and security. It concerned itself with the different aspects of nation-wide strikes: food supplies, alternative forms of transport, maintenance of essential services; and with the use of the armed forces. It had an added reason to be concerned about internal security. The unrest among the police had reached such an intensity in the Metropolitan area that the Commissioner said that in the event of labour troubles he could not depend on them.[5] The Government had little reason to be any the more confident about the use of the army. Early in the year there had been a number of demonstrations by servicemen over the pace and method of demobilization and it was unlikely that they could be relied on to support conscription.

An additional source of conflict was created when the Government attempted to discover whether it could rely on using troops

[1] Minutes of the Parliamentary Committee of the T.U.C., 8 April 1919.
[2] Mr. Lloyd George was away at the Paris Peace Conference.
[3] T.U.C. Report, 1919, p. 225.
[4] *The Times*, 17 April 1919.
[5] *Annals of an Active Life*, by Sir Nevil Macready, vol. II, p. 34.

during industrial disputes. A secret military circular had come into
the possession of George Lansbury, then editor of the *Daily Herald*,
which he promptly published.[1] Marked 'Secret and Urgent' it
stated:

(1) I am directed to request that until further notice you will furnish
information on the headings hereunder as regards the troops in your
area, and that you will arrange for a report to reach this Office without
fail not later than the first post each Thursday morning.
  (*a*) Will troops in various areas respond to orders for assistance to
        preserve the public peace;
  (*b*) Will they assist in strike breaking;
  (*c*) Will they parade for draft to overseas, especially to Russia. . . .
(2) You will, of course, understand that any material change in a
situation and any cases of disorder or indiscipline are to be reported
at once.

In explanation the circular stated: 'I am to add that the above is
required with a view to the establishment of an efficient Intelligence
Service, whereby the Army Council can keep its finger on the pulse
of the troops, and that the information desired is required for the
information of the Secretary of State.' Also on the circular was the
following:

To Station Commander ——, No. —— Area ——.
Will you please let me have the following information for the C.M.A.
—— Area as speedily as possible with regard to the Units on the
Station under your command:
  (*a*) Whether there is any growth of Trade Unionism among them;
  (*b*) The effect outside Trade Unions have on them;
  (*c*) Whether any agitation from internal or external sources is affecting
        them;
  (*d*) Whether any soldiers' councils have been formed;
  (*e*) Whether any demobilisation troubles are occurring, and if so,
        (*i*) what troops are demonstrating, (*ii*) the numbers involved, (*iii*) what
        their grievances are, (*iv*) what has been done.

(Sgd.) ——

The circular, called the Strike Breaking Circular, became the
subject of many protests from trade unions. Mr. Winston Churchill,
the Minister of War, disclaimed responsibility for it, but he defended
the military chiefs in seeking to obtain information which might be
useful to the Government in certain circumstances.[2] The circular was

[1] *Daily Herald*, 13 May 1919.
[2] *Railway Review*, 6 June 1919.

withdrawn, but not until it had been used to support the Triple Alliance's case against the Government.

The trade union protests which had begun on 26 March carried on through April and most of May without any contact being established between the Government and trade union leaders. The deputation which the Parliamentary Committee had appointed on 8 April to interview Mr. Bonar Law had to wait until 22 May before it could see him.[1] He was not in a hurry to precipitate action through an unsatisfactory reply. Law told the deputation that the Allies did not intend to interfere in the internal affairs of Russia, that Britain was to withdraw her troops from Russia at the earliest possible moment but would keep on helping Admiral Koltchak who was resisting the Bolsheviks. This contradictory statement was accompanied by unsatisfactory replies concerning the repeal of the Military Service Act and the withdrawal of the secret military circular. After the interview[2] it was plain that the real issue before the Parliamentary Committee was whether or not direct action should be used to force the Government's hand. One member moved 'that the interview is satisfactory enough to justify the Parliamentary Committee refusing to call a special conference. . . .' An amendment, asking for the request of the Triple Alliance to be met, was defeated by seven votes to five and the original motion was carried.[3] The Parliamentary Committee then decided to protest to Mr. Bonar Law about his replies over conscription and the military circular.

The subsequent developments over this issue revealed more clearly the division in the Labour Movement and, in consequence, its inability to act against the Government. The National Union of Railwaymen, the Miners' Federation, and the Labour Party protested against the Parliamentary Committee decision. The Labour Party conference deplored the continued intervention of the Allies in Russia and instructed its 'National Executive to consult the Parliamentary Committee of the Trades Union Congress, with the view to effective action being taken to enforce these demands by the unreserved use of their political and industrial power'.[4] The Labour Party executive, on which sat C. T. Cramp, Robert Williams, and two miners' representatives, quickly acted on the conference's instructions. On 9 July it met the Parliamentary Committee, which re-affirmed its opposition to direct action, then continued in session

---

[1] A description of the debate in the Labour Movement which followed this interview is contained in *British Labour and the Russian Revolution*, by S. R. Graubard, p. 72 et seq.

[2] A full report of the interview was published.

[3] Parliamentary Committee Minutes, 28 May 1919.

[4] Labour Party Annual Conference Report, 1919, p. 156.

alone. By fourteen votes to five it agreed to press for the special conference 'for the purpose of discussing whether, and by what means, direct industrial action should be taken . . .' [1]

The Labour Party in this matter was helpless without trade union support. Its position was made clear by the following official statement:

> The general view of the Executive Committee is that if the British Labour Movement is to institute a new precedent in our industrial history by initiating a general strike for the purpose of achieving not industrial but political objects, it is imperative that the Trade Unions, whose members are to fulfil the obligations implied in the new policy and whose finances it is presumed are to be involved, should realize the responsibilities such a strike movement would entail and should themselves determine the plan of any such new campaign. [2]

The Parliamentary Committee refused to be moved, though the majority against taking action remained small. At a special meeting in the House of Commons on 22 July 1919 a motion was put 'That a special Congress be convened to discuss the questions of the Blockade, Intervention in Russia, Conscription and Conscientious Objectors, and if it is found that there is a large volume of opinion in favour of industrial action being taken, before such action is taken, a ballot vote of the affiliated members is essential.' It was defeated by four votes to six. [3]

At this the Triple Alliance decided to proceed without the Parliamentary Committee in its campaign against the Government. It recommended its constituent unions to consult their members to discover whether they would take strike action in support of their demands. [4] A uniform ballot paper was prepared for the occasion which stated: 'The Government having refused to abolish (1) conscription, (2) military intervention in Russia, (3) military intervention in trade union disputes, are you in favour of withdrawing your labour to enforce the abolition of the foregoing? Please place your cross opposite "Yes" or "No" in the space provided for the purpose.' [5] The result of the ballot was to be made known by 25 August. [6] But the ballot papers had barely been distributed when a Triple Alliance conference met and decided that a strike was no longer necessary. This was on 12 August.

---

[1] Joint Meeting minutes, 9 July 1919.

[2] Labour Party Report, 1919, p. 116.

[3] Parliamentary Committee Minutes, 22 July 1919.

[4] Recommended by a conference of Triple Alliance delegates on 25 July 1919. The recommendation was accepted by 217 votes to 11.

[5] *The Times*, 8 August 1919.

[6] The National Union of Railwaymen decided not to take a ballot vote, but to obtain the opinion of branches by branch votes on resolutions.

The reason given by the conference was that a policy statement by Mr. Winston Churchill, Secretary of State for War, in a House of Commons debate on 29 July 1919 met their demands. What had Mr. Churchill said? He had spoken ironically about the threat of the Alliance to resort to strike action. He had gibed at the Triple Alliance leaders. The questions over which the threat was made were the responsibility of the War Office. Mr. Churchill quoted them separately and commented upon them in the following manner. '1. "Withdrawal of the British troops from Russia." That was decided upon at the beginning of the year and was in progress. 2. "Conscription." It was passing away, and it was always intended that it should pass away. 3. "The War Office circular inquiring whether soldiers would assist in maintaining order during strikes." That had no political significance. It was issued without any Minister having seen it, and was withdrawn. 4. "The release of the conscientious objectors." All of them, without exception, were out of gaol.' [1] Mr. Churchill then added, to the amusement of Government supporters, 'If they do not hurry up with the general strike, the Triple Alliance will have to get hold of a new outfit of grievances.' This was hardly a conciliatory speech. If it had really contained the concessions the Triple Alliance leaders desired why were they not recognized immediately—before the ballot papers were printed? Two weeks had elapsed before the strike was cancelled. What other factors, then, were involved?

One was that the Government was displaying more confidence in its ability to handle a strike situation. Both Mr. Bonar Law and Mr. Austen Chamberlain declared the Government's intention to take any necessary steps to defend the authority of Parliament.[2] The Government had cause for greater confidence. On 31 July 1919 the National Union of Police and Prison Officers declared a national strike to dissuade the Government from making law the Police Bill under which that union became illegal, policemen were prevented from joining any trade union, and under which it became a criminal act to incite policemen to strike. The strike came after a garrulous and unpleasant relationship, lasting for almost a year, between the union on the one side and the Commissioner of the Metropolitan Police and the Government on the other. The strike threat and then the strike successfully extracted material concessions from the Government for the pay and working conditions of policemen were

[1] *The Times*, 30 July 1919. The fourth factor had been left off the ballot paper.
[2] Mr. Bonar Law said in the House of Commons, on 5 August 1919, that a successful attempt by the Triple Alliance to force a decision upon political questions would mean the end of democratic government in Britain. 'It is therefore necessary to say', he proceeded, 'that it would be the duty of the Government to resist any such attempt with all the resources at its disposal' (ibid., 6 August 1919).

substantially improved. But they did not achieve their immediate purpose. The Police Bill became law on 15 August 1919. The significance of the strike to the Government was its failure to gain any real support from policemen except those on the Merseyside. Out of a total of about 60,000 policemen throughout the country only 2,365 policemen went on strike. 1,132 of these came from Merseyside towns and most of the remainder from London. The response was so small that the police authorities were able to dismiss all of the strikers from the service.

From this strike the Government learned two things. First, that the police were more loyal than had been supposed and could, therefore, be trusted in a state of emergency. And, secondly, that other groups of workers had shown no willingness to strike over a constitutional issue. The police strikers received a little money and lots of verbal support from the trade union movement; it received no official sympathetic strike support and only an isolated case of un-official strike support. This second point had a meaning for the leaders of the Triple Alliance too.

The Parliamentary Committee had initially opposed holding the special conference which the Triple Alliance demanded, because it feared, amongst other things, to test rank-and-file sentiments. In the early stages of the controversy perhaps the fear was justified. But the agitation went on too long without action being taken for an anti-Government feeling to be maintained at a high pitch. The Triple Alliance leaders realized this in August and rather than risk a partially supported strike they withdrew their challenge.

The Council of Action

The agitation to influence the Government's policy over Russia continued in September when the Trades Union Congress demanded the withdrawal of British troops from Russia and agreed to call a special congress to decide on future action, without a murmur of protest from the Parliamentary Committee. The mood of the delegates was clearly against the Government and out of sympathy with the Parliamentary Committee. The Special Trades Union Congress met on 8 December. The delegates were told that the Government regarded the commitment of £15,000,000 for military operations in Russia recently sanctioned by the House of Commons as final.[1] They decided that there should be an impartial inquiry into Russian conditions and that a trade union delegation should visit Russia. They were not in a militant mood on this occasion.

[1] Lloyd George had stated this in a speech in the House of Commons. He repeated it to a Parliamentary Committee delegation which saw him on the day before the Congress.

Events in Russia became a matter for Parliamentary debate a few months later. A dispute had arisen between Poland and Russia and the Labour Party was troubled in case Poland asked for British military aid. Lloyd George reassured the Labour Party that 'His Majesty's Government have made it clear that they do not encourage and cannot support by men, money, or material, an offensive by Polish troops into Russian territory'.[1] This was on 19 February 1920. In April 1920 a Polish offensive against Russia was launched. Labour believed that Britain was implicated. 'The marionettes are in Warsaw,' the *Daily Herald* commented, 'but the strings are pulled from London and Paris.'[2] The *Labour Leader* remarked that the 'British Government deny responsibility for this new war. This denial is a lie.'[3]

At this point trade unions again took up the issue. On 10 May London dockers at the East India Docks refused to load the *Jolly George* which was bound for Poland, because they suspected it of carrying munitions and other supplies. The following week the Triennial Conference of the Dockers' Union congratulated its London members for their action and protested 'against the export of arms to Poland and other Border States, which enables the Junkers of these countries to set the people at war in the interests of their financial paymaster . . .' The Miner's Federation executive protested strongly to the Prime Minister, while the executive of the National Union of Railwaymen told its members not to handle munitions bound for Poland. The railwaymen did not apply their decision; instead they referred the issue to the Triple Alliance. In a resolution which was fairly non-committal and did not mention direct action, the Triple Alliance asked the Parliamentary Committee to convene a Special Congress.[4]

At a meeting of the Parliamentary Committee on 16 June 1920 J. H. Thomas described the attitude of his union in relation not only to Poland but also to Ireland, where railwaymen were striking against British policy. His executive, he said, wanted the Parliamentary Committee to organize a Special Congress so 'that the whole Trade Union Movement may take a common decision to guide the N.U.R. and all other Trade Unions in their future action in connection with the Polish, Irish and similar matters'.[5] The Miners' Federation in a letter supported this suggestion; it was accepted by the Committee and a Special Congress was arranged for 13 July.

At this time the Poles were sweeping victoriously into Russia. The

[1] Hansard. 125 H.C. Deb. 5s. 1022.
[2] 30 April 1920; quoted in Graubard, op. cit., pp. 91–92.
[3] ibid., p. 92.
[4] *The Times*, 1 June 1920.
[5] Parliamentary Committee Minutes, 16 June 1920.

British Government felt no need to intervene and it seemingly paid little attention to the Labour protests, which were weakened again by sharp differences of opinion about the need for direct action. But the situation was so fluid that even in a space of a few weeks fortunes in Russia had changed so radically as to alter the need for direct action. When the Parliamentary Committee met, the need was to save Russia; less than two weeks later, when the Labour Party Conference debated British foreign policy, the Poles were being driven out of Russia. With an ease in the tension the Labour Party delegates refused to support a demand for a general strike.

Early in July 1920 the Polish Prime Minister asked the Supreme Allied Council for help. The British Government began to equivocate about its own intentions and about the use of the League of Nations. The League, it stated, was not considered to be competent to aid a retreating Polish army. The Supreme Allied Council commissioned the British Government to deliver a note to Russia requesting an immediate armistice. It did this on 12 July 1920, and added 'the British Government and its Allies would feel bound to assist the Polish nation to defend its existence with all the means at their disposal' if Poland's territorial integrity were not respected.[1]

The day after the note was delivered a Special Trades Union Congress met to discuss the Government's Irish and Russian policies. Its mood now was terse and militant. It demanded the withdrawal of all British troops from Ireland and the cessation of the production of munitions of war destined to be used against Ireland and Russia. It added that if the Government refused these demands the Congress would recommend a general 'down tools' policy. The Congress made no plans to implement the resolution, nor did it stipulate a time-limit. When J. H. Thomas, who was the chairman of the Congress, was asked what was to be done he simply replied, 'Wait and see.'[2] It waited until August just seeing and doing nothing.

This was, perhaps, because the British Government, after an initial reluctance, had accepted Russian terms for negotiations between Russia and Poland. The prospects of peace did not last for long. The negotiations collapsed and Russia continued its advance into Poland. The British Foreign Secretary, Lord Curzon, then told the Russians that if they persisted in their offensive Britain would have no alternative but to aid the Poles. The Government quite obviously had been unimpressed on this issue by trade union protests.

The next Labour move was made by Arthur Henderson, secretary of the Labour Party. He sent a telegram on 4 August to each of the local Labour Parties and Trades Councils affiliated to the Labour

---

[1] Graubard, op. cit., p. 101.   [2] *The Times*, 14 July 1920.

Party which stated, 'Extremely menacing possibility extension Polish-Russian war. Strongly urge local parties organize citizen demonstrations protest against intervention and against supply men, munitions to Poland. Demand immediate complete raising blockade, resumption trading relations. Send resolutions Premier and Press, deputize local M.P.s.'[1] The demand was for public constitutional pressure on the Government.

The following day the Parliamentary Committee of the Trades Union Congress, the Executive Committee of the Labour Party, and the Parliamentary Labour Party met together in the House of Commons and with an exceptional unanimity agreed to threaten the Government with a general strike if it pursued its policy of war. It issued an instruction to the Labour Movement which read: 'That the Executive Committees of affiliated organizations throughout the country to be summoned to hold themselves ready to proceed immediately to London for a National Conference, and that they be advised to instruct their members to down tools on instructions from that National Conference, and that a Council of Action be immediately constituted to take such steps as may be necessary to carry the above decisions into effect.' On previous occasions Labour Members of Parliament had either refused to countenance direct action or had adopted an ambivalent attitude towards it. This time no voices were raised against it. A Council of Action was formed. It consisted of twenty-four members, five from each of the bodies and nine co-opted members. All but two, Josiah Wedgewood and George Lansbury, were trade unionists of standing.[2] Representatives of the Council met Mr. Lloyd George on 10 August. Ernest Bevin, the selected spokesman for Labour, told him that Labour was opposed not only to military aid to Poland but to every form of aid. At this meeting Lloyd George made no concessions. He said he was going to speak at length on the subject that afternoon in the House of Commons. The only points he made were that the Soviet Union was threatening the independence of Poland; that Labour in Britain had always supported Polish independence; and that he could not conceive of

---

[1] Graubard, op. cit., p. 104.
[2] The composition of the Council of Action was as follows: Parliamentary Committee of T.U.C., Harry Gosling, A. A. Purcell, A. Swales, R. B. Walker, and Margaret Bondfield; E.C. of Labour Party, A. G. Cameron (Woodworkers), Frank Hodges, C. T. Cramp, Robert Williams, and John Bromley (A.S.L.E.F.); Parliamentary Labour Party, W. Adamson, M.P. (Scottish Miners), J. R. Clynes, M.P., James O'Grady, M.P. (Furnishing Trades), John Robertson, M.P. (Scottish Miners), and Josiah Wedgewood, M.P. Co-opted members were: Robert Smillie, J. H. Thomas, Ben Turner (Textiles), George Lansbury (editor, *Daily Herald*), John Ogden (Weavers), J. W. Bowen (Post Office Workers), W. H. Hutchinson (Engineers), Ernest Bevin, and A. E. Holmes. The joint secretaries were Fred Bramley, J. S. Middleton, and H. S. Lindsay.

Labour being opposed to British support being given to the Poles.[1]
When he spoke in Parliament, Lloyd George said that if no peace
were concluded because of the severity of Russia's terms, Britain
would be compelled to offer Poland counsel and material equipment,
would consider imposing economic sanctions on Russia, and would
contemplate giving generous assistance to General Wrangel who was
still fighting the Bolsheviks inside Russia.[2] There was no sign here of
a weakening in the face of a strike threat. The Council of Action
decided to summon a National Conference for 13 August.

A Conference of more than 1,000 delegates met in London, unmistakably opposed to war and determined to stop it. It presented a
spectacle of men who had been enthusiastic supporters of the Great
War displaying almost a religious fanaticism against war with Russia.[3]
Everyone seemed determined to make the Conference discussions
and decisions unanimous. Previously inveterate opponents of direct
action spoke in its favour. J. H. Thomas said, 'Direct action would
not merely mean a strike; it would mean a challenge to the whole
constitution of the country. The step was momentous, but it was
justified in order to prevent war.' [4] J. R. Clynes, a most temperate
man, declared that every member of the Parliamentary Labour Party
was prepared to commit himself to a policy of direct action.

In this mood the delegates supported the Council of Action in its
condemnation of the British Government and authorized it to call
'for any and every form of withdrawal of Labour which circumstances
may require to give effect to . . . [its] policy . . . [and] in order to
sweep away secret bargaining and diplomacy and to assure that the
foreign policy of Great Britain may be in accord with the well-
known desires of the people for an end to war and the interminable
threats of war'. The public mood seemed to be equally opposed to
war. About 350 Local Councils were formed by trades councils,
local Labour Parties, or by special local conferences. They held
demonstrations, disseminated information received from the Council
of Action and acted in accordance with its instructions, and reported
back on the production or movement of munitions, war material, or
equipment of any kind. Local Councils especially looked out for the
re-labelling of goods suspected for war use, and forwarded copies of
orders received by men called up for war service. They provided an
additional stimulus to action by pressing the Council of Action to

---

[1] Report of the Council of Action, August to October 1920 (18 October 1920).
Presented to the Parliamentary Committee of the T.U.C.
[2] Graubard, op. cit., pp. 108–109.
[3] This phenomenon impressed Mr. Philip Snowden. Cf. *An Autobiography*, vol. II,
pp. 559–563.
[4] ibid.

extend its mandate to include Ireland and asking that the Government should be given an ultimatum with a time limit.

The Council of Action did not call a general strike nor did it place an embargo on the production and transport of munitions, etc., to Poland. It stated in its final report that if open war had been declared by the British Government early in August a general strike movement would have met with a successful response, but that in the circumstances of no open war, of Government denials about its alleged intentions, and of furtive movements of munitions, the response would have been dubious. It realized that the only effective form of industrial action would involve the transport unions, but rejected this because 'taking into consideration all the circumstances the Council felt that it would be unfair to throw the whole onus upon single sections of the Movement . . .' It seemed that too many conditions had to be simultaneously present for the Movement to plan itself into a general strike.

Meanwhile, what of the response of the Government to Labour's pressure? The Council of Action asked Lloyd George early on whether he would object if it consulted with the three Soviet emissaries then in London. At first he said he would, then he changed his mind and actually used the Council of Action as an intermediary with the Russian Government. The Council, through the emissaries, urged the Soviet Government to publish its terms for peace with Poland. These were announced in the press and in Parliament on 11 August. Then Lloyd George asked Bevin and his colleagues to use their influence with the Soviet Government to keep to the published terms for peace, rather than stiffen them in view of the Soviet military successes. The Council of Action did this, and also asked the Soviet Government to waive the clause in its terms which stipulated that a Working-Class Civic Militia should be established in Poland. On both points the Soviet Government agreed to co-operate.[1] But in between the time when the Soviet Government was approached and when it gave its reply the battle situation changed. When it was approached the Red Army was on the outskirts of Warsaw, poised to march in. The French General Weygand was in Warsaw at that time on an inter-allied mission and he was ordered to assist the Poles. The Polish armies were reorganized and, under Weygand's command, defeated the Russians in the battle of the Vistula on 14 August. The Red Army was then pushed out of Poland. The Soviet Government replied to the requests made by the Council of Action at a moment of defeat.

The Council of Action played a part as an intermediary and it

[1] Council of Action Report, op. cit.

voiced the collective sentiments of the working class, but whether it, rather than an alteration in battle fortunes, caused the Government to adopt a less bellicose attitude towards Russia is hard to say. The Government's intentions would have been clearly revealed if the Russians had won the battle of the Vistula and had marched into Warsaw. But this did not happen and whatever justification the British had for intervening, apart from the desire of some to defeat the Communist Government *per se*, it disappeared with the Red Army retreat.

There was one brief spell at the beginning of August when the British Government may have seriously contemplated outright intervention, and it is likely that it hesitated because of the outraged protests of Labour and the general public's antipathy to war. It was only at the initial moment of the Government's hesitation that the Labour Movement had all the conditions to enable it to call a general strike. The realization of this may have convinced the more aggressive members of Lloyd George's Cabinet that the domestic risks of war were too great.

Labour claimed, of course, that it had prevented open war with Russia;[1] while the Government denied that the Labour threat had had any effect on its policy. Bonar Law even argued in Parliament that the policy advocated by the Council of Action and the Government policy were similar, and in the same vein Lloyd George said that the Council of Action had kicked at an open door—that a danger of war had never existed.

After August 1920 the activities of the Council of Action virtually ceased, though Britain and Russia were still not at peace. Public interest in Russia declined because it was not possible for a high emotional tension to be maintained by the public over a single issue for very long, and because other issues, portending strikes and Irish affairs, began to occupy its mind. The Council of Action had shown itself to be a useful body in the Labour Movement and some of its members wanted to keep it in existence until a permanent body had been formed to deal with emergency matters of concern to the Labour Movement. The Parliamentary Committee decided on 18 October 1920 that the Council should continue its work but it disappeared from the scene by default.

Nationalization of the Mines

Agitation for the state ownership of the mines had been carried on for many years before 1919. The Trades Union Congress first accepted a motion demanding the nationalization of the mines in

[1] Council of Action Report, op. cit.

1892 and the Miners' Federation did likewise in 1894. But the old miners' leaders did not want nationalization and the demand was dropped for some years. It became an important issue after Robert Smillie became president of the Miners' Federation in 1912. The advocates of nationalization in 1919 were aided by the fact that the mines had actually been controlled by the state during the war, and by the conclusions of the Sankey Commission Interim Report which was presented in March 1919. The Report stated: 'Even upon the evidence already given, the present system of ownership and working in the coal industry stands condemned, and some other system must be substituted for it, either nationalization or a method of unification by national purchase and/or by joint control.'

On the day this Report was presented to Parliament, Mr. Bonar Law, for the Prime Minister, said that the Government adopted the Sankey Report 'in spirit and in letter'. The final Sankey Report was issued in June and recommended that the principle of state ownership of the coal mines should be accepted. The Royal Commission had been appointed to pacify the miners, who had strike notices out. The strike was postponed and the Miners' Federation accepted the Report after a ballot vote of its membership. It seemed that the Government and the Miners' Federation were at last agreed on the most contentious item in the miners' programme.

Mr. Lloyd George might himself have been willing to go ahead with nationalization, but there were many Members in the House of Commons opposed to it and they announced their intention of fighting against it.[1] The coal owners had mobilized their forces. At this point Robert Smillie made the novel and ironic suggestion that the miners should help the Government, by a strike, to force nationalization through Parliament against the opposition of hostile political and industrial interests.[2] The Government, intent on self-preservation, went back on its word to the miners and in July 1919 decided to renounce nationalization, though Lloyd George did not say so until 18 August. His delay in announcing the change of policy was no doubt prompted by the activities of the Triple Alliance and by the strike of 150,000 Yorkshire miners in July which could have been quickly extended if a dispute over nationalization had flared up. The miners had good reason to believe that they had been deceived.

There were no local strikes against the Government decision. The miners' delegates reacted cautiously. At a conference on 3 September they stated: 'We do not at this stage recommend the miners to take industrial action to secure the adoption of the report of the Coal Industry Commission, but we invite the Trades Union Congress to

[1] R. Page Arnot, op. cit., vol. II, p. 210.   [2] *The Times*, 16 July 1919.

T.U.G.—M

declare that the fullest and most effective action be taken to secure that the Government shall adopt the majority report of the Commission as to the future governance of the industry.' [1] The Trades Union Congress, by an overwhelming majority, agreed to co-operate with the Miners' Federation, and for a time protests were made in a proper constitutional manner. A trade union deputation interviewed the Prime Minister on 10 October to demand the nationalization of the coal industry. In his reply Lloyd George said that the Government had never committed itself to a blindfold acceptance of whatever the Sankey Commission might recommend; that it would have been most inopportune anyway to press for nationalization during the Yorkshire miners' strike; that the alternative form of organization he proposed, namely unification of the industry by districts without a change in ownership, would give the miners all they claimed nationalization would give them. [2]

In its constitutional mood the Miners' Federation collaborated in 'The Mines for the Nation' campaign which the Special Trades Union Congress launched on 9 December 1919. The campaign did not make much impression, so after four weeks the miners' executive asked the Parliamentary Committee to convene a further Special Trades Union Congress to consider calling a general strike to force the Government to nationalize the mines. The Parliamentary Committee did so and the Congress met on 11 March 1920.

It seemed that a general strike might occur. The issue was a domestic one; it was viewed as a case of a broken pledge; and it involved a group of workers whose unsatisfactory working conditions drew sympathy from people in general. The Government was worried and considered what precautions it should take in the event of a general stoppage, of violence, or of revolutionary activities.

The miners, however, were divided amongst themselves. On the day before the Special Congress met, the Miners' Federation held a Preliminary Conference which decided for Direct Action but by a relatively small majority. 524 delegates were in favour and 344 against. [3] The lack of enthusiasm for a general strike was even more pronounced among the other trade unionists. The country was reaching the peak of its post-war boom and unemployment was falling to its lowest post-war level. In March 1920 only 3·6 per cent of insured workpeople in the United Kingdom were unemployed, compared with 6·6 per cent in the previous December. [4] After a year of industrial unrest and inevitable post-war dislocation, workers were

---

[1] R. Page Arnot, op. cit., p. 215.   [2] *Annual Register*, October 1919, p. 120.
[3] R. Page Arnot, op. cit., p. 218.
[4] *Aspects of British Economic History, 1918–1925*, by A. C. Pigou, p. 221.

not prepared to dissipate their newly acquired security. The delegates at the Special Trades Union Congress decided against a strike by 3,732,000 votes to 1,050,000 and agreed to concentrate on intensive political propaganda in readiness for a general election. This decision left the miners with no alternative but to do likewise for they could not force a nationalization measure on the Government by themselves.

A CHANGED ATTITUDE

Direct action was a version of the pre-1914 Syndicalism. It differed from it in two important respects. Direct action was not a political ideology and it was not conceived of to achieve revolution. It was a method used by men who were dissatisfied with society and impatient with democratic methods. In all essentials its leading protagonists were political pragmatists. A member of the Miners' Federation executive viewed direct action as a means of keeping Government Ministers to their pledges.[1] This was an apt description of the method.

The political issues which aroused trade union leaders in 1919 and 1920 were never satisfactorily settled. The significance of some just disappeared with time, but others remained unsolved for many years. Those which disappeared were replaced by other equally important issues. It was as necessary to keep Ministers to their pledges after 1920 as it was before. Yet after 1920 direct action was not used until the coal dispute in 1925 and 1926.

The reason for this can easily be explained. Direct action was a method of expediency. It had no continuing validity. A few kind words from the Prime Minister, the emergence of new political personalities, a change in economic conditions, could each undermine it. Anything which quietened tempers or deflected attention could cause it to be discarded.

The increase in unemployment in 1921, with its train of adverse effects for trade unions, was the prime cause of the rejection of direct action. Union leaders were preoccupied with domestic problems: how to keep their organizations intact and to fend off employers' attacks. There were secondary causes. Ernest Bevin's attention was taken up by the creation of the Transport and General Workers' Union; Robert Williams, secretary of the National Transport Workers' Federation, lost his influence as the Federation became defunct; Robert Smillie resigned from the leadership of the Miners' Federation. Then in 1922 the Coalition Government broke up

[1] *The Times*, 17 April 1919.

and the collective trade union animosity which it had aroused dispersed.

The General Strike in 1926 was a consequence of a continuing belief in direct action. The issue which gave rise to it was an industrial one, but the strike was a political act because it was directed against the Government and because its massive size inevitably implicated the Government.[1] The failure of the strike revealed the barrenness of direct action as a political method, but it did not altogether dispose of the notion that strikes could be used to coerce the Government. In moments of acute tension and exasperation with parliamentary methods the notion has been revived.

In the years 1932, 1933, and 1934 there were national and international trade union discussions about the use of the general strike to prevent war. A conference of International Trade Secretariats in March 1932 requested the International Federation of Trade Unions to examine the question of taking international action to prevent the transport of war materials. A similar but wider question was raised at the Trades Union Congress the same year, but no vote was taken on it because the issue was being examined by the International Federation of Trade Unions.

Discussions about the possibility of war intensified in 1933. Labour leaders were disturbed by the belligerent attitudes of Hitler and Mussolini, by the Japanese war against China, and by the apparent impotence of the League of Nations. In August the International Trade Union Congress made a strong appeal for working class unity to its affiliated members. It recognized the general strike as the ultimate weapon of the working class against war, but stated that for it to be effective it had to be called at the right psychological moment.[2]

Both the Trades Union Congress and the Labour Party in Britain carried on the debate. The Trades Union Congress in September referred for the consideration of the General Council a motion which asked for 'an organized refusal to assist in any shape or form in measures calculated to help in the prosecution of the war' if a war were declared. The General Council wanted to examine the matter in relation to its own powers.[3] It was, it seemed, using delaying tactics. Not so the Labour Party. In October 1933 its annual conference unanimously endorsed a motion pledging itself to take no

---

[1] The General Strike is described in Chapter XI, pp. 190–199.

[2] T.U.C. Report, 1933, pp. 443–444.

[3] The T.U.C. Standing Orders 8(h) stated: 'In order that the Trade Union Movement may do everything which lies in its power to prevent future wars, the General Council shall, in the event of there being a danger of an outbreak of war, call a special Congress to decide on industrial action, such Congress to be called, if possible, before war is declared.'

part in war and to consult with trade unions with a view to considering a general strike in the event of a war or a threat of war.[1]

The General Council, the Labour Party executive, and the Parliamentary Labour Party executive met together in February 1934 to decide on a uniform anti-war policy. The meeting discussed whether Labour should oppose every war and decided that in the light of events on the continent it would be wrong to lay down a definite line of action for all future emergencies. Its final statement of policy was announced by the National Joint Council in June 1934. In a detailed document on war and peace it rejected the idea of a general strike. It stated:

> Labour is fully cognisant of the various implications of a General Strike against war. The present Standing Order 8(h) of the Trades Union Congress which states that a Special Congress should be called in the event of there being a danger of an outbreak of war covers the position and in spite of the psychological difficulty of taking action once the war spirit has been roused, provides them with the best means of dealing with such a situation. The lack of an independent Trade Union Movement in such countries as Germany, Italy, Austria, etc., makes the calling of a General Strike against their Governments an impossibility. In other countries, such as Japan, the Trade Union organisation is too weak to be able to restrain its Government.
>
> It is quite possible that aggressive action might come from some of those countries. A general strike under such circumstances could not possibly be made effective by the Trade Unions in those countries.
>
> The responsibility for stopping war ought not to be placed upon the Trade Union movement alone. Every citizen who wants peace and every other section of the Labour Movement, must share the responsibility of any organised action that might be taken to prevent war.
>
> The refusal to handle munitions of war is another suggestion which has been made. Apart from the technical difficulties of defining and identifying such munitions, if conducted on a large scale by the Trade Union Movement, such a refusal would very rapidly develop into a general strike. This question is so closely bound up with that of the general strike, that it would be most unwise to go beyond the provisions of the existing Standing Order 8(h) of the Trades Union Congress.[2]

The Trades Union Congress in 1934 accepted the document with relatively little opposition. There was no further discussion about a general strike until the Conservative Government attacked Egypt in 1956. Trade union emotions were aroused and there were fears of a widespread war. There was a feeling of frustration at the inability of the Parliamentary Labour Party to take effective action against the

---

[1] Labour Party Conference Report, 1933, p. 186.
[2] T.U.C. Report 1934, p. 160.

Government and some thoughts turned to direct action. The Fire Brigades Union asked the General Council to organize a general strike in order to assist the Parliamentary Labour Party in opposing the Government, while the National Union of Vehicle Builders wanted the Trades Union Congress to take immediate action to force the Government to cease armed intervention, but did not specify how it should be done. Most calls for a general strike came from outside the Movement.

Although there was trade union discussion on this occasion about ways of exerting extra-Parliamentary pressure on the Government, there was no indication that the large trade unions seriously considered direct action. Certainly the General Council of the Trades Union Congress gave it no consideration, for the Council itself was not united in its opposition to the Government.

It is still possible for the trade union movement to take industrial action over political issues. There are no insuperable constitutional or legal obstacles,[1] but there are many other obstacles. Trade unions are large established institutions with a vested interest in the existing state of society. Some trade unions leaders may desire changes in society but mostly they are limited ones which can be achieved without damaging the fabric. An essential part of the fabric is parliamentary democracy. Trade union leaders, on the whole, have neither the desire to damage this nor the attitude of mind to make real damage possible. They accept that industrial action for political purposes is no different in principle and intent from the use of force against the Government by other means, and they realize that a prime virtue of political democracy is that it eliminates the use of force and coercion from the determination of political policy. Trade union leaders, through the nature of their work, are steeped in constitutional practices. They would, in the main, be incapable of adjusting themselves to take unconstitutional action on a scale which would challenge the Government's sovereignty. They are also realists. The Government has all the resources of the state at its command and no doubt, if the occasion demanded it, it would use them.

---

[1] A purely political strike can be declared illegal under the Conspiracy and Protection of Property Act, 1875, but illegality is not an insuperable obstacle.

Chapter Eleven

STRIKES AGAINST THE GOVERNMENT
AS EMPLOYER[1]

WHEN the Government became an employer of industrial labour it was faced with the possibility of being a participant in industrial disputes. It was possible for a public employer to make as many mistakes in its industrial relations as any private employer and there was no practical reason to suppose that workers would differentiate between situations in the two types of employment. From the workers' point of view a strike against the Government could be indistinguishable from a strike against any other employer. They could either win or lose it. The strike might be difficult to win because the Government with troops and police at its command could organize strike-breaking services, but this had happened in strikes against private employers.

The Government, on the other hand, was the sovereign body whose decisions normally formed the basis of law. If its decisions were challenged by union strikes, regardless of whether they had political or industrial ends, would not this constitute a threat to the Government's authority in general and, therefore, endanger Parliamentary democracy? Or could a practical distinction be made between the decisions of the Government as an employer and its decisions as the sovereign body so that strikes against the Government could be waged without political consequences? The answer has been provided quite clearly by the Government's experience since 1918. It has been involved as an employer in strikes on the railways, in the mines, and in the road passenger transport industry and has made concessions in the same way as an ordinary private employer without incurring any adverse political consequences. This chapter describes each of the strikes in turn and shows the conditions under which strikes against the Government as an employer have been won and lost.

THE RAILWAY STRIKE, 1919

Nine months of industrial unrest on the railways preceded the national railway strike. 1919 started with a strike threat from the

[1] The definition of employer as it applies to the Government is that which is given at the beginning of Part II, on p. 69.

171

Railway Clerks' Association, the most pacific and conservative of the railway unions. This union was the only one organizing railway workers which did not possess full negotiating rights at the end of the war. The employers were prepared to grant it recognition in the case of the lower railway clerical grades but not for the supervisory personnel, the stationmasters and agents. The union was not prepared to accept partial recognition. It was in a strong bargaining position. With 72,000 members it had organized the majority of the railway clerical staff, and out of a possible membership of 8,800 stationmasters and agents it had organized 5,300. The executive of the union declared that unless it had been given full recognition by 6 p.m. on 4 February, all clerical work on the railways would stop. The dispute was referred to the War Cabinet, which gave in to the railway clerks at 3 p.m. on 4 February 1919 on the understanding that the supervisory grades were organized in an autonomous section in the union. This was accepted and an agreement was signed.

On the day before the railway clerks' dispute was settled an Underground railway strike began in London over dissatisfaction with an eight-hour-day agreement which the Associated Society of Locomotive Engineers and Firemen and the National Union of Railwaymen had signed with the Government. There was confusion over all aspects of the strike. Traffic was dislocated not only by the strike but also by the cold snowy weather. The Government and the Railway Executive disagreed over terms for a settlement. The two unions involved adopted entirely opposite attitudes. On the second day of the strike the Associated Society of Locomotive Engineers and Firemen officially recognized it, and after three days called it off when the Government gave the union a vague undertaking about interpreting the agreement. The strike was repudiated at first by the National Union of Railwaymen, then officially recognized just as the other union was calling it off. This act extended the strike by three days but did not improve the settlement.

While the Underground railway strike was taking place, an unofficial movement was growing in the National Union of Railwaymen for a strike against the Government unless it opened negotiations on the railwaymen's national programme of wages, hours, and conditions of work. Negotiations did indeed open but broke down in March 1919. A national strike was then called, but it was postponed while representatives of the Triple Alliance negotiated with the Government on behalf of the railwaymen. In the course of these negotiations Mr. Bonar Law, who was acting for the Prime Minister, warned the Triple Alliance leaders about the political consequences of a strike when the Government was the employer.[1] This meeting nonetheless ended without agreement. A few days later the Government made an offer which the union accepted. The implementation of the complete national programme had still to be achieved.

A good deal of tension was built up amongst railwaymen as strike threats were made and not carried out, for on each occasion emotion was generated which was not released. In this situation material factors lost their precise significance. So long, then, as the railwaymen's demands were negotiated in a drawn-out piecemeal manner there was always the possibility of a strike actually taking place over some minor detail.

By the summer of 1919 the negotiations with the Government had reached the issue of the standardization of wage rates between all the railway companies. After the Associated Society of Locomotive Engineers and Firemen had threatened to strike in August, the Government concluded an agreement covering drivers and firemen but it would not give the same terms for the lower grades. Railwaymen in various parts of the country protested by threatening unofficial, sectional strike action. Under this pressure the executive of the National Union of Railwaymen sought a new offer from the Government.

The general secretary of the union, J. H. Thomas, met the President of the Board of Trade, Sir Auckland Geddes, on 16 September 1919 to discuss the issue. Thomas asked for a Government offer and said that when it 'came it should be a definite offer so that we should know exactly, having regard to the delay and long negotiations, that it was the Government's firm and definite proposal'.[2] The Government's offer came three days later. It did not meet the union's claim and in an accompanying letter Sir Auckland Geddes wrote that the proposals were 'not put forward as a basis of negotiation but as the definitive offer of the Government'. The union executive rejected the offer. It would have entailed wage reductions and it violated the principle, on which the union insisted, of levelling up wages between companies to the best wage paid for a grade. The executive was annoyed at the terms of the letter because it wanted a *definite* not a *definitive* offer.[3] A national railway strike was called for 26 September. The Government's first reaction was to show that the offer was not definitive by inviting the union to continue negotiations. In the course of these, Lloyd George said that if they failed to reach a settlement

---

[1] At a meeting on 22 March (*Railway Review*, March 1919).

[2] *Railway Review*, 3 October 1919.

[3] The letter was the responsibility of Geddes. He said that when the letter was given him to sign he altered the word *definite* to *definitive* (ibid.).

then the public would have to judge between them.[1] This is precisely what happened. A settlement was not reached and work stopped as planned. The strike had the official support of the Associated Society of Locomotive Engineers and Firemen, although its members were not in dispute with the Government.

The Government's attitude at the beginning of the strike was indicated by the following Cabinet statement:

> The Government, now that matters have reached this pass, have taken the view that the strike must be resisted and fought with all the resources of the country. A great deal of organization exists already which has been specially prepared to deal with the situation, such as, the organization of food supplies, the distribution of food supplies, arrangements for the taking by compulsory acquisition of motor vehicles, and so on. While it is hoped that the matter will be settled without civil disturbance, at the same time the Government are determined to see it through, and if necessary the armed forces of the community, as well as the community itself, will be called into use to deal with the situation. Wherever it is possible for volunteers to do the work, when they are ready to come forward, protection will be given to them. It is too serious a matter to conceal anything. This is a strike against the life of the community, under conditions which the Government consider to be unreasonable, and it is going to be fought, so long as this Government has the fighting of it, with the full resources of the community.[2]

The Cabinet issued official communiqués on the strike. It made dramatic statements and issued an appeal for the help of all citizens. Demobilization was suspended and Forces' leave was cancelled; a number of war regulations were revived; restrictions were imposed on the use of fuel; an order was made concerning food rationing; and both Field-Marshal Haig, Commander-in-Chief of the Home Forces, and Major-General Fielding, Commanding the London District, attended a Cabinet meeting, thus emphasizing the Government's determination to use troops if necessary.

The Government had been taken aback by the act of striking; it had grown accustomed to idle threats not only from the railwaymen but also from the Triple Alliance. Its reactions, once the strike had started, were based on the fear that a widespread dispute would take place which would be directed towards political ends. The contentious political issues such as conscription and British intervention in Russia which had provoked earlier threats from the Triple Alliance were by no means dead in October 1919.

The Government's fears were unfounded. The National Union of Railwaymen had no consultations before the strike with the other

---

[1] From a verbatim report in the *Railway Review*, 3 October 1919.
[2] *The Times* ,27 September 1919.

members of the Triple Alliance. The Dockers' Union recorded: 'We were not asked to give more active assistance, and, in fact, it was hinted that we were not required to do so; we agree with that policy.'[1] J. H. Thomas refused offers of help which he said would have paralysed the community.[2] But the response to the strike from some quarters might have set events in motion which were revolutionary in fact if not in intent. The early announcements of the Government and some editorials in the Press were intemperate and provocative. *The Times*, for instance, likened the strike to the war with Germany, which must be fought to a finish.[3] There was pressure for Parliament to be summoned immediately.

On the first day of the strike the Labour Research Department was authorized by the National Union of Railwaymen to publicize the railwaymen's case.[4] It was allowed to spend up to £1,500 a day on publicity advertisements in the Press. These advertisements varied between a full page in *The Times* and the *Herald* to a single column in other papers. The aim of the advertisements was to appeal to the public and to other unions, and to controvert Government statements.[5] The Labour Research Department adopted various other media for making the railwaymen's case known to the public. It canvassed newspapermen, sent out articles under the signature of J. H. Thomas, induced prominent writers to support their cause, arranged the compilation and distribution of daily news bulletins for those newspapers which would not give them editorial space. The Department also distributed posters and leaflets and sent letters to the clergy in the London area. A message from Thomas—'Railwaymen are not fighting the country . . .'—was flashed on the screens of cinemas in competition with a statement from Lloyd George on the same cinema screens that 'The Government is not fighting Trade Unionism . . .' A press-cutting service was arranged for each day so that the railwaymen's publicists knew exactly what points to counter, to elaborate, and so on.

This highly organized publicity campaign was conducted by G. D. H. Cole, R. Page Arnot, and a few other intellectuals who helped to run the Labour Research Department. Such a campaign was unprecedented. It changed the temper of the strike by drawing

---

[1] *Docker's Record*, October 1919.

[2] *Railway Review*, 3 October 1919. Robert Smillie and Robert Williams were very annoyed at the unilateral action of the railwaymen.

[3] *The Times*, 29 September 1919.

[4] The way in which the Labour Research Department tackled this job is clearly described in the *History of the Labour Research Department*, by R. Page Arnot. Appendix III.

[5] ibid., p. 47.

the Government to state its case in public. The issue lost its revolutionary significance and became a simple straightforward one about wages. Once the public had assimilated this change it grew sympathetic towards the railwaymen. The progress of the strike was illustrated by the union and Government advertisements in *The Times*.[1] Had the Government's original attitude been maintained the strike could only have ended through the capitulation of one side.

The executive of the National Transport Workers' Federation at its meeting on 30 September decided, on the suggestion of Ernest Bevin, to convene a conference of representatives of unions likely to be affected by the strike.[2] Nineteen unions were invited to attend, and all did so except the Miners' Federation.

The Conference met on 1 October, heard a statement by the general secretaries of the two railway unions involved in the strike, and unanimously resolved that it was convinced that the strike was a purely trade union fight for wages and conditions. After the railway union representatives had withdrawn, the Conference appointed a mediation committee of eleven members.[3] The committee met the Prime Minister the same day but was told that the Government considered it to be quite impracticable to continue negotiations until work was resumed. Nevertheless, Mr. Lloyd George conferred at length with the executives of the two railway unions and the mediation committee on 1 and 2 October. The Government asked for a truce of seven days during which the contentious matters could be discussed. Failing a settlement it was prepared to submit the disputed questions to arbitration. Its terms were rejected by the adjourned Conference on 3 October.

The Conference delegates then prepared to consolidate their own ranks. They agreed to convene a conference on 7 October in order to obtain the authority to take sympathetic action in support of the railwaymen. The mediation committee[4] felt sufficiently representative of the trade union movement to make strongly worded declarations to the Government. It stated on 4 October that the Prime Minister 'underestimated the power of resistance of the Railwaymen's Unions

[1] These advertisements are reproduced on pp. 178–184.

[2] Ernest Bevin was then a national organizer of the Dock, Wharf, Riverside and General Workers' Union. *Docker's Record*, October 1919.

[3] They were: H. Gosling, R. Williams, J. R. Clynes, Arthur Henderson, J. Muir, E. Bevin, J. O'Grady, J. T. Brownlie, J. W. Bowen, T. E. Naylor, and R. B. Walker. The part which this committee played in the strike is described in a *Report to the Labour Movement of Great Britain by the Committee appointed at the Caxton Hall Conference, October 1st 1919*, published by the National Transport Workers' Federation.

[4] Frank Hodges (Miners' Federation), C. W. Bowerman (secretary of the T.U.C.), and G. H. Stuart-Bunning (president of the T.U.C.) had joined it.

and the fighting spirit and capacity of the Trade Union Movement as a whole. . . . We feel bound to warn the Government and inform the nation that unless a more reasonable attitude is adopted before [the Conference meets on 7 October], it will be impossible to avert a widespread extension of the strike with all its consequences.'

After its intentions had been stated, the mediation committee arranged with the executives of the two railway unions to meet the Prime Minister on Sunday morning, 5 October. By 4 p.m. on that day the basis of a settlement had been reached. Detailed negotiations were left until after work had been resumed on the understanding that they were to be completed by 31 December 1919. Wages were to be stabilized up to 30 September 1920, not to 31 December 1919, as the Government first demanded; no adult railwaymen was to receive less than 51s. a week so long as the cost of living remained at least 110 per cent above pre-war level. The first Government proposal had been for a permanent minimum wage of 40s. per week irrespective of cost-of-living changes. The usual mutual guarantees were made about the victimization of strikers by the Government and of non-strikers by the union. Finally it was agreed that the wages of strikers, which had been withheld because the strike was a breach of contract, were to be paid after work had been resumed. The strike ended, after nine days, on 5 October.

In material matters neither side could proclaim a victory, though naturally each side did so. The railwaymen had not secured their original demand nor had the Government maintained its pre-strike terms. The Government had improved its offer during the course of the strike, but, more important than this, it had made a substantial concession in principle by negotiating and effecting a settlement. In this sense the unions were successful. The Government settled under duress but it is doubtful whether it would have done so if the unions had not made it so clear to everyone that the Government was behaving as a bad employer. Lloyd George was right. The public did in fact judge the issue.

FIGHT
FOR THE LIFE OF THE COMMUNITY.

How Every Citizen Can Help.

Maintaining supplies of food and other necessities is vital in this crisis. Every citizen must do his part. Each day volunteers will be called for by the Government. Read this carefully and follow the instructions.

Skilled volunteers are the first need.

Help by working, help also by saving petrol, light, coal, food.

Don't use the Telephone, Telegraph, or other Postal service more than you can possibly help.

Keep in good spirits. Make the best of things.

Help those who have the skill to do the work; lodge them if they need lodging; feed them if they are stranded; a broken-down supply-lorry of food or petrol by the roadside is the nation's property— guard it and help the driver on his way.

ALL PASSERS-BY SHOULD OFFER HELP.

I.—RAILWAY SERVICE.

All civilians possessing qualifications as under should get into touch with the head offices of any of the railway companies or with the local superintendent of any line.

Engine Drivers.	Telegraph Repairers.
Firemen.	Carters.
Stokers (for stationary engines).	Checkers.
Motor Drivers.	Porters.
Signalmen.	Women Employees.
Guards.	Cleaners.
Foremen.	

Stablemen (for feeding, watering, and looking after deserted horses).

Help by unloading and carting your own goods to and fro.

II.—MOTOR TRANSPORT.

1. Persons experienced in organization and control of mechanical transport, petrol and steam, on the road.

2. Engineers experienced in maintenance and upkeep of mechanical transport, steam and petrol.

3. Drivers and mechanics for steam and petrol-driven lorries.

All the above should apply at once, stating qualifications, to—

    (a) In the *London Area* to Major Chubb, Grosvenor House, Upper Grosvenor-street, W.1. Those who have already applied in response to the Food Controller's appeal need not send in a second application.

    (b) Outside the *London Area* to the Divisional Road Transport Officers or Area Transport Secretaries as follows :—

LONDON AND HOME COUNTIES DIVISION.

Division Road Transport Officer.	Address.
COL. W. RIGBY	.. 7/8 Norfolk-street, Strand

Area.	Address of Area Transport Secretary.
WATFORD	F.C.C. Offices, High-street, Watford.
BISHOP STORTFORD	Market Chambers, Bishop Stortford.
CHELMSFORD	Rainsford House, Duke-street, Chelmsford.
COLCHESTER	60, Head-street, Colchester.
ASHFORD	22, Bank-street, Ashford.
MAIDSTONE	West Borough Chambers, Maidstone.
GUILDFORD	Town Hall, Guildford.
LEWES	64, High-street, Lewes.
CHICHESTER	93, East-street, Chichester.

The Government hope that many demobilized officers and men who have recently had valuable experience in this branch of transport will respond to this appeal.

III.—APPEAL TO USERS OF MOTOR SPIRIT.

During the railway strike it is essential to make extensive use of motor transport for the supply of food and vital necessities. It is of utmost importance to conserve the supplies of motor spirit.

The Government urgently appeal to all users of motor spirit to restrict the use of motor-vehicles to absolutely necessary purposes and to limit consumption to the lowest possible amount.

Every gallon of petrol used needlessly means less food for the people.

Don't keep any empty cans. Return them at once.

Don't Hoard Petrol.
Don't Drive for Pleasure.

IV.—SPECIAL CONSTABLES.

Able-bodied men can render useful services as Special Constables, and so help the civil authorities to maintain order and protect necessary public services. All willing to serve should apply at the nearest police station and offer himself for enrolment.

V.—COMMUNICATIONS.

Wireless operators who have had experience in the Army or Air Force and are willing to render continuous service where required in the event of an emergency arising should communicate their names and addresses at once, for registration, to the Chief Signal Officer, Headquarters, York, Chester, Salisbury, Aldershot, or Edinburgh, or to the Army Signal Officer, Horse Guards, Whitehall, S.W.1.

Save Food—Save Petrol—Save Coal.

HELP FIGHT
for the Life of the Community.

WHY
DID THE RAILWAYMEN
STRIKE ?

THE GOVERNMENT PROMISED

No Reduction in War Wage except under sliding scale based on the cost of living or settled by any other way that might be arranged between the Government and the Railwaymen.

NO REDUCTION AT ALL

(*a*) before December 31st, 1919;

(*b*) **even after that date, unless the cost of living falls to 110 per cent.** above the pre-war level and remains below that figure for 3 months;

(*c*) **no reduction at any time** below a figure which will on the average give every grade twice as much as it got before the war, even when the cost of living gets back to pre-war prices.

THE PUBLIC AND THE RAILWAYMEN

Don't blame the Railwaymen for the strike, blame the Government that forced the strike upon them!

Railwaymen showed they were public spirited by postponing their National programme for better wages and conditions when the War began.

The Prime Minister said there must be **"A land fit for heroes to live in"**!

Does he make "the land fit for heroes" by forcing down Railwaymen's wages?

If the Government set the example **every private employer will follow suit.**

Your wages will be reduced next.

Is this the way to recompense Labour's service during the War?

Is this the way to increase production?

You know the scandal of profiteering.

Brow-beating the poorest workers is worse than a scandal.

It is a crime!

Insist on fair and equal treatment for all!!

Issued by the

NATIONAL UNION OF RAILWAYMEN

Unity House, Euston Road,
London, N.W.1.

The Prime Minister said :

There must be a land fit for heroes to live in.

Better social conditions depend on better wages.

The Government now say that as prices fall wages must fall. It has not even said how much.

The Prime Minister said on September 25th: "I am one of those who have always believed that the Railway Workers before the war, certainly very large numbers of them, were disgracefully paid."

If the Government proposal is accepted some "Disgracefully paid" Railwaymen may receive in 1920 a wage equivalent to that of 1914.

"Disgracefully paid" workers should be substantially **better off** than before the War, not merely as well off.

Issued by the National Union of Railwaymen, Unity House, Euston Road, London, N.W.1.

The Railway Strike

Two Declarations by the Prime Minister:

1. To Railwaymen

(In a telegram to a correspondent)

"Reference your telegram this morning, you can certainly assure Railwaymen in your district that wages will not be reduced before end of March. This promise was already indicated in the Government's offer to Railway Executive.

"D. LLOYD GEORGE."

2. To All Workers

"The Government is NOT fighting Trade Unionism. Trade Unionism is a recognised factor in the industrial life of the country. What the Government is fighting for is to prevent the Extremists of any industrial body from attempting to gain their ends by attacking the life of the Community, and so bringing untold misery upon thousands of innocent people.

"D. LLOYD GEORGE."

WHO IS SPEAKING THE TRUTH ?

The Government says it offers

	Government Offer Standard Wage	War Wages Bonus	Total of Government Offer
Porters - - -	40s. to 49s.	9s. to 6s.	49s. to 55s.
Parcel Porters -	45s. to 54s.	8s. to 9s.	53s. to 63s.
Ticket Collectors -	45s. to 54s.	9s. to 10s.	54s. to 64s.
Passenger Guards	48s. to 60s.	10s. to 8s.	58s. to 68s.
Goods Guards -	48s. to 60s.	10s. to 8s.	58s. to 68s.
Shunters - - -	46s. to 60s.	7s. to 4s.	53s. to 64s.
Goods Porters - -	40s. to 47s.	13s. to 12s.	53s. to 59s.
Checkers - - -	46s. to 55s.	8s. to 9s.	54s. to 64s.
Carmen - - -	45s. to 52s.	8s. to 10s.	53s. to 62s.
Platelayers - - -	40s. to 50s.	14s. to 7s.	54s. to 57s.

It is not true that the figures in Column 3 are, as the Government says, its "offer."

They include the very War Bonus in Column 2 which the Government is attacking.

WORKERS IN OTHER TRADES!

Do you want **your** wages to be reduced in the same way!

Remember what the Prime Minister said: "Whatever we lay down with regard to the Railwaymen you may depend upon it is going to be claimed throughout the Country."

YOUR TURN COMES NEXT.

STAND BY THE RAILWAYMEN.

Issued by the

NATIONAL UNION OF RAILWAYMEN,

Unity House, Euston Road, N.W.1.

THE GOVERNMENT OFFER

TO THE

Classes of Railwaymen involved in the present dispute.

THIS shows the Pre-War Wage, the Present Wage, and the Minimum Wage. The present wage is guaranteed till 31st March, 1920, after which the Government have offered to adjust it either according to the present scale, depending on the cost of living, or by Court of Arbitration, or by any other method which may be agreed between the Government and the Railwaymen.

	Pre-War Wage :	Till 31st March, 1920 Present Wages Guaranteed.	After 31st March, 1920. Minimum wage which will not be reduced however much the cost of living falls.	War Bonus which continues till cost of living falls and then can only be altered by agreement or arbitration.
Porters - -	16s. to 22s.	49s. to 55s.	40s. to 49s.	9s. to 6s.
Parcel Porters -	22s. to 30s.	53s. to 63s.	45s. to 54s.	8s. to 9s.
Ticket Collectors -	21s. to 31s.	54s. to 64s.	45s. to 54s.	9s. to 10s.
Passenger Guards -	25s. to 35s.	58s. to 68s.	48s. to 60s.	10s. to 8s.
Goods Guards -	25s. to 35s.	58s. to 68s.	48s. to 60s.	10s. to 8s.
Shunters -	20s. to 31s.	53s. to 64s.	46s. to 60s.	7s. to 4s.
Goods Porters -	20s. to 26s.	53s. to 59s.	40s. to 47s.	13s. to 12s.
Checkers -	21s. to 31s.	54s. to 64s.	46s. to 55s.	8s. to 9s.
Carmen -	20s. to 29s.	53s. to 62s.	45s. to 52s.	8s. to 10s.
Platelayers -	21s. to 24s.	54s. to 57s.	40s. to 50s.	14s. to 7s.

NOTE I. The lower rates apply chiefly in the country: the higher rates in industrial areas.
NOTE 2. As the cost of living falls the pound is worth more and real wages increase: that is, your pound purchases more.

Why have the leaders of the Railway Unions forced a strike now?

IS THE STRIKE JUSTIFIED?

THE COAL DISPUTES

The Government's attitude towards the coal-miners was not that solely of an employer. For a number of reasons it thought about them in political terms. The Miners' Federation was led after 1918 by powerful advocates of direct action. Whenever they threatened or called a strike they were understandably suspected by the Government of having political motives, irrespective of the actual content of the miners' grievances. The nature of the miners' post-war claims tended to confirm the Government's suspicion, for industrial and political demands were usually included in the same claim. For instance, the ballot paper distributed to miners in February 1919 on the question of a national strike had five items, among which were an application for a 30 per cent increase in wages and a demand for the nationalization of the mines.

The suspicions were given point by the aggressiveness of the miners themselves. The miners' leaders reflected the feelings of the men in the pits. But this was not all. The Miners' Federation was a member of the Triple Alliance and displayed every intention of using it.

The National Coal Strike, October 1920[1]

The Miners' Federation, in June 1920, pressed for an increase in wages and a reduction in the price of coal. This was submitted as an indivisible demand; that is, the miners said they would insist on a larger wage increase if the Government failed to reduce prices. The miners were acting, they said, on behalf of the consumer. The Government uncompromisingly rejected the claim, whereupon the miners voted by a large majority for a strike.

The Triple Alliance unions met on the day the result of the miners' strike ballot was declared. They decided to support the miners' claims, but restricted themselves, for the time being, to forming a publicity committee which decided to use the services of the Labour Research Department. The following week, on 8 September, the annual Trades Union Congress announced that the miners' claims were both reasonable and just.

Meetings with the President of the Board of Trade continued intermittently, during which the miners were advised to submit their wage claim to arbitration, and the miners, after rejecting the advice, modified the claim, only to have that rejected. Other features of

[1] See *Labour in the Coal-Mining Industry*, by G. D. H. Cole, Chapter VIII, and *The Miners—Years of Struggle*, by R. Page Arnot, p. 236 et seq., for detailed descriptions of the strike.

the dispute became apparent during the third week of September 1920 when the Government's advice to the miners to submit their wage demand to arbitration caused a split in their ranks. Robert Smillie and a minority on the executive of the Miners' Federation were in favour of accepting the advice. The differences were carried into the open at the miners' conference on 23 September, and caused divided opinion in the Triple Alliance which Lloyd George effectively utilized when he quoted Smillie in support of the Government's case.

The Triple Alliance unions decided, on 23 September, that they would not strike in sympathy with the miners. The Government then made elaborate preparations to meet a coal strike. Coal exports were restricted and big reserve stocks were built up.[1] Emergency arrangements were made just in case there should be sympathetic strikes, and a Bill conferring exceptional powers on the Government in cases of emergency was prepared. In view of the unfavourable situation the Miners' Federation executive approached the Prime Minister and then accepted his suggestion to suspend the strike notices and meet the coal owners. No settlement was reached and on 16 October 1920 the miners went on strike—alone. Moreover, they were not wholeheartedly in the strike. Robert Smillie had opposed it and on the day before the strike he had handed in his resignation. The resignation was withdrawn, but the incident was publicized to the detriment of the miners' case. The Government made no attempt to break the deadlock although it was pressed in Parliament to do so.

The situation was profoundly changed by a decision of the National Union of Railwaymen on 21 October to strike in support of the miners unless the dispute was settled by 23 October, and by the intervention of the Parliamentary Committee of the Trades Union Congress on 22 October when it arranged for a conference of trade union executives to be called the following week to consider the dispute. Lloyd George said that a resumption of negotiations had been made more difficult by the railwaymen's decision, and as if to emphasize this fact the Government introduced the Emergency Powers' Bill into the House of Commons on 22 October. Yet at the same time Lloyd George asked the miners to confer with him.

The miners accepted the invitation to confer at first unofficially and then officially. In view of the possibility of a negotiated settlement the railwaymen were asked to delay taking sympathetic action until further notice. An agreement with the Government was reached on 28 October while the special conference of trade union executives

[1] Cole, op. cit., p. 157.

was actually sitting. It was reluctantly accepted by the members of the Miners' Federation and the strike ended on 3 November.[1]

The Government had reached a settlement under the threat of widespread strike action, as during the railway strike. But it had only negotiated a patched-up peace and had settled none of the outstanding issues. The miners received the wage increase they had asked for but it was related to output, and this they disliked. Moreover, they were to negotiate a permanent wages scheme with the coal owners by 31 March 1921. This was an almost impossible task, for the miners' premise was that wages should be determined nationally, while the coal owners believed in district settlements.

The 1921 Dispute[2]

This dispute occurred partly because of precipitate action by the Government and partly because of the unsatisfactory nature of the 1920 settlement. The Mining Industry Act of 1920 stipulated that the Government control of the mines was to continue until 31 August 1921, and the negotiations over a wages scheme were conducted with this date in mind. The economic boom ended in the winter of 1920 and with it went the prosperity of the coal industry. The industry became a financial liability to the Government. In January 1921 the Miners' Federation was informed by the President of the Board of Trade that the Government intended to decontrol the coal industry before 21 August. The miners objected and so did the coal owners, who needed government financial support to maintain profit levels because of the decline in the demand for coal. The actual date of decontrol was not given until 22 February. It was to be 31 March 1921. The employers acquiesced but the miners continued to object.

The negotiations over a wages scheme had not made any real progress, and there was no possibility that the difference would be eliminated by 31 March. The decision to remove controls determined the employers to pay wages according to the financial state of each district, with no national arrangements for evening-out district variations as had existed under government control. Even if there had been no recession there would have been wage reduction in some districts. Under the economic conditions of March 1921 large wage reductions were involved in almost every district.

[1] More than half of the miners wanted to reject the terms of the settlement, but under the rules of the Miners' Federation a two-thirds majority was necessary to start and continue a strike.

[2] The Government in this and the 1926 coal dispute was not directly in control of the mines. It had, however, a financial interest in the disputes and was a negotiating party. If the miners had obtained concessions the Government would have had to meet their cost. The Government acted, thus, as an employer.

The coal owners, without negotiation, published district schedules of wage rates which were to operate from the date of decontrol. The miners rejected the schedules; they wanted a National Wages Board maintained either by a form of government control or by a government subsidy to the industry. The Government refused to intervene, so on 31 March 1921 work stopped in the mines. This was in effect a lock-out. It could be called a strike only if the right of the coal owners to manipulate mining conditions as they pleased were granted.

The stoppage was more complete than on previous occasions, because the coal owners had issued notices to all mineworkers, including those who were responsible for the safety of the mines, and the Miners' Federation had insisted that all workers should refuse to accept the terms. During previous disputes the safety workers had remained at work. There were outcries that the miners were declaring war on the community by endangering the safety of the mines.[1] In fact very little damage was done to the mines, but the miners alienated much public sympathy through their act. Their case was further complicated by the nature of their claim. They wanted the Government to interfere in the direction of the coal industry, and although the request was directly related to the inability of the mining industry to pay reasonable wages, it was construed as a political claim and aroused controversy. The other part of the claim was against a reduction in wages. This by itself was a clear enough issue, but few people, in the early stages of the dispute, could say what the extent of the reductions would be. The figures varied between districts and between grades within districts. The miners' case suffered from its complexity.

The determined way in which the Government had passed the Emergency Powers Act in the 1920 strike and the patched-up nature of the settlement conveyed the impression that it was preparing to tackle the Miners' Federation once for all. The precipitate way in which it ended controls as soon as the industry met financial difficulties, its refusal to assist the industry in any way, and its use of the Emergency Powers Act emphasized the impression. A Royal Proclamation was issued under the Act declaring a state of emergency on the day the stoppage began, and on 4 April the Emergency Regulations were issued disclosing that the Government had taken upon itself drastic powers. Troops were moved into the coal-fields and measures were taken to make sure that the country's food supply was maintained.

Yet it was a jittery Government which embarked on the dispute.

[1] Cole, op. cit., p. 201.

It thought there was going to be a revolution and it was not mentally prepared to tackle one. Out of fear, it set out to divide the members of the Triple Alliance against each other and banked on J. H. Thomas's giving it the utmost help. At first Thomas failed to create any division or even to carry his own union with him. The Miners' Federation had called for the support of the Triple Alliance, and by 8 April all of its constituent parts had decided to take sympathetic strike action at midnight on 12 April.

The transport workers and the railwaymen wanted a settlement, not a strike, and they persuaded the miners to re-enter negotiations. While the negotiations were on, the strike notices were suspended. But the negotiations broke down and all seemed set for a strike on 15 April. Unions not in the Triple Alliance and the executives of both the Trades Union Congress and the Labour Party expressed their support of the miners. Even J. H. Thomas was resigned to a wide, almost general, strike.

The day before the strike was due to begin Frank Hodges, the miners' secretary, made a statement at a meeting in the House of Commons which was interpreted as meaning that the miners might consider a temporary settlement on a district basis. When the news was conveyed to Lloyd George he immediately invited the miners' executive to confer with him. What Hodges said was disputed and the Miners' Federation executive promptly rejected the Prime Minister's invitation.

This decision had far-reaching consequences because it gave those union leaders who were opposed to the strike an opportunity to back out. Some delegates from the transport and railway unions, whilst prepared to help the miners resist wage cuts, had little sympathy with the claim for a National Wages Board, which they regarded as a political issue and they considered the miners' executive to be unreasonable in refusing to meet the Prime Minister. Other delegates supported all the miners' demands but feared the consequences of a Triple Alliance strike and were glad of a chance to avoid them. There was also a minority of delegates which had consistently opposed the strike. This minority, led by J. H. Thomas, successfully used the behaviour of the miners' executive to exploit doubts and fears. The Triple Alliance strike was cancelled on the day it was due to begin, Friday, 15 April, and the day became known as Black Friday.

Once again the miners were striking on their own, and this time the Government was in no hurry to reach a settlement. It retained its emergency powers. At the end of April and during May the transport unions and railwaymen placed an embargo on 'tainted' coal but it was ineffective. The miners were worn down and on 1 July 1921 accepted defeat and ended the dispute. The terms of settlement were worse than could have been obtained by negotiation in the early days of the dispute.

The 1926 Coal Dispute and the General Strike

The 1926 coal dispute resembled that of 1921. The strategy of the Miners' Federation, which was to obtain the widest possible backing of organized workers, was unchanged and the Government was drawn in to take up the coal owners' case in the same manner. The dispute was the culmination of a series of incidents which started after the recommendations of a court of inquiry into mining wages in May 1924, which were favourable to the miners, had been embodied in a National Wages Agreement. The employers were determined to get the agreement changed and in November 1924 they initiated talks with the miners to investigate the condition of the industry. The investigation produced no satisfactory results and it ended in June 1925. On the last day of June the miners received notice that the National Wages Agreement of 1924 was to be terminated from 31 July 1925.

The employers made proposals which included wage reductions and which the miners promptly rejected. The Government then stepped in. First it appointed Mr. W. C. Bridgman, First Lord of the Admiralty, as a mediator. He was unsuccessful. Then it appointed a court of inquiry into the dispute. The miners refused to collaborate and the court's findings, published on 28 July, came to nothing.

In the meantime the miners had been busy collecting support. The Miners' Federation had approached a number of unions in transport and heavy industry in April 1925 to form an Industrial Alliance for joint action. The Alliance had not materialized by July, but the indications then were that it would be formed. Neglecting no source of support, the Miners' Federation put its case to the General Council of the Trades Union Congress on 10 July. Support for the miners took a material form when the transport and railway unions agreed to place an embargo on the transport of coal if the coal owners did not withdraw their notices by 31 July. The operation of the embargo was placed under the control of the General Council, which then conducted the trade union side of the dispute.

The miners' case on this occasion was without complications. It was simply a refusal to accept wage reductions and trade unionists sympathized with it. The General Council did not possess the authority to order industrial action, so a conference of trade union executives was called for 30 July. The conference empowered the

General Council to issue strike notices. Neither the mine owners nor the miners would make concessions. Instructions for the operation of the embargo were issued, but in the evening of 31 July, a few hours before the embargo was due to start, the Prime Minister, Mr. Baldwin, announced that the Government would subsidize the industry until 1 May 1926; that the coal owners had agreed to suspend their notices; and that an inquiry into the coal industry would take place.

The 31 July was named Red Friday. Trade unions were jubilant and proclaimed a victory over the Government. Mr. Baldwin's decision formed the basis of controversy which went on for many years. Mr. Baldwin, when asked by his biographer, G. M. Young, why he gave the subsidy, answered simply, 'We were not ready.' [1] This was confirmed by Baldwin's Cabinet assistant and confidant, T. J. Jones, who wrote that 'the Government was, in fact, buying time to prepare the national defences against the possible recurrence of this threat'.[2] The Home Secretary, Sir William Joynson Hicks, amplified the Government's attitude. 'The danger', he said, 'was not over. Sooner or later this question had got to be fought out by the people of the land. Was England to be governed by Parliament and by the Cabinet or by a handful of trade union leaders?' [3] Mr. Churchill, the Chancellor of the Exchequer, spoke similarly and said '. . . if you are going to embark on a struggle of this kind, be quite sure that decisive public opinion is behind you . . .' [4]

The Government took elaborate anti-strike precautions during its nine months' grace.[5] It took no practical steps to improve the position of the coal industry. It did appoint a Royal Commission on the Coal Industry, under the chairmanship of Sir Herbert Samuel, but as the Commission did not report until 10 March 1926, there was little time left to settle the miners' and coal owners' differences before 1 May. Mr. Baldwin stated on 24 March that the Government accepted the recommendations of the Royal Commission provided the other parties did also. These recommendations disappointed both sides. The Commission displeased the employers because it favoured national wage agreements and wanted the industry to be reorganized, and it displeased the miners because it was opposed to the subsidy being continued and proposed that wages should be reduced. So Mr. Baldwin simply handed the issue back for the employers and miners to resolve.

[1] *Stanley Baldwin*, p. 99.   [2] *Lloyd George*, by Thomas Jones, p. 217.
[3] Quoted in Arnot, op. cit., p. 382.
[4] Hansard, vol. 187, cols. 1684–1685, 6 August 1925.
[5] Cf. Chapter VII, above, p. 126.

In the middle of April the coal owners announced that they would seek district agreements when the coal subsidy ended on 30 April and in most districts they posted notices to terminate the existing contracts on that day. Unless the miners accepted the employers' revised terms of employment, which consisted of district agreements, wage reductions and an increase in the length of the working day, then they were not to be employed. This was notice of a lock-out. A series of negotiations took place in which government representatives played a prominent part. At the end of April the Government was negotiating on employers' proposals while the General Council was acting with the Miners' Federation.[1]

The last day of negotiations involving the coal owners and the miners was 30 April. The negotiations hinged on the order of precedence to be given to two recommendations of the Samuel Commission on the Coal Industry. The coal owners wanted the miners to accept a wage reduction pending the reorganization of the industry, whereas the miners said they would not countenance a wage reduction before anything else was done. The Government refused to continue the subsidy. That night the Prime Minister, who had been involved in the negotiations during the day, told the union representatives that he did not think any useful purpose would be served by continuing the negotiations.

A conference of trade union executives which had been meeting since 29 April was told of the breakdown in the negotiations and then, on 1 May, considered a scheme for co-ordinated action which had been hurriedly prepared by Ernest Bevin and A. A. Purcell.[2] The scheme provided for a cessation of work at midnight on 3 May in the transport trades, the iron and steel industry, the printing industry, the metal and heavy chemical groups, and the building trade. Certain essential services were to be maintained. A second-line withdrawal of labour involving other unions was to be effected at the discretion of the General Council. The scheme was accepted excitedly and almost unanimously by the executives. At five o'clock that evening strike notices were sent out to the various unions. A Royal Proclamation under the Emergency Powers Act was also issued on 1 May and the Government set its anti-strike organization in motion. The miners' representatives handed over the conduct of the dispute to the General Council and dispersed to their various districts to prepare for the strike. Everything on 1 May seemed set for action.

[1] See Page Arnot, op. cit., pp. 405 et seq., for a description of the events leading up to the General Strike.

[2] Member of the T.U.C. General Council and organizer for the Furnishing Trades Association.

The General Council, however, had no intention of concluding the negotiations. It issued a manifesto declaring that it still believed an honourable settlement could be reached, and at 8 p.m. it sent a deputation to meet the Prime Minister and some members of the Cabinet. At the Prime Minister's suggestion it was agreed that negotiations should be continued with three representatives from each side. J. H. Thomas, A. B. Swales, and Arthur Pugh represented the T.U.C., while Baldwin, Steel-Maitland (Minister of Labour), and Lord Birkenhead spoke for the Government, with Walter Citrine and Sir Horace Wilson as their respective secretaries. At a meeting between these in the early hours on 2 May, Baldwin proposed a formula which the trade unionists were inclined to accept and submit to the miners; it was that 'The Prime Minister has satisfied himself as a result of the conversations he has had with the representatives of the T.U.C. that, if negotiations are continued (it being understood that the notices cease to operate), the representatives of the T.U.C. are confident that a settlement can be reached on the lines of the [Royal Commission] Report within a fortnight.' [1]

The miners' executive was recalled to London by telegram on 2 May to discuss the formula. In the meantime it was re-examined by the six negotiators and the matter of a wage reduction, omitted from the formula, was raised. Baldwin wanted it to be understood that if the formula was accepted it would mean that the miners would accept a wage reduction. The Negotiating Committee, however, did not categorically commit itself and it was not clear whether it accepted that there should be a wage reduction or that it was a fit subject for discussion. It was agreed that if the owners withdrew their lock-out notices the general strike notices would be recalled too.

The Cabinet also discussed the formula on 2 May. At a meeting at noon there was immediate hostility to it from Ministers who had not been present when it was drawn up. Some thought it was too vague and indefinite; others that it amounted to a capitulation under a threat of strike. A note was drawn up at a Cabinet meeting later in the day which specifically mentioned that 'some interim adjustment of hours and wages was inevitable' and added that the strike notices which had been sent out involved 'a challenge to the constitutional rights and freedom of the nation. The Government must . . . therefore require from the Trades Union Congress an unconditional withdrawal of the threat before it can continue negotiations.' [2] The negotiating Ministers were allowed to decide themselves whether this note should be used. Mr. L. S. Amery, who was a member of the

---

[1] G. M. Young, op. cit., pp. 113–114. [2] ibid., p. 115.

Cabinet, stated that opinion in the Cabinet hardened very much during the Sunday meetings.[1]

Not long before midnight a second formula which went some way towards meeting the feelings in the Cabinet was drafted by Lord Birkenhead and presented to the T.U.C. negotiating representatives. It stated: 'We [the T.U.C.] will urge the Miners to authorize us to enter upon a discussion, with the understanding that they and we accept the Report as a basis of settlement and we approach it with the knowledge that it may involve some reduction in wages.' While this second formula was being discussed the miners' officials and executive arrived at Downing Street and the T.U.C. negotiators adjourned to meet them and the rest of the General Council. At the same time Baldwin reported the proceedings to the Cabinet. While the Cabinet was in session the news came through to it that printers in the office of the *Daily Mail* had refused to print a leading article about the General Strike under the heading 'For King and Country'. This, Amery stated, 'tipped the scale. It was clear that the only issue that now mattered, for the Government and for the Public, was whether Government and Parliament were to surrender to coercion.' [2]

The Cabinet decided to face a General Strike. The note, drawn up earlier, was revised and stiffened. It stated that negotiations could not be continued unless interference with the Press was repudiated and the General Strike called off. The note was handed to the T.U.C. representatives by Baldwin just after 1 a.m. on 3 May—before the miners' leaders or the General Council had been able to examine the second formula.[3] The Cabinet had dispersed. Baldwin then went to bed. At about 3.30 a.m. on 3 May the General Council replied to the Government that it had no knowledge of the *Daily Mail* printers' act and reminded it that the workers had a right to cease work in defence of their interests. It stated that 'the public will judge of the Government's intentions by its precipitous and calamitous decision . . .'

A General Strike, to all intents and purposes, was on. The General Council had not weighed up the details or possible consequences of the strike: how long the strike might last; how it could coerce the Government; what form a Government capitulation would take; what the political consequences would be; what would be put in place of the Government if it were defeated; whether concessions could be wrested from the coal owners without first defeating the Government. Possibly its members thought differently about these

[1] *My Political Life*, by L. S. Amery, p. 484.   [2] ibid.
[3] *The General Strike*, by Julian Symons, p. 47.

things. Some may have thought that the Government would give way as in 1925, and that there would inevitably be a last-minute settlement. Others who had had experience of the Labour Government's inability to prepare against the contingencies of strike action may have thought that the Government could not take adequate precautions and would give in soon. Or they thought of the Government's ineffectual behaviour in 1919. There would have been some who thought only in terms of sympathetic action and not about consequences. Others may just have been bluffing.

The industrial crisis was discussed at length in the House of Commons on 3 May, after the end of negotiations and before the strike actually began. In the debate both Baldwin and Churchill expressed their opposition to the strike in constitutional terms. Baldwin, describing the course of the negotiations, said:

> I have recounted now the history of the last few days, I hope fairly. Stripped of all accessories, what was the position in which the Government found itself? It found itself challenged with an alternative Government . . . when you extend an ordinary trade dispute in this way, from one industry into a score of the most vital industries in the country, you change its character . . . I do not think all the leaders when they assented to ordering a general strike fully realised that they were threatening the basis of ordered government, and going nearer to proclaiming civil war than we have been for centuries past . . . it is not wages that are imperilled; it is the freedom of our very Constitution . . .[1]

Churchill explained that the question of a subsidy was one which only Parliament could competently decide. 'I see no difference whatever', he said, 'between a general strike to force Parliament to pass some Bill which the country does not wish for, and a general strike to force Parliament to pay a subsidy . . . it is a conflict which, if it is fought out to a conclusion, can only end in the overthrow of Parliamentary Government or in its decisive victory.'[2] Labour spokesmen denied these contentions. J. H. Thomas said: 'I know the Government's position. I have never disguised that in a challenge to the Constitution, God help us unless the Government won . . . but this is not only not a revolution, it is not something that says "We want to overthrow everything." It is merely a plain, economic, industrial dispute. . . .'

The debate in the House of Commons unmistakably revealed the attitude which the Government was to adopt during the strike. It considered two disputes to be in progress: a coal dispute and the General Strike; and while the strike lasted the coal dispute would

---

[1] Hansard, vol. 195, cols. 70, 71, 72, 3 May 1926.   [2] ibid., cols. 121, 124.

be relegated to the background. It considered the strike to be a challenge to the constitution which had to be defeated. This attitude precluded negotiations over the end of the strike. On the other hand, from the outset the General Council set out to deny that the strike was a constitutional challenge. Thomas's speech on 3 May was a denial. Thomas was expected to say this, but even John Bromley,[1] reputedly one who had pressed to have the strike notices sent out, said on 5 May that 'any suggestion that this dispute is a challenge to constitutionalism or an endeavour to overthrow the Government is quite wrong . . .'[2] The General Council went out of its way to establish the constitutional propriety of its action and used the *British Worker* on a number of occasions for this purpose.

The response to the strike call was complete. It was estimated that on 4 May about 2,300,000 workers were on strike.[3] This astounded all the prophets, for in most industries even in a strike where the issue directly affected the workers a higher proportion of blacklegs would have been expected than occurred on 4 May. The solidarity of the workers raised problems for the Government, for it became necessary for it to take steps to defeat the strike. If the strike response had been weak the Government could have just waited for its collapse. All members of the Government were united in insisting on an unconditional surrender, but they were not united on how to achieve it. There were in the Government such men as Churchill and Birkenhead who wanted to suppress the strike; there were others, led by Baldwin, who wanted to be firm where it was necessary but who desired to appear as men of peace.

Baldwin's views prevailed. Emergency powers were invoked, troops were displaced but kept mainly out of sight, volunteers for running the public services were recruited, and order was maintained without too much provocation. The Government spokesmen were cautious and moderate in the main. When, for instance, on 5 May, Sir W. Joynson-Hicks announced the terms of the emergency regulations, he justified their content by reference to similar acts of the Labour Government in 1924. When Mr. Baldwin broadcast to the nation he adopted a conciliatory tone, while at the same time emphasizing the constitutional aspect of the strike. He said:

> I do not believe that any honest person can doubt that my whole desire is to raise and not to lower the wages of every worker. . . . I want to repeat, therefore, that the Government is not fighting about wages at

[1] General Secretary of the Associated Society of Locomotive Engineers and Firemen, a member of the General Council, and a Member of Parliament.

[2] Hansard, vol. 195, 5 May 1926.

[3] 'Narrative of the General Strike of 1926', by D. H. Robertson (*Economic Journal*, September 1926, p. 384).

all . . . it is fighting because, while the negotiations were still in progress, the Trades Union Council declared a General Strike in order to try to force Parliament to bend to its will. . . . The Trades Union Council declares that this is merely an industrial dispute. But their method of helping the miners is to fight the Government and attack the community. . . . The General Strike must be called off absolutely and without reserve. The mining industry dispute can then be settled. . . .

The Government did not even pronounce about the legality of the strike. On 6 May, Sir John Simon, a lawyer and former Liberal Attorney General, announced to the House of Commons that the General Strike was illegal. 'Every trade union leader', he said, 'who has advised and promoted that course of action is liable in damages to the uttermost farthing of his personal possessions.' [1] Simon's opinion carried much weight, though it was thoroughly disputed by Sir Henry Slesser. [2] When, on 10 May, the Home Secretary was asked whether the Government had considered the legality of the strike, he replied that the question was being examined. The next day Mr. Justice Astbury, a Chancery Judge, declared that the strike was illegal, but the Government did not exploit the ruling. Rumours spread about the Government's intentions. For instance, it was said that the strike leaders were to be arrested, but at no time were arrests seriously contemplated. [3] The determination of the few to end the strike by bold and dramatic action got no further than the Cabinet room.

Only the *British Gazette*, the Government strike bulletin edited by Mr. Churchill, gave public expression to an intemperate attitude. Churchill had been given this job by Baldwin to keep him occupied and relatively harmless. [4] The *British Gazette* repeated many times the cry that the General Strike was an attack on the constitution. On 8 May it went further and stated: 'All ranks of the armed forces of the Crown are hereby notified that any action which they may find it necessary to take in an honest endeavour to aid the Civil Power will receive, both now and afterwards, the full support of His Majesty's Government.' Even King George V protested to the War Office about this unnecessarily provocative statement. [5]

The solidarity of the strike also raised problems for the General Council. It was not enough just to withdraw men from work; they had to be kept from work with constant justification, disciplined and not allowed to idle. They had to know the pattern of strike activity; where their weaknesses lay and how they could be overcome. It was

---

[1] Hansard, vol. 195, col. 585, 6 May 1926.   [2] ibid., 10 May 1926.
[3] Lord Waverley (interview with writer).   [4] ibid.
[5] *King George V*, by Harold Nicolson, p. 418.

necessary, then, for the General Council to construct a nation-wide strike organization. The General Council had made no plans before the last week in April, so it had to improvise. The central direction of the strike organization was entrusted to a committee run by Ernest Bevin and A. A. Purcell.

There were inevitable defects in the strike organization owing to its hurried construction. But its most serious defect arose from the weakness of the strike leadership. An effective organization could only be constructed by men who wanted to win the strike, and few members of the General Council had this intention. The General Council set about controlling activities in the provinces more from the desire to contain the strike and restrain the strikers than to co-ordinate their activities.[1] From the outset some members of the General Council were afraid that the solidarity of the strikers would be exploited by extremists. The organization tended to be centralized without adequate channels of communication. In order to keep the strikers occupied, the General Council suggested only that sports and entertainments should be arranged for them, yet it knew that morale could only be maintained by engaging as many of the men as possible in prosecuting the strike; in perfecting local organizations and picketing. A strike is a class struggle, not a game. The General Council's half-heartedness in its picketing arrangements permitted the Government to organize a relatively effective 'volunteer' road transport system. Clearly, the determination of the leaders came nowhere near to matching that of the strikers.

Some General Council members moved to settle the strike behind the scenes and there was no end to the would-be mediators who wanted to meet them.[2] 'The Parliamentary Executive of the Labour Party met each day of the strike,' Philip Snowden wrote, 'ready to use any influence they might have to bring the dispute to an end under conditions which would save the Trade Union Council from abject surrender.'[3] The most important mediator was Sir Herbert Samuel, who had been chairman of the Royal Commission on the Coal Industry earlier in the year. Samuel failed completely to get the Government to support his intervention but, even so, he succeeded in meeting the General Council for discussions in the house of Sir Abe Bailey, the South African mining magnate and friend of J. H. Thomas.[4] Samuel drafted a memorandum which the General Council regarded 'as a satisfactory basis for the re-opening of

[1] cf. Symons, op. cit., p. 64.
[2] See *Laughter in the Next Room*, by Osbert Sitwell, pp. 199–243, for some illustrations.
[3] *An Autobiography*, by Philip Snowden, vol. II, p. 731.
[4] Samuel gives an account of the discussions in his *Memoirs*, pp. 183–192.

negotiations', but the miners refused to accept it. On the morning of 11 May, Samuel wrote a long letter to the Prime Minister describing his unsuccessful attempt to mediate but the letter was not sent, for in the afternoon he heard that the General Council was on the point of acting independently of the miners. That night the General Council found the Miners' Federation executive to be uncompromising and decided finally to break with them. On 12 May at 12.20 p.m. a General Council deputation told the Prime Minister that the strike was ended. No guarantees were received about resuming negotiations with the miners or about victimization. The end was unconditional.

There was much bewilderment and anger amongst the strikers at the decision of the General Council, for although some union leaders sought to justify their behaviour by statements that the strikers were weakening, they had little supporting evidence.[1] The strike could have been carried on for a longer period. It would not have been wholly successful, of course, for the Government had committed itself too deeply to defend the constitution to give way. But a written assurance could, perhaps, have been obtained which committed the Government to resume negotiations with the miners at the end of the strike and which protected strikers on their return to work. This would have been a substantial concession compared with the actual ending.

The end did not come because the strike was weakening, or because the union leaders feared arrest or were frightened by the statement that the strike was illegal. It came because the General Council had entered a strike which it was afraid of winning. This, and not its conduct of the strike, was the General Council's basic mistake. As soon as the mistake was realized, the General Council grasped the first plausible excuse it could find to escape.[2]

The miners remained in dispute, though their position was hopeless. Mr. Baldwin sent proposals for a settlement to their leaders on 14 May. These included wage reductions and district settlements, but they were treated in the same manner as earlier proposals. Some parts of the proposals were also rejected by the mine owners, who added:

> The proposals of 14 May, calculated as they are to limit freedom of administration, will not be helpful in securing the increased efficiency of the industry. It will be impossible to continue the conduct of the industry under private enterprise unless it is accorded the same freedom from political interference as is enjoyed by other industries.[3]

---

[1] cf. Symons, op. cit., pp. 207–212.   [2] See also Chapter X, p. 168.
[3] Arnot, op. cit., p. 462.

The Government responded to this censure by contracting out of the coal dispute, except when it could show preference for the mine owners. It renewed the emergency regulations each month as the lock-out continued. Occasionally it offered to bring the parties together, knowing full well what differences divided them. At the end of June 1926 it forsook any semblance of impartiality by introducing a Parliamentary Bill to increase the miners' hours from seven to eight, thus achieving for the coal owners one of the objects of their lock-out. The dispute was not closed until the end of November 1926, when the miners returned to work, defeated, as in 1921. The Miners' Federation was broken and bankrupt. That was one measure of the Government's success.

STRIKES SINCE 1945

The Government employed more industrial labour after 1945 than ever before but not until 1955 was it actually faced with a national strike of its employees. This was when the Associated Society of Locomotive Engineers and Firemen went on strike from 28 May until 15 June 1955, over wage differentials. An award of a Court of Inquiry in January 1955 had narrowed the gap between the wages of the lower-paid workers and those of the engine drivers and firemen. The National Union of Railwaymen accepted the award but the Associated Society of Locomotive Engineers and Firemen rejected it. The strike was not supported by the other railway unions; indeed, it was in part an inter-union dispute and at no time could the Minister of Labour, Sir Walter Monckton, persuade the two operatives' unions to meet together to discuss a settlement.

The strike was treated seriously by the Government. The Prime Minister, Mr. Anthony Eden, broadcast on the first day that the Government would do all it could to protect the nation from the worst effects of the strike. A state of emergency was proclaimed, though there was no question of troops being used.[1] The right of the railwaymen to strike, however, was not questioned by the Government. It did not call it an attack upon the sovereignty of the Government. Its representatives acted primarily as conciliators and it was difficult to discern the Government's financial interest in the strike. A settlement was reached at the Ministry of Labour when the union and the British Transport Commission agreed to submit their differences to an independent arbitrator.

The Government at this time still retained some of the trade union goodwill which had been accorded to Sir Winston Churchill's

[1] *The Times*, 1 June 1955.

Conservative Government after 1951 and its motives were not seriously questioned. The squabble between the railway unions diverted attention from the Government's responsibility.[1]

Conditions had changed considerably by the time of the next official strike against the Government as an employer. Relations between the Government and trade unions were strained and no matter how hard the Government tried it could not detach itself from the dispute.

The London Bus Strike, 1958

Early in 1957 resolutions were passed in London bus garages calling for substantial wage increases. The resolutions were not embodied in a wage claim until 17 October, when the Finance and General Purposes Committee of the Transport and General Workers' Union agreed to submit a demand to the London Transport Executive for a pay increase of 25*s.* a week for all London busmen.

This wage claim affected the Government in three ways. First, because London Transport was a part of nationalized transport, the Government held the ultimate financial responsibility for it. Secondly, the Government was applying an anti-inflationary policy and was rejecting wage claims from others in its employ. Thirdly, the claim was part of what seemed to be a leap-frogging process with provincial busmen which was inflationary.[2] The act of submitting the claim appeared as a challenge to the Government.[3]

The claim was presented on 1 November. It was based on the increase in living costs which had occurred since the last pay increase, the skill and hazards of the work, and the relationship of London bus wages with wages in other industries. The London Transport Executive rejected the claim outright after consultation with the British Transport Commission. The busmen who, the union's assistant general secretary said, had lost faith in arbitration after recent Government pronouncements on wage claims,[4] instructed their representatives to go back to the London Transport Executive to press again for an offer.

The union leaders were in a difficult position. They were making

[1] See Chapter V for a description of the Government's responsibility to the railwaymen.

[2] In July 1957 there was a strike of provincial busmen who wanted to reduce the wage differential between themselves and the London busmen. The strike ended when the provincial busmen were awarded a pay increase of 11*s.* a week by the National Arbitration Tribunal. The strike had a direct bearing on the London demands, for if the London busmen were granted 25*s.* a week extra the differential would be wider than previously. The object of the strike would have been defeated.

[3] *Manchester Guardian*, 18 October 1957.

[4] *The Times*, 10 December 1957.

the pace in current wage claims with one which was large and unlikely to be popular with the public; and they were confronted by a Government which was unusually rigid in its attitude. They knew, too, that a strike was a likely outcome of the dispute.

The claim was rejected for the second time on 8 January 1958. Both parties then approached the Chief Industrial Commissioner, Sir Wilfred Neden, to discuss their difficulties. The Government had so far been backstage in the negotiations. Now it appeared as the conciliator but there was not much it could do. The London Transport Executive wanted the claim deferred but, failing this, preferred arbitration; the busmen wanted the claim to go on and declined arbitration.

The busmen were not of one opinion. The resignation of some busmen from the Communist Party over the Russian intervention in Hungary in 1956 had made them eligible to stand for office in the Transport and General Workers' Union. A few returned to the posts they had held before the union proscribed Communists from holding office. They were respected and powerful advocates of militant action. On the other hand there were rank-and-file leaders who had arisen in the interim who advised moderation. The second group showed its authority at a busmen's delegate conference on 17 January when a motion that the claim should be put before a committee of investigation to be appointed by the Minister of Labour was approved by 110 votes to 20.

The London Transport Executive agreed to accept a committee of investigation and Mr. Macleod, the Minister of Labour, was informed. At this point the issue was taken up by the Cabinet and examined in relation to the Government's wage policy. It was understood that differences of opinion within the Cabinet about what action to take delayed the announcement of a Government decision. On 24 January 1958, however, the Cabinet met and later in the day the Chief Industrial Commissioner sent a letter to the union giving the decision of the Minister of Labour. The letter stated:

> ... In the circumstances the Minister finds great difficulty in setting up a committee, the purpose of which would be to deal with the wages situation in London in isolation from the rest of the road passenger transport industry. He has, therefore, decided it would be inappropriate to set up a committee for the purpose suggested.
>
> If all the parties concerned were to request a more general inquiry into the wages situation in the whole of the road passenger industry, the Minister would not wish to rule out such a possibility. It is realized that other interests would be involved in such a wider inquiry.[1]

[1] *The Times*, 27 January 1958.

There was a spontaneous union protest at the terms of the letter, for it had been assumed that the appointment of the committee was a mere formality. This assumption was made because the Chief Industrial Commissioner had been present at the meeting between the parties when the proposal for a committee had been made and accepted. He was considered to have given it at least his tacit approval. The union rejected the Minister's suggestion for a wider inquiry. The union leaders were annoyed because they felt they had been placed in a difficult position with their members, who had been persuaded to shelve their militancy for a course of action which had been rejected. The implications of the decision must have been clear to the Government. It was, it seemed, prepared to risk a strike.

Mr. Macleod insisted that he had taken the decision on his own responsibility, although he had consulted some of his senior colleagues. In any case the decision was a Government one and it brought the Government into direct conflict with the union. The question before the union was whether the Government had a right to impose its wages policy on the union any more than a private employer had. It decided unequivocally that it had not.

When the busmen met to discuss the Minister's decision on 3 February a motion demanding a strike was narrowly lost.[1] The union officials were opposed to strike action, but the men's negotiating committee was divided so strongly that it was unable to make a firm recommendation to the delegate conference. Mr. Cousins asked the delegates to submit their claim to arbitration by the Industrial Court and in this he was supported by some of the ablest rank and file busmen. After a loud and acrimonious discussion the proposal for arbitration was accepted by 92 votes to 40, but only on condition that nothing but a 'fair' award would be accepted.

The decision was welcomed by the Government. The Industrial Court met on 24 February and heard the arguments of both sides. The union case was similar to that presented to the London Transport Executive in November. The employer's argument was that it could not finance a wage increase without increasing fares, and to increase fares would accentuate a decline in the demand for London Transport services. The number of passengers on London Passenger Transport services had fallen by 17·1 per cent between 1950 and 1958. At the end of 1956 the Executive had an accumulated deficit of about £16 million.[2] The Court made its award on 11 March. It gave the

---

[1] Motions at a busmen's conference can only be carried if at least two-thirds of the delegates are in favour. On this occasion 83 were in favour of the motion and 48 were against it—that is the motion received 5 votes short of the required majority.

[2] L.T.E. statement, quoted in *Manchester Guardian*, 26 February 1958.

drivers and conductors employed on buses and trolleybuses in the Central Road Services of the London Transport Executive an increase of 8*s*. 6*d*. a week and rejected the claim for other sections of London Transport.[1] 34,000 of the labour force of 47,600 were to benefit from the award.

The Government, through the Minister of Transport, immediately made it clear that if the award were implemented the money, about £1 million, would have to come from economies and increased efficiency and not from increased fares. Mr. Cousins and the London busmen's negotiating committee opposed the award because it did not apply to the maintenance and country service workers and because, in any case, they thought it was inadequate. They approached the London Transport Executive for a revision of the award but made no progress. On 17 March the talks reached a deadlock. The next step depended on the decision of the busmen's delegate conference called for 24 March.

A few days before the conference was held Mr. Cousins voiced his opinion about the activities of the Government. He said that the union would not allow any circumstances to deflect it from protecting the interests of members who were adversely affected by the Government's actions. 'We shall not, of course, seek conflict,' he added. 'We believe that . . . one ought to be able to settle most problems without resort to the withdrawal of labour, but that can be done only if two sides think in that way. We are not prepared to accept that the price of peace in industry is our acceptance of policies with which we fundamentally disagree.'[2]

The London busmen were disgruntled but disciplined. There were no unofficial strikes for the negotiating committee held the initiative. The delegates at the conference unanimously rejected the Industrial Court award and asked the general executive council for plenary powers to take every step necessary to achieve an increase of 10*s*. 6*d*. for all staff covered by the claim. At its meeting on 2 April the union's Finance and General Purposes Committee gave the busmen plenary powers and decided to call a strike for 4 May.

While discussions about the Industrial Court Award were going on there were signs of unrest on the railways. The Railway Staff National Tribunal met on 17 March to consider a railwaymen's claim which the British Transport Commission had rejected, and in anticipation of an unfavourable award railwaymen in some parts of the country were preparing for strike action. The Manchester district council of the National Union of Railwaymen, representing 23,000

---

[1] Industrial Court Award 2680.
[2] In a speech at Bristol on 22 March (*Manchester Guardian*, 24 March 1958).

workers, set up a strike committee in readiness. Representatives from all the London branches of the union called for a national strike if their claim was rejected. The Tribunal's findings were not known when the busmen took their strike decision. They were published on 10 April and rejected the railwaymen's claim.

It was too early, the general secretary of the National Union of Railwaymen said, to talk of a strike,[1] but some of his members were less patient. Delegates in the west of Scotland urged the union to call a national strike at midnight on 4 May if further negotiations were unhelpful. Railwaymen in the east of Scotland and in the Manchester area also wanted to take strike action. It seemed possible that the railwaymen and the London busmen would strike together.

The Government made a distinction between the two disputes. It did not rule out further negotiations with the railway unions; it simply repeated Mr. Thorneycroft's policy of the previous October, that if the Transport Commission granted a wage increase it would have to find the money from its own resources or economies. The representatives of the three railway unions met the chairman of the British Transport Commission again and together they talked with the Prime Minister, were shown around the garden of No. 10 Downing Street, and admired the Prime Minister's magnolia tree. Mr. Cousins was not privileged with such high-level negotiations. The Government adopted an uncompromising attitude over the busmen's case. 'Voluntary arbitration by the Industrial Court', Mr. Macleod stated, 'has always rightly been regarded as the final stage in the settlement of a dispute. . . . I cannot take any action which would have as its object a variation of the Industrial Court Award.' [2]

The chairman of the London Transport Executive, Sir John Elliot, had said on 2 April: 'We will apply the award, the whole award, and nothing but the award.' His attitude, however, was not so rigid as that of the Government. Later in April he spoke of re-examining in the autumn the wage rates of the grades to whom the award gave nothing, and just before the strike he said he was willing to look at the wages of the Green Line drivers, who were in that group, earlier than the autumn, perhaps in July.

The union offered concessions too. First it substituted its demand for an increase of 25s. a week by one of 10s. 6d. a week. In the week before the strike Mr. Cousins stated that the union would be prepared to accept a redistribution of the total cost of the Industrial Court's award so that all grades would receive an increase of 6s. 6d. Sir John Elliot rejected this because he considered it would lead to

---

[1] *The Times*, 11 April 1958.
[2] ibid., 17 April 1958.

other claims. The Central London busmen also rejected the suggestion. They wanted a reasonable wage increase as well as an equitable
one and they were prepared to strike for it.

The 48,000 London busmen and bus conductresses solidly supported the strike call. On the first day no buses ran in London, as
only four drivers and five conductors reported for work. Although
the workers had been warned by Mr. Cousins that the strike would
most probably be a long one the strikers' morale was high. But a
solid strike and a high morale were not enough.

In a strike involving the Government the attitude of the public
plays an important part in determining the issue, for the Government,
more than private employers, is responsive to public demands.
Where the public are directly inconvenienced by the strike the strikers
cannot expect to get sympathy easily. But it can be obtained by a
judicious exposition of the trade union case, by exemplary strike
behaviour and, sometimes, by an unbroken display of unity.

The Transport and General Workers' Union made no obvious
effort to gain public sympathy for the London busmen. It adopted
the attitude normally adopted by British trade unions that if the
workers' case is sound it will not need publicizing. But a case often
has to be proved sound and it has to appear to be reasonable.
Publicity may be necessary to fulfil both of these tasks. The railwaymen in the 1919 strike showed how true this was. The Government,
with its pronouncements on the sanctity of arbitration awards and
its expressions of concern about the community's interest, seemed to
have the public on its side. It certainly had the support of most of
the national press.

When the London busmen first went on strike they inconvenienced
many thousands of normal bus travellers. The inconvenience was
short-lived for many, because London passenger transport was part
of a transport system. When it ceased to operate, its former passengers walked short distances, used cars or transferred to the
Underground railway. The lack of serious inconvenience to the
public strengthened the Government's hand, because it reduced
the pressure for a compromise settlement.

Mr. Cousins did not help the strikers' case by making the issue
into a political one. Instead of emphasizing the Government's
responsibility as an employer and stating that it did not matter
what the Government's politics were its responsibilities remained
unaltered, he continued to criticize the Government's policy.[1] The

[1] On the day the strike began he said: 'We are . . . not prepared to go backwards
at the behest or instruction of a government not of our political feeling.' He added
that the London busmen were fighting the fight for all trade unionists (*Manchester
Guardian*, 5 May 1958).

issue was taken to the floor of the House of Commons with his encouragement. On the first day of the strike the leaders of the Parliamentary Labour Party tabled a motion which deplored 'the refusal of the Minister of Labour, in pursuance of the economic and industrial policy of Her Majesty's Government, to attempt to bring about a settlement of the London bus dispute, which is causing great inconvenience and hardship to the general public'. None of Mr. Cousins' predecessors in the Transport and General Workers' Union would have countenanced such a move. The House of Commons, in the minds of Bevin and Deakin, was not a place in which an industrial issue could be soberly examined. The debate on 8 May confirmed this opinion.

The Government was under greater pressure from other sources than the Labour Party. It was disturbed by the possibility of a railway dispute which it could not readily settle without risking offending the Conservative back-bench M.P.s who were insisting that Mr. Thorneycroft's policy of not financing wage increases should be followed. The formal negotiations in the railway dispute had ended when, unexpectedly, Mr. Macleod invited the representatives of the three railway unions to confer with him and persuaded them to defer taking action over their claims for four days to enable the Cabinet to discuss the dispute. The Cabinet was having second thoughts. There were rumblings of dissatisfaction from the rank and file among the railwaymen and signs that the London busmen were contemplating calling on other members of the union to support them.

The Cabinet decided to offer the railwaymen a pay increase of 3 per cent as from the end of June.[1] Two railway unions, the Associated Society of Locomotive Engineers and Firemen and the Transport Salaried Staffs' Association, quickly accepted the offer. The National Union of Railwaymen, under pressure from its militant members, went back to the British Transport Commission for an improved offer but it failed to get anything and finally, on 15 May, accepted the offer. Thus the railway dispute ceased to be an active issue for the time being. There was a little dissension among Conservative back-bench M.P.s at the manner of the settlement but it petered out. The London busmen were isolated.

The Government was in no hurry to settle the bus strike. When, on 5 May, the Minister of Labour was asked in the House of Commons whether he proposed to bring both sides in the dispute together, he replied that he would decide when the time was opportune to intervene. Eleven days later, he said that he would be ready to step

---

[1] The full settlement included a promise of a major inquiry into wages at a date to be decided.

in if he saw 'a single chink of light'. Exploratory talks between the two parties were initiated by the Chief Industrial Commissioner, on 20 May, after consultation with Mr. Macleod, but no progress was made. The Government remained inactive, the exploratory talks apart, until the end of May.

The strike was uneventful for the first three weeks. The General Council attempted to give moral support to the busmen, and at the same time satisfy Mr. Cousins that press reports implying that some members of the General Council had no sympathy for the strikers were unfounded, by stating on 7 May that the 'Government policy has brought London's buses to a standstill. Having mismanaged the economy, the Government has chosen the pay claim of London's busmen as an opportunity to put pressure on a public employer to conform to its policy of holding down wages. . . .' [1] Verbal support came from some unions and financial support from others. There were rumours that Underground railway workers in London were contemplating unofficial action, but they came to nothing.

The Oil Trade Section of the union took action to cut off the oil supplies of coaches which were running services considered to be 'black', but it experienced difficulties in making its action effective. The union attempted during the first three weeks to publicize its case by distributing leaflets explaining the strikers' case, but the public seemed to have lost interest in the strike. The union's strike bulletin on 22 May aptly mentioned the 'silent determination' of the strikers to win. The General Council issued on 21 May an appeal for financial support to unions affiliated to the Trades Union Congress, but only after some hesitation. [2]

The strike came out of the doldrums through the impatience of the busmen's negotiating committee. The committee, at its meeting on 24 May, decided to ask the railway unions whether they considered that the effect of the strike was being minimized by an excessive use of the Underground railway. It also agreed to call together the senior full-time officials of the union who dealt with petrol distribution in London and the generating stations supplying power to the Underground railways, to see whether they could make the strike more effective. The railway unions refused to take any action to support the strikers. Within the union preparations were made to extend the strike. On 28 May Mr. Cousins told Sir Vincent Tewson, the general secretary of the Trades Union Congress, that the possibility that

---

[1] T.U.C. Report, 1958, p. 130.
[2] ibid., p. 131. It was suggested on the General Council that to support a local strike involving a comparatively small number of workers might create 'a dangerous precedent'.

the strike would be extended to London petrol tanker drivers and workers employed in the generating stations if it were not settled by 31 May, was greater than the union had so far disclosed to the press.[1] He asked for the General Council to intervene either by effecting a negotiated settlement or by co-ordinating an extension of the strike.

The General Council met on 29 May and after hearing Mr. Cousins state that they could not leave the busmen 'to fight the battle of the Trade Union Movement alone any longer', agreed to send a deputation to the Minister of Labour. Mr. Macleod made no concessions to the deputation so the next day it appealed to the Prime Minister to intervene.

As soon as it appeared that the strike might be extended to oil-tanker drivers the Government took measures to maintain oil supplies. The Ministry of Fuel and Power on 30 May issued a statement advising motorists to conserve petrol and to use cars only for essential purposes; while the War Office stopped the weekend leave of 6,000 troops, most of whom were drivers. The Prime Minister explained that these decisions were not intended to be provocative but were simply precautions.[2]

Mr. Macmillan met representatives of the General Council to discuss the strike on the same day as the Government precautionary measures were announced. He outlined the terms on which he thought the strike could be ended. They were: the acceptance of 8*s.* 6*d.* for the Central London busmen, the inclusion of the 720 Green Line drivers in this settlement, and negotiations to be resumed to fix a definite date for the review of the wages of those still excluded from the settlement. Thus the Government was now prepared to discard the Industrial Court Award though it did not say so explicitly. The Green Line drivers were to be offered an immediate but undefined wage increase.

Some members of the General Council were sufficiently impressed with these terms to prevail upon Mr. Cousins to resume negotiations with the London Transport Executive. Negotiations went on for two days. Both sides made slight concessions. Sir John Elliot agreed to review the pay of the sections excluded from the award on the morning of a return to work and to complete the review within a month. The busmen's negotiating committee was prepared to accept a token increase of 4*s.* a week for the workers concerned in the review until the review was completed. The concessions were not enough and the negotiations ended on 1 June. Afterwards Sir John Elliot said: 'My attitude is a tough one. I feel that public opinion is behind

---

[1] ibid.   [2] *The Times*, 31 May 1958.

me and I do not care for surrender. The strike is a flop. London is managing. Otherwise Mr. Cousins would not want to expand it.' [1] The prospect of a negotiated settlement seemed more remote than ever.

Representatives of the General Council saw the Prime Minister again on 3 June but his attitude was unchanged. On the following day the General Council held a special meeting to discuss the strike. The question before them, posed by Mr. Cousins, was 'how soon was this strike going to be developed into something that somebody was going to take notice of'. [2] The strike, he said, was getting into the position where it must be extended or collapse. If it was extended it would inevitably involve the unions of General Council members. What had the General Council to say about this?

Views were expressed about extending the strike and about the nature of the conflict with the Government. A decision to extend the strike, Mr. Cousins was told, could only be made by the executives of the separate unions, not by the General Council. The members of the General Council were convinced that an extension of the strike would transform it into a wide conflict with political implications. They

> disagreed with Mr. Cousins in that they did not think that the wages and standards of living of all workers in all industries depended on the outcome of the busmen's strike or that a determined threat to extend the strike would make the Government take a different attitude towards wage increases in general. On the contrary they thought that an extension of the strike, which would necessarily bring the unions concerned into direct conflict with the Government, would end in a failure which would be disastrous for the whole Trade Union Movement. . . . [3]

The advice tendered to the busmen was not to extend the strike to other groups of workpeople.

Although Mr. Cousins disagreed with the General Council, he accepted its advice. He opposed a majority recommendation by the busmen's negotiating committee that the strike should be extended and then advised bus delegates against voting for an extension. The delegates by 71 to 60 votes opposed an extension but approved a motion to stay on strike. [4]

Sir John Elliot had said on 1 June that the review of the wages of those excluded from the award could be completed within a month, that is by 1 July. When the General Council representatives saw Mr. Macleod on 12 June he reiterated Sir John Elliot's offer and terms, thus reducing the time-lag to two weeks. He said that if an

---

[1] *The Times*, 2 June 1958.
[3] ibid., pp. 136–137.
[2] T.U.C. Report, 1958, p. 136.
[4] On 6 June 1958.

increase were conceded it would be payable from 2 July. Moreover, he added that the union knew that the excluded busmen would get an increase and were aware of the limits within which the increase would fall.[1] When Mr. Cousins was told what Mr. Macleod had said he retorted, 'Why did not Sir John Elliot say so.' Nothing more precise was said to Mr. Cousins and a chance of ending the strike was passed by.

It seemed that the Government was going to succeed. Mr. Cousins told a bus delegate conference on 13 June that the union had been placed in a difficult position by the attitude of the General Council and by the refusal of the Government to allow the London Transport Executive to make an improved offer. With the consent of the negotiating committee he advised the delegates to vote to return to work. They accepted a motion, by 94 votes to 32, which stated that in view 'of the forces ranged against us, the conference is of the opinion that to continue the struggle would not be in the interests of the members. . . .' No mention was made in the motion about the precise terms on which the strikers were to return to work. The resolution was referred to the garages to be voted on.

The strikers rejected the advice of the delegate conference and surprised everyone, even the union leaders. Sixty-four garages voted to continue the strike and fifty-four garages voted to end it. Detailed voting figures would have shown a more pronounced determination to prolong the strike, for in most garages which voted to end the strike there were large minorities in favour of carrying on. The minorities in the garages which voted to continue the strike were not so large. Two factors influenced the voting: first, dissatisfaction with the proposal to return to work without a specific and improved offer; and, secondly, indignation at the temerity of the London Transport Executive in posting notices in the garages announcing cuts in the services and revised schedules, on the assumption that the strike was ending.

The busmen's decision introduced a new element into the strike. The strike had been so quiet and orderly that the mood of the strikers had been ignored. The busmen's negotiating committee had seemed to have full control of the situation and all attention had been focused on its behaviour. The decision of the negotiating committee had been influenced by factors not associated with the terms of the return to work, for instance the need to conserve the union's resources and the strategic value of a united return to work. These factors carried little weight with the ordinary workers. For them the terms of the return to work were of paramount importance. They made it clear

[1] T.U.C. Report, 1958, p. 52.

that they had not suffered privation to achieve an illusory tactical victory, and in doing so evoked respect even from people who disagreed with them.

The Government and the London Transport Executive had to decide whether they wanted to prolong the strike indefinitely or offer the busmen more favourable terms for a return to work. They chose the latter method. The London Transport Executive could not afford an indefinite stoppage. It was losing about £1 million a week in passenger receipts.[1] It was not spending, of course, on wages and fuel, but it was losing profit and its vehicles were deteriorating through standing idle. The loss of profit on London Transport meant that the British Transport Commission was losing money on all of its main activities.

After the vote Sir John Elliot, whilst not stipulating a precise wage increase for the busmen excluded from the award, did promise an increase which would not leave them 'in an unfavourable position' compared with other staff employed by the London Transport Executive. It was reported that in his conversations with the union leaders Sir John Elliot went further than this and said that the increase would 'closely approximate' to the figure of 8*s*. 6*d*.[2] With this concession the strikers, on 20 June, voted by a large majority to return to work. The strike had lasted almost seven weeks.

The strike ended with the union maintaining the principle of something for all and with the reasonable expectation that the something would not be much lower than the 10*s*. 6*d*. a week demanded at the beginning of the strike. After such a long strike it was meaningless to talk of victory, but the union could point with satisfaction to the settlement, the high morale and independence of the strikers, and the disciplined return to work. The Government, on the other hand, could say that the Industrial Court award had been accepted in so far as a return to work had been agreed upon before the actual increase for those excluded from the award had been determined.

The subsequent negotiations were unpleasant for the union. When the strike settlement was announced Sir John Elliot remarked that the losses from the strike and the cost of wage increases would amount to more than could be obtained from economies made and planned so far. The London Transport Executive, he said, would have to apply for more 'headroom' in fares, that is, for fare increases. On the same day Mr. Harold Watkinson, the Minister of Transport, made a speech in which he said that the Government policy had not changed; that 'the London Transport Executive are fully aware that any settlement has to be held by savings, cuts, or economies within

[1] *The Times*, 31 May 1958.   [2] *Manchester Guardian*, 20 June 1958.

the strict limits laid down last autumn. . . .' [1] The next day Mr. R. A. Butler, the Home Secretary, spoke of the inflationary effect of an increase in fares. Other members of the Government took exception to Sir John Elliot's statement about fares. The labour sub-committee of the Conservative's 1922 Committee in the House of Commons objected strongly to the statement and obtained from Mr. Macleod an assurance that fares would not be raised.

In the face of this criticism Sir John Elliot had to negotiate the wages of the busmen who were not given a wage increase in the strike settlement. He offered the Green Line bus drivers an increase of 7s. 6d. a week and the others 5s. a week. The offer was turned down by the union as being inadequate and because it 'departed so much from the spirit of the discussions between Sir John and Mr. Cousins before the strike ended'.[2] The offer, made on 1 July, was finally accepted on 17 July. In between there was much recrimination about unfulfilled assurances and misinterpretations. The union leaders appealed to the Chief Industrial Commissioner to intervene but he refused. The union could not call another strike on the same issue as before. It had been, it felt, the victim of renewed political pressure.

THE MAIN CHARACTERISTICS

A strike between a trade union and a private employer is normally a trial of economic strength. This is not so when the Government is the employer; if it were the Government would never lose. The most important factor in determining the outcome of a strike against the Government as an employer is the public impression created during the strike. The Government in a political democracy is normally susceptible to public pressure, and if opinion during a strike turns against it then it is likely to make concessions.

The issue turns then on what determines the attitude of the public. In Britain people believe in a system of selecting and controlling a Government rather than in a Government as such. Consequently they react against anything which is likely to damage the system and thus they protect the Government from unconstitutional pressure, such as strike action. The Government as an employer, however, has never been accorded any special rights which private employers have not possessed, so that it has always been considered permissible for Government employees to protest about their conditions of work to the extent of striking.

---

[1] *The Times*, 21 June 1958.
[2] Stated by Mr. Harry Nicholas, assistant general secretary of the T. & G.W.U. (*Manchester Guardian*, 2 July 1958).

T.U.G.—P

The problem, therefore, is to distinguish between strikes which constitute a political challenge and strikes which are purely industrial protests by Government workers. It may be said that the problem should not be difficult to resolve because by definition a strike against the Government as an employer is a strike about employment conditions. The difficulty arises because strikes involving the Government never appear at the outset as uncomplicated industrial issues, even if they are. Unless unions take special steps to ensure that there can be no doubt that their motives are purely industrial, the public is likely to get an impression that the issue is political and it will place its support firmly on the side of the Government. Trade unions stand no chance against such odds. The responsibility for complicating the issues rests with both sides.

In every strike against it as an employer the Government has tried to avoid its responsibilities by treating the strike as a threat to its authority, as an attack on the welfare of the community, or simply by denying that it is the employer. The national railway strike was called in 1919 after negotiations over wages had broken down between the National Union of Railwaymen and the Government. As soon as the strike started the Government claimed it was an attack on the life of the community. Its attitude was in part due to the political atmosphere in 1919, but no one in the Government, least of all Lloyd George, seriously believed that J. H. Thomas would lead such an attack. The Government reacted similarly but with more justification during each of the coal stoppages. On the day the strike of railway engine drivers and firemen started in 1955 the Prime Minister, Mr. Anthony Eden, said the Government would do all it could to protect the nation from the worst effects of the strike. And during the 1958 bus strike the Prime Minister, Mr. Macmillan, just denied that the Government was a principal in the dispute. Each time the Government viewed its role in broad, sweeping terms as if it were always above petty industrial differences. It regarded itself as the protector, the mediator, the one to pronounce on the merits of a dispute.

Trade unions have helped to complicate matters by mixing their industrial claims with political issues. The Government, with its propensity to highlight the political aspect of a strike, has seized on any political content which has appeared either in a claim or in its prosecution. The miners after the First World War were the biggest culprits in this respect. In 1920 they wanted a wage increase and a price reduction; in 1921 they resisted a wage reduction and wanted a National Wages Board; and in 1926 they resisted a wage reduction and wanted a Government subsidy. The second part of each claim was construed as a political issue and alienated not only public support but also, in one instance, trade union support as well. The issue was plainly industrial during the 1958 bus strike, but it was complicated by the leaders of the strike when they attributed the dispute to the Government's economic policy. The General Council of the Trades Union Congress, normally chary of introducing political issues into industrial disputes, made the same mistake when it published its statement of support for the busmen.

If a trade union is to have a reasonable chance of success against the Government it must not only have a simple industrial issue to fight over; it must make this patently clear to the public. The 1919 railway strike illustrated how important this point was. No other British strike has ever been so successfully publicized as that one. The odds were heavily against the strikers at the beginning; then, through selective and organized publicity, not only was the charge that the strike was against the life of the community destroyed but the Government was compelled to answer the railwaymen's case. The need for trade union publicity during a strike is made greater by the fact that the Government has easy access to publicity media and is not hampered by expense.

Another way in which trade unions have assisted the Government to complicate strike issues, has been through seeking to obtain sympathetic support from workers not directly affected by the initial claims. This factor arose in some form in all except the 1955 railway strike. As soon as sympathetic action has been threatened, the Government has found justification for taking precautionary measures without provoking public protests. It has been able to talk of constitutional threats without appearing to be a blatant distorter of facts. The more widespread is the support which is promised to the workers in direct dispute, the more easily can the Government turn an industrial dispute into a political challenge. The General Strike gave the clearest possible illustration of this process of distortion. Even if the Trades Union Congress had maintained an efficient propaganda service to focus attention on the miners' grievances, it could not have countered the Government's contention that the strike was a threat to its authority. If a General Strike has any meaning at all it is as an instrument to coerce the Government, blatantly and without compunction. It has no meaning as a method of protest. This is also true of lesser degrees of sympathetic strike action directed against the Government. Unless Government workers want to jeopardize their chances of success in disputes with their employer, they must be prepared to strike alone.

It can be said, then, that a dispute between the Government and its employees is a struggle for the support of public opinion. If a trade union can reveal the Government unmistakably as an employer, and an unjust one at that, then it can win its case. If it in any way mixes its industrial aims with political issues or extends the dispute until it constitutes a threat to Government authority, then it will, in all probability, lose its case. The validity of this analysis, however, depends on there continuing to be only isolated cases of actual strikes against the Government by its employees. If for any reason there were frequent and widespread legitimate strikes against the Government, it is possible that they would have political consequences and would be treated differently.

4

TRADE UNIONS AND
LABOUR GOVERNMENTS

THE first chapter in Part IV is an introductory one dealing very briefly with the relationship between trade unions and the Labour Party before the formation of the first Labour Government. The other chapters examine the relations between trade unions and each of the Labour Governments. An attempt is made in them to reveal the main features of the relationship; to bring out the basic differences and similarities and to show why they existed.

Chapter Twelve

TRADE UNIONS AND THE
LABOUR PARTY TILL 1924

THE trade unionists who pressed for the formation of an independent political party by the trade union movement at the end of the nineteenth century had mixed motives. Some were Socialists who, in the undefined future, envisaged a working-class millennium; others feared for the legal security of trade unions; and some saw extended political action as the only means of achieving the day-to-day objectives of their unions. In 1899 the Trades Union Congress passed a resolution to call a conference of Co-operative, Socialist, Trade Union, and other working-class organizations to 'devise ways and means for the securing of an increased number of Labour Members in the next Parliament'.[1] The conference met on 27 February 1900 in London and agreed to sponsor Parliamentary candidates. Those elected to Parliament were to establish '. . . a distinct Labour group in Parliament, who shall have their own whips, and agree upon their policy . . .'[2]

The Labour Representation Committee was formed. It endorsed fifteen candidates in the 1900 general election, but only two were successful, and they differed radically in their political opinions.[3] Determined opposition to trade unions by employers and the damaging House of Lords decision in the Taff Vale case in 1901 persuaded hesitant unions to support the Labour Representation Committee. The electorate, too, gave it more support, and in the 1905 general election it had twenty-nine successful candidates. In 1906 the Labour Representation Committee was renamed the Labour Party.

The early role of the Labour Party in Parliament was as a pressure group. Its policy was to support the party which legislated in favour of the working class and to oppose the party which pursued any contrary measures. It did not possess its own coherent policy and did not regard itself as an alternative to the Government. Until 1918 the Labour Party never presented more than seventy-eight candidates in an election.

[1] See *The Origins of the Labour Party, 1880-1900*, by Henry Pelling, Chapter X, for a description of the political activities of trade unions in this period.
[2] ibid., p. 221.
[3] They were Keir Hardie and Richard Bell, general secretary of the Amalgamated Society of Railway Servants.

In February 1918 the Labour Party adopted a new constitution. Until then it was an affiliation of trade unions and socialist parties and membership could only be obtained through membership of one of those organizations. Trade unions controlled the Labour Party conferences through their large votes, and their members dominated the Parliamentary Labour Party. The new constitution retained the affiliated membership but permitted individual membership through local Labour Parties. The Labour Party aimed to become a nationally organized party.

There was trade union opposition to the new constitution, led by Tom Shaw of the United Textile Factory Workers' Association.[1]

> He wants the Labour Party [Beatrice Webb stated] to remain a close preserve of the officials of the great Unions, acting as a select group in the House making terms with either of the principal parties and securing places for leading Trade Union officials either as ministers or as permanent officials. He dislikes the advent of the ambitious middle-class politician and the intrusion of the missionary Intellectual.

A small group of trade union leaders unsuccessfully agitated for the formation of a Trade Union Labour Party at the 1918 Trades Union Congress.[2] The Independent Labour Party, on the other hand, opposed the constitution because it wanted a 'People's Party' with trade unions being absorbed into local constituency organizations. The constitution was primarily Arthur Henderson's creation. He wanted the financial support of the trade unions combined with the initiative and enthusiasm of local members. The constitution was accepted by the unions after a period of contemplation. From 1918 the composition of the Labour Party broadened and its leadership became the preserve of intellectuals.

1918 was a year of change for the Labour Party, for in June it also endorsed a comprehensive programme called 'Labour and the New Social Order', and for the first time possessed a national policy to put before the electorate.[3] When the general election was sprung on the nation in December 1918, the Labour Party was able to enter 361 candidates. Some had hopes of seeing a post-war Labour Government, but they were not based on a realistic political appraisal of the situation. The Labour Party had not significantly increased its numbers in the House of Commons since 1906; some of its leading members were unpopular because they had opposed the war; and its main political opponent, Mr. Lloyd George, was a national hero.

[1] *Diaries, 1912–1924*, by Beatrice Webb, p. 106.
[2] T.U.C. Report, 1918, p. 251.
[3] See *Fifty Years' March*, by Francis Williams, pp. 280–283, for a description of the programme.

Only fifty-seven Labour Members of Parliament were elected and the hopes of having a Labour Government in the near future were dispelled at a stroke.

The political situation altered after 1918. From the early part of 1921 unemployment became an important political factor and an election issue. In addition, the Government failed to fulfil the postwar aspirations which had figured so prominently in Lloyd George's 1918 election programme. The Labour Party increased its support in the country. It endorsed 414 candidates in the general election in November 1922 and had 142 returned successfully. The next election came quickly and unexpectedly, long before the Labour Party had recovered from the financial strain of the preceding one, for Parliament was dissolved in November 1923 to enable the Conservative Party to go to the electorate for a mandate to implement a policy of tariff protection. The election was held on 6 December and with a great effort the Labour Party put up 427 candidates: 191 of these were elected. No party emerged with a clear majority. The number of Conservative seats fell from 346 to 259, while the Liberal Party increased its representation from 117 to 159. The outcome in Parliament depended upon the attitude of the Liberal Party towards each of the other two parties. After some dithering the Liberal Party decided to support the Labour Party. On 22 January 1924, the first Labour Government was formed.[1]

When the general election took place in 1923, the Labour Party had direct contact with unions which were affiliated to it and it had an organic connection with the Trades Union Congress through the National Joint Council and three joint departments, all of which were established under a reorganization scheme in 1921. The National Joint Council consisted of three representatives from the General Council and three from the Labour Party Executive. The joint departments were for international affairs, research, and press and publicity. They were jointly financed and were controlled by committees with representatives from both bodies.

There were factors making for harmony between the Labour Party and trade unions. To start with, they both had the same broad aims and they consisted largely of the same people. Trade unionists were active at all levels of the Labour Party. Their ideas and attitudes were impressed on trade unions and the Labour Party alike. This introduced some symmetry into the relationship. The official convergence of policies was brought about by the representative Labour Party policy-making conferences.

[1] For details of its formation see *The First Labour Government*, by Richard W. Lyman, Chapters IV, V, and VI.

There were also factors making for discord. The Labour Party had an organization which was distinct from trade unions; it had developed practices and loyalties; it possessed its own staff. In consequence it tended to move under its own momentum and to reach decisions in its own peculiar way. The Labour Party conference policy decisions were interpreted by the national executives of the Trades Union Congress and the Labour Party. The membership of these two executives was not the same. It was not permitted to be the same.[1] The Labour Party Executive at that time consisted mainly of trade unionists who were not merely dutiful second-string trade union leaders but were forceful and independent politicians. And for this reason strong differences of approach to day-to-day and general short-term issues could arise between the Trades Union Congress and the Labour Party.

The Parliamentary Labour Party, constitutionally, was independent of both other bodies. Its members were to be found on the General Council of the Trades Union Congress and the Labour Party Executive. It, too, was capable of taking independent action. It was possible, therefore, for there to be three collective viewpoints within the Labour Movement on a single labour problem.

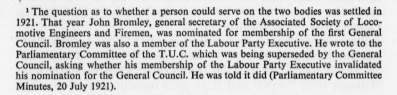

[1] The question as to whether a person could serve on the two bodies was settled in 1921. That year John Bromley, general secretary of the Associated Society of Locomotive Engineers and Firemen, was nominated for membership of the first General Council. Bromley was also a member of the Labour Party Executive. He wrote to the Parliamentary Committee of the T.U.C. which was being superseded by the General Council, asking whether his membership of the Labour Party Executive invalidated his nomination for the General Council. He was told it did (Parliamentary Committee Minutes, 20 July 1921).

Chapter Thirteen

RELATIONS WITH THE FIRST LABOUR GOVERNMENT, 1924

MOST Labour politicians and trade union leaders in 1923 expected to have a Labour Government at some stage but none anticipated having it in 1924. Even Mr. Sidney Webb, one of the most optimistic in 1923, could not envisage the Labour Party having a majority of the votes cast until 1926.[1] The next year Ramsay MacDonald, speaking at a Labour Party Conference, said, 'Had [Sidney Webb] told you that he had made a calculation or had had a vision that within seven months of his addressing you your representatives in Parliament would form the Government . . . your comments . . . would have been of the nature of "Poor old Webb" and in the evening you would have filled your glasses to drink to his memory. And yet that apparently insane miracle has happened . . .'[2]

The possibility of the Labour Party being called upon to form a Government was discussed by Labour politicians soon after the election. The most influential of them, with the exception of Arthur Henderson, were apprehensive about taking office, but considered that MacDonald ought not to refuse to form a Government if invited to do so.[3] The General Council was less exuberant about the election result than the Labour Party Executive, but it confirmed the executive's view that 'in the event of Labour being invited to form a Government, the Parliamentary Party should at once accept full responsibility of the Government of the country without compromising itself with any form of Coalition'.[4] The next day a joint meeting of the General Council and the Labour Party Executive, after being addressed by MacDonald, reassured itself that 'should he be called upon to assume high office he will in all his actions consider the well-being of the nation in seeking to apply the principles of the Labour Movement'. The trade union movement, officially, was prepared in principle to receive a minority Labour Government.

[1] At the 1923 Labour Party conference he said 'that a continuation of the rising curve of Labour votes from the 62,698 of 1900 through the 323,195 of 1906 and the 505,690 of January 1910, the 2¼ millions of 1918, and the 4¼ millions of 1922, would produce a clear majority of the total votes cast in Great Britain somewhere about 1926'. (Conference Report, 1923, p. 175.)
[2] ibid., 1924, p. 106.   [3] Beatrice Webb, op. cit., p. 255.
[4] General Council Minutes, 12 December 1923.

Government-Forming

A Labour Government had been an abstract conception until the task of actually forming a Government began. Few people had thought of it in terms of personalities they knew. There had been no period during which trade union leaders had been able to condition themselves to working with a Government composed of members of the Parliamentary Labour Party. This would not have been so important if the Parliamentary Labour Party had been a body which the unions trusted and respected. But there were few Labour Members in Parliament to whom unions would give their allegiance.

The trade union movement was divided then, as ever, into militant and non-militant factions. The militant faction was dominant. Its members regarded the moderate trade union Parliamentarians, J. R. Clynes, Arthur Henderson, and J. H. Thomas, with some contempt and much distrust. Frank Hodges was a new Member of Parliament, but he was already in disfavour with the miners; Harry Gosling and Ben Tillett, both of the Transport and General Workers' Union, were in Parliament but neither had much authority in the union. Nine members of the General Council of the Trades Union Congress were Members of Parliament, but, apart from Robert Smillie, there were no men of outstanding merit among them and even he was no longer a man of power in the Miners' Federation.[1] Some trade union Members of Parliament aroused no deep feelings in the Movement at all, but this only made it more difficult for trade union practitioners to envisage them in possession of Government authority.

Trade unions nevertheless expected to be prominently represented in the new Government. They had sponsored 101 out of the 191 members of the Parliamentary Labour Party.[2] Outside of Parliament the unions dominated the Labour Party. They largely financed it and through their preponderant share of votes at Labour Party Conferences, they determined the fate of policy issues. Fifteen of the twenty-two members of the Labour Party Executive were trade unionists, and included such men as C. T. Cramp (National Union of Railwaymen), Robert Williams (National Transport Workers' Federation), and A. J. Cook (Miners' Federation).

[1] The other members of the T.U.C. General Council in Parliament were: Miss Margaret Bondfield (chairman), A. Hayday (N.U.G.W.), A. A. Purcell (Furnishing Trades), W. Thorne (N.U.G.W.), B. Tillett (T. & G.W.U.), H. Gosling (T. & G.W.U.), B. Turner (N.U. Textile Workers), and J. H. Thomas (N.U.R.).

[2] The proportion was less than after previous elections. The Parliamentary Labour Party after the 1918 election had forty-nine trade union sponsored members out of a total membership of fifty-seven. After the 1922 election eighty-seven of the 142 successful candidates were sponsored by unions.

The Cabinet-making and general Government-forming activities of J. Ramsay MacDonald have been described elsewhere.[1] He was given the freedom to allocate the Ministerial offices as he wished because it was constitutional practice and not because his colleagues nearest in authority thought it desirable.[2] Then he retired to Lossiemouth in Scotland, unimpressed with the quality of material in the new Parliamentary Labour Party and intent on appointing non-trade unionists to all the best offices.[3]

There were twenty members in the 1924 Labour Cabinet, of whom seven were trade unionists. Only one of the seven, J. H. Thomas, was a member of the General Council. There were thirty-nine Government posts, excluding the Cabinet, and trade unionists filled seventeen of them. Two members of the General Council were among the seventeen.[4] Miss Margaret Bondfield, who was the chairman of the Trades Union Congress, became the Parliamentary Secretary to the Minister of Labour and Harry Gosling became the Minister of Transport.

Outside the Cabinet only two trade unionists, Gosling and F. O. Roberts (Typographical Association), were Ministers in charge of Departments; the rest held positions where they could exercise little influence.[5] Perhaps MacDonald made the most out of the available material. Nevertheless, according to Snowden, trade unionists resented their relatively small and uninfluential share in the Government and the inclusion in the Cabinet of men who had no record of service in the Labour Movement.[6]

Trade Union Expectations

What did trade unions expect of the Labour Government? Ideally the Labour Government should have been part of the last stage in the fulfilment of Labour aspirations. But this was not an ideal situation. It was a minority Government, continuing at the whim of Liberals, and unable to legislate for a contentious Socialist policy. It was controlled by men who were distrusted by a number of the most prominent union leaders. But with all its limitations it was a *Labour* Government and an infectious enthusiasm for it spread among rank-and-file Labour supporters.[7]

[1] See Beatrice Webb, op. cit., p. 255 et seq.; *An Autobiography* by Philip Snowden, p. 594 et seq.; Lyman, op. cit., Chapter VII, and biographies and autobiographies of contemporary Labour politicians.
[2] Snowden, op. cit., pp. 596–597.   [3] ibid., pp. 594–595 and p. 598.
[4] The members of the General Council resigned on being appointed to Government posts.
[5] A list of these Members and the Government posts they held is given in Appendix III at the end of this chapter. Robert Smillie (Miners' Federation) stated that he refused a Government post (cf. *My Life For Labour*, by Robert Smillie, p. 303).
[6] Snowden, op. cit., p. 607.   [7] Lyman, op. cit., p. 88.

Official trade union responses were restrained. The Iron and Steel Trades Confederation commented: 'A Labour Government can do much to help the workers of this country, even if it does not possess the whole-hearted support of either of the other parties. Its difficulties will commence at an early date when it has to bring in a Budget, but in the meantime the recognition of Russia and the facilitation of trade between the two countries ought to bring a considerable amount of work to unemployed work people here.'[1] The Railway Clerks' Association stated: 'It goes without saying that the Labour Party as the Government will differ from the Labour Party as the Opposition . . . the taking over of office usually brings with it more responsibility and less freedom. . . . We sincerely hope that the rank and file of the Labour Party will give the Government a fair chance and not expect too much . . .'[2] The Trades Union Congress General Council, in the middle of the year, stated: '. . . there are those who, because of the advent of the Labour Government, minimize the necessity for effective industrial organization. They take the mistaken view of regarding the political Labour Movement as an alternative, instead of an auxiliary to the Trade Union Movement. Such an attitude is extremely dangerous . . . the best safeguard for our political liberties is to be found in a vigilant and active Trade Union Movement.'[3]

In trade union matters which fell within the province of Government, unions expected greater understanding and sympathy from the Labour Government, consultation and greater freedom of access to it, and even some concessions. But their expectations were tempered by the facts of the situation. We can now see how far they were met.

The relationship between trade unions and the Labour Government mainly concerned four issues: unemployment, industrial legislation, representation on committees, and the impact of strikes on the welfare of the community.

Unemployment

Britain, in January 1924, was in the doldrums, a state of relative stability characterized by a hard core of unemployment.[4] Since the deep depression of 1921 unemployment had fallen to a fairly constant, but still high figure of 1¼ million in 1923. In the month of the general election, December 1923, it represented 10·5 per cent of the insured working population and was lower than it had been

---

[1] *Man and Metal*, January 1924.   [2] *Railway Service Journal*, February 1924.
[3] T.U.C. Report, 1924, p. 81.
[4] *Aspects of British Economic History 1918–1925*, by A. C. Pigou, Part II, Chapter IV.

since 1920. The unemployment was concentrated in the export industries: in steel manufacture, general engineering and founding, marine engineering, shipbuilding and ship repairing, and in the cotton industry.[1] Consequently it was localized and was of particular concern to certain sections of the trade union movement.

Trade unions and the Labour Party had protested continually and vigorously at the timidity and inadequacy of the previous Government's policy to reduce unemployment. After the election, but before the resignation of the Government, the Trades Union Congress and the Labour Party had joined in pressing for information about the Government's plans to reduce unemployment. The Labour Party had propounded its unemployment policy—massive public works schemes in the short run and Socialism in the long run—so that when the Labour Government was formed there was some hope of a constructive approach to the problem.[2]

The level of unemployment did fall slightly during the spring of 1924 but the lowest monthly rate still remained as high as 9·2 per cent in May and June. At no time during its brief spell in office could the Labour Government say that it had a practical policy for unemployment. This is the more surprising because the President of the Board of Trade, Mr. Sidney Webb, who had some responsibility for Government action in the matter, had reflected on the problem of unemployment for more than thirty years. He could think of nothing other than a revival of trade as a solution. His wife defended the Government's inactivity on the ground that a policy for unemployment 'could only be developed slowly through a long course of years and with great deliberation and continuity of action'.[3] The General Council, however, was impatient. On 2 May 1924 it sent a deputation to meet the Prime Minister to express 'its deep dissatisfaction with the Government's plans for dealing with the prolonged and widespread unemployment . . .'[4] Another deputation went to see him on the same matter late in May. MacDonald candidly admitted, in the House of Commons on 29 May, that it is one thing to have a policy in opposition and quite another to implement it.[5] The General Council persisted in badgering the Government. It interviewed the Cabinet Committee on Unemployment on 26 June but still got no satisfaction. The unemployment rate rose from 9·2 per cent in June to 10·8 per cent in October 1924.

---

[1] *Survey of Industrial Relations*, Report of Committee on Industry and Trade (H.M.S.O.), 1926, p. 227.

[2] cf. Lyman, op. cit., Chapter IX, for an examination of the Labour Government's unemployment policy.

[3] *Diaries 1924–1932*, pp. 28–29.   [4] T.U.C. Report, 1924, p. 111.

[5] Lyman, op. cit., p. 138.

Industrial Legislation

The main items in the Government's programme for industrial legislation were Bills for regulating hours of work and factory conditions. Within two weeks of the formation of the Government a General Council deputation informed the Minister of Labour that it wanted the Government to legislate immediately for a legal minimum working week for wage-earners. The deputation quoted various authoritative bodies, the Peace Conference of Versailles, the 1919 National Industrial Conference, and the Washington Convention of the International Labour Organization, to support its demand. Mr. Shaw, the Minister of Labour, said that he intended soon to submit a Bill to the Cabinet to ratify the Washington Convention and that he would take trade union objections into account. He added that he had already seen the employers about it.[1] The Washington Convention had decided in favour of a legal eight-hour day and forty-eight-hour week, subject to certain reservations based on technical, climatic, and economic considerations. Mr. Shaw himself had been chairman of the Washington Hours Convention.

When the General Council met on 27 February, the general secretary said that he had heard nothing further from the Minister of Labour but he gathered from press reports that the Government was waiting until there could be a simultaneous international ratification of the Washington Hours Convention. The General Council told its general secretary to press the Minister of Labour to take the initiative and to provide it with advanced copies of his Bill so that it could make representations to him. The Minister refused to let the General Council see the Bill before it was presented to Parliament.

At the same time a similar situation had been reached over a Factories Bill. A deputation of representatives from seventeen organizations concerned with the welfare of women and girls went to the Home Office on 8 February 1924 to press for a new Factory and Workshop Bill. They wanted three main changes: a forty-eight-hour week; improved lighting, temperature, washing facilities, and outdoor clothing; and an increased inspectorate. The Parliamentary Under-Secretary who saw them said that the Home Secretary, Arthur Henderson, would favourably consider their request.[2] A Factory and Workshops Bill was drafted which proposed many alterations in factory conditions and aimed to consolidate existing legislation. The General Council asked to see a draft copy of the Bill before it was submitted to Parliament but its request was refused on the grounds that it was a breach of constitutional procedure.

[1] T.U.C. Report, 1924, p. 190.   [2] *The Times*, 9 February 1924.

The General Council discussed the attitude of the Minister of Labour and the Home Secretary on 26 March 1924. It was annoyed by the rebuffs and informed the Prime Minister that it wished to see him and the Ministers concerned as soon as possible. That same night A. A. Purcell, the chairman of the General Council, spoke to MacDonald, but instead of protesting he assured the Prime Minister that the General Council was prepared to give the Government all the assistance it could to reduce the number of industrial disputes.[1] Subsequently, however, a General Council deputation was given a verbal undertaking that the Council would be provided with draft copies of proposed bills.[2] The General Council did not record any further dissatisfaction but W. M. Citrine stated later that the matter remained unsatisfactory.[3]

Representation on Committees

The Government continued to be generally unwilling to make formal concessions to trade unions. It created annoyance over small matters, perhaps in some cases through thoughtlessness, though its members should have known better. On the other hand the Ministers may have been trying to display a national consciousness by obviously disregarding their class allegiances. Such seemed to be the case when Mr. Sidney Webb appointed the Balfour Committee on 28 July 1924, 'to inquire into the conditions and prospects of British industry and commerce, with special reference to the export trade', without consulting the General Council about the Committee's composition. Webb invited the General Council to submit evidence to the Committee in September 1924, and in doing so evoked strong feelings from its members. A first reaction was to reject the invitation outright without any explanation. In the end the General Council refused to give evidence, advised its affiliated members to do the same, and told Sidney Webb their reason for acting in this way.[4]

When still in this disapproving mood, the General Council discussed the Home Secretary's decision to set up a committee to inquire into the operation of the Factory Inspectorate and decided to ask for representation on the committee 'to the extent of one-half of the members to be appointed'. The general secretary was then instructed to raise with the Prime Minister, the general principle of representation on Government Committees. The Government, by this time, 24 September, was nearing the end of its period in office. It was defeated in Parliament on 7 October and resigned. The

[1] General Council Minutes, 26 and 27 March 1924.   [2] ibid., 9 April 1924.
[3] Memorandum on the National Joint Council, 12 December 1931.
[4] General Council Minutes, 24 September 1924.

discussion about Government consultations with the General Council was suspended until 1929.

Strikes

The most publicized aspect of trade union and Government relations in 1924 was over trade disputes. There was a belief, shared alike by trade unionists and those politically opposed to the Labour Party, that the Labour Government would be inclined to make concessions to union demands and to treat striking workers with understanding. There was to be much opportunity for this belief to be tested.

The Labour Government started in office with a strike in progress. The railway companies had submitted an application to the National Wages Board of the railway industry in December 1923 for a revision of the pay and working conditions of locomotive men. The Associated Society of Locomotive Engineers and Firemen refused to accept the award by the Board and issued strike notices to take effect at midnight, 20 January 1924. The General Council of the Trades Union Congress intervened as a mediator before the strike notices expired but with no effect. The strike began as scheduled and was in full swing, involving about 75,000 workers, when MacDonald formed his Government on 22 January. Two members of the General Council, who on 18 and 19 January had been involved as mediators, became Ministers; a third member, J. H. Thomas, who also joined the Government, was directly implicated in the dispute as the general secretary of the National Union of Railwaymen which had condemned the strike and had instructed its members to continue working. The new Government did not intervene though at one stage there were rumours that it intended to do so. On 25 January the General Council resumed its role as mediator, brought the contending parties together and materially assisted in ending the strike on 29 January.

In January 1924 Ernest Bevin submitted a claim for an increase in wages and a guaranteed working week for dockers in the Transport and General Workers' Union. When he failed to get a satisfactory reply from the port employers, Bevin called the whole of his dock membership out on strike. The strike lasted from 16 until 25 February. Involving 110,000 dockers, it had the complete backing of the union and was waged to win, regardless of community costs. Bevin flatly refused to compromise over the settlement.

The General Council deserted its role of mediator and congratulated the dockers 'on their magnificent stand for the defence of a living wage for dock employees'.[1] The Government was of a dif-

[1] T.U.C. Report, 1924, pp. 131–132.

ferent mind. It was perturbed about the flow of food supplies and
the increases in food prices. The Prime Minister said on 18 February
that the Government would not fail to do what was necessary to
transport food supplies.[1] It explored the possibility of regulating
food prices and it gave Colonel Wedgwood, Chancellor of the Duchy
of Lancaster, the permanent job of Chief Civil Commissioner to
act as a liaison officer between Government Departments during
industrial disputes. Wedgwood warned the union that the military
would be used to keep food supplies moving if the strike continued.[2]
The Government took steps to operate the Emergency Powers Act.
At the same time the Minister of Labour endeavoured to act as a
mediator and on 18 February he set up a Court of Inquiry to report
on the dispute. Three days later the Prime Minister said that the
emergency measures would not be applied because he hoped to be
able to announce a settlement that day.[3] A settlement was reached on
25 February when the port employers granted a wage increase and
agreed to set up a committee to investigate the problem of dock
labour decasualization.

Ernest Bevin clearly resented the intrusion of the Government. At
the end of the strike he is reported as having said, 'I only wish it had
been a Tory Government in office. We would not have been frightened
by *their* threats. But we were put in the position of having to listen
to the appeal of our own people.' [4] Bevin was not deterred from
further strike action by the presence of a Labour Government.

A dispute arose in March over a claim for a wage increase by
London tram and bus workers. The Transport Union intended to
issue strike notices on 13 March but held them up for six days at the
request of the Minister of Labour in the hope of getting a satisfactory
offer from the employers.[5] No offer came, so the London tram and
bus workers came out on strike on 22 March 1924. The Minister of
Labour, already taking part as a mediator, again set up a Court of
Inquiry to investigate the merits of the dispute. While the Court was
sitting the Prime Minister with the Ministers of Labour and Transport
intervened to get negotiations resumed. They made no impression
on the situation. Indeed it got worse. Members of the Associated
Society of Locomotive Engineers and Firemen who worked on London's Underground railways agreed, on 26 March, to strike in
sympathy if necessary—in response to a request from Bevin. The

[1] *The Times*, 19 February 1924.   [2] Lyman, op. cit., p. 219.
[3] Hansard, vol. 169, cols. 1974–1975.
[4] *Ernest Bevin*, by Frances Williams, p. 122.
[5] London Tramway Authorities, the London General Omnibus Co. Ltd., and its
Associated Companies.

Electrical Trades Union was also prepared to take sympathetic action.

The Government was obviously in a dilemma. It wanted to assist in the settlement of the dispute through mediation, but it also wanted to stop the strike spreading and to provide a rudimentary transport service to meet the public's essential needs. When the Minister of Labour was questioned in the House of Commons about the dispute he said, '. . . it would be unwise in the highest degree for a Minister, who may be called upon at any moment to act as an impartial chairman for the parties, to express any opinion whatever . . .' [1] The Government, at the same time, was preparing to issue a Proclamation under the Emergency Powers Act. This step was regarded as provocative by the General Council of the Trades Union Congress and the executive of the Labour Party. At a joint meeting on 27 March, they stated:

> That this Joint Meeting, whilst deploring the Government's declaration of the possible necessity for putting into operation the Emergency Powers Act, strongly urges His Majesty's Government that in the event of this Act being put into operation it should be used for the purpose of carrying on the ordinary transport services, with ordinary men at the wages and conditions asked for, pending the report of a Committee which should be immediately set up to determine the lines upon which a permanent solution of the Transport difficulties in London could be settled. [2]

This was a novel but not unreasonable suggestion for the use of emergency powers, which the Government ignored. The Government did not consider itself to be under any obligation to favour the strikers. 'From the first day of this dispute,' J. R. Clynes said, 'we have done everything possible by acts of mediation to compose the differences, and in that sense have played properly the part of a national Government, and not of a class Government . . .'. [3]

A special Government committee was set up to establish an emergency organization to cope with difficulties created by the strike, and a Privy Council meeting was hurriedly held at Knowsley Hall where the King was staying with Lord Derby, to obtain the King's signature for the Proclamation. But by the time Lord Thomson, a member of the Cabinet, had arrived back in London with the Proclamation the strike had ended. The employers had made an offer of a wage increase which the strikers had accepted by a majority of two to one. It was then 31 March 1924.

[1] Hansard, vol. 171, col. 1410 (26 March 1924).
[2] Minutes of Joint Meeting.
[3] Hansard, vol. 171, col. 1452 (26 March 1924).

This was not the end of the matter. Ernest Bevin, whose strong disapproval of the Government's action in the two strikes was reinforced by his intense personal dislike of MacDonald, took a small deputation from his union to a General Council meeting to make a complaint. Bevin stated:

> that in view of the recent disputes and certain overtures on the part of the Government, his Executive thought some attempt should be made to get agreement as to policy between the Government and the General Council. It was not fair that any one union should be put in the position of having to decide whether to withdraw a strike because the Government was embarrassed. The Government should be made to understand that in matters of this kind the General Council were the right body to be approached.[1]

The General Council concurred with Bevin and agreed to inform the Prime Minister, adding that it would be prepared to discuss the matter with him if he so desired. MacDonald did not meet the General Council and yet another problem of relationship remained unresolved.

Many other trade disputes occurred. One arose in the coal industry when, in March, the miners refused to renew a national wage agreement unless it embodied substantial alterations. The coal owners made an offer to the miners but it was rejected by a small majority after a national ballot. There was no question of a strike, but the Minister of Labour, on the recommendation of Mr. Shinwell, the Secretary for Mines, set up a Court of Inquiry to review miners' wages. The subsequent report favoured the men, negotiations were resumed on the basis of it, and a settlement was reached in May.[2] The Government in this matter acted as well as it was able. The miners wanted a Minimum Wage Act and a Nationalization of the Mines Act more than a temporary wage settlement, but although they pressed these demands on the Government they got neither.

A strike of engineers and other shipyard workers in Southampton resulted in a national lock-out of about 100,000 shipbuilding workers throughout the country from 12 to 23 April. In the same month there was an unofficial strike over wages by 5,000 building workers at the Wembley Exhibition; early in June 6,500 railway shopmen in London and South Wales struck for a wage increase; then a national work stoppage occurred in the building industry and lasted from 5 July till 25 August. There was a larger number of strikes and lock-outs involving more than 5,000 workers in 1924 than in any other year since 1920.

---

[1] General Council Minutes, 9 April 1924.   [2] See also Chapter XI, p. 190.

The Government was much criticized for its inability to obtain the allegiance of its own electoral supporters. There is no evidence to show that union leaders deliberately embarked on strike action simply because they expected Government support, though they may have been more confident about its results. It seemed that, by and large, they disregarded the political nature of the Government. The Labour Government came into office just as the unions, encouraged by a slight improvement in trade after a prolonged depression, were attempting to recoup some of the losses workers had experienced during the depression. Ernest Bevin explained in April 1924 how this operated in the case of his union. He wrote:

> The Union has had to face criticism from various quarters because it has pursued a vigorous industrial policy while its own political friends are in office in the State. We welcomed a Labour Government as keenly as anyone, and have made our contributions to the building up of a Labour political movement which has made that Government possible. We appreciate the importance of political action. Nevertheless the industrial situation has not been altogether of our making, and to a great extent trouble has been due to the unreasonableness of the employers. They took full advantage of the slump period to drive the workers' standards down to the lowest possible level, and that created, after the war experience, a feeling of deep bitterness and resentment. Forward movements were, therefore, inevitable, and most of them began with the first indications of trade improvement and long before a Labour Government was thought possible.
>
> These movements could not have been checked, nor would it have been wise to have held them up because a Labour Government assumed office. After all, the demands made were and are perfectly legitimate . . . to check the movement would be to dispirit the workers, to weaken their faith in industrial action, and to encourage the employers to encroach still further on the present standards.[1]

The Railway Clerks' Association thought that 'the success of political Labour at the poll has had the effect of stimulating and giving confidence to the trade unions in their efforts to regain some of the ground they have lost since the war . . .' [2] It added that the Government stood only to gain a temporary advantage by damping down the industrial revival and gaining a transient industrial peace: 'No one desires peace more than the trade unionist and the trade union leader; but it cannot be too clearly emphasized that the aim of the Labour movement is not industrial peace, but social justice. . . .' [3]

The Government in turn did not show any special sympathy towards trade union aims. It needed to avoid, more than previous

[1] *The Record*, April 1924.   [2] *Railway Service Journal*, April 1924.
[3] ibid., June 1924.

Governments, the appearance of strike-breaking, but it regarded its primary duty as being to the community. The desire to act as protector to the public influenced the Minister of Labour's handling of industrial disputes. During each of the important disputes he first attempted to mediate himself and then set up a Court of Inquiry. Seven Courts of Inquiry were held in 1924 compared with a total of six for all the previous years since the Industrial Courts Act was passed in 1919. In justifying his record to the House of Commons, Shaw said, '. . . in all cases where the public interest is affected, the public has the right to know the facts . . .' [1]

There was pressure in Parliament when disputes were in progress for MacDonald to set up an Industrial Commission to collect facts about industry and to offer services in industrial disputes. Both Henderson and Snowden had at various times advocated the establishment of an industrial parliament to obtain industrial peace within a capitalist system,[2] but either they altered their opinion when in office or they were unable to impress MacDonald with its value, for the Prime Minister did not respond favourably to the suggestion.[3]

THE RELATIONSHIP IN GENERAL

There was no formal relationship between trade unions and the Government, though the National Joint Council could have been used as a means of communication between them. Two members of the National Joint Council, Sidney Webb and Margaret Bondfield, resigned when they joined the Government. MacDonald ignored its existence. The Council met only twice in 1924 and transacted little and relatively unimportant business.

Some union leaders came into contact with Ministers through their membership of joint Trades Union Congress and Labour Party advisory committees. The function of these committees was to advise the executives of the two national bodies on economic and political problems. When the Labour Government was formed, several Ministers expressed a desire to maintain a connection with the appropriate advisory committees in order to keep in touch with informed Labour opinion. As a consequence, the secretary and chairman of the Joint Research and Information Committees, Mr. Arthur Greenwood and Mr. Sidney Webb, circulated a letter to each

[1] Hansard, vol. 176, col. 2576 (4 August 1924).
[2] ibid., vol. 171, col. 1403.
[3] On one occasion, on 27 February, he said he would consider the suggestion to set up an Industrial Conference if employers and workers' organizations wanted one (Hansard, vol. 170, col. 466). On later occasions he refused outright.

Minister, suggesting ways in which contact could be maintained.[1] Most of the Ministers responded favourably, and informal discussions between Ministers and advisory committees took place. The committees were not, however, allowed to make recommendations to Ministers on policy which had not already been endorsed by the General Council or the Labour Party Executive.

In the main, contact was maintained between unions and the Government through deputations to Ministers. They differed from deputations to Conservative or Liberal Ministers only because there was a familiarity between the leaders of the deputations and the Labour Ministers. This familiarity led to strain rather than ease in relationships. When the General Council disapproved of a Government act it tended to protest peremptorily and impatiently. The Government, too, showed impatience with the unions. Having union leaders as members of the Government did not assist matters, for they were among those who were most conventional and endeavoured to stand above class differences. Moreover, they were not particularly good Ministers.

Informal relations between union leaders and Ministers were unsatisfactory. The personal animosities which had characterized the Labour Movement before Labour took office continued at the expense of informal contact. Fred Bramley, general secretary of the Trades Union Congress, claimed, for instance, that he did not have five minutes' conversation with MacDonald during his whole spell as Prime Minister.[2]

Personal conflicts were underscored by basic differences in approach to economic and social problems. Trade union leaders showed a marked propensity to underrate the value of political action, while politicians had just as strong feelings about industrial action. It was unfortunate for the relationship between the two wings of the Labour Movement that events should reveal this cleavage at the outset.

MacDonald deplored all strikes and blamed union leaders for them. 'The problem', he said, 'was to show these people that if they did strike, they could not win in the present circumstances.' [3] The union leaders, on the other hand, displayed their preference for industrial action by leading large strikes. There was little chance of a mutually co-operative relationship existing between the industrial

---

[1] Statement on 'Advisory Committees and Interviews with Ministers' by the Acting Secretary of the Research Department and Advisory Committees, May 1924 (T.U.C. File).

[2] Memorandum drawn up by Bramley in 1925 on T.U.C. and Labour Party relations (T.U.C. File).

[3] *After All*, by Norman Angell, pp. 243–244. See also *Call Back Yesterday*, by Hugh Dalton, p. 148.

and political leaders of the Labour Movement while they were so widely at variance over methods.

The Government as a whole was a harassed one. Harassed by the enormity of administrative tasks and responsibilities, and by its own almost complete inexperience. It did not welcome suggestions and pressure for new legislation, particularly that of a nature to bring it into conflict with Liberal opinion, on whose favour it depended. 'There were so many things [the Government] wanted to do,' MacDonald told a trade union deputation, 'and so many opportunities of compelling them to go slowly.' [1] To Sidney Webb, when offering him the Ministry of Labour, MacDonald wrote: 'As little legislation as you can do with, please, though you will need some. . . .' [2]

Trade unionists were slow to realize the effect which the responsibilities of office had on the implementation of an Opposition programme. 'If', one general secretary asked, 'it was possible for the Labour Party in the House of Commons, when another Government was in office in 1923, to ask for a double-barrelled Bill [on hours of work] . . . why was it not possible with a Labour Government in office to do it now?' [3] Fred Bramley reacted strongly against the Labour Party on similar but more general grounds. 'Experience of the Labour Government when in office,' he wrote, 'made it quite clear that the policy of the T.U.C. General Council could not permanently remain in the present association with that of the Labour Party. . . . The Labour Party cannot have it both ways. If when in office we are to be detached from the Labour Movement, we cannot be treated as an integral part of that movement when Labour is out of office.' [4]

Appendix III

TRADE UNION SPONSORED MEMBERS OF THE LABOUR GOVERNMENT IN 1924[5]

Cabinet

J. R. Clynes (National Union of General Workers)—Lord Privy Seal and Deputy Leader of the House of Commons.

[1] T.U.C. Report, 1924, p. 115.

[2] Beatrice Webb, op. cit., p. 259. MacDonald advised Webb to get a legislative programme from the leading employers' representative in the country, Sir Allan Smith. No mention of the General Council.

[3] J. Hallsworth (National Union of Distributive and Allied Workers) at the Labour Party Conference, 1924. (Report, 1924, p. 141.)

[4] Memorandum on Joint Departments with the Labour Party, 1925 (T.U.C. File).

[5] Only the persons whose candidatures were officially and financially supported by

Arthur Henderson (National Union of Foundry Workers)—Secretary of State for Home Affairs.

J. H. Thomas (National Union of Railwaymen)—Secretary of State for the Colonies.

Stephen Walsh (Miners' Federation)—Secretary of State for War.

William Adamson (Miners' Federation)—Secretary of State for Scotland.

Vernon Hartshorn (Miners' Federation)—Postmaster-General.

Thomas Shaw (United Textile Factory Workers' Association)—Minister of Labour.

Not in Cabinet

Harry Gosling (Transport & General Workers' Union)—Minister of Transport.

F. O. Roberts (Typographical Association)—Minister of Pensions.

Frank Hodges (Miners' Federation)—Civil Lord of the Admiralty.

Margaret Bondfield (National Union of General Workers)—Parliamentary Secretary to Minister of Labour.

R. J. Davies (National Union of Distributive and Allied Workers)— Under-Secretary of State for Home Affairs.

J. Lawson (Miners' Federation)—Financial Secretary to the War Office.

C. G. Ammon (Union of Post Office Workers)—Parliamentary Secretary to the Admiralty.

W. R. Smith (National Union of Boot and Shoe Operatives)—Parliamentary Secretary and Deputy Minister of Fisheries.

W. Lunn (Miners' Federation)—Parliamentary Secretary to the Overseas Department of Board of Trade.

R. Richardson (Miners' Federation)—Charity Commissioner in the House of Commons.

G. Middleton (Union of Post Office Workers)—Second Church Estates Commissioner.

J. Robertson (Miners' Federation)—Lord Commissioner.

F. Hall (Miners' Federation)—Lord Commissioner.

G. H. Warne (Miners' Federation)—Lord Commissioner.

J. A. Parkinson (Miners' Federation)—Comptroller of the Household.

T. Griffiths (British Iron, Steel and Kindred Trades Association)— Treasurer of the Household.

J. E. Davison (National Union of Foundry Workers)—Vice-Chamberlain of the Household.

trade unions are listed in this Appendix. In each of the Labour Governments there have been some trade unionists who have been supported only by constituency Labour Parties.

Chapter Fourteen

TRADE UNIONS AND THE SECOND LABOUR GOVERNMENT
1929–1931

A GENERAL election was held on 30 May 1929 after the Conservative Party had been in office for almost five years. There were 569 Labour candidates in the election and the Labour Party emerged as the largest single party in Parliament with 287 seats. It formed a Government and, for the second time, was dependent upon support from the Liberal Party for a Parliamentary majority.

Trade union attitudes towards the second Labour Government were influenced by the experiences of 1924 and by subsequent economic and political developments. The enthusiasm for a Labour Government had not disappeared but it was dampened. Union leaders still urged their members to vote Labour, but they did so more dispassionately because of their previous experience. They looked to a Labour Government more to remove specific grievances rather than to hasten progress towards the millennium.

The position of trade unions in 1929 was adversely affected by events after 1924. Their membership, which had fallen sharply between 1920 and 1924, continued to fall.[1] The Trades Union Congress itself had lost nearly three million affiliated members in nine years and organized not much more than one-sixth of the total working population in 1929. The decline in membership, although its incidence varied between unions, affected all unions to some extent and decreased their influence in industry and, therefore, with the Government. The position was worsened by the ignominious end to the General Strike and the attitude which the Government displayed by passing the Trade Disputes and Trade Unions Act in 1927.

The executives and headquarters staffs of the Trades Union Congress and the Labour Party were physically closer than they had been in 1924, for after 1927 they were accommodated together in Transport House. But the joint working arrangements which had existed since 1921 had ceased through trade union dissatisfaction. At the end of March 1926 the Trades Union Congress withdrew from the three joint departments for research, press and publicity, and

[1] From 8,348,000 in 1920 it fell to 5,544,000 in 1924 and then to 4,858,000 in 1929 (*Ministry of Labour Gazette*, September 1939).

international matters, and the joint committees controlling the departments and joint advisory committees were disbanded. Only the library and the telephone operator stayed under combined trade union and Labour Party control. The remaining constitutional link between the Trades Union Congress and the Labour Party was the ineffectual National Joint Council. When the Labour Government was formed in June 1929 the National Joint Council had not met for 1½ years.

There had been few changes in the leadership of the Labour Movement. MacDonald, Henderson, Thomas, Snowden, Clynes, and Webb still dominated the Labour Party. The General Council had acquired some new members. Ernest Bevin, A. J. Cook (Miners' Federation), C. T. Cramp (National Union of Railwaymen), J. Hallsworth (National Union of Distributive and Allied Workers), and H. H. Elvin (National Union of Clerks) had all joined the General Council since 1924. But all of those who were prominent in 1929 had been so in 1924. The only new leader of significance to emerge was W. M. Citrine, who had succeeded Fred Bramley as general secretary of the Trades Union Congress in 1926. The old animosities, personal and bitter, remained between union and political leaders. There was much scope in 1929 for suspicion, acrimony, and resentment to exist in the Labour Movement.

The trade union sponsored members of the Parliamentary Labour Party were still numerous but formed a lower proportion of the total membership than after previous elections. They numbered 115, comprising 40 per cent of the Party membership of 287. After the elections in 1923 and 1924 trade unionists had constituted 53 and 58 per cent of the total. There were no new trade unionists of marked ability in the new Parliament.

The speculation which had been made by trade union leaders about the composition of the first Labour Cabinet did not exist over the second. There was some uncertainty arising from the ambitions of Arthur Henderson and J. H. Thomas to be Foreign Secretary, but little else was uncertain. Ramsay MacDonald's preferences and his dislike of trade unionists were known. Six trade unionists were in the Cabinet, one less than in 1924, and five of these had held Cabinet rank in 1924. The solitary newcomer was Miss Margaret Bondfield, who became Minister of Labour. She had been Parliamentary Secretary to the Minister of Labour in 1924. In the Government but not in the Cabinet were eleven trade unionists, compared with seventeen trade unionists in the 1924 Labour Government.[1] F. O.

---

[1] See Appendix IV at the end of this chapter for a list of trade unionists in the 1929 Labour Government.

Roberts (Typographical Association) who was Minister of Pensions in 1924 held the same post in 1929. No other trade unionist in 1929 held Ministerial rank outside the Cabinet; and only two had not been in the previous Labour Government.[1] Three members of the General Council, J. H. Thomas, Margaret Bondfield, and Ben Turner, had Government posts.

Industrial Disputes

The Labour Government was formed in June 1929 and ended in August 1931. In that time there were two large disputes in the cotton textile industry, one in the wool textile industry, and two in the coal-mining industry. These disputes accounted for approximately two-thirds of all the workers directly involved in disputes in Great Britain and Northern Ireland for the three complete years, 1929, 1930, and 1931. As 1,250 disputes began in those three years it can be seen that most of them were of a minor character.

(*i*) *The Textile Industries*. The Prime Minister intervened directly in the cotton textile disputes. On the first occasion he induced the employers to make concessions in favour of the workers. About 380,000 cotton operatives had been locked out on 29 July 1929 for refusing to accept wage reductions. No progress was made towards a settlement until 10 August, when MacDonald asked the employers' representatives to confer with him in Edinburgh. Arising out of this meeting the employers agreed to submit their case to arbitration and to suspend the application of the wage reduction until the arbitration award was known.[2]

The second dispute was also a lock-out and arose over an attempt by Burnley mill-owners to increase the number of looms attended by each weaver. 120,000 cotton operatives were involved directly. The dispute started on 5 January 1931 as a local Burnley dispute and spread, despite the attempts of the Minister of Labour to contain it. The Prime Minister took a hand in it on 29 January 1931 but this time he had no success. The lock-out was ended when the employers gave in and discontinued the Burnley experiment in the middle of February.

The Government intervened in the wool textile dispute strictly according to the letter of the law. The Minister appointed a Court of Inquiry in January 1930 to inquire into a dispute in the industry arising from attempts by employers to enforce wage reductions. The

---

[1] They were Ben Turner (National Union of Textile Workers) and Ben Smith (Transport and General Workers' Union). Turner had been president of the Trades Union Congress in 1928.

[2] The Arbitration Board recommended a wage reduction which was half of that proposed by the employers (*Ministry of Labour Gazette*, September 1929).

Court concluded that wage reductions were inevitable and recommended a reduction of about 9 per cent. The recommendation was rejected by 72·1 per cent of the operatives in a ballot vote. In consequence the employers posted notices that the reduction would be enforced and the workers withdrew their labour on 12 April 1930.

Having performed the task which the Industrial Courts Act required of her, the Minister of Labour, Margaret Bondfield, let the dispute take its own course until 16 May, when she wrote to the employers' and workers' representatives: '. . . whatever the loss which has so far been suffered by both sides, the time has come when permanent and irreparable harm to the industry will result from a continuance of the present situation. . . . It is not for me to express any view upon the merits of the dispute. . . .' [1] She hoped the trade unions and employers would re-open negotiations but her hope was not fulfilled.

The woollen textile workers were attempting to resist the full impact of the recession which affected all sections of the woollen trades. Many Yorkshire people were suffering acute social and economic privations. Yet this was of no apparent concern to Miss Bondfield. The dispute dragged on in a most unsatisfactory manner. It ended when the workers, unregulated and dispirited, returned to work. At the peak of the strike 120,000 workers were involved; 40,000 were still on strike in June, 3,000 in July, and some workers were still out in August.

(*ii*) *Coal-Mining.* The other large industrial disputes resulted from the application of the Coal Mines Act of 1930. Working hours in the mines were regulated by Acts of Parliament. The Coal Mines Regulation Act, 1908, fixed the normal maximum period during which miners should be underground at eight hours; the Coal Mines Act, 1919, reduced this figure to seven. The hours were again revised by the Coal Mines Act of 1926 which stipulated that until 8 July 1931 they should be eight.

The Labour Party, when it took office, was pledged to restore the seven-hour-day for miners. It was faced with a difficult task, for the coal-mining industry was in a state of severe depression; in some districts as many as one-third of the miners were unemployed. But the Government could not ignore the pledge altogether, for the Miners' Federation, with forty-one sponsored candidates in the House of Commons, was the most politically powerful of unions. It responded by introducing a Coal Mines Bill in December 1929 which contained proposals for marketing schemes, for setting up a

---

[1] *Ministry of Labour Gazette,* June 1930, p. 202.

National Wages Board for the Industry, and for reducing working hours to $7\frac{1}{2}$ a shift until the Coal Mines Act of 1926 expired in July 1931.

The Bill was the subject of many consultations between the Government, the coal owners, and the Miners' Federation, and of much criticism from the Liberal Party and the House of Lords. The House of Lords submitted many amendments which the House of Commons rejected, but it used its power to delay the passage of the Bill in order to induce the Government to accept two of them, one of which concerned working hours. The House of Lords wanted to give colliery owners the right to extend working hours up to a maximum of eight on any day, so long as the total hours worked in a fortnight did not exceed 90. This was called a spread-over of hours. After negotiations between the Government and the House of Lords, it was agreed that the spread-over could only be operated after agreement between the Coal Owners' Association and the Miners' Federation. The Bill became law on 1 August 1930, and the provisions regarding working hours were applied from 1 December 1930.

The Miners' Federation executive had tried to negotiate with the coal owners for a $7\frac{1}{2}$-hour day without loss of pay, in order to obtain full benefit from the Act, but it had failed. The only way, therefore, in which it could prevent miners' wages from falling was to extend hours above $7\frac{1}{2}$ through spread-over agreements. A single agreement could not be negotiated, because there were marked variations between districts, so the executive recommended to a Miners' Federation delegate conference that districts should be allowed to negotiate their own agreements. The delegates wanted a $7\frac{1}{2}$-hour day without loss of pay and would have nothing to do with spread-over agreements. This meant, according to the Act, that any variation of the $7\frac{1}{2}$-hour day was illegal.

The Government was placed in an awkward position. It had intended to use the coal marketing schemes as a means of financing the shorter working day, but the reduction in hours came before the schemes could be operated. The coal owners, on the other hand, refused to finance the shorter day themselves. Strikes were called on 1 December by three districts which objected to having spread-over agreements. 76,000 miners went on strike in Scotland, 6,000 in North Staffordshire, and 1,100 in Shropshire, but they all went back to work when a miners' conference refused to support them with a national strike.

An anomalous situation developed over the spread-over agreements. The Miners' Federation delegate conference maintained its refusal to permit districts to contract their own agreements, so local spread-over agreements remained illegal. Nevertheless, districts did contract local temporary agreements. The South Wales Miners' Federation concluded one for a month from 1 December; other districts had them for various periods, even from day to day. Only in this way could the miners prevent or lessen wage reductions.

From the Government's point of view the whole situation was unsatisfactory. The Prime Minister appealed to the miners to allow the Act three months to get into operation, because strikes and temporary agreements which could quickly give rise to strikes would endanger the operation of the marketing schemes and other proposals in the Act. For political reasons the Government could not delete the hours clause, nor could it take the right to veto spread-over agreements away from the Miners' Federation. All it could do was to assist in mediating between coal owners and miners as disputes were threatened.

In the respite which the temporary agreement had given the coal owners and miners in South Wales they tried and failed to negotiate a long-term agreement. So on 1 January 1931 about 150,000 South Wales miners stopped work and remained on strike until 17 January. A deputation from the South Wales Miners' Federation on 5 January asked the Government to invoke the Emergency Powers Act against the coal owners so that the mines could be opened on the miners' terms but the Government would not agree.

Mr. W. Graham, President of the Board of Trade, succeeded in bringing about a resumption of negotiations on 7 January.[1] While Graham was busy conciliating, the Prime Minister criticized the coal owners and said they were setting a bad example by not accepting the Coal Mines Act in full. He said, 'The Government does not want any dispute at the present moment, but the Government is going to interfere in no way which would make injustice a condition of peace.'[2] A compromise settlement was eventually reached at the Board of Trade on 15 January and the miners returned to work two days later.

Unrest in the coal-fields was only temporarily eased. Wage reductions were enforced in several districts, and the position became so serious that a special Miners' Federation report was made to the General Council of the Trades Union Congress in April.[3] It stated that the Minimum Wage Act of 1912 was a dead letter and that

[1] Mr. Shinwell, who had been active in the earlier negotiations, had excluded himself from being the principal Government arbiter because of some indiscreet remarks he had made about the temporary spread-over arrangements (*The Times*, 1 January 1931).

[2] ibid., 8 January 1931.

[3] General Council Minutes, 22 April 1931.

legislation was necessary to bring it up to date. The Act only covered underground workers and it stipulated that the minimum wages fixed should be related to the actual wages paid. Thus low actual wages resulted in a low minimum. The Government presented a Coal Mines (Minimum Wage) Act, 1912 (Amendment) Bill to the House of Commons but it made no progress.

The miners continued to agitate about working hours. The legislation regulating hours was due to lapse on 8 July 1931, and the Miners' Federation told the General Council in May that unless and until further legislation was passed the miners would revert to the seven-hour day which was worked before the 1926 Coal Mines Act.[1] The coal owners stated that if a seven-hour day were enforced they would demand wage reductions in every district. The miners, already dissatisfied with the level of wages, did not want to be faced with additional reductions. They therefore asked the Government to legislate for a guaranteed weekly wage.[2]

A special Cabinet Committee conferred with committees of both the Mining Association and the Miners' Federation in an attempt to settle the problem. In the absence of an agreement and without at least an extension of the existing legislation, a general stoppage of work on 8 July seemed likely. No agreement was reached, so the Government, in the last few days of grace, introduced a Coal Mines Bill which was simply a device to enable negotiations to continue. It provided for a continuance of the $7\frac{1}{2}$-hour day for a further twelve months or until such time as another Act came into force ratifying the proposals on working hours in the mining industry of an International Labour Convention. It also arranged for the maintenance of existing minimum wage rates.

The Government did more to please the miners than it did for any group of workers. It attempted whatever the Miners' Federation asked of it. But the miners were in a pernickety mood and were not altogether consistent in their attitude. The Government, tied by Liberal Party support and badgered by the Miners' Federation, could only move from one expedient to another.

Unemployment Insurance

As a high level of unemployment came to be viewed as a persistent, if not a permanent, feature of British industrial life, so unions turned more anxiously to unemployment insurance provisions. The Trades Union Congress had a standing committee on Social Insurance and a

---

[1] General Council Minutes, 20 May 1931.
[2] ibid.

Social Insurance Department with a full-time secretary, examining the problem for the greater part of the 1920s. The Labour Party was well acquainted with the Trades Union Congress views on unemployment insurance and its manifesto for the 1929 election stated that it would 'amend the Unemployment Insurance Act so as to afford more generous maintenance for the unemployed, and [would] remove those qualifications which deprive them of payments to which they are entitled'.[1]

The Government acted quickly. The Minister of Labour, in July 1929, appointed a committee under the chairmanship of Sir Harold Morris, K.C., to consider the administration of the Unemployment Insurance Acts. The President of the Trades Union Congress, Mr. A. Hayday, was appointed to the committee and the Trades Union Congress presented detailed evidence to it. The gist of the evidence was that there should be a more effective and understanding treatment at Employment Exchanges; that provided an applicant for benefit established that he was unemployed and available for work he should not have to prove that he was not malingering or, as the Act stated, 'not genuinely seeking work'; that the State should make a more effective use of trade unions as placing agencies and use them for the administration of State unemployment benefit; that specialized Employment Exchanges should be established; and, lastly, that the constitution of Courts of Referees should be improved.

The committee, so far as its terms of reference permitted, made recommendations broadly along the lines of the Trades Union Congress evidence. In November 1929, a Bill to amend the Unemployment Insurance Acts was read. It aimed to remove the 'not genuinely seeking work' provision and to raise rates of benefits. A joint General Council and Labour Party Executive sub-committee consulted with the Minister of Labour about the Bill and made a number of suggestions which were accepted by the Minister. The committee continued in being until the Bill became law in March 1930. The Trade Union Group in the House of Commons, which had been reformed in December 1929, was used to watch the progress of the Bill.

The reasonably amicable relationships which existed between the Government and the unions over this issue were suddenly disrupted by a Government decision to set up a Royal Commission on Unemployment Insurance late in November 1930. The General Council was taken completely by surprise. It saw no need for a Commission in view of the number of inquiries which had been conducted

[1] Labour Party Report, 1929, p. 305.

into the subject since 1923. It considered the act as an affront, for the General Council had not been consulted about the desirability of having a Royal Commission, its terms of reference, or its composition.

The General Council discussed the matter on 26 November and again on 17 December. At the second meeting trade union anger was translated into decisions. Affiliated unions were asked to have nothing to do with the Royal Commission until they had again heard from the General Council, and the following protest was sent by Citrine to the Prime Minister:

> The General Council have instructed me to convey to you their very strong protest against the manner in which this Commission has been set up and also against its terms of reference. Unemployment Insurance is an important and vital issue to the whole Trade Union Movement, and they resent very much the fact that the Government, not only decided to set up such Commission, but have settled the terms of reference and personnel without consultation with the General Council.
>
> They expected that on a matter of this character there would have been a greater degree of co-operation and sympathetic understanding between the Government and the General Council.
>
> There have been a number of incidents which have occurred during the life-time of the present Government and which have caused perplexity and uneasiness to the General Council, but the Council, conscious as they have been of some of the difficulties confronting the Government, have refrained from any action which might have had the effect of embarrassing the Government. The Council feel they can remain silent no longer, and the way in which they have been treated in respect of this Royal Commission shows an absence of appreciation on the part of the Government of the responsibilities of the General Council's own position.
>
> So seriously do the Council regard this matter that they have appointed a deputation to meet you for the purpose of having a frank discussion in respect of the whole question. I shall be glad if you will inform me as to a date upon which you can receive the deputation, in order that I may make the necessary arrangements.[1]

The General Council was not satisfactorily reassured by the Prime Minister; it grudgingly consented to give evidence before the Commission and, before the Commission's work was completed, it stood prepared to raise strong objections to any suggestion that the rate of unemployment benefit should be cut. The Royal Commission's first report, made on 1 June 1931, aroused deep hostility in the trade union movement and gave a preview of its response to the financial

---

[1] General Council Minutes, 17 December 1930.

policy of the Government later in the summer. The report recommended, amongst other things, that contributions should be increased and that benefits should be reduced and paid for a shorter period. The General Council arranged protest conferences throughout the country.

The Prime Minister took notice of the trade union protests and announced that the Government would not implement the Royal Commission's report.[1] Instead it introduced a Bill to deal with certain anomalies in the operation of the Unemployment Insurance Acts to which the report had drawn attention. In the case of this Bill the General Council was fully consulted and was given recognition in it as one of the bodies, with the National Confederation of Employers' Organizations and the Treasury, to be represented on an Advisory Committee to report on regulations necessary to remove the anomalies.[2] The Bill became law on 31 July 1931.

The Trade Disputes and Trade Unions Act, 1927

The repeal of this Act was demanded by the Trades Union Congress in 1927 and 1928. It figured in the Labour Party election manifesto and was an issue, though not a major one, in the election campaign in May 1929. After the Labour Government had been formed the General Council reminded it that nothing less than the full restoration of the law as it stood before 1927 would be satisfactory.

The General Council formed a special sub-committee to negotiate with the Government over the repeal of the Act. It met the Lord Chancellor and the Attorney-General and was kept fully informed about the Government's intentions. No Bill was introduced during the Government's first session. There were two main reasons for this.

First there were demands on the Government for legislation for education, raising the school-leaving age, unemployment, and pensions. The Government, like its predecessor in 1924, was handicapped by being a minority Government and was not able to manœuvre independently of the Liberal Party. In addition it was hard pressed for Parliamentary time. At one period it seemed that a choice would have to be made between an Education Act and the repeal of the Trade Disputes and Trade Unions Act.[3] The General Council disliked being placed in this dilemma, for it was publicly committed to educational reform but it insisted that its own Bill should take precedence over others in the 1930 autumn session of Parliament.

[1] T.U.C. Report, 1931, p. 175.   [2] ibid., p. 341.
[3] ibid., 1930, p. 375.

The second reason for delay was more important. A joint meeting of the Labour Party Executive and the General Council was held on 29 May 1930 to discuss the repeal of the Act but it could not agree on whether or not revolutionary strikes should remain illegal. The Prime Minister stated at the meeting that the Government would like to introduce a Bill without any provision except to wipe out the existing Act but he did not think that it was possible. 'The question', he said, 'was whether the unions would prefer the Bill to be defeated or whether they would agree to such a clause making political and revolutionary strikes illegal, but being so worded as not to interfere with the pursuit of an industrial strike.' [1] The General Council refused to accept any restrictions on the trade union right to strike.

The General Council had its way. A Bill was drafted to restore the pre-1927 position and was presented to Parliament on 18 October 1930. It was clear after the First Reading of the Bill that the Liberal Members of Parliament would not support it as it stood. The General Council was told this in December 1930. [2] The question which was bothering the Liberals most was that which was put by Sir John Simon. If the Bill became law, he asked 'would a national strike similar to that of 1926 now be illegal?' The General Council answered that it would not. [3]

The General Council's reply to Sir John Simon's question really settled the fate of the Bill. A number of Liberals voted against it at its Second Reading and the official Liberal Party spokesman intimated that it would have to be amended drastically to secure Liberal support. A Liberal amendment to Clause I, aiming to make any strike illegal which adversely affected the interests of the community, was carried on 26 February. [4] The General Council wrote to the Prime Minister the next day that the Liberal amendment would put trade unions in a worse position than at any time since 1871 and that the Bill as amended was wholly unacceptable to the trade union movement. MacDonald did not reply to this letter, [5] but on 3 March 1931 the Attorney-General stated that the Government had decided to withdraw the Bill. This ended the Labour Government's attempt to repeal the 1927 Act. Recrimination about the failure of that attempt, however, was carried on and intensified. It was felt by some trade union leaders that the Government should have been prepared to resign rather than make concessions on the Bill.

---

[1] Report of Joint Meeting of the Labour Party Executive Committee and the General Council of the T.U.C., 29 May 1930.

[2] T.U.C. Report, 1931, p. 254.   [3] General Council Minutes, 28 January 1931.

[4] John Bromley, M.P., member of the General Council, alleged that some members of the Government had had a hand in drafting the Liberal amendment (General Council Minutes, 25 March 1931).   [5] ibid.

The Financial Crisis

On the day the House of Commons rose for the Summer Recess, 31 July 1931, Mr. Snowden, the Chancellor of the Exchequer, emphasized the gravity of Britain's financial position. That day he had received the report of the Committee on National Expenditure which had been presided over by Sir George May. Snowden said the Report 'would come as a shock to the country'.[1] He intimated that the Government would need the co-operation of all other Parties to enable it to carry through drastic reductions of expenditure. The next day, when Parliament had dispersed, the May Committee Report was published. In the orthodox but fallacious belief that sound national finance required a balanced budget, the Report painted a gloomy and alarming picture of Britain's financial position. It forecast a budget deficit of £120,000,000 by April 1932 which would have to be cleared by severe taxation or economy, or both. Increased revenue from taxation amounting to £24 millions and a reduction of expenditure totalling £96 millions were proposed. The Report had an immediate impact on Britain's financial position. A form of economic hysteria developed and spread. Foreign investors became nervous and withdrew their money and Britain's gold reserves fell at an increasing rate.

MacDonald and Snowden, not in anticipation of a crisis but as a general precautionary step, had formed an Economy Committee of the Cabinet on the last day of the Parliamentary Session. It consisted of MacDonald, Snowden, Henderson, Thomas, and Graham and was scheduled to meet on 25 August after its members had had a holiday. Snowden stayed in London and, witnessing an incipient foreign exchange crisis, wired MacDonald on 7 August to call an immediate meeting of the Committee. MacDonald returned to London and, with Snowden, sought the advice of some prominent bankers. On 12 August the Economy Committee met and decided that the next year's budget would have to be balanced and that every section of the community would have to make proportionate sacrifices.[2] Interviews with the leaders of the Conservative and Liberal Parties, who had also had their holidays interrupted, were arranged. Whatever was in fact happening, it was by this time generally believed that Britain was in the process of a serious crisis.[3]

It was a peculiar crisis with many cross-currents about which all manner of interpretations, guesses, and estimates were made. It was

[1] Snowden, op. cit., p. 930.   [2] ibid., p. 937.
[3] See *Britain Between the Wars*, by Charles Lock Mowat, pp. 379 et seq., for an account of the crisis.

a situation rife with suspicion and class antagonisms. In all essentials it was a political crisis. Bankers were consulted in the first few days, maybe because a symptom of the crisis was a withdrawal of foreign exchange; leaders of other political parties were consulted early, assumedly because the Government needed full Parliamentary support for its measures. But the main proposals for economy involved the unemployed. Out of an aggregate saving of £96 millions, £66·5 millions were to come from a reduction in unemployment benefit and an increase in unemployment contributions. To the Trades Union Congress and the Labour Party, both in Parliament and out of it, this proposal was of fundamental political importance. The Cabinet Economy Committee met almost daily and maintained contact with Opposition leaders. Yet no Labour organization was consulted until 20 August.

At the suggestion of Arthur Henderson, and not through an intrinsic desire to consult with Labour organizations, the Cabinet Economy Committee met the General Council, the Labour Party Executive, and the Consultative Committee of the Parliamentary Labour Party on 20 August. Snowden recalls: 'I went to this meeting with the Trade Union Congress Committee with great reluctance. I had never recognized the right of the Trade Union Congress Committee to be consulted on matters of Cabinet policy.' [1] The Cabinet, the day before, had agreed on certain economies, but it had rejected a proposal of the Cabinet Economy Committee to reduce unemployment benefits.

The meeting began with a general statement by MacDonald, who said that 'The pursuit of economies would mean an increase in unemployment up to 20,000 or 30,000. The alternative was much worse. If the crisis was met by taxation only, the taxation must be so high that confidence would be destroyed still more . . . the principle must be borne in mind that there must be some kind of equality in the sacrifices imposed. The tremendous cost of dealing with unemployment which fell on the Exchequer was disturbing the minds of people outside the country. . . .' [2] After he had made his statement, MacDonald asked for questions but he got no response. The General Council wanted consultation, and this, Citrine stated, 'could only take place if the Council was placed unreservedly in possession of information on which the Cabinet was to make its decisions. . . . To tell the Council that there were three possible ways in which remedies might be sought for the situation, was to tell them no more than had already appeared in the leading articles of many papers. . . .' Snowden then described the possible economies—on unemployment

[1] Snowden, op. cit., pp. 940-941.   [2] Report of Meeting (T.U.C. File).

insurance, teachers' salaries, the pay of the police and armed forces, grants for public works, salaries of Cabinet Ministers and Members of Parliament, and in other minor ways too. There was no specific proposal to cut unemployment benefit. The General Council took this to mean that the Government had decided not to cut it. Snowden, however, simply meant to convey that the question was still open.[1] The meeting then adjourned to examine the proposals.

The opposition to reductions in unemployment pay which had been expressed in the Cabinet was magnified many times on the General Council, and was extended to nearly all the suggestions made by Snowden. The General Council refused firmly to 'acquiesce on any new burdens on the unemployed'. It considered alternative proposals to those outlined by Snowden and dispatched a deputation, with Citrine and Bevin as spokesmen, to present them to the Cabinet Economy Committee that same evening. The Trades Union Congress proposals were:

  (i) As an alternative to increasing unemployment insurance contributions or limiting benefit it was decided to appeal to the Government to consider the principle of the scheme put forward by the General Council to the Royal Commission on Unemployment Insurance. Under this scheme the present method of contributions from worker, employer and State would be replaced by a graduated levy upon profits, incomes and earnings.

  The Government could, without adhering to every detail of the scheme suggested, ensure that all classes of the community should contribute.

  It was felt that it was impracticable to attempt to place the Unemployment Fund on an insurance basis, having regard to its history and the accumulated debt.

  It was also pointed out that any increase in contribution would fall very heavily on the exporting industries, while in coalmining in particular, owing to the method of ascertainment of costs, practically the whole of the extra burden would really fall on wages.

 (ii) It was agreed to suggest that new taxation upon fixed interest securities and other unearned income should be imposed, since the fall in the price level had greatly enhanced the real value of such holdings.

(iii) It was felt that in the existing emergency the suspension of the Sinking Fund would be justified. This would mean a saving of nearly £50,000,000 which would otherwise have been devoted to extra repayments of debts.

(iv) The question of a Revenue Tariff was discussed, and it was agreed that a matter of such fundamental importance could not be de-

---

[1] Snowden, op. cit., p. 941.

cided by the General Council. It was felt that Congress decisions in the past precluded the General Council from pronouncing upon this matter.[1]

MacDonald and his colleagues received the deputation at 9.30 p.m. The General Council's views were summarized by Citrine, while Bevin intervened to make additional points. When Snowden said 'apparently the clear statements made by Mr. Citrine meant that the General Council were opposed to all the economies that had been suggested that afternoon', he was told cryptically that the General Council had not discussed such proposals as a reduction in Cabinet Ministers' salaries.[2] In a subsequent discussion Snowden and Bevin disagreed over the basic approach to the crisis and about the domestic consequences of the collapse of sterling. Bevin, and the General Council, believed that it was wrong to tackle the crisis by continuing a policy of deflation. During the meeting Snowden revealed what he meant by equality of sacrifice. He referred to the General Council suggestion that a tax on fixed interest securities would be an equitable means of increasing revenue as the holders of these securities had had the real value of not only their interest but their capital enhanced by the fall in prices, and said: 'Incidentally, as the argument had been applied to rentiers, why not apply the same argument to teachers and to unemployment benefit, namely, that as prices had fallen, it was equitable to make a reduction.' There was no analogy, said Bevin. At the end of the meeting MacDonald said that nothing the General Council representatives had suggested touched the actual problem which faced the Government.

It was clear to the General Council representatives that the Government had no intention of seeing them again.[3] They were not popular with members of the Cabinet. 'The General Council', Sidney Webb (then Lord Passfield) said, 'are pigs, they won't agree to any "cuts" of Unemployment Insurance benefits or salaries or wages. . . .'[4] Snowden said their attitude was based upon a pre-crisis mentality.[5] The collective views of the Cabinet were expressed in a letter from MacDonald to Citrine on 21 August. The letter stated:

> The Cabinet met again this morning, and its Sub-Committee, whom you saw, reported what you said to it. It felt bound, however, to proceed with its examinaton of the scheme about which the Chancellor and

[1] T.U.C. Report, 1931, p. 514.
[2] Report of Meeting of the General Council Sub-Committee and the Cabinet Economy Committee at 10 Downing Street on Thursday, 20 August 1931 (T.U.C. File).
[3] T.U.C. Report, 1931, p. 515.   [4] Beatrice Webb's *Diaries, 1924–1932*, p. 281.
[5] Snowden, op. cit., p. 942.

myself talked to the joint meeting yesterday. It did this in the belief that if it took another course the situation would steadily worsen, and unemployment would rapidly increase—far more rapidly than we have known it even during this terrible time of depression. As you know, nothing gives me greater regret than to disagree with old industrial friends, but I really personally find it absolutely impossible to overlook dread realities, as I am afraid you are doing.[1]

The Cabinet resigned *en bloc* on 23 August. It had been told on the previous day by MacDonald and Snowden that only reductions in unemployment benefits would satisfy the Opposition, and it was this issue which was crucial. The Bank of England had approached the Federal Reserve Bank of New York for credit to tide it over its difficulties. The Americans, in a reply by telegram, stipulated conditions which entailed bigger enonomies than the Cabinet had already agreed upon, including a 10 per cent reduction in unemployment benefits.[2] The Cabinet was divided almost equally over this last issue. Eleven Ministers were prepared to support a reduction; ten were not.[3] The six trade union members of the Cabinet were equally divided. J. H. Thomas, Thomas Shaw, and Margaret Bondfield favoured the cut, while Arthur Henderson, J. R. Clynes, and W. Adamson opposed it. Clearly the General Council opinion carried no weight with those most recently connected with it, namely Thomas and Miss Bondfield.

A surprising feature of the crisis was the weakness of not only the Trades Union Congress but also the Labour Party Executive and the Parliamentary Labour Party. After the crucial meeting with the General Council and the Cabinet Economy Committee on 20 August, the Labour Party Executive decided to leave the main question, for the moment, in the hands of Henderson and Clynes, who were in the Cabinet.[4] No special Labour Party Conference was called to express its opinion about the situation or to prescribe a course of action. The Parliamentary Labour Party did not even meet. When Arthur Henderson asked for it to be summoned immediately he was told that there was not time.[5] The General Council did at least make its views known to the Cabinet.

The position was all the more extraordinary because even the Cabinet was in ignorance of some of the most important developments. The Cabinet had resigned on a Sunday evening, and Mac-Donald said he would notify the King. The next day, 24 August, the Cabinet, at its last meeting, received the unsuspected news that

[1] T.U.C. Report, 1931, p. 515. [2] Mowat, op. cit., p. 392.
[3] ibid. [4] *Call Back Yesterday*, by H. Dalton, p. 269.
[5] T.U.C. Report, 1031, p. 401.

MacDonald had agreed to form a 'National' Government with Conservatives and Liberals; that it had lost office with the Parliamentary Labour Party. Not even Snowden or Thomas anticipated this, though they, with Lord Sankey, were invited to join MacDonald and did so. Only one other ex-Cabinet Minister, two non-Cabinet Ministers, and eight ordinary Members of Parliament supported MacDonald. The bulk of the Parliamentary Labour Party, after consultation with the General Council and the Labour Party Executive, went into official Parliamentary Opposition.

THE RELATIONSHIP IN GENERAL

Not long before the election in 1929 the General Council had discussed what form of contact ought to be established between it and the various committees of the Parliamentary Labour Party which would be engaged on drafting industrial legislation, if a Labour Government should be returned. Citrine was instructed to confer with the Labour Party leaders on this issue so as to make sure that the mistakes of 1924 were not repeated. After the election but before the Government had been named, the question of some form of liaison between the Trades Union Congress and the Labour Government was raised at a meeting between the executives of the Labour Party and the Parliamentary Labour Party. J. H. Thomas opposed it 'because it would give countenance to the idea that the Government was under outside dictation . . .' [1] It was unanimously agreed not to establish any form of liaison. The General Council was still discussing its relations with the Government at the end of June, and on 1 July Citrine was instructed to discuss the question with the Prime Minister. No form of liaison, however, was set up.

With no formal relations between the Trades Union Congress and the Labour Government consultations between the two depended upon the attitude of the Government. MacDonald said that he had issued instructions that Ministers must consult the General Council on any matter directly affecting the interests of trade unions. [2] Such an instruction was not uniformly carried out, and the most persistent culprits were those who were trade unionists themselves. The trade union members of the Cabinet did not consider that unions should be treated differently by the Government simply because it was a Labour one. They made it plain that they were concerned with national, not sectional, interests and, as if to make up for their pasts

[1] Snowden, op. cit., p. 762.
[2] Memorandum on the National Joint Council, by W. M. Citrine, 12 December 1931 (T.U.C. File).

and to cover up their apparent allegiances, they denounced class solutions more vigorously than others in the Cabinet. Strangely, it was MacDonald, in his occasional interventions in strikes, who displayed most bias in favour of the working class.

In 1924 some Labour Ministers were considered to have been dominated or unduly influenced by the civil service heads of their departments. To prevent this recurring in 1929 it was suggested that Ministers should draw some of their private secretaries from the Labour Movement.[1] The suggestion was not taken up and similar criticisms were again directed at Labour Ministers in 1929.[2]

During the tenure of the 1929 Labour Government J. R. Clynes, Margaret Bondfield, and J. H. Thomas were the Ministers who had most cause to consult and meet union leaders. J. R. Clynes, as Home Secretary, was involved with factory legislation and he, like Henderson in 1924, refused to let the General Council see draft copies of a proposed Factory Bill. He was also criticized for continuing a legislative provision which gave the Home Secretary the prerogative of permitting women and young persons to be employed on a two-shift system. He had been the most persistent critic of this provision when he was in opposition. Clynes worked on the principle that it was preferable to get a Bill passed than to lose it by overloading it with what he called 'Labour perfections'.

Margaret Bondfield's behaviour was erratic. She consulted the General Council about the provisions of an Hours of Industrial Employment Bill, but she did not show it the actual final wording. She was criticized most, however, for her lack of tact in handling deputations. On one occasion she broke into a violent denunciation of the Miners' Federation before a meeting of officials;[3] at another time in November 1929 she met a joint deputation from the Labour Party Executive and the General Council about unemployment insurance without having read their memorandum and then cut the meeting short to rush off to another engagement.

Although the attempt to repeal the Trade Disputes Act of 1927 failed, the General Council was consulted to its satisfaction. The General Council was never approached about a Road Traffic Bill, but the transport unions were consulted. The task of dealing with the unemployment problem was given to J. H. Thomas. In so far as he tackled it, he did so without seeking the help of trade unions, apart

---

[1] Memorandum on the National Joint Council, by W. M. Citrine, 12 December 1931 (T.U.C. File).

[2] Margaret Bondfield was singled out as being particularly influenced by civil servants.

[3] Beatrice Webb's *Diaries, 1924–1932*, p. 231.

from an initial burst of enthusiasm for consultation. On 28 November 1929 Thomas, unaccompanied by Government officials, had an informal meeting with the General Council to consider the question of unemployment. Thomas talked, then he engaged in discussion. He said he would like to see the General Council or a committee of it at any time. There is no record that he ever met the General Council again.

The Chancellor of the Exchequer, Snowden, with a colossal ignorance of trade unions and no sympathy towards them, never paid lip-service to consultation. 'I sometimes despair about the working-class', he told the Soviet Ambassador in August 1930; 'next week I have to meet the General Council of the T.U.C.; they want more wages, shorter hours, a greater expenditure on social services—here and now. . . .' [1] The Prime Minister, like Thomas, started with a flourish. He invited the whole General Council to dine with him at 10 Downing Street soon after the Government was formed. But it ended there, and MacDonald retired into the company of aristocrats.

The Government was inconsistent over consultations about the appointment of trade unionists to its committees. In July 1929 it sent personal invitations to Ernest Bevin and Arthur Pugh to sit on the Colonial Development Committee and the Consultative Committee on Employment Schemes. Bevin and Pugh informed the General Council, which in turn told the Prime Minister that in the first instance all invitations should be made to the General Council for their submission of lists of names to the Government. [2] Later Snowden issued a personal invitation to the Assistant General Secretary of the T.U.C. to sit on a Royal Commission on the Civil Service. The General Council turned down the invitation. [3]

Yet on other occasions the T.U.C. protocol was followed closely. Snowden asked the General Council for the names of trade unionists to sit on the Macmillan Committee on Finance and Industry in October 1929, as did the Prime Minister in respect of the Economic Advisory Council in February 1930. It seemed that the Government was simply unconcerned about whether it annoyed the General Council or not.

There was an inquest after the resignation of the Labour Cabinet, on the failure of the Government to establish relations with the General Council. It started at a joint meeting of the General Council and the Labour Party Executive on 10 November 1931 and was continued at a meeting of the resuscitated National Joint Council in December 1931. On each occasion the General Council expressed

---

[1] ibid., p. 249. [2] General Council Minutes, 24 July 1929.
[3] ibid., 30 August 1929.

its view, no longer as a suppliant but as a representative of the principal partner in a weakened, shocked, though wiser Labour Movement. At the first meeting Citrine said:

> There had been a manifest reluctance on the part of the late Labour Government to have contact with the General Council. That state of affairs must be righted . . . They did not seek in any shape or form to say what the Party was to do, but they did ask that the primary purpose of the creation of the Party should not be forgotten. It was created by the Trade Union movement to do those things in Parliament which the Trade Union Movement found ineffectively performed by the two-Party system.[1]

Citrine related his criticisms in a memorandum. He repeated what Bramley had said in 1924: that whereas the relations between the Trades Union Congress and the Labour Party in opposition were generally satisfactory, when the Party was in office they were unsatisfactory. 'It is essential, therefore, at the outset, that the General Council should be regarded as having an integral right to initiate and participate in any political matter which it deems to be of direct concern to its constituents.' He gave examples of the absence of consultation and added that they 'show the necessity, first, of Ministers being given to understand that their policy should be to help the Trade Union Movement in every manner possible, and, secondly, to act decisively even in the face of departmental inertia or opposition'. He suggested that the National Joint Council should be reconstituted to play a role in Labour Party and future Labour Government policy-making. He wanted the power of a future Labour Prime Minister to be weakened by taking away his unfettered right to appoint his Cabinet and compelling him to consult, say, the National Joint Council about Cabinet appointments.

These proposals suited the mood of trade unionists. There was a feeling of anger at the betrayal of the Movement by MacDonald, Snowden, and Thomas, which, in Thomas's case, was reflected in his ignominious dismissal from his union post of general secretary.[2] There was general agreement in the trade union movement that such major defections should not be allowed to occur again. But fourteen years passed before Labour came back into office and in that time memories lapsed, tempers subsided, and attitudes mellowed.

[1] Report of Meeting (T.U.C. File).
[2] See *Power in Trade Unions*, by V. L. Allen, pp. 237–239, for a description of the dismissal.

Appendix IV

TRADE UNION SPONSORED MEMBERS OF THE LABOUR GOVERNMENT IN 1929

Cabinet

Arthur Henderson (National Union of Foundry Workers)—Secretary of State for Foreign Affairs.

J. H. Thomas (National Union of Railwaymen)—Lord Privy Seal.

J. R. Clynes (National Union of General and Municipal Workers)—Secretary of State for the Home Department.

Thomas Shaw (United Textile Factory Workers' Association)—Secretary of State for War.

William Adamson (Miners' Federation)—Secretary of State for Scotland.

Margaret Bondfield (National Union of General and Municipal Workers)—Minister of Labour.

Not in Cabinet[1]

F. O. Roberts (Typographical Association)—Minister of Pensions.

Alfred Short (Boilermakers' Society)—Under-Secretary for the Home Department.

W. Lunn (Miners' Federation)—Under-Secretary for Colonial Affairs.

Walter R. Smith (National Union of Boot and Shoe Operatives)—Parliamentary Secretary to the Board of Trade.

J. J. Lawson (Miners' Federation)—Parliamentary Secretary to the Minister of Labour.

G. H. Hall (Miners' Federation)—Civil Lord of the Admiralty.

Ben Turner (National Union of Textile Workers)—Secretary for Mines.

J. Alan Parkinson (Miners' Federation)—Junior Lord of the Treasury.

Charles Edwards (Miners' Federation)—Junior Lord of the Treasury.

Ben Smith (Transport and General Workers' Union)—Treasurer of the Household.

Robert Richardson (Miners' Federation)—Charity Commissioner in the House of Commons.

---

[1] The Parliamentary Secretary to the Admiralty, C. G. Ammon, had been an official of the Union of Post Office Workers but was not sponsored by that union in 1929.

Chapter Fifteen

TRADE UNIONS WITH LABOUR IN POWER
1945–1951

THE result of the general election which was declared on 26 July 1945 showed a complete change in the balance of political power. A Parliament which had been dominated by the Conservative Party was replaced by one in which the Labour Party had a majority of 145 over all other parties. For the first time in its history the Labour Party was able to form a Government with unilateral power to control Parliament and to implement the whole of its election programme. The election result also altered the relationship between the trade union and political wings of the Labour Movement.

The Labour Party had been heavily dependent upon the trade union movement since the 1931 election, when it had had only forty-six members returned to the House of Commons. Its recovery had been slow, for at the dissolution in 1945 it had only 154 members in Parliament. The trade union movement had also suffered during the early 1930s, when its membership fell to not much more than half of what it had been in 1920, but it had substantially improved its position by 1945. Its membership increased from just over $4\frac{1}{2}$ million in 1931 to almost eight million in 1945 and its status in relation to the Government was higher than it had ever been.

The two wings of the Labour Movement had experienced a fairly close and amicable association while the Labour Party formed the Parliamentary opposition. The defection of MacDonald, Snowden, and Thomas had removed a source of conflict and the replacement, by 1936, of all the old political leaders had ended connections with a past of strained relations. The new political leaders[1] and the most influential members of the General Council had worked relatively closely together on the resuscitated National Council of Labour and had produced a series of policy documents in a manner which was never possible in the 1920s. New frictions arose, of course. Some were centred on personalities, as in the case of Bevin and Morrison, while others were the product of deep-seated prejudices such as anti-intellectualism. But none was seriously disruptive.

---

[1] C. R. Attlee, Herbert Morrison, Hugh Dalton, and Arthur Greenwood—not one a trade unionist.

The exigencies and developments of the Second World War reduced both the opportunity and the need for significant differences between union leaders and Labour politicians. Some of these men were brought together as administrators in various emergency tasks and learned to respect each other's qualities. Others were too preoccupied with their wartime tasks to engage in the politics of the Labour Movement. Trade unions, moreover, were experiencing and enjoying a new kind of political independence through the lavish scale of consultations the Government had instituted with them. They had relatively little interest in what the Labour Party was doing. However, on two occasions significant disagreements occurred.

The first disagreement arose out of the attempts by the Trades Union Congress to obtain changes in the 1927 Trade Disputes and Trade Unions Act.[1] The General Council had continued to press for the complete repeal of the Act after 1931 but without success. Then when Ernest Bevin became the Minister of Labour in the wartime Coalition Government trade union hopes were raised, for Bevin had been a consistent advocate of the repeal of the Act.

The hopes were not realized. The General Council discussed the issue in September 1940 and agreed to seek an interview with the Prime Minister, Mr. Churchill. He told the Council in April 1941 that the Cabinet had decided to do nothing about the Act; that its repeal would arouse controversy and that an interim measure would be unsatisfactory.[2] Citrine informed Churchill that bad feeling would be created in the Labour Movement if the presence of Labour representatives in the Government had no effect on its policy. The Labour representatives, however, supported the Cabinet decision. What is more, when, in August 1943, the General Council threatened to contravene the Act by accepting the Union of Post Office Workers into affiliation, Attlee, Bevin, and Morrison were prepared to enforce the punitive provisions of the Act against civil servants.

Frequent discussions took place between the General Council, the Labour Ministers, and Labour Party representatives which produced nothing but strained relations.[3] There was talk about the possible effects of forcing the Government's hand, of destroying the Coalition and of the kind of general election which would follow. Citrine complained that the Labour Party had not considered the repeal of the Act to be a first-class political issue until the General Council had taken action.[4] He believed that the Labour Ministers could have

---

[1] See Chapter 4 above, pp. 79–80, for the relationship between civil servants and the Government during this affair.

[2] General Council Minutes, 10 April 1941.

[3] The Conservative and Liberal Parties also entered into the discussions.

[4] General Council Minutes, 8 June 1943.

done something to avoid the controversy and added that they had provided the General Council with inadequate information about the Government's attitude. Citrine said that they 'could get that [a revelation of what was happening] from the Conservative Ministers on the most high and fundamental questions that affected the well-being of the State. When it came to their own colleagues it was very difficult.'[1]

The General Council and the Labour Party Executive did their utmost to prevent their differences from being portrayed as disunity. And when the general election drew near they acted more tolerantly towards each other. The Labour Party stated in its draft election programme that it was in favour of repealing the Act. In response, the General Council discussed whether the demand for repeal would have electoral consequences. Only three of its members thought that the repeal of the whole Act ought to be demanded, whatever the consequences. The rest considered either that the Trades Union Congress should demand the repeal of particular clauses or that the Labour Party should be left to use its discretion in the matter. It was felt that if the repeal of the whole Act were demanded, the Conservatives would claim that unions wanted to organize a general strike and would make it an election issue. They decided in favour of the Act being completely removed from the Statute Book, but agreed that the Labour Party should advocate at the election only the removal of Clauses 5 and 6.[2]

The second occasion was just before the dissolution of Parliament in 1945. The General Council wanted to act in a consultative role to the British delegation to the United Nations Conference in April 1945 in the same way as the American and Russian trade unions acted in their delegations. Mr. Eden, the Foreign Secretary, was consistently opposed to the request, saying that it had to be assumed that the Government represented the whole of the people. The Cabinet accepted this view, and, despite trade union protests, the Government's decision remained unchanged.[3]

The matter was discussed at a General Council meeting on 23 May 1945. Citrine said that he thought Mr. Attlee held the same view as Mr. Eden. When Attlee had been approached at San Francisco he had stated that if representation were accorded to the British trade union movement then it would also have to be given to scientific bodies. Mr. George Tomlinson, a Labour member of the Govern-

---

[1] General Council Minutes, 19 August 1943.

[2] ibid., 28 March 1945. Clauses 5 and 6 prohibited civil service unions from affiliating to the T.U.C. or the Labour Party and made it illegal for membership of a trade union to be a condition of employment in any local or public authority.

[3] See T.U.C. Report, 1945, p. 116 et seq.

ment and a British assistant delegate, had informed Citrine that as he was a trade unionist he would express the trade union point of view at the Peace Conference.[1] The General Council would not accept Tomlinson's view. It thought that the issue, if not resolved to its satisfaction, might have repercussions on the relationship between trade unions and the Government. But it was on the attitude of Labour Party leaders that the General Council mainly concentrated. Citrine stated:

> that it was the view of the Labour Ministers in the Cabinet that the Trade Union Movement should have no part whatever in the making of the peace and he felt it imperative that the General Council should ascertain whether that view was held by the Labour Party as a whole. The issue which emerged from the controversy was that because Labour representatives were in the Government they alone should express the views of the Trade Union Movement, but that position could certainly not be accepted. The Trade Union Movement had seven million members whilst the Labour Party had two and a half millions, and both bodies held different points of view. It was essential that the T.U.C. should have the right to express their point of view to any Government.[2]

These opinions were accepted by the General Council but it refrained from expressing them publicly because of the imminence of a general election. The General Council did not want to embarrass the Labour Party, but it did want to make clear what it expected from the Labour Party in the event of a Labour election victory.

Later the same day the General Council met the Labour Party Executive, but they did not discuss the matter fully in case unguarded remarks about their relationship leaked out to the press. Citrine, speaking for the General Council, repeated broadly what he had said earlier and emphasized that the General Council could not accept a situation in which the Trade Union Movement only had access to the Government through the Labour Party.

He went on to protest about the treatment of trade unions in the Labour Party election manifesto. He agreed that it had been drafted in a hurry under abnormal circumstances, but unions were only mentioned in reference to the Trade Disputes Act, 1927. The General Council wanted to appeal to trade unionists through a promise of industrial improvements—a 40-hour week, two weeks' holiday with pay, a more adequate Workmen's Compensation Act, and a guaranteed working week. To this, the chairman of the Labour Party, Mr.

---

[1] Mr. Tomlinson, who was the Parliamentary Secretary to the Minister of Labour, had been a weaver and belonged to the United Textile Factory Workers' Association.
[2] General Council Minutes, 23 May 1945.

Harold Laski, replied that 'The Labour Party who were fighting the Election, regarded as their right the ultimate responsibility for the manifesto.' [1] The manifesto was nevertheless re-drafted to the satisfaction of the General Council. When the basic issue of consultation cropped up again there was an altogether different situation, for the Labour Party was in office, in a dominant and superior position.

Government-Making

The proposal made in 1931 to restrict the power of any future Labour Prime Minister in the formation of a Government was forgotten in 1945 and Mr. Attlee was left to act as he pleased. He did not start with a strong prejudice against trade unionists as Ramsay MacDonald had done.

The Parliamentary Labour Party from which he chose his Government contained 120 trade union sponsored members.[2] Few of these were counted among the Movement's most prominent leaders, as a result of the indifference of unions towards Parliamentary activities for two decades. The only obvious union candidate for high office was Ernest Bevin. The size and quality of the trade union representation in Parliament no doubt influenced Mr. Attlee, but his prime initial concern was with obtaining men with experience of Government. He gave posts to twenty-eight of the thirty-three members of the Parliamentary Labour Party who had had experience either in the Coalition Government or in the previous Labour Government. Amongst the thirty-three there were fourteen trade unionists, of whom ten received Government posts.

Altogether twenty-nine out of about eighty-one Government posts were given to union sponsored members of the Parliamentary Labour Party.[3] Six of them were in the Cabinet. Two of the union members of the Cabinet had not had previous Government experience. These were George Isaacs, president of the Trades Union Congress in 1945, who became Minister of Labour, and Aneurin Bevan, whose abilities had been displayed only in opposition,[4] who became Minister of Health. Outside the Cabinet the most important trade union newcomer to office was James Griffiths, the Minister of National Insurance.

[1] Minutes of Joint Meeting, 23 May 1945.

[2] The proportion of trade unionists in the Parliamentary Labour Party was less than in previous years, because the unions had concentrated on safe electoral seats and had not gained from the Labour Party's successes. The electoral gains and losses were carried by the constituency parties. After the 1931 election, only fourteen of their candidates were among the forty-six members of the Parliamentary Labour Party; the rest were trade unionists.

[3] See Appendix V for a list of these members.

[4] *As it Happened*, by C. R. Attlee, p. 154.

During the Labour Party's tenure of office there were many changes in the composition of the Government through deaths, resignations, retirements, and displacements. New members of the Parliamentary Labour Party had ample opportunities to show their talents. The most rapid progress was made by young intellectuals who were initially drawn into the Government as Parliamentary Private Secretaries or Parliamentary Secretaries. Towards the end of the Government's life they were prominent in it. In 1951 there were only four trade unionists in a Cabinet of seventeen and outside the Cabinet they held eighteen of the sixty-six posts. Only two of the eighteen were in charge of departments. This decline was due to a shortage of competent trade unionists upon whom Mr. Attlee could call to fill vacancies. Mr. Attlee had his preferences[1] but he would not have disregarded trade unionists of marked political ability in favour of lesser men with public school and university backgrounds.

Formal Contact

There was no single piece of consultative machinery established to deal with all the issues which arose. Sir Walter Citrine met a number of new Labour Ministers informally and talked to them about Government relations with the General Council. His impression was that the Government would be co-operative.[2] The General Council appeared to be satisfied with this state of affairs. An attempt was made to establish contact between the National Council of Labour and the Government by forming a Liaison Committee on which sat two members of the Government. But the National Council of Labour had little influence and, in any case, it was a composite body on which trade union opinions could be in the minority.[3]

The General Council had no desire to deal with problems, for which it had specialist committees, through one piece of consultative machinery. This had been made clear in 1944 when the Minister of Labour had tried to make the Joint Consultative Committee of the National Joint Advisory Council into such a body.

> The General Council [Citrine wrote] have always been opposed to confining their contacts with the Government through one Department; neither have they agreed to confining their contact with one Department to one body, particularly a joint body with the employers. I recommend that the Joint Consultative Committee should consider only those

---

[1] Mr. Attlee wrote that when he was selecting a Parliamentary private secretary for himself 'There was a wide choice, but, other things being equal, I saw no reason why I should not select someone from my old school. For the first time there were Old Haileyburians in the Labour Party in the House of Commons . . .' (*As It Happened*, p. 156).　　　　　　　　　　[2] General Council Minutes, 6 September 1945.
[3] The Co-operative Union was now represented on it.

matters with which the Minister of Labour is primarily concerned, and which do not directly conflict with the work and activities of specialist committees of the General Council.[1]

This recommendation was adopted by the General Council and later re-affirmed, in spite of protests by Bevin.

The Minister of Labour, in May 1946, wanted to do what Bevin had tried in 1944. The General Council not only opposed the idea, it complained to the Prime Minister that Ministers were neglecting to use its specialist advisory committees. 'It was the desire of the General Council', one of its members said, 'to give the maximum assistance to the Government but to make this possible all Ministers must be reminded of the necessity of using the joint machinery which existed between the Government and the T.U.C.'[2] A deputation met Mr. Attlee on 29 November 1946 and asked him to circulate a note about consultation to all Departmental Ministers. He did this, urging 'Ministers to be vigilant in ensuring that the T.U.C. and, in suitable cases, individual trade unions, are fully taken into consultation wherever appropriate at the earliest possible stage.'[3] But, as in the case of Ramsay MacDonald's directive, the effectiveness of this one depended largely upon the personalities of the Ministers.

THE MAIN POINTS OF CONTACT

All members of the Government were committed to a general policy which had been determined in consultation with the unions. There were different conceptions within the Labour Movement as to precisely what that policy entailed, but they did not always involve unions, and when they did they were relatively unimportant. The most important matters which did involve the unions concerned the application of policy.

Some Legislative Acts

(a) *Conscription.* This, which was covered by expiring legislation, concerned unions through its impact on industry, particularly on apprenticeships. Late in October 1946 the Prime Minister and the Minister of Defence designate met the chairman, vice-chairman, and general secretary of the Trades Union Congress informally and said that there was going to be a reference in the King's Speech to continuing conscription after the expiration of the National Service (Armed Forces) Act on 1 January 1949. They arranged a meeting

---

[1] Memorandum by Sir Walter Citrine on the Joint Consultative Committee to the Minister of Labour, 24 July 1944 (T.U.C. File).
[2] General Council Minutes, 25 September 1946.
[3] T.U.C. Report, 1947, p. 299

with the General Council at which the Prime Minister stated the case for maintaining conscription. No one on the General Council opposed it, though a few of its members said they were unwilling to accept conscription for an unlimited period. A motion was eventually accepted which stated that the General Council felt there was justification for continuing conscription for a limited period beyond January 1949.

During his statement to the General Council the Prime Minister said 'that it had always been the desire of the Labour Government to work in the closest co-operation with the industrial side of the Movement, and to consult with the T.U.C. on major questions of policy. He desired the present matter to be treated with the utmost confidence.' [1] But, of course, the Government was not seeking the advice of the General Council about conscription because it had already made its decision. It was simply providing advance information on a matter which was to be made public a week later.

(*b*) *Restoration of Pre-War Practices.* The Restoration of Pre-War Trade Practices Act, 1942, placed on employers the obligation to restore trade practices relaxed during the war period, within two months of the expiration of the Act. The 'war period' meant the period beginning on 3 September 1939 and ending not later than the date on which the Emergency Powers (Defence) Act, 1939, expired. As this Act was due to expire on 24 February 1946 and as the Government considered it to be unpropitious to declare the war period to be at an end on that date, the Minister of Labour wrote to the General Council to get it to agree to delay bringing the 1942 Act into operation. The General Council agreed to a Government suggestion that the Restoration of Pre-War Practices Act should not be applied until December 1947. Then, because of the severe economic situation in 1947, it agreed to a further postponement of the Act. It was not until 1951 that the Act was applied.

The General Council's willingness to delay applying the 1942 Act did not involve trade unions in making undue concessions. The Act referred to workshop practices, most of which were covered by national or local agreements between employers and unions in the engineering and shipbuilding industries, and over which the Government had no control whatever. Many of these agreements, especially the local ones, were changed as industrial conditions altered after the war and in their new form they were excluded from the jurisdiction of the Act.[2] In so far as the 1942 Act had any meaning

---

[1] General Council Minutes, 5 November 1946.
[2] The National Joint Advisory Council decided in October 1949 that agreements concluded after the end of the war would not be covered by the Act.

after the war it was in helping to maintain the sense of urgency in solving production problems. The General Council simply displayed its desire to co-operate with the Government by delaying the application of the Act.

(*c*) *Trade Disputes and Trade Unions Act, 1927.* This matter was decided by the election result. The repeal of the Act was mentioned in the King's Speech on 15 August 1945 and in May 1946 it was put into effect. The General Council expressed its gratitude publicly for the Government's prompt and uncomplicated action.[1]

(*d*) *Order 1305.* The Government had to act fairly quickly over this piece of expiring wartime labour legislation. The Conditions of Employment and National Arbitration Order 1305 was made in July 1940 under the emergency powers conferred on the Government which were due to lapse on 24 February 1946. The future of the Order was also of immediate concern to the Trades Union Congress, for at its 1945 meeting it had agreed to press for the abolition of its main provision, namely compulsory arbitration.

The Minister of Labour told the Joint Consultative Committee that the Government could either (*a*) continue the Order for a limited period after 24 February 1946, (*b*) allow it to lapse, leaving the Industrial Court to function under its existing constitution, i.e. without compulsory powers, or (*c*) allow the Order to lapse and to reconstitute the Industrial Court on lines similar to the National Arbitration Tribunal.[2] The Government preferred the first method, and the union representatives on the Committee, without having time to consult the General Council, agreed to continue the Order until such time as the T.U.C. and the British Employers' Confederation desired its termination. A Supplies and Services (Transitional Powers) Bill was drawn up which provided for the retention of a number of Defence Regulations, including the one under which Order 1305 was made.

The decision to accept a continuation of the Order was endorsed by the General Council, despite the resolution of the Trades Union Congress in 1945. The General Council stated that there had been no serious demands from unions for the complete revocation of the Order. Indeed, a number of union leaders wanted some of its provisions, for instance the one compelling employers to observe National Arbitration Tribunal decisions, retained permanently. It added that it did not want to damage the system of controls which had been instituted during the war. And as one of the conditions on which unions had accepted the Order in 1940 was that the Government should introduce price controls and rationing, the General

[1] T.U.C. Report, 1946, p. 24.   [2] General Council Minutes, 19 December 1945.

Council felt that the withdrawal of the Order would encourage the campaign for the elimination of price controls which was then being conducted. It agreed to re-examine the situation periodically.

Each year until 1951 the General Council agreed to accept the Order. Its reasons varied, for the system of wartime controls had been seriously damaged by 1951. It continued to accept the restrictions on the right to strike which the Order imposed, because it wanted to assist the Government to reduce the volume of strike action and it regarded the Order as a restraining influence. But the members of the General Council had a feeling of apprehension about the penal clauses in the Order. Even the Order's most ardent supporters, such as Arthur Deakin, disliked the idea that strikers should be punished. So it was surprising when the Government suddenly embarked on two provocative sets of prosecutions against strikers within a period of five months, without, in one case, even informing the General Council of its intention.

The first case occurred just a month after the Trades Union Congress had endorsed the Order by a large majority. On 16 September 1950 about 1,700 gas maintenance workers went on strike against a wage settlement of $1\frac{1}{2}d.$ an hour which had been signed by their union, the National Union of General and Municipal Workers. The strike seriously interfered with the supply of gas and the Cabinet decided to prosecute the strike leaders, but twice postponed the application of its decision in the hope that the strike would be settled. The decision was applied on the seventeenth day of the strike when ten of the strikers were summoned under the Conspiracy and Protection of Property Act of 1875 and Section 4 of Order 1305. The strikers had contravened the 1875 Act by depriving the public of its supply of gas and they had infringed the Order because they had not given the Minister of Labour twenty-one days' notice of the intention to strike. Only the summonses relating to the Order were proceeded with and, on 5 October, each of the men was sentenced to one month's imprisonment. On the same day the strikers agreed to return to work. The convicted men appealed against the sentences, which were altered to fines of £50.

There were some trade unionists who had a genuine desire to preserve their right to strike and who regarded the Order 1305 as a trespass on this right; there were others who disliked the Order because they wanted to increase and intensify strikes against the Government and employers. The Government's action joined these two groups and put a solid body of trade union opinion behind them. A powerful agitation against the Order started which the General Council could not ignore. The Government, foolishly breaking faith with the General Council, stimulated the agitation by a second act about four months later.

On 8 February 1951 seven dock members of the Transport and General Workers' Union were arrested for conspiring 'with others unknown to incite dock workers to take part in strikes in connection with trade disputes contrary to Article Four' of Order 1305. The union's general secretary, Arthur Deakin, was not consulted, or even officially informed, about the arrests. He first read about them in a morning newspaper.[1] Many dockers expressed their indignation by staging one-day strikes during the court hearings. The decisions of the jury on different counts were inconsistent and for this reason, it was announced, the prosecutions were withdrawn.

The damage to Order 1305 was complete, for the prosecution of strikers was not tolerated even in wartime. The General Council's dislike of the prosecutions, however, was not wholly emotional. Trade unionists who were dissatisfied with the official union policies were forming their own unofficial bodies and it was these bodies which were engaging in strike action. If they conformed to Order 1305 and gave the Minister of Labour notice of the intent to strike then they would further undermine the official leadership of unions. So the General Council raised the question of amending the Order with the Minister of Labour. The Government, even if it had desired it, was in no position to insist on the retention of the Order with its penal provisions, for an official union disregard of the Order would have rendered it inoperative. The Courts could not have sent hundreds of thousands of trade unionists to prison. On 2 August 1951 the Minister of Labour, Mr. Alfred Robens, announced that Order 1305 had been withdrawn and that a new Order, without provisions making strikes or lock-outs illegal, had been introduced.[2]

Nationalization

The number and types of industries selected by the Labour Party in 1945 for nationalization were not questioned, in the main, by trade unions. A few unions were disappointed at the omission of their particular industries, but most considered the programme to be sufficiently intensive to keep the Labour Government fully occupied. The arguments about the form of nationalization which had reached a high pitch in the early 1930s had subsided. In general it was agreed that the 'public corporation' form should be adopted. Little consideration, whether by unions or by the Labour Party, had been

---

[1] Quarterly Report to the General Executive Council of the T. & G.W.U., March 1951. The strikes in which the dockers had been involved were unofficial and strongly opposed by the union executive.   [2] See T.U.C. Report, 1951, pp. 232–234.

given to the actual implementation of nationalization. This was left to be worked out when Labour gained power to legislate.[1]

Trade union interests in the process of nationalization were mainly guarded by the various unions directly concerned, and the appropriate Government departments established contact with these unions. In this way many minor difficulties were removed. On issues of principle with a relevance beyond the confines of a single industry, the Trades Union Congress acted for the unions. One such issue was appointments to nationalized boards; another concerned the clauses in Nationalization Bills to establish negotiating machinery; and the third was about compensation for workers made worse off by nationalization.

(*i*) *Boards of Nationalized Industries.* The question of appointments to nationalized boards had been raised in discussions about workers' control at the Trades Union Congress from 1932 to 1935. In 1932 the General Council stated, in a report on 'Trade Unionism and the Control of Industry', that 'Boards of management of socialized industries or services should consist of persons appointed by the Government solely on the ground of their fitness for the positions, not excluding persons from any class but not selected as representing particular interests. Advisory Committees should be constituted to represent particular interests including trade unionism.' [2] This statement was criticized but no decision about it was taken. The next year the General Council admitted that there was 'a strong desire that the Trade Unions should, by statute, be given an adequate place on the Board of Management responsible for the general control and direction of each socialized industry or service'.[3] It pointed out the difficulties in applying this principle and concluded that it should be exercised after consultations between the responsible Minister and the trade unions concerned. This view was still criticized by unions. By 1935 the General Council had adopted the majority view of unions, namely that they had a right to be represented on Boards of Management of nationalized industries and that it should be 'secured by statute'.[4]

[1] Mr. Emanuel Shinwell, who had the job of nationalizing the mines in the Labour Government, commenting on this matter, said: 'For the whole of my political life I had listened to the Party speakers advocating state ownership and control of the coal mines, and I had myself spoken of it as a primary task once the Labour Party was in power. I had believed, as other members had, that in the Party archives a blue-print was ready. . . . I found nothing practical and tangible existed . . . I had to start on a clear desk' (*Conflict Without Malice*, pp. 172–173).

[2] T.U.C. Report, 1932, p. 219.   [3] ibid., 1933, p. 210.

[4] See T.U.C. Report, 1935, p. 211. In 1933, Arthur Pugh, for the General Council, said that a questionnaire had been sent out to affiliated unions asking their views on workers' participation in the control of industry. A majority had criticized the General Council.

The issue was revived in 1944 when the General Council pointed out to the Trades Union Congress that no decision had been taken about the implementation of the right claimed by the unions, and suggested 'that the statutory obligation of the Minister should be limited to consultation with the T.U.C. in the appointment of one or two members of each Board constituted to control a socialized industry or service. The T.U.C. would in turn consult with the appropriate Unions.'[1] This suggestion was accepted by the Congress.

When the Labour Government was in the process of implementing its nationalization programme, the composition of boards of management raised important practical questions for trade unions. How many trade unionists should sit on each board? What should their relationship be to their trade unions? How should they be selected? And what kind of men should sit with them to enable the boards to function effectively? The questions did not come up immediately, nor did they all have direct implications for the Government as well as unions. The relationship between union members of boards of nationalized industries and their respective unions was a matter for debate within the trade union movement.

The Government pursued a policy of requiring board members to be responsible only to the industry they were serving. The General Council supported this and stated:

> It is essential that the Trade Union Movement should retain its complete independence of the executive and employing authority of a nationalized industry. Only thus can unions exert their power of independent criticism and perform, without divided loyalties, their primary functions of maintaining and advancing the working conditions of workpeople. In these circumstances it is desirable that trade unionists who are selected to serve on the Boards of Public Corporations should sever their formal connection with unions in the industries concerned.[2]

This attitude remained unaltered, although its merits were debated at various times. The boards, trade unionists generally believed, should be influenced by union attitudes and thought. But in the absence of direct representation how surely could this be achieved?

Quite soon after some of the Nationalization Acts had begun to operate there was union dissatisfaction at the paucity of trade unionists on the boards. Some trade unionists regarded this as a reflection on the ability of union leaders by the Government, and they loudly criticized Sir Stafford Cripps, President of the Board of Trade, when he said:

> From my experience there is not as yet a very large number of workers

[1] *T.U.C. Interim Report on Post War Reconstruction,* 1944.
[2] T.U.C. Report, 1949, p. 213.

in Britain capable of taking over large enterprises. . . . It has always been extremely difficult to get enough people who are qualified to do that sort of job, and, until there has been more experience by the workers of the managerial side of industry, I think it would be almost impossible to have worker-controlled industry in Britain even if it were on the whole desirable.[1]

The Trades Union Congress, however, did not dispute the general validity of Cripps's statement. At its meeting in 1947 it asked the Government to provide the fullest participation by workers in the management of nationalized industries, but it also instructed the General Council 'to review and enlarge the educational opportunities open to trade unionists, so as to give the workers the necessary background and qualifications for the greater responsibilities which of necessity fall upon them'.[2]

The question arose again at the Trades Union Congress in 1948 when a motion was accepted, heavily supported by the railway and miners' unions, stressing the need for greater workers' participation in the nationalized industries. The discussion was mainly about union representation on the boards, and the complaints were about under-representation.[3] Neither the speakers nor the motion indicated how many trade unionists should sit on the boards. But a figure was stated by others at different times. In 1950, for instance, the Association of Supervisory Staffs, Executives and Technicians asked for at least one-third of the members of boards to be representatives of the trade union movement.[4]

The case for having a higher percentage of trade unionists on the boards of nationalized industries was stated, with slight variations, at different Congresses. J. B. Figgins outlined it in 1948. He said: 'It is not merely a question of having technical knowledge and administrative ability . . . you must win efficiency, and if you are to win efficiency, then you must get the enthusiastic co-operation of the workers.'[5] Other union leaders made much of the need to make nationalization a success. But if it were believed to be true that more experienced and able trade union officials on the boards would have

---

[1] *The Times*, 28 October 1946.
[2] T.U.C. Report, 1947, pp. 472–473.
[3] Mr. J. B. Figgins, general secretary of the National Union of Railwaymen, quoted the boards in his own industry as examples of under-representation. He said 'we have only got one representative . . . out of five full-time members on the British Transport Commission. On the Railway Executive Committee it is more thoroughly weighted against us, because we have only one representative out of seven full-time members . . .' Mr. Abe Moffat, a Scottish miners' leader, said that the boards had 'a very insignificant number of trade union representatives playing a very insignificant part in . . . determining the policy of the Boards . . .' (T.U.C. Report, 1948, pp. 371–373).
[4] ibid., 1950, p. 514.　　　　　　　　　　[5] ibid., 1948, p. 372.

increased their efficiency, why did not the General Council press the Government more assiduously for greater trade union representation on the boards?[1] And why, if this were so, in view of the desperate need for increased efficiency, did not the Government do this in any case?

The main difficulty lay in the inability of trade unions to spare their experienced and most able officials for even the noblest of causes outside the trade union movement. Sir Stafford Cripps was aware of this. He wrote that he had had difficulty even in getting enough trade unionists to man a single working-party. 'Those who are qualified are already, most of them, hopelessly overworked on their own trade union affairs and just cannot be spared.' [2] Mr. Lincoln Evans made a similar point in a Trades Union Congress debate in 1950.[3] In any case, some officials did not want to leave their union posts. Arthur Deakin, for instance, refused to go on the Transport Commission. And after the National Union of Mineworkers had successfully persuaded the Government to add another trade unionist to the two already serving on the National Coal Board, no suitably qualified miners' leader could be found who was willing to leave his union.

The General Council was not satisfied with the manner in which all the trade unionists were selected to serve on the boards of nationalized industries. In October 1945 it established a Fuel and Power Advisory Committee, at the invitation of Mr. Shinwell, the Minister of Fuel and Power, to advise him informally. At the Minister's first meeting with the Committee he was reminded that there was no clause in the Coal Industry Nationalization Bill requiring him to consult with the Trades Union Congress about the selection of trade unionists for the National Coal Board. He said he was unwilling to make such a statutory provision but that he would consult with the Trades Union Congress and the National Union of Mineworkers about the appointment of one member from each body.[4] He did so and Sir Walter Citrine and Mr. Ebby Edwards were appointed.[5] The

---

[1] When the Coal Industry Act was passed in 1949, the Minister of Fuel and Power was given the authority to increase the size of the National Coal Board. A General Council delegation asked the Minister, Mr. Hugh Gaitskell, whether trade unions could have extra representation if the authority were used. Mr. Gaitskell told the delegation what was obviously the Government view, 'that, whilst a balanced representation must be secured, experience in the organization of workpeople would continue to be regarded as an important qualification' (T.U.C. Report, 1949, p. 228). The delegation was satisfied.   [2] *The Times*, 17 January 1947.

[3] General secretary of the British Iron, Steel and Kindred Trades Association and Chairman of the Economic Committee of the General Council of the T.U C. (T.U.C. Report, 1950, p. 517).

[4] T.U.C. Report, 1946, p. 209 and p. 218.

[5] Mr. Edwards had been general secretary of the Miners' Federation, later National Union of Mineworkers, since 1932.

General Council expected consultation on appointment to boards to be extended to other nationalized industries as a result of Mr. Shinwell's assurance.[1] It was disappointed. It complained to the Government in 1948, and in 1949 stated its view that the 'T.U.C., as representing the viewpoint of organized workers in general, expects to be consulted by the Minister concerned when persons are being appointed to the Boards of Public Corporations'.[2] This was more than consultation about the appointment of trade unionists.

In some cases the individual unions were consulted about appointments. The determinants here were the attitude of the Ministers and the power of the unions involved. The National Union of Bank Employees, with less than 26,000 members and no negotiating rights with the big banks, wanted to be consulted about the appointment of trade unionists to the Court of the Bank of England. When it complained, late in 1947, about the lack of consultation the General Council replied that the Chancellor of the Exchequer had not even consulted it about appointments. The Chancellor of the Exchequer, when told about this, replied that it was important to avoid

> anything which might be construed as representation of sectional interests on a body with such wide responsibilities as the Court of the Bank of England. In these circumstances the procedure, which had been adopted with some public bodies, of inviting the General Council to submit several names from which appointments might be made, was not appropriate. Nevertheless, he would be glad to keep in touch with the General Council informally so that any names which the T.U.C. cared to put forward from time to time might be taken into consideration, along with others, before final selection was made.

This reply was accepted by the General Council as being reasonable. The General Council said that it, in turn, would ask the National Union of Bank Employees for advice.[3]

There was no difficulty of this kind where the National Union of Mineworkers was involved. It was invariably consulted and its advice carried weight. When a successor was being chosen for Lord Hyndley, chairman of the National Coal Board, in 1951, the union supported the candidature of Sir Hubert Houldsworth and he was appointed although he did not possess all the qualities which made for a successful chairman of a nationalized industry.

Another grievance against the Government was over its selection of the other members of boards. 'Some of the people appointed', one speaker said at the Trades Union Congress in 1947, 'have been the grimmest and bitterest opponents of the Trade Union Movement

---

[1] T.U.C. Report, 1946, p. 218.   [2] ibid., 1949, p. 212.
[3] ibid. 1948, p. 239.

in the strikes and struggles of the past. . . .'[1] Undoubtedly many men sat on the boards who had never professed sympathy for trade unionism or even nationalization, and they tended to hold the most important positions on most of the boards. Of the forty-seven full-time members on twelve national boards in 1951, thirteen had been company directors, ten managers and engineers, four civil servants, three military men, three accountants, two solicitors, nine trade unionists, and three others.[2] Five of the twelve boards had no trade unionists among their full-time members. There was a comparable distribution of occupations among the part-time members. No board had a majority of left-wing sympathizers. This was the situation all the time the Labour Government was in office, despite continued trade union protests.

(*ii*) *The Establishment of Negotiating Machinery by Statute.* This issue arose over the inclusion in the Civil Aviation Bill in 1946 of clause 19, which was intended to ensure that each of the Airways Corporations to be established by the Bill should, 'in the determination of questions affecting the wages, working conditions, safety, health, and welfare of their workpeople, conform to the principles and practices of collective negotiation and agreement with the appropriate Trade Union or Trade Unions'. A similar clause had been included in the Coal Industry Nationalization Bill.[3]

The Amalgamated Engineering Union, which organized civil aviation workers, protested to the Trades Union Congress that the Government had not asked it for advice about the clause. The Trades Union Congress, it was discovered, had not been consulted by the Government either over that clause or any similar clause in other Bills nor had any other union in civil aviation heard beforehand about the clause. The National Union of Mineworkers knew about it but had made no comment.

It rankled with the Trades Union Congress that it should be ignored by the Government. Then it was realized, giving the complaint greater point, that the meaning of the clause was obscure and was likely to create difficulties. A part of the clause stated that each Corporation should seek consultation 'with any organization appearing to the Corporation to represent a substantial proportion of persons . . .' Who was to decide which unions these were? The employers alone? the employers and trade unions in concert? or the law courts?

The issue which this clause raised was a fundamental one to the

[1] See T.U.C. Report, 1947, p. 475.
[2] *The Men on the Boards*, by the Acton Society Trust, 1951, p. 6.
[3] See T.U.C. Report, 1946, pp. 218–219.

Nationalization 277

Trades Union Congress. There were two unions in civil aviation not affiliated to the Trades Union Congress and not considered by it to be *bona fide* unions. Any interpretation of the clause which resulted in either or both of these unions being given negotiating rights would have created inter-union conflicts and could have disrupted the machinery of negotiation. In any case the Trades Union Congress wanted to have control over its own preserve, without having to seek interpretations at law. It wanted the clause to be withdrawn or amended satisfactorily.

A series of protests to the Government started in June 1946. The Lord Privy Seal, Mr. Arthur Greenwood, was in charge of the Civil Aviation Bill in Parliament and the General Council representatives saw him first. He regretted his failure to consult the Trades Union Congress and undertook to alter the wording of the clause.[1] The alteration did not satisfy the General Council, so Greenwood was approached to get the clause deleted. He repeated his regret about the lack of consultation but added that the Bill had reached a stage in Parliament where it was politically unwise to withdraw the clause. There was nothing the General Council could do apart from protest to the Prime Minister.

Mr. Attlee asked George Isaacs, the Minister of Labour, for his view before replying to the General Council. Isaacs, in a note, stated that he disagreed with the General Council and considered the amended clause to be a suitable one. This opinion, and those previously expressed by Greenwood, were included in Attlee's reply. The General Council gained no concessions, but at the end of his letter Attlee stated: 'I hope that the General Council will be satisfied with this explanation and I would add that, in any further extensions of our nationalization policy, the T.U.C. General Council and such organizations as they feel are directly concerned, will be consulted before any clause affecting industrial relationships is finally drafted.' [2]

(*iii*) *Compensation for Displaced Workpeople.* This issue also concerned the terms of Nationalization Bills. After the return of Labour to power the General Council discussed how workers could claim compensation if they became redundant through industrial reorganization. It decided that whereas legislation would be unsuitable for workers in private undertakings, in nationalized industries it would be a practical way of ensuring that compensation was paid. This method had been tried satisfactorily in the Electricity Acts of 1919, 1922, and 1928 and in the London Passenger Transport Act, 1933 and the Local Government Act, 1933. The General Council, in

[1] Finance & General Purposes Committee Minutes (T.U.C. General Council), 12 June 1946.   [2] ibid., 22 July 1946.

T.U.G.—T

1946, wanted compensation terms not less favourable than those included in the London Passenger Transport Act.

The Coal Industry Nationalization Bill, the Government's first measure to transfer an industry to public ownership, did not contain a compensation clause for workers so the General Council approached Mr. Shinwell. He refused to alter the Bill, considering 'that the general legislative provisions to meet this problem might be exploited by interests without a genuine claim for benefit . . .' [1] This statement conflicted with Trades Union Congress policy and the matter was taken to Mr. Attlee in March 1946. He accepted the responsibility for providing 'adequate protection' to workers in the transference of industries from private to public ownership, but preferred to undertake it in the case of the coal industry by giving the Minister the power in the Bill to issue Regulations to cover compensation. The General Council was satisfied by this statement but the Bill was amended without further consultation. There seemed to be no end to irritation from this source. As the General Council had not seen the draft of the amended clause it asked if it could see the draft of the Regulations before they were issued. Shinwell replied that this request was premature and that, in any case, consultation should be with the National Union of Mineworkers rather than with the Trades Union Congress. [2] The irritation was not eased by this reply.

The points at issue with the Government, besides that of consultation, were whether compensation provisions should be expressly stated in each Act or whether they should be covered by Regulations; whether the actual financial loss should be calculated, as the General Council claimed, or whether a claimant for compensation should have to consider 'prospects of alternative employment' and prove 'substantial hardship'. The General Council had agreed to the issue of Regulations in the case of the coal industry and it felt it had made a considerable concession to the Government. Eventually, after an exchange of letters with the Prime Minister and two meetings with him, it agreed to accept the issue of Regulations in every case. It expected the Government to make a concession in return.

Mr. Attlee had stated, in a letter dated 16 June 1946, that in calculating provision for compensation two factors should be taken into account: that the working population in general would benefit from the nationalization and full employment policy of the Government; and that 'nationalization schemes must not be hampered by unduly onerous compensation provisions which might lead to frivolous claims . . .' [3] The General Council refused to accept the

[1] T.U.C. Report, 1946, p. 209.   [2] ibid., 1946, p. 209.   [3] ibid., 1946, p. 217.

first point on the ground that the precise result of those Government policies was not measurable in the case of individuals. Nor could it accept the second which was used to justify making claimants for compensation prove 'substantial hardship'. The phrase had no precise meaning. The Government, however, refused to budge from its position.

Then the General Council informed the Prime Minister that it and the unions concerned would have to reopen negotiations in the case of each nationalization measure. It asked to meet him again in view of the strong feelings which unions had about compensation. When a deputation saw him in March 1947 it told him that 'there would be considerable resentment in the industries concerned if the Labour Government were to provide compensation on less favourable terms than had been provided for in previous negotiations'.[1] He then conceded that there ought to be a precise standard for assessing compensation and that some account should be taken of previous legislative provisions. Agreement was also reached over consultation. It was decided that the actual discussions on draft Regulations should take place between the unions and the Government departments involved, once the method of assessing the actual amount of compensation to be paid had been settled by informal discussions between the officials of the Trades Union Congress and the Government.

Thereafter the Trades Union Congress became involved in discussions about compensation through its separate advisory committees. Negotiations took place between unions and the Government over draft Regulations for the Bills nationalizing the transport, electricity, gas, and iron and steel industries, and the health service and national insurance. Difficulties with the Government over compensation did not wholly cease. For instance, in February 1948 the Fuel and Power Advisory Committee of the Trades Union Congress met the Prime Minister to protest against the inadequacy of the provisions in the Gas Bill as compared with those in the Electricity Act of 1947. The Government made a slight concession which was accepted. But in the main the going was smooth. The Bills and their compensation clauses became law and an appeals machinery was set up in September 1948 to deal with complaints about the operation of the clauses.

(*iv*) *Extent of Nationalization.* Before the general election in 1950 the policy of nationalization was re-examined separately by the Labour Party and the Trades Union Congress, and jointly through joint committees and common meetings. The point at issue was not

---

[1] ibid., 1947, p. 269.

the form nationalization should take, or its practical application, but the extent of further nationalization proposals. After 1945 various unions demanded that their respective industries should be nationalized. The armaments industry, fire insurance, shipbuilding, the rubber manufacturing industry, shipping, the engineering industry, and the chemical industry were each listed by one union or another as being suitable for nationalization. The Trades Union Congress, on advice from the General Council, treated these demands with caution, sometimes apprehension. Most were rejected or quietly passed over after being remitted to the General Council. At no time was there sufficient trade union feeling in favour of extending nationalization to bring the Trades Union Congress into conflict with the Government policy of simply executing its electoral mandate. Nor did any serious differences arise over the formulation of future nationalization policy for the general elections in 1950 and 1951.

Government Economic Policy

The economic problems which faced Britain after the war could not have been tackled effectively without Government intervention. A transition had to be made from war to peacetime production. The country had to rebuild and restock its damaged and depreciated industries; regain its export markets and divert goods to them from the domestic market; and it had to prevent inflation. In order to tackle its problems the Government needed a behaviour from trade unionists which was contrary to some of their traditions and practices and to much of the advice they had been given by their leaders in the past. Trade unionists were distrustful of requests to increase productivity because productivity was positively related to profits and it was considered wrong to increase profits; they were opposed to, sometimes hostile about, the introduction of new methods or machines which led to redundancy because they had lived under conditions of unemployment or under-employment; they jealously guarded restrictive practices which they had struggled to establish because they were a protection against the whims or motives of employers and against the exigencies of economic fluctuations. In addition, trade unionists had a long-lived, deep-seated objection to Government interference in wage determination.

Trade union behaviour had become more tolerant about these things during the war as a result of war conditions and, to a lesser extent, the guarantees and concessions made by the Government. But when the war ended the main force making for collaboration disappeared and the Government was confronted with the task of overcoming inhibitions, removing prejudices and winning the confidence not simply of union leaders but of the rank-and-file members who saw all problems in their local context. The Labour Government started with the goodwill of workers but it did not thereby automatically obtain their collaboration.

Late in January 1946, the Minister of Labour telephoned Citrine to ask whether the General Council would agree to call a conference of trade union executives in the spring to meet Bevin and himself to discuss some production problems. A few days later he told a group of General Council representatives 'that the Government proposed to start a campaign throughout the country to enlighten people as to the present precarious position; to urge a production drive; to appeal to the women to return to industry temporarily. Before embarking on that campaign, however, it was felt that the Trade Union Movement should be taken into the confidence of the Government . . .' [1] The General Council agreed to convene a conference but it was not prepared to commit itself to a statement of policy on all the issues which would be raised, nor did it want to give the impression that it endorsed the Government statements which would be made. It therefore listed the items on which it wanted the Government's opinion, and drew up a motion to be put to the conference which would clear it of any responsibility for what was said.

The conference was held on 6 March 1946. Nothing was said by the Government spokesmen which was contrary to the General Council's policy, and at the end a long motion was endorsed which declared a determination to tackle various economic problems 'in accordance with the policy laid down by the Trades Union Congress . . .' and instructed the General Council 'to give careful consideration to the statements made by the Ministers and the discussion arising therefrom with a view to affording guidance to the affiliated unions on the subjects which had been raised'.[2] It was clear that this type of co-operation was not going to help the Government very much.

The Government, however, did not intend to have its plans for the nationwide campaign rendered innocuous by trade union indifference. It made arrangements to call regional conferences of workers' and employers' representatives and then asked the General Council to support them. The General Council, of course, protested at the lack of consultation and stated that it did not like the idea of mixed conferences. The Minister of Labour said he would suggest to the Lord Presidents' Committee of the Cabinet that either separate conferences of trade unionists and employers should be held or, if

[1] F. & G.P.C. of the General Council Minutes, 5 February 1946.
[2] T.U.C. Report, 1946, p. 197.

mixed conferences were to be held, that they should be addressed by a Minister with no questions or discussion.[1] The arrangements in hand were not altered: the conferences were mixed, were addressed by Cabinet Ministers, and were open to questions and discussion.

The General Council at the end of the war insisted on implementing the Trades Union Congress demand for a forty-hour week. It decided to encourage and assist unions to obtain the forty-hour week by voluntary collective bargaining, and at the same time to approach the Government for legislation to make the practice general. Affiliated unions were asked for details about their efforts to get a forty-hour week and discussions were held with the Labour Party in March 1946. The Labour Party delegation, containing three members of the Cabinet, pointed out the adverse effects on production which reduced hours might create, but the General Council had already considered and rejected similar arguments and was prepared to take its case to the Government.

The General Council's complacency about the country's economic problems was also shown by its attitude to wages. When, for instance, the Government stated in a White Paper in January 1947[2] that production should be increased before there was any general increase in the level of profits or wages, the General Council simply informed the Minister of Labour that 'Unions would reserve the right to continue to be free to make wages applications as formerly and to negotiate such claims'.[3]

The precarious state of Britain's economy was apparent late in 1946. The American Loan was being consumed rapidly by rising prices, and the foreign trade deficit was taking the form of an acute shortage of dollars. But it still seemed that the transition from war to peace would be made without large-scale unemployment of the kind which marked the transition after the First World War. Then came the awakening. Britain had a fuel shortage. The Minister of Fuel and Power announced to the House of Commons on 7 February 1947 that electricity supplies would have to be cut because of the coal shortage. Without fuel, industries had to close down. The total number of insured persons registered as unemployed on 9 December 1946 was 362,976; by 22 February it had risen to 1,874,061.[4] When weather conditions had improved and coal could be transported the number of unemployed fell. It went below the December level, to

[1] General Council Minutes, 12 March 1946.
[2] Statement on the Economic Considerations Affecting the Relations Between Employers and Workers.
[3] General Council Minutes, 22 January 1947.
[4] *Ministry of Labour Gazette,* January and June 1947. In February an additional 503,200 persons were said to be unemployed but they did not register.

331,543, by 12 May. This transitory break in the state of full employment reminded union leaders how quickly and easily the economic
strength of their unions could be swept away. The high membership
of trade unions was in part a product of full employment, the
maintenance of which was determined by several factors involving
labour. Union leaders saw clearly that the size and power of their
organizations and the state of the economy bore a direct relationship
to each other.

One of the first signs that the General Council was prepared to
adapt its demands to suit national economic needs was shown in its
attitude to hours. The fuel crisis had started by the time the General
Council met the Government to state its case for a forty-hour week.
It realized that the demand was politically as well as economically
untenable and that the Government was likely to ask unions to agree
to work longer hours. So it dropped its demand and spent its time at
the meeting discussing the possibility of increasing working hours. It
did not make any more concessions, however, until 1948.

It was becoming evident as the year 1947 slipped by that the
Government would have to take some action over wages. The fuel
crisis was followed by a critical foreign trade situation in July and
August 1947. Under the terms of the American Loan Britain was
required to make sterling freely convertible into other currencies on
15 July 1947. Convertibility increased the already excessive demand
on Britain's dollar reserves to such an extent that crisis dimensions
were reached and, on 20 August, the Chancellor of the Exchequer
announced that the free convertibility of sterling into dollars was
suspended. The Government clearly needed to take steps to reduce
or at least stabilize British prices in order to boost the sale of exports.
It acted by trying to restrict demand in the home market.

The Prime Minister did not think that the Government should
attempt to regulate wages. This was Ernest Bevin's opinion and he
had impressed it on Mr. Attlee.[1] None of the influential union
leaders nor the Labour Party Executive wanted a wages policy.[2] But
nor did any of them offer a feasible alternative suggestion. The
General Council heard about the Government's difficulties with
sympathy but did not consider that it was its job to attempt to
formulate a policy. The Government, on the other hand, was loath
to intrude into heavily guarded trade union territory. Many meetings
between the representatives of the two bodies were held during 1947.
When the General Council met on 6 August it agreed to a reintroduc-
tion of a Control of Engagements Order and, given satisfactory

---

[1] Interview between the writer and Lord Attlee, 17 July 1957.
[2] Labour Party Conference Report, 1947, p. 144.

consultation with the Government, it was prepared to accept some direction of labour. It also issued a statement to the Press urging trade unionists to work harder.

On that same day Mr. Attlee, in a House of Commons debate on the State of the Nation, appealed to workers in all industries not to press for increases of wages or changes in conditions of work simply to maintain differentials.[1] This was the first significant public appeal from a Government spokesman for wage restraint. In his eagerness to communicate the appeal to quarters where it might have the greatest effect, the Minister of Labour sent letters to both sides of some national negotiating bodies, asking them to bear the Prime Minister's statement in mind. The General Council construed the letters as an interference in the negotiating rights of trade unions and immediately protested to the Prime Minister, who agreed that the letters should not have been sent out. The Prime Minister, in his reply, asked the General Council to meet the Minister of Labour and Sir Stafford Cripps, then Minister for Economic Affairs, to discuss wage movements.[2] A meeting subsequently took place at which Cripps asked the General Council 'to give very serious consideration to the possibilities of securing some greater stability in wages'. The General Council promised to do so.

The General Council became aware in the autumn of the need for a Trades Union Congress declaration of policy on wages, profits, and food subsidies.[3] The Government could not go on much longer without making a public statement on wages and it was clear that if such a statement were made before the Trades Union Congress view was known, and it was contrary to that of the Trades Union Congress, the General Council would be placed at a disadvantage. So the Crisis Committee of the General Council, established initially to review the fuel crisis, was instructed to prepare a report on the issues in question for submission to the executives of affiliated unions.

An *Interim Report on the Economic Situation* was approved by the General Council in December 1947. It wanted the Government to continue with food subsidies but recognized that the Government could not be expected to pay subsidies to meet rising costs 'regardless of the effect upon costs of movements in wages and profits over which the Government itself had no direct control nor any assurance that effective control was being exercised'.[4] It recommended 'the responsible executive committees of Trade Unions to exercise even greater moderation and restraint than hitherto in the formulation and pursuit of claims for wage increases', and added that the General

[1] Hansard, vol. 441, col. 1489.   [2] T.U.C. Report, 1948, p. 289.
[3] General Council Minutes, 22 October 1947.   [4] T.U.C. Report, 1948, p. 289.

Council was 'giving consideration to the representations to be made to the Government on the means by which more extensive and stringent control of prices and profits could be developed for the purpose of maintaining future price stability'. This was a vague declaration of policy. Moderation and restraint were undefined and no explicit guarantees about prices or profits were mentioned.

All this was too slow and uncertain for Cripps. He felt that the unions themselves must be convinced of the need for restraint.[1] As a result of his persuasion, Mr. Attlee, on 4 February 1948, made a second statement on wages, which was later published as a White Paper called the *Statement on Personal Incomes, Costs and Prices*.[2] Its theme was about the need to prevent dangerous inflation which was caused primarily by rising wages. It aimed to convince trade unions that wage increases should be determined on their national merits. Mr. Attlee made only a passing reference to profits, and price control was not mentioned explicitly. The General Council had not been consulted by Cripps about the details of the Statement, which it considered to be ambiguous and unsatisfactory. Its London members tried to get clarification on some points from Mr. Attlee, and later they met Cripps and George Isaacs to discuss the Statement's emphasis and omissions. At this meeting Cripps offended the union leaders by his discourteous behaviour. He explained the Statement and then departed from the meeting abruptly without discussing its merits, leaving George Isaacs, equally bewildered, to carry on.[3]

Such an affront could have seriously impaired the desire of union leaders to collaborate with the Government for union leaders became more intemperate over the manner in which the Government handled their relationship than over the subject matter of their discussions. Cripps should have known, as Attlee certainly knew later, that it was desirable to keep union leaders 'sweet'.[4] Fortunately the General Council was willing to support the principle of wage restraint and its most prominent members were prepared to be loyal to the Government irrespective of the petulance of Government Ministers.

The Crisis Committee of the General Council, after a number of meetings with Government representatives, recommended that the General Council should record its endorsement of the policy of general stabilization as set out in the White Paper and accept the principles which that statement proposed should be applied to wage claims, on condition that the Government pursued 'vigorously and

---

[1] *The Life of Richard Stafford Cripps*, by Colin Cooke, p. 367.   [2] Cmd. 7321.
[3] *Trade Union Leadership*, by V. L. Allen, p. 127.
[4] In an interview with the writer, 17 July 1957.

firmly a policy designed not only to stabilize but to reduce profits and prices'.[1] It also enumerated five conditions under which trade unions would consider it justifiable to claim wage increases.[2] They included all the major contingencies, so that any trade union which wanted to pursue a wage increase could do so without compunction. The General Council accepted the recommendations which, on 24 March 1948, were also endorsed by a Special Conference of Trade Union Executive Committees.

This was the beginning of a new phase in trade union behaviour in relation to the state. During the First World War the leaders of some unions had been prepared to make concessions to the Government to assist in prosecuting the war but they had been out of step with their members and their attempts to suspend union practices received strong rank-and-file opposition. No further concessions were made until the Second World War. Then officials and ordinary members, more closely in accord, collaborated to increase production. No concessions, however, were made over wages. Now, in 1948, not only members of the General Council but rank-and-file members of union executives, agreed to exercise wage restraint. Although it could be argued that by their action they were helping to stabilize prices and were therefore maintaining real-wage levels, their decision was equivalent to a suspension of the basic function of unions. The determination of money wages had always been regarded as the *raison d'être* of union activity; real wages and prices fell outside its scope.

In taking their decision, the union executives may have been influenced by the concessions made by Cripps in negotiations with the General Council after the publication of the White Paper. Cripps had announced in a parliamentary debate on 12 February that the Government intended to achieve price stability, if possible price reductions, through a more rigorous enforcement of Government price controls and by appealing to the representatives of manufacturers, wholesale distributors, and retailers. He also appealed for a limitation to be placed on dividends. The members of the executives, doubtless too, found wage restraint more palatable because of the conditions on which the General Council had accepted it. Nonetheless, by trade union standards, the decision was a momentous one. It was even more remarkable that in general the decision was applied.

The General Council rejected other traditional attitudes in its campaign to assist the Government. It urged unions to become actively engaged in increasing productivity and it encouraged the

[1] General Council Minutes, 18 February 1948.
[2] See T.U.C. Report, 1948, pp. 290–291, for the conditions.

extension of payment by results schemes. When sterling was devalued in September 1949, the General Council urged unions to exercise even greater restraint and suggested that wage claims and sliding-scale arrangements should be adapted to hold wage rates stable whilst the Interim Index of Retail Prices remained between the upper and lower limits of 118 and 106.[1] This recommendation went beyond any previous attempt to assist the Government, for it was made without a stipulation about price control or a restraint on profits. It was endorsed by a Special Conference of Trade Union Executive Committees on 12 January 1950, but only by a small majority.[2] As further evidence of their loyalty to the Government, union leaders faced unofficial strikes by groups of their members against the wages policy they were pursuing.

The trade union attitude towards wage restraint changed in the course of 1950. The proposals made in January had proved to be unworkable, for unions with sliding-scale agreements would not suspend them without a guarantee that unions without agreements would withhold wage demands. No such guarantee could be obtained, for many unions were beginning to revolt against applying a policy which provided no immediately visible economic returns and which encouraged dissension within their ranks. The craft unions had an additional reason for rejecting the policy, for it operated to narrow the differential between the skilled and unskilled. The General Council's own view was changing too. It realized that wage restraint could not be a permanent feature of union wage policy, and it resented the manner in which the Chancellor of the Exchequer tended to take wage restraint for granted in his calculations. Then, during the summer, the effect of the Korean war was seen in rising prices. The General Council presented a modified view of wage restraint at the Trades Union Congress in September, but it did not go far enough for the majority of the delegates, who revolted and rejected the wage restraint policy altogether.

THE RELATIONSHIP IN GENERAL

The relationship between trade unions and the Labour Government went through three broad phases. The first, from 1945 to late 1947, was marked by an attitude of critical but friendly detachment by trade unions. This was really a continuation of wartime collaboration. Trade unions were willing to make concessions in return for concessions, but in the sphere of wage bargaining they insisted on

[1] *Trade Unions and Wages Policy.* Report of the Special Conference of Trade Union Executive Committees, 12 January 1950.   [2] By 4,263,000 votes to 3,606,000.

retaining their independence. The General Council, dominated by Citrine and deeply concerned about protocol, felt free to criticize the Government whenever it thought fit. Its members were loyal members of the Labour Movement but they were men who had grown up with the practice of treating all Governments alike. Some of them had had experience of an earlier Labour Government and were not wholly impressed by the thought of another. The Labour Party, on the other hand, having spent fourteen years as a dependent partner in the Labour Movement, was anxious to prove to the country at large that it was not dominated by unions once it had been returned to power.

In the first phase the Government and unions were faced with a situation possessing novel characteristics to which they had to get accustomed. Trade unions were in a wholly new peacetime environment containing full employment, acute national economic problems, and a Labour Government with power to implement its election programme. The Government, however, for all its power, still needed to seek the collaboration of trade unions in order to solve its economic difficulties, so it could not pursue independence too far. It was not long before it realized this and made gestures for trade union co-operation. These were met at first by caution. Then the trade union attitude changed and a phase of close collaboration began.

The responsibility for the second phase lies completely with the General Council of the Trades Union Congress, for it made all the concessions. The period 1947–1950 was one with numerous economic and political reasons for a close relationship between unions and the Government, but it is doubtful whether it would have occurred if the composition of the dominant group on the General Council had not altered. Sir Walter Citrine relinquished the general secretaryship of the Trades Union Congress in 1946 to become a member of the National Coal Board. Without Citrine the power situation within the General Council became fluid. The position was more unsettled by the fact that between 1945 and 1947 the General Council lost ten of its members, including some of its most able advocates. When the situation settled, Arthur Deakin was filling Citrine's role. He was the central figure of a small but influential group of union leaders whose unions accounted for almost half of the total affiliated membership of the Trades Union Congress. Not only could this group dictate the proceedings of Congress, it could apply the decisions of the General Council in practical union affairs through its control over individual unions. It is not necessary to look beyond this change in the General Council power situation to find the prime reason for the phase of collaboration with the Government which followed.

The focal personality, however, was not Deakin but Ernest Bevin. During the war Bevin and Attlee were brought together as members of the Coalition Government, and they developed a deep personal friendship which transcended the squabbles about status and power which took place in the Labour Party.[1] Bevin loyally accepted Attlee's leadership and intolerantly opposed anyone who dared to challenge it.[2] This loyalty was recognized by Attlee, for Bevin became not only the Foreign Secretary but also Attlee's confidant and adviser. Attlee invariably consulted Bevin over labour problems and used him as a means of assessing and influencing trade union opinion.[3]

Trade union leaders normally lose their influence with unions when they leave their union posts for industry or politics. Bevin was an exception. Right until his death he carried some influence over union behaviour. In his own union, the Transport and General Workers' Union, a mythology grew up which attributed to Bevin the credit for developing the union and none of the criticisms associated with its current activities. But in practical terms the most important factor was the attachment of Arthur Deakin to Bevin, whom he had succeeded as general secretary of the union.

Arthur Deakin became Bevin's most powerful practising trade union ally. The personal loyalty which Deakin had for Bevin was extended to the Government to which Bevin belonged, and was reinforced by his own loyalty to a Government which he considered epitomized the Labour Movement. The power which the massive Transport and General Workers' Union possessed in industry and the Labour Movement, and the authority which Deakin exercised over the deliberations of the General Council, were placed unreservedly at the disposal of the Government.

The second phase was one of almost complete uncritical acceptance of the Government's main policy by the General Council; even legitimate criticisms were stifled. Government actions which would have caused irritation, annoyance, perhaps anger, in other circumstances, were ignored. The Government, however, did not give preferential treatment to unions. The General Council, for instance, made its annual Budget proposals and received its annual disappointment about their partial or complete rejection. The Government respected the negotiating power which full employment gave unions, but no more than the wartime Coalition Government had done, nor indeed than the Conservative Government did between 1951 and

---

[1] The friendship was a new one. Even as late as 1939 Bevin had criticized Attlee's leadership (*The Fateful Years*, by Hugh Dalton, p. 218).

[2] See Dalton, op. cit., p. 405 and pp. 467–468 for illustrations.

[3] Interview of the writer with Lord Attlee, 17 July 1957.

1956. It used formal channels of communication except when it wanted to get unions to adopt a special aspect of Government policy. Then it exerted informal pressure, mainly through Ernest Bevin.

Trade union protests were always received more sympathetically by the Prime Minister than by any other Minister. Sometimes he embarrassed his Ministers by his response. He agreed, for instance, to the withdrawal of the letter sent by George Isaacs to negotiating bodies in 1947,[1] and when Isaacs sent a similar letter to Wages Councils in March 1949, urging them to take cognizance of the Government's economic policy in their deliberations, Attlee agreed to that letter being withdrawn too, leaving Isaacs to accept full responsibility for it. Where the Prime Minister could not take immediate decisions over protests he sometimes gave assurances, but he was frequently not in a position to see that they were carried out. Individual Ministers had much scope for discretion in their treatment of trade unions, and the evidence shows that they used it freely and by no means always in favour of unions. The administrative day-to-day relations between unions and the Ministries were not altered by the presence of a Labour Government, and this was so even in the Ministry of Labour.

The third phase of the relationship started in 1950 when unions rebelled against the policy of wage restraint. The General Council was still dominated by the same people in 1950 as in 1948 and, by and large, their views had not changed. Their hold over other unions had weakened, however. In the autumn of 1950 and during 1951 wage increases were common, and all union leaders, even Arthur Deakin, had to make sure that their members shared in them.

Unions also started being less conciliatory over disputes with employers. For the first time during the Labour Government's period in office they seriously contemplated calling official national strikes. The Confederation of Shipbuilding and Engineering Unions took a ballot of its members in the summer of 1950 to decide whether it should submit a wage claim to arbitration or strike, and early in 1951 the railway unions took action which could have led to an official strike in a dispute with the British Transport Commission.

The period of close collaboration had ended, but the Government still needed a moderate wages policy and industrial peace to enable it to combat inflation. It approached members of the General Council in 1951 in order to test their feelings about establishing a national representative body with employers' and workers' representatives to examine the country's problems. The idea was amiably discussed but it was not accepted, in the main, because prices were

---

[1] See also above, p. 284.

rising too steeply for the General Council to ask workers to be moderate again in their wage demands. The Labour Party went out of office before the suggestion could be pressed.

The third phase was marked, too, by a decline in the influence of trade unionists in the Government. After the death of Ernest Bevin, there was no one in the Government who either had any influence over union leaders or could speak with authority about union attitudes and aspirations. The Government had lost its key link with the trade union movement.

Trade unions and the Labour Government did not spoil their record of unprecedented collaboration, for the Labour Government went out of office before the full effects of the situation after 1950 could be felt. But the flaws which had appeared were becoming more prominent. Had the Labour Government continued in office it would have had to forge a new type of relationship or else be faced, like any Conservative Government, with an independent, perhaps refractory, trade union movement.

Appendix V

TRADE UNION SPONSORED MEMBERS OF THE LABOUR GOVERNMENT IN 1945

Cabinet

Ernest Bevin (Transport and General Workers' Union)—Secretary of State for Foreign Affairs.

George Isaacs (National Society of Operative Printers and Assistants)—Minister of Labour.

J. J. Lawson (National Union of Mineworkers)—Secretary of State for War.

Ellen Wilkinson (National Union of Distributive and Allied Workers)—Minister of Education.

Aneurin Bevan (National Union of Mineworkers)—Minister of Health.

Tom Williams (National Union of Mineworkers)—Minister of Agriculture and Fisheries.

Not in Cabinet

A. Creech Jones (Transport and General Workers' Union)—Under-Secretary of State for the Colonies.

W. J. Edwards (Transport and General Workers' Union)—Civil Lord to the Admiralty.

J. B. Hynd (National Union of Railwaymen)—Chancellor of the Duchy of Lancaster.

G. H. Oliver (Transport and General Workers' Union)—Under-Secretary of State for Home Affairs.

Ness Edwards (National Union of Mineworkers)—Parliamentary Secretary to the Minister of Labour.

James Griffiths (National Union of Mineworkers)—Minister of National Insurance.

G. S. Lindgren (Railway Clerks' Association)—Parliamentary Secretary to the Minister of National Insurance.

Wilfred Paling (National Union of Mineworkers)—Minister of Pensions.

W. A. Burke (National Union of Distributive and Allied Workers)—Assistant Postmaster-General.

George Mathers (Railway Clerks' Association)—Treasurer of His Majesty's Household.

William Whiteley (National Union of Mineworkers)—Parliamentary Secretary to the Treasury.

Joseph Henderson (National Union of Railwaymen)—Lord Commissioner.

Frank Collindridge (National Union of Mineworkers)—Lord Commissioner.

T. Fraser (National Union of Mineworkers)—Under-Secretary of State for Scotland.

George Buchanan (United Pattern Makers' Association)—Under-Secretary of State for Scotland.

George Tomlinson (United Textile Factory Workers' Association)—Minister of Works.

F. Marshall (National Union of General and Municipal Workers)—Parliamentary Secretary to the Minister of Town and Country Planning.

R. J. Taylor (National Union of Mineworkers)—Lord Commissioner.

Sir Ben Smith (Transport and General Workers' Union)—Minister of Food.

Arthur Jenkins (National Union of Mineworkers)—Parliamentary Secretary to the Minister of Education.

Ellis Smith (United Pattern Makers' Association)—Parliamentary Secretary to the President of the Board of Trade.

E. J. Williams (National Union of Mineworkers)—Minister of Information.

William Foster (National Union of Mineworkers)—Parliamentary Secretary to the Minister of Fuel and Power.

Appendix VI

TRADE UNION SPONSORED MEMBERS OF THE LABOUR GOVERNMENT AT ITS DISSOLUTION IN OCTOBER 1951

Cabinet

Tom Williams (National Union of Mineworkers)—Minister of Agriculture and Fisheries.

George Tomlinson (United Textile Factory Workers' Association)—Minister of Education.

James Griffiths (National Union of Mineworkers)—Secretary of State for the Colonies.

Alfred Robens (Union of Shop, Distributive and Allied Workers)—Minister of Labour.

Not in Cabinet

W. J. Edwards (Transport and General Workers' Union)—Civil Lord to the Admiralty.

Fred Lee (Amalgamated Engineering Union)—Parliamentary Secretary to the Minister of Labour.

G. S. Lindgren (Railway Clerks' Association)—Parliamentary Secretary to the Minister of Local Government and Planning.

George Isaacs (National Society of Operative Printers and Assistants)—Minister of Pensions.

Ness Edwards (National Union of Mineworkers)—Postmaster-General.

Tom Fraser (National Union of Mineworkers)—Under-Secretary of State for Scotland.

William Whiteley (National Union of Mineworkers)—Parliamentary Secretary to the Treasury.

R. J. Taylor (National Union of Mineworkers)—Lord Commissioner.

George Brown (Transport and General Workers' Union)—Minister of Works.

Frank Collindridge (National Union of Mineworkers)—Comptroller.

Ernest Popplewell (National Union of Railwaymen)—Vice Chamberlain.

A. J. Champion (National Union of Railwaymen)—Parliamentary Secretary to the Minister of Agriculture and Fisheries.

H. Neal (National Union of Mineworkers)—Parliamentary Secretary to the Minister of Fuel and Power.

H. B. Taylor (National Union of Mineworkers)—Parliamentary Secretary to the Minister of National Insurance.

C. J. Simmons (National Union of General and Municipal Workers)—Parliamentary Secretary to the Minister of Pensions.

T. F. Cook (Electrical Trades Union)—Under-Secretary of State for the Colonies.

C. R. Hobson (Amalgamated Engineering Union)—Assistant Postmaster-General.

W. A. Wilkins (Typographical Association)—Lord Commissioner.

5

SUMMARY AND CONCLUSIONS

Chapter Sixteen

AN OUTLINE OF THE RELATIONSHIP

THIS chapter summarizes the main factors which have contributed to bringing trade unions and the Government into contact with each other and it shows briefly the form the contact has taken.

The relationship between the Government and trade unions has resulted from the progressive interaction of several economic and political factors. The working class gained political power and trade unions established their own political party. Trade unions grew into large, national, relatively tightly organized bodies. Industry became more complex and concentrated while the parts of the economy became more interdependent, thus giving union action wide repercussions. The Government increasingly intervened in economic affairs and became the nation's largest employer. Wars and economic crises gave organized labour enhanced power because labour became a scarce and highly sought after commodity. Trade union attitudes, methods, and purpose changed. And on the whole complex process a few union leaders and politicians left the imprints of their personalities.

The relationship can be traced back to the emergence of the 'New Model' unions after 1850: to the days of the Sheffield outrages, the appointment of a Royal Commission to investigate trade unions and to the Reform Act which extended suffrage in the working class. Trade union leaders established contact with the Government and because of the growing political importance of the working class after the Reform Act of 1867 the contact bore results. Trade unions were given legal recognition in 1871.

During the nineteenth century trade unions were mainly small and localized and their influence was diffused and weak. Their organizations were rudimentary. This was largely so even at the beginning of the twentieth century. Many workers had not been touched by trade unionism and it is probable that less than 10 per cent of the total working population was organized. There were few unions which were national in scope. Trade union leaders went to the Government for concessions with an air of confidence which belied their true position. They were in fact suppliants.

The growth of trade unionism was facilitated in the twentieth century by the increase in the size of industrial and financial units

and by the spread of industry. More members of the working population became workers in industrial undertakings which were relatively
easy to organize. Trade unionism, too, was encouraged by the spread
of class consciousness.

Trade union membership increased in the aggregate and as a
proportion of the total working population. It became concentrated
in vital national industries such as the coal and dock industries and
the railways. Unions established federations and alliances, then
through mergers and amalgamations built up closely knit organizations. Their ability to control the supply and behaviour of labour
improved, while a deepening class consciousness gave them the
impulse to use their newly acquired ability. By 1914 the docks, the
mines, and the railways had at different times been closed down by
union action.

Ever since legal recognition had been obtained in 1871 unions had
been political pressure-groups. Their leaders had lobbied Members of
Parliament from both political parties, and election candidates had
been canvassed for their support, all to obtain an *ad hoc* amelioration
of working class conditions. Deputations, unwieldy and burdened
with grievances, had waited annually on Ministers. But the Government was not compelled to listen to trade union complaints and the
extent to which unions were satisfied depended largely upon the
fortuitous presence in the Government of liberally-minded persons.

The frustrations which attended constitutional pressures drove
trade unions to seek direct Parliamentary representation. The Labour
Representative Committee was formed in 1900. It gained a relative
success in the 1906 election and was renamed the Labour Party. It
was still necessary for unions to canvass for support from Conservative and Liberal Members of Parliament, but after 1906 this became
progressively more difficult. During the 1906 Liberal Government's
period in office class divisions in Parliament and the country
hardened. The political parties developed a greater cohesion and in
Parliament the discipline of parties became tighter. In consequence
Members of Parliament lost much of their freedom of action. It
became a waste of time for unions to ask individual Members of
Parliament to support measures which their Parliamentary Party
officially opposed. Trade unions therefore had to rely much more on
the use of Labour Party representatives to get issues raised and aired
in Parliament. Nevertheless, trade union access to the Government
became easier after 1906. Mr. Campbell Bannerman and Mr.
Asquith, the two Liberal Prime Ministers after 1906, received trade
union deputations willingly and courteously; while Mr. Lloyd George
and Mr. Winston Churchill intervened in disputes on an unprece-

dented scale. The Government made progress by forming an industrial conciliation service; while at the same time it intervened provocatively in strikes by using troops to preserve law and order and to maintain food and coal supplies, but in a manner which assisted employers. By 1914 the Government had a continuing interest in trade union activities.

The forces which brought trade unions and Governments closer before 1914 were reinforced by the war conditions. Trade unions grew rapidly and spread to unorganized sections of industry. Their total membership rose from approximately two million in 1900 to four million in 1914. By 1918 it was about 6½ million. The expansion occurred mainly among semi-skilled and unskilled workers. Truly national and large organizations emerged from the war period. The National Union of Railwaymen, for instance, had 402,000 members, the Workers' Union possessed a membership of 380,000, while the Miners' Federation surpassed them all with 650,000 members.

Labour became a scarce commodity during the war and the Government was compelled in consequence to seek the collaboration of unions in various ways. A few representatives of labour joined the Government and others became members of the network of committees which the Government set up to perform wartime tasks. The Government approached union representatives to obtain a relaxation of restrictive practices and their support in obtaining and preserving industrial peace. Compulsory arbitration was introduced and the Labour Department's conciliation activities were extended. The Labour Department was made into the Ministry of Labour. The Government became a large-scale employer of labour. It had an interest in every facet of labour activities.

If the position of trade unions had been assessed in November 1918 a trend might have been detected which the war had emphasized. Trade unions were growing, acquiring more power, assuming greater responsibilities. The Government had forsaken its nineteenth-century *laissez-faire* function, was interested in preserving general welfare as well as protecting economic interests, was becoming involved in the organization of society. It might have been seen that as a result of these processes unions were being accorded a political status within the existing constitutional framework which they were accepting and utilizing. But a look at the scene twelve months later would have given a different impression, for the trend was an illusory one.

Soon after the war the wartime labour regulations were revoked, committees were disbanded, compulsory arbitration was ended, and the system of industrial relations moved back almost to its pre-war state. It was as if the wartime experiences had provided no lessons. Joint negotiating machinery was established in some industries according to the Whitley Committee proposals, but it was some years before it operated effectively. There was one difference from pre-war conditions. The militancy before 1914 had been generated by rank-and-file activity. Some of the strikes, as a result, had had lots of inspiration but no organization or singleness of purpose. After 1918 the direction came from union leaders with the full support of their organizations.

The Government's eagerness to discard its wartime role was due to pressure from employers to return to an unrestricted private enterprise economy. Trade unions did not take such a calculated step back to their pre-war industrial attitude. If the Labour Party had substantially increased its representation in the House of Commons in the general election after the Armistice, union leaders would possibly have thought that their aspirations were capable of being satisfied by constitutional action within the foreseeable future. The Labour Party, however, suffered a crushing defeat. Trade union leaders, always with a preference for industrial methods which gave speedy solutions, turned away from party politics and pursued a policy of direct industrial action.

Early in 1919 the Government faced a belligerent trade union movement which had witnessed a workers' revolution in Russia. Despite its overwhelming electoral victory the Government was nervous. It did not relax until midway through 1926. In the interim the Government regarded most major strikes as challenges to its authority. In this situation a formal relationship with trade unions was out of the question.

The Government's first reaction in 1919 was to gain time. It inaugurated the National Industrial Conference early in February and set up the Sankey Commission on the coal industry shortly afterwards. After it had gained a respite from industrial troubles it rejected the proposals of both bodies. Then followed a series of strikes or strike threats until April 1921, all directed against the Government. The Government used extensive emergency powers and took military precautions.

The Miners' Federation, the most militant of trade unions, was engaged in two long disputes in 1921 and 1926 which depleted the union's funds, exhausted the miners, and impaired their organized ability for many years. The second of these coal disputes was the occasion of the General Strike, the culmination and anticlimax of the movement for direct action. The Government was prepared for the General Strike and it used successful tactics. The strike showed a magnificent feeling of sympathy and solidarity for the miners but the General Council of the Trades Union Congress, scared of the possible consequences, ended the strike unconditionally and left the miners to struggle not only in isolation but also in a movement bitter with recrimination and rankling from defeat.

As a consequence of the General Strike the Trade Unions and Trade Disputes Act was passed in 1927. A general strike, sympathetic strikes, and strikes which were aimed to harm the community became illegal. Restrictions were placed on civil servants and employees of local and public authorities, and all trade unionists had to contract to pay the political levy instead of paying it automatically unless they contracted out. This Act featured in many trade union protests to the Government.

Long before the defeat of 1926, however, direct action had lost much of its practical significance. Unemployment had started to increase late in 1920 and became acute in 1921. It became a permanent feature of the remaining years until the Second World War. Trade union membership fell considerably and unions had to concentrate on protecting the wages, hours, and working conditions of their members, which were under pressure from employers. The Government was forgotten by individual unions during most of their struggles until the 1925 coal dispute and the General Strike, and then it was largely forgotten by them again until 1939.

The Government played a minor role in industrial relations in this period. It maintained an interest in conciliation but the enthusiasm which had been present immediately after the publication of the Whitley Committee Report on joint industrial councils, and which sent Ministry of Labour officials around the country in an endeavour to convert trade unionists and employers to the Report's recommendations, had considerably diminished. The Government's main contact with labour occurred through the civil service.

In 1924 and 1929–1931 the trade union movement had two generally unsatisfactory experiences with Labour Governments. Both Governments were handicapped by being dependent upon the Liberal Party for a Parliamentary majority. As far as some union leaders were concerned, the Governments were also handicapped by being led by politicians whom they disliked and in whom they had little faith. Trade union influence in the Governments was negligible, for even the Ministers who had been union leaders did their utmost to forget their pasts. The miners exerted the greatest influence on the Governments, but then there were a large number of miners in the Parliamentary Labour Party. The influence of other unions was almost non-existent. If any union leaders harboured beliefs that their own party would try to set a standard of behaviour based on Socialist ethics, they were disillusioned.

With the experience of the General Strike and two Labour Governments behind them, the principal members of the Trades Union Congress set about establishing a fresh relationship with the Government. They were convinced that unions should deal with every Government, regardless of its politics, and they aimed to make the Trades Union Congress the medium through which unions and the Government approached each other. They claimed that the Trades Union Congress represented the views of the trade union movement and that the movement was sufficiently large and important to justify its giving advice on all labour questions to the Government. Sir Walter (now Lord) Citrine, the general secretary of the Trades Union Congress, was responsible for establishing and organizing this claim for recognition. The Trades Union Congress obtained some success before 1939.

When the Second World War came the trade union movement was equipped to play a responsible role. Trade unions had become firmly established institutions with a vested interest in the existing form of society. Their immediate past was not associated either with pacificism or political opposition to war. In the mid-1930s they had rejected the use of the general strike against war after a mild flirtation with the idea and they had become conditioned to the thought of a war against Nazism. The class war had ceased to animate anyone except the militant fringe of the trade union movement. The war caught the trade union movement in the course of a rather dull but solid development. Trade union leaders behaved much like responsible statesmen. The Government had no doubts about their willingness and capacity to co-operate.

It was not until May 1940, however, that the Government drew on the trade union movement for full-scale co-operation. Then, as in 1915, union leaders entered the Government as one of the costs to the Government of trade union concessions. There was a difference between the two wars. In the First World War union leaders were flattered and feted in a manner which exploited their political immaturity and were easy victims to the guile and intrigues of the ruling clique. Once trade union concessions had been secured in statutory form, union leaders were gradually discarded or ignored. It was not so in the Second World War, for then the Government was dealing with a different type of union leader. Ernest Bevin, who became Minister of Labour, was a high-powered personality with a proved intellect. He worked on the basis of equality with the most influential of the governing élite and became a power inside the Cabinet.

Outside the Government stood Sir Walter Citrine, unlike Bevin in many ways, but of proved ability too. Citrine, jealous of trade union rights, agreed to make concessions only in return for concessions. Trade unions in the Second World War bargained from a position of strength.

The enhanced wartime importance of labour created the primary need for contact between trade unions and the Government, but other factors operated too. Trade unions, benefiting from full employment and the peculiar stimulus to trade union expansion which the atmosphere of war created, increased their aggregate membership from 6,300,000 in 1939 to 8,200,000 in 1943. The distribution of membership showed an increasing degree of concentration which put union power in the hands of fewer trade unionists. The Government came into direct contact with unions through its intensive and widespread intervention in industry and its large-scale employment of industrial labour. Trade union influence appeared to be real and pervasive in the economy.

In 1939 the Government established the National Joint Advisory Council to the Minister of Labour consisting of union and employers' representatives. A sub-committee of this, the Joint Consultative Committee, became, from 1940, the principal formal means of contact between unions and the Minister of Labour. Trade unions established relations with many Government departments and consultations between them became frequent. The aim of the Trades Union Congress to get its nominees on Government committees was realized. Trade unionists were consulted on all matters appertaining to labour questions.

The principal wartime factors which had placed unions in positions of power continued in peacetime and were multiplied. Full employment continued and, with the demobilization of the armed forces, the aggregate membership of trade unions increased. In 1948 it was 9,300,000. The needs of war were replaced by the needs of an acute economic situation. Labour retained its importance. The Government needed to seek the collaboration of the trade union movement more even than in war, for during the war there had been a moral force making for unity which did not exist afterwards. A compensating factor, however, was the return of a Labour Government in 1945. Trade unions and the Labour Party owed each other traditional allegiances. It was expected that unions would be willing to collaborate with the Labour Government. Some of the earlier experiences had been forgotten. This Government, moreover, was in the hands of different politicians and it possessed full political power.

Frequent direct contact between the Government and trade unions continued after 1945. The Government, in an endeavour to plan its economic policies, retained controls and instituted advisory committees on which trade unionists served. It nationalized substantial segments of British industry and became a permanent peacetime employer of industrial labour on a large scale. The political nature of the Government did not affect its formal relations with trade unions; they continued largely as during the war. There was, of course, much more informal contact than there would have been with any other Government. Ernest Bevin continued to be the most influential trade union personality in the Government, and in the trade union movement Arthur Deakin took the place of Sir Walter Citrine. Bevin and Deakin had close personal ties, and through these a high degree of trade union collaboration with the Government was effected.

During the years of the third Labour Government a new peacetime pattern of relations was established. Trade union leaders had easy access to Ministers, whom they approached on terms of equality and with whom they discussed topics beyond the confines of labour problems. Official deputations still waited on Ministers but they had given way to representation on committees and the like as the main form of formal contact with the Government. The Parliamentary Labour Party ceased to be used as a medium for influencing the Government because unions preferred to rely on direct contact with the Government.

This pattern continued after the defeat of the Labour Party in the 1951 general election. The Conservative Government until 1955 appointed trade unionists to its consultative committees more freely than even the Labour Government and a fair measure of informal consultation took place too. The Government agreed with the trade union disapproval of House of Commons debates on labour questions and encouraged direct consultation. Both Sir Winston Churchill, the Prime Minister, and Sir Walter Monckton, the Minister of Labour, deliberately pursued a conciliatory policy towards trade unions. One change in the pattern of relations was the emergence of the Minister of Labour as the main link between the Government and the trade union movement.

The economic elements of the immediate post-war situation continued to operate when the Conservative Government was in office. Full employment was maintained. Trade unions increased their membership and in 1952 reached the record figure of 9,524,000. The Government still intervened in economic affairs but on a smaller scale and in a different manner from the Labour Government. It employed a smaller industrial labour force because the iron and steel

industry and a part of the road transport industry were denationalized, but it was still by far the largest single employer in the country
and retained in its employment such militant groups as the miners
and the railwaymen. The same economic problems plagued the
country and labour retained its importance in their solution. These
elements were largely unchanged up till 1960.

The political environment changed, however, after 1955, and with
it industrial appearances altered. New trade union and political
figures made their impact. The Conservative Governments under Sir
Anthony Eden and Mr. Harold Macmillan pursued Conservative
economic policies more aggressively than their predecessor, and in
doing so aroused the opposition of unions. For the first time since
the 1930s official national strikes were called. A good deal of cross
criticism went on which appeared to sour a relationship which had
been reasonably amicable for ten years. The General Council of the
Trades Union Congress grew disinclined to meet Ministers and the
Parliamentary Labour Party was encouraged by union leaders to
display a greater interest in industrial relations. But these were small,
perhaps temporary, changes in the relationship between trade unions
and the Government. The system of direct communication which
was established by Ernest Bevin in 1940 remained basically unaltered.

Chapter Seventeen

AN ESTIMATE OF INFLUENCE

THERE are a number of aspects of the form outlined in the previous chapter which need to be evaluated and summarized. Trade unions have exerted pressure on the Government to influence its decisions. How effective have they been? What special problems have arisen and in what way are they likely to influence the relationship in the future?

Precise answers cannot be given to these questions because there are always many forces operating on a Government and it is often impossible to isolate their effects. Moreover, the real reasons for a Government decision may be obscured for tactical political reasons. In some cases the Ministers themselves may not be able to account for their actions. They may be impulsive by nature or they may simply be incapable of rational decision-making. Still, there is enough evidence to point to answers.

Trade unions have used three main methods to influence the Government. They have used the strike weapon, constitutional representations, and party political pressure. All three methods are still in use and are likely to continue so in the future.

Strikes

The use of the strike weapon is severely limited. By the time trade unions were capable of waging highly organized national strikes the Government was capable of countering them with the full use of the resources of the state if necessary. The strike as an instrument of force, however, has been blunted more by a change in attitudes than by the prospect of the Government's counter-measures. The country has grown to accept Parliamentary democracy as the way in which it wants to be governed. All forms of coercion are contrary to the standards of Parliamentary democracy and this has been accepted by trade unionists and non-trade unionists alike. Trade unionists, as vigorously as other sections of the community, have deprecated the use of strikes as a means of getting the Government to accept their political views. When, as in the General Strike, union leaders found themselves attempting to coerce the Government they backed down at the first opportunity. The unwillingness of most union leaders even to appear to challenge the Government was revealed during the 1958 bus strike.

There were occasions shortly after the First World War when some union leaders were willing to challenge the Government through strike action. The challenges were over specific issues, were not clearly thought out, and were not coherently related. They were never fulfilled. The only occasion when the Labour Movement was united in its intention to strike against the Government was over British intervention in Russia in August 1920. The strike was not carried out because the Government changed its policy. Whether the Government responded to pressure is difficult to say. It is doubtful, moreover, whether the strike threat could have been made effective if the need had arisen. The emotion which stimulated the initial protest very quickly dispersed.

It would be wrong, despite the strong forces acting against them, to suppose that political strikes will not occur in Britain in the future. If the Government took steps to involve the country in a widely condemned war and did not quickly retreat in the face of public opposition, it is possible to conceive of trade unions taking direct action against it. The strike is the ultimate emergency sanction which can be applied against the Government. But in such a case it is not really a trade union weapon. It is a public protest arising out of a combination of intense emotion and deep frustration.

It is possible, too, to imagine a Government inadvertently directing a strike against itself. The most frequent occasions on which violence has been used by strikers in Britain have been when their solidarity has been violated by blacklegs. If a Government intervened in a dispute to encourage strike-breaking it would encourage violence; if it gave troop protection to blacklegs it might direct the violence against itself.

Strikes against the Government as an employer do not offend political democratic morality and can be successful. Such strikes, to be successful, have to be plainly industrial and nowadays confined to the workers directly affected by the Government's employment policy. But even when they satisfy these conditions they are difficult to win because the Government invariably adopts a constitutional attitude which gives it automatic protection. The Government employees who strike successfully are those who reveal to all and sundry the falseness of this position.

The desire to maintain political democracy also acts in favour of unions by protecting their general right to strike from indiscriminate Government action. The right to strike is an essential democratic function which is possessed by all workers except those employed in water, gas, and electricity supply undertakings. There have been many pressures to curb this right but it would be a foolhardy

Government which succumbed to them without the collaboration of unions, unless, of course, it wanted to destroy political liberties.

Where a strong, independent, trade union movement exists, a Government cannot legislate effectively to make strikes illegal unless either the unions agree to accept the legislation or the Government is prepared to take special steps to enforce it. This was borne out by the Government's experiences during both World Wars. The British judicial system is built on the assumption that laws will only be broken by a small proportion of the population acting as individuals. It has no provisions for organized mass infringements of the law. So when in 1915 and 1944 there were large-scale illegal strikes the Government could do nothing about them. If it wished in the future to make strikes illegal it would have to establish special courts supported by an extensively organized force, in order to apply the legislation. In other words, it would have to operate a police state.[1]

Constitutional Representations

These are used continually and are the principal means of exerting pressure on the Government. They involve informal and formal activities, sometimes complementary, at other times separately. Their success depends on many things. In the first place unions have to have some national significance to gain access to the Government. When this has been done, whether or not they are listened to depends on their economic or political power. The factor which decides whether the views are accepted and applied is the extent to which they coincide with the Government's views. That is, it is not only necessary for a pressure group to have economic or political strength, it must also have some affinity with the Government. The merits of a case and the manner of its presentation may have some bearing on its treatment, but they are likely to be slight. This does not mean that there must be a Labour Government before trade unions can exert effective pressure, only that with a Labour Government the chances of success are greater than with any other Government.

Trade union interests cover a wide range of topics, but they are significant to the Government mainly in the field of labour and, to a lesser extent, in related subjects. A Prime Minister, during a Cabinet discussion of say, food subsidies, may ask the Minister of Labour

[1] In order to curtail strike action it has been suggested that a law could be enforced making it compulsory for trade unions to hold secret ballots before strikes could be called. This is based on the false assumption that in many strikes ordinary members do not want to strike and if allowed to express their opinions secretly they would say so. In any case if workers wanted to strike before holding secret ballots nothing but a repressive penal system could stop them.

what the union attitude is. The Minister of Labour will then give his view of the trade union view. He may have received a deputation over the issue and perhaps have read a memorandum which came with it. The view he expresses will be noted and the Cabinet discussion will go on. The ultimate decision of the Cabinet will be determined by issues which accord with its broad lines of policy. If the Government is fundamentally opposed to food subsidies then nothing the unions may say will make it alter its mind. No trade union view may be asked for at all during Cabinet discussions about issues not concerned with labour.

The position is different when trade unions can influence the application of Government policy. On matters concerning wages, unemployment, factory conditions, productivity, and so on, the Government will listen readily to trade union opinions because trade unionists have a special knowledge of these issues and because not to do so would create an appearance of arbitrariness which might be regarded as undemocratic. Indeed the Government often *seeks* the advice of unions over these matters. This is a practice, however, which is applied to most pressure groups with specialist knowledge.

No problem in Government decision-making occurs if the Government views tally with those of trade unions. But what if they disagree? If it is a matter of policy and not the application of policy, a Government, no matter what its political complexion, will rarely give way on essentials. It may make concessions on minor items, or give guarantees about the application of the policy. It may 'sweeten the pill'. On the other hand it may ignore trade union protests altogether. The Conservative Cabinet in the autumn of 1957 decided to pursue a wages policy which it knew would arouse strong trade union opposition, and a year later it abolished compulsory arbitration in the face of protests. That Government, however, gave way to union pressure on some issues because it did not think it worth while to offend unions over minor matters.

Four qualifications need to be made. First, if economic circumstances are particularly precarious then trade union pressure may be given exceptional consideration. But this is only likely if unions are actually in a position to jeopardize a policy of which they disapprove. Mr. MacDonald paid no attention to trade union protests in 1931. Secondly, while unions may be unsuccessful in changing Government policy, they may get a measure speeded up or delayed. In some circumstances this can be a significant effect. Thirdly, most union representations to the Government are made by the General Council of the Trades Union Congress and usually concern matters of general interest to the trade union movement. There are cases, however, where an individual union protests to the Government and this can carry much weight if it is influential in a vital industry. The National Union of Mineworkers, under conditions of full employment, and with a shortage of coal, was undoubtedly listened to intently by the Government. Lastly, a number of union policy declarations, which are the subject of memoranda to the Government and the substance of protests, may be disregarded by a Government, but through insistence they may gradually permeate Government policy-making. The belief in full employment and its acceptance by Conservative as well as Labour Governments is the most outstanding illustration.

Through the membership of Government advisory committees, trade unionists are in a position to influence Government policy-making and its application without having to make direct representations, but in most cases they do not utilize their opportunities. Because of the Trades Union Congress policy of claiming representation on every conceivable Government committee and its unwillingness to appoint any but General Council members to serve on the committees, its nominees sit on far too many committees, most of which hold no special interest for them. Consequently, many union leaders either do not attend the meetings or they attend without giving adequate attention to the subjects under examination. There are a few exceptions but there would be many more if the Trades Union Congress confined its attention to those committees in which it has a special interest and for which it has qualified nominees.

Party Political Pressure

Trade unions have used the Parliamentary Labour Party and their own members who have been Members of Parliament to raise issues and air grievances before the Government, but their preference has been for direct contact with the Government. The ideal theoretical conception of direct contact has been contact with a Labour Government. Now, after the experience of three spells of Labour rule, it is possible to see how the ideal has materialized.

The main advantage for trade unions from having a Labour Government is that their broad social aims converge and that there is also general agreement over the means of pursuing those aims. For instance, they agree that the use of public ownership, physical conrols, and budgetary manipulations are desirable and necessary. So, provided an election programme is drawn up which satisfies unions, and the Labour Party obtains sufficient electoral support to govern independently of the other parties, unions will get a degree of satisfaction from a Labour Government which it will not normally get from a Conservative Government.

It is possible, however, to have a Conservative Government with many of the main attributes of a Labour Government in so far as trade unions are concerned. This is becoming more likely as the policies of the two political parties converge. A Labour Party which is exhausting its social inspiration and an adaptable Conservative Party can be remarkably similar. This was so during the period of Sir Winston Churchill's post-war Government. It could be so again and will be unless the Labour Party obtains a new momentum. Trade unions, however, so long as they are intimately associated with the determination of Labour Party policy, will continue to prefer a Labour Government to any other.

During the course of a Government's life there are occasions when a new policy has to be formulated, or an old policy has to be re-orientated. All policies, moreover, have to be administered. What advantages in these respects do trade unions get from a Labour Government? How much greater is their influence in the process of governing?

The evidence of three Labour Governments indicates that union influence is determined primarily by their economic strength at the time, as with other Governments. With full employment, inflation, and a balance-of-trade problem, trade union influence is greatest. Other things being equal unions are likely to have more influence with a Labour than with a Conservative Government, to the extent that a Labour Government will be less willing to offend unions out-right and will therefore incline to offer concessions and make safe-guards. But if the policy of a Labour Government is contrary to trade union wishes it is no more likely to be changed than would be the policy of a Conservative Government. If union pressure is publicly obvious, a Labour Government may be especially unwilling to alter its policy, in order to illustrate its independence of the trade union movement.

How is it that, with union leaders in the Cabinet, a Government policy can run counter to union wishes? First, the intellectual influence of union leaders in the Cabinet has never been very great except in the case of Ernest Bevin. Secondly, union leaders, when they become Government Ministers, usually try hard to act in what they consider to be the national interests and discard their sectional loyalties. They do not say that what is good for the working class is good for the country. Conservatives, on the other hand, have con-vinced themselves that the solutions to their own particular problems are national solutions. There is a profound difference of approach here which has caused trade union politicians to shy away from recognizable class solutions to national problems.

What about consultation? Is not this more effective because of the already existing familiarity between union leaders and the members of a Labour Government? There is undoubtedly much informal consultation, and formal access to Ministers is simplified. The quality of the consultation, however, can be adversely affected by the very same factors which make consultation easier. Labour politicians often meet union leaders not to listen to solutions to labour problems but to expound solutions. Labour Governments suffer from a surfeit of labour specialists. The loyalty of unions is taken for granted and consultation, therefore, is sometimes considered to be unnecessary. This has not been the case with some Conservative Ministers. These have not professed to know the minds of union leaders and they have listened to their advice in a manner which has impressed and perhaps flattered union leaders, even if in the end the advice has been rejected. Formal consultation between union leaders and the union members of a Labour Government has sometimes been adversely affected by the personal relations between them. It is difficult for a union leader to get accustomed to the transition of a fellow union leader, perhaps from a smaller union or one with a subordinate union position, to the exalted rank of Government Minister.

The main advantages from a trade union and Labour Government relationship have gone to the Government. Trade unions from 1945 to 1951 were loath to exert pressure on the Government, because they did not want to embarrass it and they made concessions to enable the Government to implement its policy. The extra benefits they obtained did not accrue from the exercise of influence, but depended on the nature of the policy which the Government pursued. This means that the part which unions play in determining the electoral policy of the Labour Party when Labour is out of office is important. The more they are successful in getting a policy formulated which satisfies trade union demands, the greater will be the benefit they will get from a Labour Government.

The Legend of Power

It may be asked why it is that any Government can ignore the protests of such a large and highly organized movement. There has always been in the trade union movement a belief in the might of the working class. It is a belief founded on the knowledge that if all workers act in unison and stop work the economy will cease to function. In this sense the belief is legitimately held. But the practical use of working-class might is curbed in many ways and particularly by a general acceptance of the standards of political democracy.

Nonetheless, the belief has been perpetuated until it has become legendary. It is now one of the forces which helps to provide trade union morale and maintain unity.

Outside the trade union movement the legend has been encouraged by politicians who are not in sympathy with unions, that trade unions are excessively powerful and a threat to political democracy. By this means they have hoped to convince the electorate that by voting for the Labour Party it will be increasing trade union power.

Both of these factors have helped to create much misinformed opinion about unions and have diverted attention from those who have held real power in the community; from industrialists, the church, the press, the establishment, and the aristocracy. Trade unions normally react to economic movements, they do not create them. The power which they have is restricted to the activities which are their direct concern; it is applied not in changing the policy of an elected Government but in altering its administration. It would be preferable if the power of other organized groups in society were as constrained and directed with such social purpose.

INDEX

Abramovitz, Moses, 74n
Acton Society Trust, 276n
Adams, Rex, 103n, 105n
Adamson, W., 161n, 238, 254, 259
Advisory committees: and nationalized industries, 271, 274, 279; to Government, 27 et seq., 266, 304; T.U.C. and Labour Party, 235–236, 240
After All (Norman Angell), 236n
Allan, William, 5
Allen, E. J. B., 147n
Allen, V. L., 24n, 27n, 123n, 258n, 285n
Amery, L. S., 193, 194n
Ammon, C. G. (later Lord), 238, 259n
An Autobiography (Philip Snowden), 162n, 198n, 225n
Anderson, John (later Lord Waverley), 126n, 197n
Angell, Norman, 236n
Annals of an Active Life (Sir Nevil Macready), 121n, 153n
Annual Abstract of Statistics, 1957, 72n
Annual Register, 151n, 152n, 166n
Applegarth, Robert, 5, 27
Arbitration, 82, 203, 241; government interference with, 67, 107; on the railways, 97–100, 113; in wartime, 131–135; see also compulsory arbitration
Arbitration Acts, 46
Arnot, R. Page, 20n, 120n, 121n, 137n, 165n, 185n, 191n, 192n, 199n; in 1919 railway strike, 175
Ashton, Thomas, 55n
As It Happened (C. R. Attlee), 264n, 265n
Askwith, Sir George (Later Lord), 55n, 58n; as Government conciliator, 53, 54, 56, 57
Aspects of British Economic History (A. C. Pigou), 166n, 226n
Asquith, H. H., 10, 11, 22, 119, 298
Astbury, Mr. Justice, 197
Attempts at General Union (G. D. H. Cole), 145n

Attlee, C. R., 260n, 261, 262; forming a Government, 264–265; and consultation with T.U.C., 266, 277, 278–279; and wage restraint, 283 et seq.; relations with Bevin, 289
Avoidance of Stoppages of Work (Committee on Production), 130–131

Bailey, Sir Abe, 198
Baldwin, Stanley: and civil service arbitration, 83; and strike precautions, 125; and the 1927 Trade Disputes Act, 126; during the coal disputes and General Strike, 191 et seq.
Balfour, A. J., 10, 18, 27
Balfour Committee, 229
Bank Employees, National Union of, 275
Barnes, G. N., 29, 38
Beatrice Webb's Diaries, 1912–1924, 38n, 220n, 225n; *1924–1932*, 227n, 253n
Bell, Richard, 219n
Benbow, William, 145–146
Bevan, Aneurin, 95, 96, 264, 291
Bevin, Ernest, 31, 38, 161, 163, 167, 176, 192, 198, 207, 240, 257, 260, 266, 281, 283; and Labour Government, 33, 230–234, 264, 289–290, 291, 304, 311; as Minister of Labour, 12, 35, 64, 134, 143–144, 261, 302–303, during 1931 crisis, 252–253
Birch, Alan, 109
Birch, Nigel, 112n
Birkenhead, Lord, 151, 193, 194, 196
Black Friday, 189
Blacklegs, 117, 206; in General Strike, 196; protected by troops, 119, 121–123, 125, 307; troops as, 118
Blake, Robert, 151n
Board of Trade (see also Labour Department), 45, 122, 132; and a Labour Administration, 47 et seq.
Board of Trade Journal, 48
Boilermakers, United Society of, 110, 259

315